PRIMITIVE CONSECRATION.

ALSO BY THE SAME AUTHOR.

A MANUAL OF ECCLESIASTICAL HISTORY, FROM THE FIRST TO THE TWELFTH CENTURY INCLUSIVE. Oxford. Parker, 1851.

WHAT IS THE CHURCH? OR, THE COUNTER-THEORY. Oxford and London. Parker, 1853.

CHRISTENDOM'S DIVISIONS. Parts I. and II. Longmans & Co., 1865-7.

LETTERS TO ARCHBISHOP MANNING· 'THE CHURCH'S CREED' and 'THE ROMAN INDEX.' In 1 vol. cloth. London. Hayes, 1868-9

Or, separately—

THE CHURCH'S CREED OR THE CROWN'S CREED? Sixteenth Thousand

THE ROMAN INDEX AND ITS LATE PROCEEDINGS. Sixth Thousand.

IS THE WESTERN CHURCH UNDER ANATHEMA? Third Thousand. London. Hayes, 1869.

DIFFICULTIES OF THE DAY, AND HOW TO MEET THEM. Eight Sermons preached at S. Augustine's, Queen's Gate. London. Hayes, 1871.

THE ATHANASIAN CREED: BY WHOM WRITTEN AND BY WHOM PUBLISHED. With an Appendix. London. Hayes, 1871.

⁎ *Copies of those still in print may be had from Mr. Hayes*

PRIMITIVE CONSECRATION

OF THE

Eucharistic Oblation

WITH

AN EARNEST APPEAL FOR ITS REVIVAL.

BY THE

REV. EDMUND S. FFOULKES, B.D.

VICAR OF S. MARY THE VIRGIN, OXFORD.

'Join them one to another into one stick, and they shall become one'
Ezek xxxvii 17.

WIPF & STOCK · Eugene, Oregon

Wipf and Stock Publishers
199 W 8th Ave, Suite 3
Eugene, OR 97401

Primitive Consecration of the Eucharistic Oblation
With an Earnest Appeal for Its Revival
By Ffoulkes, Edmund S.
Softcover ISBN-13: 978-1-6667-3362-4
Hardcover ISBN-13: 978-1-6667-2843-9
eBook ISBN-13: 978-1-6667-2844-6
Publication date 8/6/2021
Previously published by J. T. Hayes, 1885

This edition is a scanned facsimile of
the original edition published in 1885.

PREFACE.

It was not to reopen or to accentuate controversy that I sat down to this investigation: but only to get, if possible, to the bottom of a problem to which the cream of my life—three times fifteen years—has been devoted: fifteen years from my matriculation at Oxford to my departure from it as Fellow and Tutor of the College where my undergraduate days were spent: to pass fifteen years in the Church of Rome, where I was assured a better Christianity was taught; and then to find myself at the end of that time, to my unspeakable wonder and contentment, occupying my former old seat in the Church of S. Mary the Virgin, to teach and heartily maintain the same doctrine that I had listened to, from almost inspired lips, with fervour as an undergraduate.

Some people may call this a waste of time: and a waste of time it would doubtless have been, were there no other world beyond this. But with a better world in prospect, no man in his senses who believes it could consider time wasted in endeavouring at any cost to secure that pearl of great price. I learnt many things in the Church of Rome which I hope never to forget or to cease to practise, no law forbidding them. But I learnt one lesson which personal experience could alone teach me: namely, that there were just about as many things which the Church of Rome might profitably learn from the Church of England as the Church of England from the Church of Rome; and that there were just as many good Christians to be found in the one as in the other.

When I found it was considered treason in the Church of Rome to say this, I applied to the authorities of the Church of England to readmit me; and to their kindness and large-heartedness my sincere thanks are due for this resumption of my studies in a place which, in spite of all the changes forced upon it by pressure from without, and of all the various forms of eccentric action consequent upon them from within, still for freedom of thought and speech, encouragement of learning and science, earnest and heroic work done for Christ and His Gospel, retains enough of its pristine type to endear it to its alumni, and is still second to none.

No better nucleus could be desired, nor any better found elsewhere, than exists, by the fact of its new phase, made to hand in this place, for organising the grandest, yet the quietest and surest, movement for reuniting Christendom that has yet been seen: let reunion only be desired as a thing worth the effort by all. Let the members of every Christian Church, Eastern and Western, be encouraged to send their sons to Oxford, not to proselytise by driblets from one Church to another—which recent events show its alumni would resent—but to learn to respect and cultivate acquaintance with each other while their hearts are young: so that should they become Fellows and Professors together as time goes on, they may be able to discuss all the points at issue between their respective communions in a friendly way, and in a spirit of love for their common Master, with a view to their better understanding and ultimate removal. Few and far between are the emoluments left in this place for which a talented member of any Christian Church might not compete with success, and hold without any reference to his creed, and not forfeit by taking Holy Orders and ministering in any communion to which he might belong. Few and far between are the Colleges where he would not be welcomed cordially, and receive courteous treatment, and have his full rights given him. Few and far between are those members of the University who would regret the drastic changes introduced by the late Commissioners into Colleges and University, should the healing of the divisions of Christendom sooner or later ensue from their adoption. Members of the Church of England were never more in earnest about their religion in this place than they are now: yet never were they more tolerant or tender towards all honest upholders of a creed slightly or widely different. And it is certain that in most cases their attitude would neither be the effect of indifference to dogma, nor of distrust in their own creed.

Great pains have been taken in every part of this work to advance nothing without adequate proof, and to pass over nothing in silence that ought to have full weight given it on the other side; and, above all, to impute sinister designs to none, for acts or events in which they clearly could have taken no part, and only defend from misconception of their true character, and misplaced belief in the genuineness of the authorities cited in their support.

Not for the world should a word drop from me to question either the good faith or the Christian lives of such; nor even to impute to their Churches any conscious deflection from 'the faith once for all delivered unto the saints.' For of this I am most thankful to have been permitted to make practical and personal proof by living among them: enabling me to say that in the lives of intelligent and sensible members of the Roman and Anglican Churches—and of the Eastern too, so far as my experience went—I could see no perceptible difference, beyond what education and nationality would explain, and *in principle* certainly there is none whatever, as to what they consider themselves bound to believe of God and to practise by man.

At the same time many facts brought to light in this book cannot fail to be regarded with as great surprise by most as they were by me when first discovered. I was far from prepared for the *dénouement* to which they led. No doubt they will be subjected to the closest scrutiny by others; and possibly not a few slips will be detected in the account that I have given of them, or the use to which I have turned them. But if everybody will read my first four chapters attentively, they will, it is hoped, be willing to consider my major premise proved; and then errors of detail in the next four, containing historical proofs of the minor, will hardly be such as to derogate from the appeal founded on the *résumé* contained in the last. In that case the solemn character of the appeal could hardly be disputed, as few would then deny that a special act of reparation was due from us all in the West—Anglicans and Romans alike— to God, in the Person of the Holy Ghost, whose prerogatives we have so long acquiesced in ignoring; and in the Person of the Son, whose words we have so long acquiesced in misapplying. This, however, we have done, not from choice, nor because our forefathers elected to do so, but because our forefathers were beguiled into doing it, through no fault of their own, on false pretences, and then handed on their mistaken teaching to their immediate descendants, till at last our living authorities became possessed of it, nothing doubting of its truth, and we imbibed it in all good faith from them. But error is *not* sin in any case till it has been obstinately maintained after having been unmasked and exposed. And this work, I trust devoutly, from history read aright, to have achieved in the last half of my book; so that henceforth, unless my reading of history can be set aside, the *fons mali* will have been made patent to all. It was the Gallicanism of the ninth century with its forged documents, that has brought us all to this pass. One generation after another has plunged deeper into the snare laid for it by the '*deceiver of the whole world*,' unconscious of its mistake, and for the teaching and ritual of the Church of the Fathers substituted the teaching and ritual forced upon the French Church in the ninth century, based upon pseudonymous or heterodox works. All we can say of it is, that it is not of our own making, but has descended to us, and been accepted by us in perfect good faith, and in utter ignorance of its source. One more fact ought in fairness to be stated: namely, that Rome was the last of all the Churches of Europe to accept this change; nor did it obtain footing there till Gallican influences got the upper hand in her midst, and dictated both the Canon of the Mass and the Creed used at Mass in the precise form in which both are said now.

E. S. FFOULKES.

CONTENTS.

CHAPTER I.

DOCTRINES OF THE INCARNATION AND THE TRINITY.

PAGES

Doctrine of the Trinity—Revealed in Scripture, confirmed in Nature—Triple character of the mind—Work of each member of the Godhead—Only the Son became man—His Body prepared by the Holy Ghost—His works done through the Holy Ghost—Up to the time of His death—Gives the Holy Ghost on Easter Day—Sends Him after His Ascension—Theology best expressed in Greek 1–12

CHAPTER II.

APPLICATION OF THE INCARNATION.

Works reserved by the Holy Ghost—His work in Baptism and the Eucharist—Incorrect renderings of S. John xvi. 15—Testimonies to S. John by S. Paul—Subjective gifts of the Holy Ghost—Action of the Holy Ghost in the Sacraments—In Baptism and Confirmation—In the Eucharist—Spiritual action all through—Liturgical allusions and phrases 13–23

CHAPTER III.

WORKS ASSIGNED TO THE SON AND TO THE HOLY GHOST.

Affronts offered to the Son and Holy Ghost—The Holy Ghost the Vicar of Christ—His Epiklesis all but forgotten by us—Dr. Neale the first to recall it—Excellent work by Dr. Hoppe—

xii   CONTENTS.

PAGES

Confounding Persons in the Godhead—Confounding offices equally wrong—Baptismal and Eucharistic Epiklesis—The Epiklesis of the Greek rituals—In 'the Orthodox Confession—Latin forms in the Gelasian Sacramentary—The Eucharistic Epiklesis—The words of our Lord fulfilled by it—Its twofold object—Illustrated in Latin Sacramentaries—Illustrations of its effects—Further illustrations—The term 'Canon' declined by S. Gregory—Latin names for the Epiklesis—Illustrations continued—Down to the ninth century—New ideas appearing in old forms—New words introduced—Words banished from primitive Liturgies—The old charge brought against Christians —Our union with Christ—A union of souls with His Body   .   24–51

CHAPTER IV.

ON THE EUCHARISTIC EPIKLESIS.

Uno ore consensus Patrum—Starting from S. Justin—His Logos the Holy Ghost—His notion derived from the Seventy—The Word of the Old Testament—His account of the Eucharist—S. Irenæus agrees with him—Prayer of one, the Epiklesis of the other—S Irenæus got his name for it from S. Polycarp—The Pfaffian fragment—The witness to it of heretics—Origen clear-spoken for once—S. Firmilian writing to S. Cyprian—S. Cyprian and his testimony—S. Cyril of Jerusalem—His Catechetical Lectures—His fifth Mystagogical—Celebration of the Eucharist described—Holy things for holy persons—Directions for communicants—Modern Liturgy compared with his—Consecration, by Whom ?—*He, not* man, shall glorify Me —Further testimonies—S. Cyril no semi-Arian—Passages from S. Ephrem—The Greek Jerome—The Alexandrian Eusebius—S. Theophilus translated by S Jerome—S Isidore of Pelusium —S. Nilus for Egypt and Constantinople—S. Cyril of Alexandria—His mystical eulogia—Other senses of eulogia—What S. Cyril quotes from his Liturgy—What Rome borrowed from him—S. Cyril as a controversialist—Explains himself to Theodoret—His query to Nestorius—Reserve practised by him—Explains himself to the Orientals—Passages from S. Augustine —The African a Latin-speaking Church—Liturgical quotations —S. Augustine misinterpreted—S Optatus of Milevis—S. Fulgentius of Ruspe—The Oblation of the whole Church—Sanctified by the Holy Ghost—S Isidore of Seville—The Christian sacrifice—The Liturgy described by him—The mystical prayer

CONTENTS. xiii

—S. Ildefonse of Toledo—S Hilary of Poitiers—Invariably
'sub mysterio'—Travestied by S Eligius—S Agobard of Lyons
—Theodulph, Bishop of Orleans—Maxentius, Bishop of Aquileia
—Testimony from Alcuin—Testimonies from Bede—From S
Gregory the Great—Anecdote told of him—His own statements—'At the voice' means 'at the prayer'—Teaching of
Pope Gelasius—First Celebration at Jerusalem—And the language Greek—Latin when first used at Rome—Decisive statement of Innocent I—agrees with the East and West—Testi-
monies of Leo not specific—Singular anecdote of Pope Agape-
tus—Pope Vigilius at Constantinople—His letter to Profuturus
—The canonical prayer—In what sense composed by a Scholastic—S. Gregory the Great interpreted—Testimonies from S.
Ambrose—From his genuine works—His prayer drawn from
his Liturgy—S. Gaudentius of Brescia—Well known in the
East—S. Jerome at Constantinople—S. Jerome at Rome—S.
Basil the Great—Theodore of Mopsuestia—Mark the Eremite
—Theodoret the Church-historian—Liturgical bearings of his
dialogues—Anastasius Sinaita—The Nestorian anaphora—The
writings of S Chrysostom—Only the earlier cited here—His
Whitsunday sermon—Consecration everywhere the same   . 52–149

CHAPTER V.

CONTROVERSY MUST NOW BE FACED.

The words of Christ used in distribution—Never in consecration
—Tertullian misquoted—S. Cyprian misquoted—Mistakes of
Mr. Maskell and Martene—Tridentine Catechism corrected—
Words of our Lord—Outspoken or unrecorded—Dethronement
of the Holy Ghost—Pope Liberius and the Macedonians—
Eustathius of Sebaste—Arian devices—Exposed by Didy-
mus—Calumnies against S Athanasius—Interpolations of the
Fathers—Eusebius of Emesa—His homilies translated into
Latin—Reviewed by Oudin—Divided into two sets—His
Easter and Palm Sunday sermons—Did S.Chrysostom copy from
them ?—Two recensions of his sermon—The words of institu-
tion—Explained by both alike—Earlier teaching of S. Chryso-
stom—Another specimen of his later—His hesitating tone
noteworthy—Tract of S. Proclus—Its authenticity confirmed
—Its liturgical statements—Liturgies of S. James and S.
Clement—The Clementine, why so called ?—The Eighty-fifth
Apostolical Canon—Reticence of S Epiphanius explained—

xiv   CONTENTS.

PAGES

First Christmas sermon of S Chrysostom—Christmas · why kept by him on December 25—Statement of S Proclus verified—The three Liturgies compared—The words of institution—Followed, *not* preceded, by the Epiklesis—Completeness of the parallel—Nestorian Liturgies characterised—Want the words of institution—Consecration-prayer of the Clementine—Copied by S. Basil and S. Chrysostom—Other parts avoided by them—Its Arianism exposed—Ascribed to S. James the Greater—Cardinal Newman on Arianism—Letter of Arius translated by him—Epithets reserved to the Father—Not to be given to the Son—The only-begotten God—The Word-God—The Son not even the Demiurge—But only the Assistant—The Clementine Preface—Unlike any other—Yet composed by no mean hand—Its formula for consecration—Its minor blemishes—Its composition and date—Its probable author—Brought out by his biographer—George intimate with Eustathius—And Eustathius with S Basil—Eusebius of Emesa copied by Diodorus—S. Chrysostom a pupil of Diodorus—S. Chrysostom's patronage—How different from that of S. Basil—S. John of Damascus—Extract from his great work—Quotation from S. Gregory Nyssen—Misconstrued by Waterland—Quotation from S. Ephrem—Not word for word as preached by him—Quoted as though part of the Liturgy—Sermon and Liturgy compared—Liturgy copied from the Sermon—Sermon copied in a hymn also—In neither connected with S. Ephrem—Attributed to S. John Damascene—Cardinal Humbert and Nicetes—Conduct of Constantinople 150–234

CHAPTER VI.

ROMAN CANON AS NOW USED.

Conflicting accounts of its authorship—S. Aldhelm first witness to its contents—Venerable Bede the next—S. Gregory the Great the next—His own hand in it—Place given in it to the Lord's Prayer—The Gelasian Sacramentary—What Strabo says on that subject—Words attributed to S. Leo—The revision by S. Gregory—Commenced at Constantinople—Liturgies seen there by him—Evidences of his use of them—Changes afterwards made in his revision—In one case perhaps from Bede—The prayer 'Supplices Te rogamus'—Recast by S. Gregory—And where placed by him—Eighth-century proof of this—Parallel from the Mozarabic Liturgy—That Liturgy, too, re-

CONTENTS.

vised at Constantinople—Facts relating to Leander its author
—His revision and that of S. Gregory compared—Testimony
from the Caroline Books—And from Paschasius Radbertus—
This prayer a puzzle to moderns—Parallel of the Gothic Missal
—Vestiges of it in others—The latest witnesses to its teaching—Druthmar and Ratramn—Rabanus, Archbishop of Mayence—Ælfric, Abbot of Cerne—Facts relating to him—Throwing light on his words—True to the Fathers—Yet calls
Amalarius a wise doctor—Anglo-Saxon Liturgies—Attested
by their fragmentary remains—Changes in them how brought
about—Private prayers of S Anselm—His letter to the Abbot
of Westminster—'De Sacramento Altaris'—Outer and inner
part of the sacrament—Another letter claimed for him—' De
Corpore et Sanguine Domini'—Fragment given by Mr Maskell
—His excellent remarks on it—Absence of the word 'spiritual' 235-284

CHAPTER VII.

HOW THE WESTERN CHURCH WAS GALLICANISED.

Aim and conduct of Charlemagne—Rejects the Second Nicene
Council—The Caroline Books on the See of Rome—Books sent
into France from Rome—Roman Mass not introduced as yet—
Creed not as yet used at Mass in Rome—Statement of Ademar
—Statement of Abbot Hilduin—He refers to the Clementine
Liturgy—Letters of bishops of Rome to French bishops—
Statement of Hilduin measured by facts—Remark of Sismondi—Forgeries under Charlemagne—His quadrilateral—
Prime specimens—The Epitome of Canons—Described by Le
Cointe—The Dionysian collection—Contention of the Ballerini
respecting both—Canons of General Councils omitted—Weight
thereby given to Sardican Canons—Policy dictated this volume—Counter-gift of Charlemagne—When and by whom
presented—Gelasian decree of A D. 494—Discredited by
Charlemagne—His own two pseudonymous Creeds—The first
interpolated also by him—The second first quoted against
the Greeks—His own clergy to learn it by heart—The Capitularies of Adrian or Angilramn—Angilramn's visit to Rome
—Return of Riculfus from Spain—Notices of Riculfus—What
called at Court—Letters of Alcuin disclosing important facts
—The Book of Riculfus used at Rome—His own hand in what
took place there—The Capitulary ' De Purgatione,' &c.—The

xvi CONTENTS.

PAGES

scene described in another—The False Decretals known to
Charlemagne—And to Alcuin and his friends—False Decretals never named by Benedict—Other sources open to him—
False Decretals why not published sooner—Modern suppressions—Letter of Leo to Riculfus—Riculfus and Autcar related
—Neither Benedict nor Riculfus forgers—The False Decretals
reflect their age—And favoured the aims of Charlemagne—
Full of harm to the Church—Triumphed at the Council of
Troyes—System designed by Charlemagne—Details of the
Council of Frankfort—Adoptionism a ground for meddling in
Spain—Rejection of the Second Nicene Council—Previously
concealed from the Pope—Council of Paris under the Emperor
Lewis—Equally self-willed—Lewis teaches the Pope his duty
—Papal ordinance for papal elections—Carried out in electing
Gregory IV —Parallel under Charlemagne—Gallicanism in the
Mediæval Church—Reconciliation attempted by Gratian—' Concordantia discordantium canonum '—Misgivings betrayed by St.
Bernard—Contrast between S. Peter and his successors—Greek
works translated by Eugenius III —New edition of Gratian
in 1582—False Decretals left in it untouched .   . 285-357

CHAPTER VIII.

THIRD PART OF THE DECRETUM ON CONSECRATION.

But one passage cited for the old form—Citations under false
names—The pseudo-Cyprian—The pseudo-Ambrose—Conceals
his rank and Church—His triumphant tone—Interpolations
of two works by S. Ambrose—His sermons like those of S. Cyril
—Yet drawn from the Emisene Eusebius—The Emisene Eusebius praised by S Jerome—Design of the pseudo-Ambrose—
Precise date of his work—Products of Metz and Mayence—
Amalarius and Paschasius—Synod of Aix, A D 816—First
work of Amalarius—The ritual of the Church of Metz—His
work on the Antiphonary—His new Canon and comments on
it—How his new Canon became law—Its thoroughly Gallican
tone—Record of his acts—Opposed by Florus of Lyons—Apocryphal writings—Circulated under names of the Apostles—
Amalarius and his plausible plea—Milan threatened by Charlemagne—Vestiges remaining of the old Canon—Amalarius and
his contemporaries—Agobard and Florus—Their joint opposition and concessions—Rabanus Maurus traduced—Haymo
plain-spoken — Walafrid Strabo—Character of Paschasius—

CONTENTS. xvii

PAGES

Character of his work—First and second editions confused—
Exposed by Ratramn—The abbot and the monk—The MS.
used by Ratramn—The Gallican tangle unravelled—Destruction
of old Office-books—Views new and old mixed—Famous letter
of Charles the Bald—Two versions of the stock-passage—Its
probable date—Parties in France then threefold—Perfect
calm at Rome—Teaching of Pope Nicholas—The Berengarian
controversy—Imported by French Popes to Rome—Roman
Council under Gregory VII.—Gregory VII. 'a disciple of
Berengarius'—Burnings of Christians in France—Changes in
the Roman Pontifical—Rejected in advance by Pope Nicholas
—Revelations of palimpsests—Discreditable practices at
Rome—Sardican Canons given up at last 358–417

CHAPTER IX.

GENERAL SUMMARY.

Primitive consecration—Outward and inward parts—Revision of
Liturgies in the East—Insertion of the words of institution—
Similar revisions in the West—The West more loyal than the
East—Leander and S Gregory together—The interpolated
Creed—Pope Theodore on altering the Creed—Wisdom of the
Council of Chalcedon—Wisdom of the Council of Constantinople—Work
of the ninth century—Gallicanism, ancient and
modern—Charlemagne mimics Jeroboam—Creed of S Jerome
—Creed of S. Athanasius—Its phrase '*suis* corporibus'—Authorship
of the False Decretals—Designed to subserve temporal
interests—End with Popes Gregory III and Zacharias—
'Codex Carolinus' begins where they end—Council of Aix, A.D.
816—Amalarius on ecclesiastical offices—The Imperial Official
—Result of his acts—Paschasius and the Official—Convict
each other—The Real Presence held by Berengarius—Sad results
of the new teaching—The Holy Ghost denied to be a
principle—Court divines—In the days of Constantine and
Charlemagne—Crowned heads and the Reformation—Crowned
heads and the Mediæval Church—England and Rome compared—Forgeries
gradually brought to light—Must all be
abandoned—Fathers buried alive by Gratian—Wholly forgotten
in the West—Beautiful Western hymns—No exceptions
to the rule—Splendid witness of the Greek Church—Attention
first called to it by Dr Neale—Dr Neale eulogised by Dr
Daniel—When divisions became permanent—Eucharistic con-

troversies all European—The Fathers that have been quoted—Their testimony recapitulated—Cannot be resisted—Has Rome really broken with them?—Council of Trent and its Catechism—Benediction in the old ritual—Interpreted by Cardinal Pullen—First Prayer-Book of Edward VI.—Communion-office by Bishop Jeremy Taylor—Fuller than that of Edward VI.—Teaching of Calvin to the same effect—Edwardine Catechism to the same effect: A.D 1553—Omissions may become sins—Resumption of missionary work—More proselytes than heathen converts—No national conversions now—Intercommunion therefore necessary—Let England and Rome join forces—Christianity demands it of both . . . 418–484

PRIMITIVE CONSECRATION

OF THE

EUCHARIST OBLATION.

CHAPTER I.

THE studied reserve practised by the Fathers in speaking of the Eucharist—partly due, without doubt, to its mysterious character, but partly likewise to its being celebrated when none but the faithful were present—was, anyhow, one reason why their teaching on it never found expression in the public Creeds, like their teaching on baptism. For the Creed was placed in the hands of the catechumen previously to his being brought to the font; whereas the ritual of the Eucharist was kept a profound secret from all, till, after having received baptism, they were finally prepared for Communion. Yet, in point of fact, whether they realised it or not, what was taught by the Fathers on the Eucharist was based on, and still finds its natural interpretation in, the twofold doctrines of the Incarnation and the Trinity, which were formulated in their Creeds. It is to those doctrines, accordingly, that we must have recourse for its fundamental conception; and hence we must, at starting, endeavour to place those doctrines in the clearest light for that purpose. To begin, then, with the Trinity. The teaching of the Fathers on this august subject was of course drawn from the Scriptures of the New Testament, as being its authoritative revelation; which, nevertheless, much that they saw around them, much that they read in books, must have doubly confirmed. For even Aristotle, who left no philosophical system earlier than his own unsifted, and laid bare the errors and unrealities of each in turn—and among them all the visionary speculations of the Pythagoreans about numbers—all at once proclaimed himself in agreement with them on the practical importance given throughout nature to the number Three. The line lay between two points, and had a centre. Three lines were the fewest that could enclose a space: and space thus enclosed took the form of a triangle. Out of triangles were formed all figures, like words out of letters. Every solid body was, as it were, labelled with its triple dimensions of length, breadth, and thickness, each and all essential to its existence, by which its uses too were severally determined: sometimes its length, sometimes its breadth, sometimes its thickness, had to be consulted *most*; but never to that extent that either of the other two could be left out; the co-operation of all three being in all cases indispensable. A single passage from him may suffice to cover the whole ground, given in the exquisite French of M. Saint-Hilaire. It occurs in the first chapter of the first book of his treatise 'De Cœlo.'

'On entend par continu tout ce qui peut se diviser en parties toujours divisibles: et le corps est ce qui est divisible en tous sens. C'est que, parmi les grandeurs, l'une n'est divisible qu'en un sens unique, c'est la ligne: l'autre l'est en deux, c'est la surface: l'autre l'est en trois, c'est le corps.

'Il n'y a pas des grandeurs autres que celles-là: parce que trois est tout, et que trois renferme toutes les dimensions possibles. En effet—ainsi que le disent le Pythagoriciens —*l'univers entier, et toutes les choses dont il est composé, sont déterminées par ce nombre, trois.* A les entendre, le fin, le milieu, et le commencement, forment le nombre de l'univers; et ces trois termes représentent le nombre de la triade. Dès alors, *recevant de la nature elle-même ce nombre, qui résulte en quelque sorte de ses lois,* nous l'employons aussi à régler les sacrifices solennels que nous offrons aux Dieux. C'est encore de cette même manière que nous exprimons les dénominations et les dénombrements des êtres. Car, lorsqu'il n'y a que deux êtres, nous les désignons en disant, les deux. Et alors les deux signifie l'un et l'autre. Mais dans ce cas nous ne disons pas tous. Et nous ne commençons seulement à appliquer cette dénomination de tous que quand il y a trois êtres au moins. Nous ne suivons du reste cette marche, ainsi qu'on vient de le dire, que *parce que c'est la nature même qui nous conduit dans ce chemin.*'

Such is the deliberate, matter-of-fact conclusion of Aristotle, derived from a close survey of the material world. He avows himself a trinitarian, so far as its constructional principles are concerned. For every solid body that it contains, of whatsoever kind, is a unit whose dimensions are necessarily *threefold.*[1] Accordingly S. Augustine, speaking for the Fathers, says: 'Oportet igitur ut creatorem per ea quæ facta sunt intellectum conspicientes, Trinitatem intelligamus; cujus in creaturâ, quo modo dignum est, apparet vestigium.'[2]

Taking a Bible, then, into our hands reverentially, we shall see that it may be so studied as to testify to the ordinances of nature and the mysteries of revelation—to the truths discoverable by philosophy, and the truths proclaimed by religion, in the same breath. For our eyes, by contemplating its external structure, may assist our souls in grasping what our Maker discloses to us within about Himself. Length, breadth and thickness are the constituents of its external frame—three dimensions appertaining to it; and neither fewer nor more than three—all obviously necessary to its existence as a book: so that one could not be taken away

---

[1] Τὸ δὲ πάντῃ καὶ τριχῇ διαιρετὸν κατὰ τὸ ποσὸν σῶμα. *Metaph* iv. 6 This was repeated by Euclid 100 years later.
[2] *De Trin* vi 10.

without involving necessarily the removal of the other two: and each by itself determining the external uses respectively to which it shall be turned by us. It is thus a perfect illustration of what our Maker tells us about Himself inside that book of books, though it is no more than an illustration.

But corporeal evidences of the Triune Godhead were for many reasons avoided, as a general rule, by the Fathers, who decided, even in interpreting the Mosaic account of the creation of man, that it was not his body, but his soul that reflected the image of his Maker [1] Accordingly, they took a subjective view of themselves, and noticed how each man might say: 'I understand; I remember; I desire. And each of these acts proceeds from a distinct faculty within me, though my whole mind co-operates in each of these acts, as they are taken in hand.' It mattered indeed little what the illustration was, for the principle was in all cases identic.

These facts within themselves, and in the world around them, therefore, must have contributed in no small degree to secure their assent, when Revelation speaking with authority required them to believe that the Godhead was also threefold, and that its members—the sharers of its essence—were distinct from each other. On the same principle they were further told—and this, again, was illustrated by what they felt in themselves, and perceived in nature—that its members, while They never acted but with the collective power of all, assumed by mutual consent each a separate part in the conduct of the world and all things in

---

[1] Hence this distinction —'Inter imaginem et vestigium Trinitatis ita distinguunt Theologi, ut per vestigium intelligant obscuram ac pertenuem quandam Trinitatis representationem per imaginem verò similitudinem ejus expressiorem, quæ nimirum pertingat usque ad propriam quandam rei significatæ representationem . Reperitur vestigium Trinitatis in omni prorsùs creaturâ Imago Trinitatis, quam diximus esse propriam quandam Trinitatis representationem, non in omni creaturâ, sed in solâ intellectuali reperitur Sunt in omni intellectuali creaturâ hæc memoria, intelligentia, voluntas

' Estius, *In Sent IV.* Dist III 9-10 Moderns perhaps will consider the corporeal representation the more decisive

it, which They had created out of nothing also by joint concert.

This concert, which Tertullian in his day called 'οἰκονομίας sacramentum,'[1] we may perhaps reverentially call 'etiquette,' by which each member of the Godhead has an official character and work assigned Him in Scripture, peculiar to Himself, in dealing with man; yet harmonising and falling in with all elsewhere revealed to us of Their mutual interdependence.[2] Thus, He who is called the Father is exhibited as the Fountain-head of the whole Godhead and in the character of the Supreme Deity throughout. The Son and Holy Ghost are sent in turn by Him, but He never is sent Himself. The Son and Holy Ghost work as His joint agents: first in creating men, and then in reconciling man with God —represented in the Person of the Father, but always intended to include Themselves as well. Hence the formula running through the writings of St. Cyril of Alexandria,[3] which Hooker reproduces[4] as that of the Fathers generally. 'Life, as all other gifts and benefits, groweth originally from the Father, and cometh not to us but by the Son: nor by the Son to any of us in particular but through the Spirit.'

Thus the parts assigned to each member of the Godhead are distinctly traced, and must be kept distinct by us; though, owing to Their intimate communion with each

---

[1] *Adv Prax* c 2

[2] 'Hæc namque est,' says S Maximus of Turin, 'ut credimus, incomprehensæ dispensatio Trinitatis ut, cum omnia simul Pater, et Filius, et Spiritus Sanctus, ejusdem Deitatis affectu, inseparabiliter operentur, quædam tamen specialiter singulis tribuantur'—*Serm* xlviii, *De Pent* 2

[3] *Ep* v *ad Euseb*; *Ep* xxiv *ad Heracl.*; *In Lucam*, iii. 21; *In Johan.* xv. 1; *In I Cor* i 21 It is put into the mouth of S Thecla by her biographer, Basil of Seleucia, contemporary with S Cyril, as part of the teaching she had imbibed from S Paul Migne, *Patrol Gr* lxxxv 551 The monk Job, whose work *De Verbo Incarn.* is largely quoted by Photius (*Bibl Cod* ccxxii 14), calls the Father, *Causa Primaria*; the Son, *Operatrix Causa*; the Holy Ghost, *Causa Perficiens* Faustus of Riez, *Serm de Trin*: 'Dixit Deus, faciamus hominem et iterum, creavit Deus hominem · et tertiò, benedixit ei Deus. Dixit Deus, fecit Deus, benedixit Deus Dixit Pater, fecit Filius, benedixit Spiritus Sanctus Propter tres Personas ter, iterum una Divinitas.

[4] *E P* v. 56-7.

other, Their official relations seem at times to overlap. Our Lord Himself, for instance, designated the Holy Ghost His 'alter ego,' when He styled Him 'another Comforter;'[1] though He is our authority for calling the Third Person of the Trinity by that name which is restricted to Him personally, viz. that of the Holy Ghost.[2] In the Incarnation, the parts assigned to the Son and Holy Ghost are much too distinct to be confused, though requiring to be stated with extreme delicacy just at the point where they begin to interchange.

It was the Son, and only the Son, who was made flesh. Though the whole Godhead concurred and assisted in the Incarnation, it was never allowable to assert that either the Father or the Holy Ghost had assumed human nature with the Son;[3] nor, again, to substitute for definite profession of the personal union of the human and Divine, from henceforth subsisting in the Son, such vague phrases as that the Omnipotent or the Infinite, the Demiurge or the Deity, became man.

On the other hand, it was by operation of the Holy Ghost that the flesh assumed by the Son was prepared.[4] This, indeed, was not affirmed in the Creed of Nicæa, but it was afterwards introduced into that Creed at Constantinople,

---

[1] S John xiv 16

[2] As St Anastasius says 'Spiritûs quidem Sancti hic est proprius character, qui hâc appellatione significatur Est enim Spiritus Sanctus Spiritum autem sanctum, totum sic dictum et vocatum, non invenies alium   Deus autem, ut antea dixi, dicitur Spiritus, et Deus dicitnr sanctus ; ambo tamen nomina composita congruunt ei, qui proprie dicitur Spiritus Sanctus Sicut nomen Patris convenit principio et nomen Filii ei, qui immediate ex principio *Et hæc nomina non commutantur inter se*   Cætera omnia moventur et immutantur'—*In Trin Orat* 1 22, as translated by Turrianus

[3] Οὐ γὰρ ἐπειδήπερ ἐστὶν ὁμοούσιος ἡ ἁγία καὶ προσκυνουμένη Τριὰς, ταύτῃ τοι καθ' οὗπερ ἂν ἕλοιτό τις προσώπου, τὸν τῆς ἐπανθρωπήσεως καθοριεῖ λόγον Γέγονε γὰρ ἄνθρωπος οὐκ αὐτὸς ὁ Πατὴρ, οὔτε τὸ Πνεῦμα τὸ ἅγιον, μόνος δὲ ὁ Υἱός. Οὕτως ἡμᾶς αἱ θεῖαι μεμυσταγωγήκασι γραφαί – S Cyril Al *Glaph. in Gen* 11 7

[4] Ib *In Isa* 1 *Orat* v 3 "Ὅτι γὰρ ἐξ ἁγίου Πνεύματος τὸ πανάγιον ἐκεῖνο διεπήγνυτο σῶμα τὸ ἐνωθεν τῷ Λόγῳ, πῶς ἂν ἐνδοιάσειέ τις. S Augustine touches on a further point 'Si a me quæratur unde acceperit animam Jesus Christus, mallem equidem hinc audire meliores atque doctiores · sed tamen pro meo captu libentius responderem " unde Adam, quàm de Adam "   '*De Gen ad lit.* x. 18.

to be confirmed at Chalcedon. The baptismal Creed of the West, meanwhile, was explicit from the first. 'De Spiritu Sancto, ex virgine, nascitur,' as Rufinus says, commenting on its words, which he repeats. It was the Holy Ghost [1] who really '*prepared*' the soul and body which the Son assumed. It was not allowable to affirm that the Father, or even the Son Himself, had taken active part in preparing and consecrating that human nature which was to be united by the Son in His own Person to the Divine.

As this point brings us to the very threshold of the sojourn of our Lord on earth, and is of the highest import, therefore, to our immediate subject, we must pause to develop its full significance before proceeding further. The first chapter of the New Testament opens with an announcement in plain terms of a new mystery, which had hitherto been kept veiled—the revelation of the Holy Ghost in His personality—yet that truth is, without preface, stated as a simple fact. 'Joseph, thou son of David, fear not to take unto thee Mary, thy wife; for that which is conceived in her is of the Holy Ghost.'[1] '*Incipe jam hinc intelligere etiam Sancti Spiritûs dignitatem*,' is the forcible remark of Rufinus on the article setting it forth in the Creed.[2] St. Luke tells us to whom, and by whom, this announcement was first made. 'How shall this be?' said the mother of our Lord to the angel who prepared her for it. 'The Holy Ghost shall come upon thee,' was the immediate reply, and it had a reassuring effect at once. 'Behold the handmaid of the Lord: be it unto me according to thy word.'[3]

Further, the act which followed was literally the first personal act of the Holy Ghost revealed as such, inaugurating a new dispensation for man, a new era for the world; the literal commencement of the kingdom of heaven on

---

[1] S. Matt. i. 20
[2] And repeated in an explanation of the Creed to catechumens in France, preceded by this further observation: 'Spiritus ergo Sanctus refertur Dominicæ carnis et templi creator.'—*Missal Gall. Vet.* ap. Muratori, *Lat* ii 712.
[3] S. Luke i. 38.

earth; God come down from heaven to pitch His tabernacle within man; a spiritual in lieu of a carnal system; an appeal, no longer to the senses, but to the mind; a Gospel of good tidings for all nations, instead of a law enforced by penalties on a single race. And, further, all manifestations of the Godhead in a visible form ceased on earth when the Incarnate Word—the Jehovah of the Old Testament, as a *consensus Patrum* taught [1]—had once for all returned to heaven. Thus the manner of His becoming man, and His official career upon earth as man, are both of them points of the utmost relevancy to be stated, though of the utmost delicacy to state.

The conception of our Lord by the Holy Ghost, then, was not an isolated act; it was consistently maintained all through His sojourn upon earth. His recognition by the Baptist as the Son of God was based on the fact that he had seen the Spirit 'descending and remaining on Him'—descending, as all four Gospels alike record; remaining on Him, as the fourth Gospel records, and only the fourth. Yet this, according to the Fathers, was literally the characteristic distinguishing the second Adam from the first: for the first Adam, they said, received the Holy Ghost in receiving his soul, though the Holy Ghost only remained with him for a time and left him when he sinned. With the second Adam the Holy Ghost came, but to remain.[2] All four Evangelists testify to the fact, though S. John alone states it in express

---

[1] See their statements of it collected, with its abuse by heretics, in Petavius, *Dogm de Trin* vii 2, Comp Pearson *On the Creed*, notes to pp 184–6 on the word 'Jehovah'

[2] On this point Petavius (*Dogm de Trin* viii 5, 6) and Bishop Bull (Discourse V, 'The State of Man before the Fall') are agreed As S. Cyril says on Joel, c 35 Οὐ γὰρ ἔρημον προφητικοῦ Πνεύματος εὑρήσομεν τὸν Ἀδάμ, οὔπω τὴν θείαν ἐντολὴν παραβεβηκότα . Ἀλλ ἤργησε μὲν ἡ ἀνθρώπῳ δοθεῖσα χάρις. Ἀνεκαινίσθη δὲ ἐν Χριστῷ, ὃς καὶ ἔστι δεύτερος Ἀδάμ . Δέδοται μὲν γὰρ, ὥς ἔφην, τὸ Πνεῦμα τῷ Ἀδὰμ ἐν ἀρχῇ, πλὴν οὐ μεμένηκε τῇ ἀνθρώπου φύσει. Διανένευκε γὰρ εἰς τὸ πλημμελὲς, καὶ παρώλισθεν εἰς ἁμαρτίαν Ἐπειδὴ δὲ ἑπτάχευσε, πλούσιος ὢν, ὁ Μονογενὴς, καὶ μεθ' ἡμῶν ὡς ἄνθρωπος τὸ ἴδιον, ὡς ἐπακτὸν, ἐδέξατο Πνεῦμα, μεμένηκεν ἐπ' Αὐτόν And again, *Adv Anthropomor* c 10 Ἀποδέδοται μὲν γὰρ τῇ ἀνθρώπου φύσει τὸ ἐν Ἀδὰμ ἐν ἀρχῇ· τουτέστιν ὁ ἁγιασμός.

terms. The first three Gospels are unanimous in declaring that it was by the Spirit that Jesus was taken into the wilderness to be brought face to face with Satan. S Luke prefaces his statement of that fact by declaring that He returned 'full of the Holy Ghost from Jordan,' and then appends this unique but decisive commentary to it all by recording that 'Jesus returned in the power of the Spirit into Galilee,' and on reaching 'Nazareth, where He had been brought up,' and standing up, as His custom was, in the synagogue to read, when the book was delivered into His hand, He opened it at the place where it was written, 'The Spirit of the Lord is upon Me.' Jesus Himself added, as He closed the book: 'This day is this Scripture fulfilled in your ears.'[1]

Later, His words to the Pharisees are, 'If I cast out devils by the Spirit of God, then *the kingdom of God is come unto you* . . . .'; and again, with enhanced explicitness in concluding them, 'Whosoever speaketh a word against the Son of Man, it shall be forgiven him; but whosoever speaketh against the Holy Ghost, it shall not be forgiven him, neither in this world, neither in the world to come.'[2]

Later still, S. Luke tells us that 'Jesus *through the Holy Ghost* gave commandment unto the Apostles, whom He had chosen. . . .' In taking leave of them He bade them 'not depart from Jerusalem till they had received the promise of the Father, which, said He, ye have heard of Me.'[3] From S. John we learn the words in which this promise was conveyed. 'The Comforter, the Holy Ghost, whom the Father will send in My name, He shall teach you all things, and bring all things to your remembrance, whatsoever I have said unto you.'[4] S. Paul tells us, finally, speaking of the sacrifice made for man by Him, that He, the Christ, offered Himself without spot to God through *the Eternal Spirit.*[5] Up to this point Jesus, to translate literally the forcible

---

[1] S Luke iv 14, &c [2] S Matt xii 28 and 32
[3] Acts i 2 and 4 [4] S John xiv. 26. [5] Heb. ix. 14

term employed by S. Paul, had '*emptied Himself*'[1]—had, in a manner, suspended or suppressed His own Divinity during His sojourn upon earth: preaching the Gospel, working miracles, choosing and commissioning apostles, 'in the power of the Spirit,' as S. Luke puts it—of that Spirit whom, as S. John tells us, the Baptist saw 'descending on Him' at His baptism, and 'remaining on Him.' Analogy would suggest—though the expression itself is not quite decisive, nor are the Fathers agreed in interpreting it thus—it was by the same Spirit that His soul was 'quickened,'[2] and went and preached to the 'prisoners of hope,'[3] while His body lay in the tomb. But, anyhow, with His resurrection we enter upon a new phase; for, first, it is always God, or the Father[4]—never the Holy Ghost—who is the agent whenever Christ is said to have been 'raised from the dead'; besides which, other passages declare that it was foretold of Him that *He should rise*: or else assert, as matter of fact, that He *did rise*[5]—namely, by His own act. And the same phrases occur in describing His ascension.[6] Secondly, when he passed through closed doors, where His official representatives were assembled on the evening of Easter Day, His first act was to 'breathe' on them and to say, 'Receive ye the Holy Ghost,'[7] adding subsequently, 'Behold *I send* unto you the promise of My Father.'[8] In other words, He became, thenceforward, the Giver of the Gift that He had,

---

[1] Philip ii 7 On this see Bishop Bull, *De J C Divin* § 19-20, a condition of things exactly represented by S Irenæus in the phrase ἡσυχάζοντος τοῦ Λόγου (*Hær* iii. 19), quoted with wider application by Theodoret (*Dial* iii p 232)

[2] 1 Peter iii 18-19; comp ib iv 6

[3] Zach ix 11-12

[4] Acts i. 32 'This Jesus hath God raised up'; ib iii 15 and 26; iv. 10; v. 30, x. 40; xiii 30, Rom x 9, 1 Cor vi. 14; Gal i. 1; Eph. i 20 'Whom God raised from the dead'; Rom. viii, 11

'The *Spirit of Him*, who raised up Jesus from the dead', 2 Cor iv 14 'He which raised up the Lord Jesus'

[5] S. Luke xxiv. 46 'It behoved Christ to rise'; Acts xxvi 23 'That He should be the first that should rise' S Matt xxviii. 6; S Mark xvi. 6, Rom viii 34 'is risen.' Rom. xiv. 9, 1 Cor. xv 4; 1 Thess iv 14 'rose'

[6] S Mark xvi. 19; Acts i. 2 'was taken up' S John iii 13; vi 62, xx 18, Eph. vi 10 'ascend.'

[7] S John xx 22.

[8] S Luke xxiv 49.

in entering on His earthly ministry, received Himself. As it had been prophesied of Him, ages before, by the Psalmist,[1] 'Thou art gone up on high: Thou has led captivity captive and received gifts for men.'

Still, in reading these words and in dwelling on their fulfilment ('He shall baptise you with the Holy Ghost,' as the Baptist puts it [2]), we must never lose sight of their relation to, nor their complete harmony with, this twofold truth: that as the Son was equally God with the Holy Ghost when the Holy Ghost descended on Him at His baptism as man, so the Holy Ghost was equally God with the Son when sent by Him from heaven on His ascension to apply the benefits of His Incarnation to His elect on earth.

The manner of His incarnation may now be described in a few words, as it as been explained by the Church. Two natures, the human and Divine, were combined in one Person—namely, the eternal Son. The human soul and the human body 'prepared' for Him had never been joined before they found their union with Him. Yet, though united in Him who was Divine, they remained separate from His Divine nature, so that His manhood was never absorbed by His Godhead, nor His Godhead ever confused with His manhood. At the same time their intercommunion in Him was always such that the properties appertaining to each might be predicated with equal truth of the other. God was born of a woman and died for man; the Son of man was in heaven, whilst He walked on earth. And we have this teaching illustrated to us in our own persons. 'For, *as* the reasonable soul and flesh is one man, *so* God and man is one Christ.'

One more remark in conclusion. The marked inadequacy for dealing with theological subjects of the Latin language which comparison with the Greek brings out, is illustrated nowhere more clearly than in connection with the subject from which we are just parting. 'Incarnatio,' the

[1] Ps. lxviii. 18. [2] S Mark i. 8.

the Latin word for expressing it, is at once lowering and incomplete—lowering, because concentrating attention on the inferior part of human nature thus assumed; incomplete, because suggesting no thought of the higher. Then, again, the opposition between 'flesh and spirit' in the natural man, recognised throughout the New Testament, adds to its inappropriateness. The Greek word ἐπανθρώπησις embraces everything and confuses nothing. 'Hypostasis' has a similar advantage over 'persona,' when applied to the Trinity.

CHAPTER II.

THE application of the Incarnation to the individual is the last remaining preliminary to our immediate subject. Our Lord designed His own human life upon earth to be reproduced, through union with Him, in each individual redeemed by Him. That union with him was ordinarily to be effected through the two sacraments ordained by Him for that purpose, and entrusted, for their external administration, to His Apostles and their successors; but whose life-giving power and efficiency the Holy Ghost was sent down officially from heaven to supply. Though Christ ordained both sacraments Himself previously to His ascension, the Apostles had ten days to wait for the descent of the Holy Ghost before they were permitted to administer them. 'Ye shall receive power after that the Holy Ghost has come upon you,'[1] said the Saviour on leaving them; and yet this power which they received on the day of Pentecost had its limitations: and much that the Holy Ghost came from heaven to impart He reserved strictly to Himself. In the first place, the Apostles are never said to *bestow* the gift that passed through their hands. 'Then laid they their hands on them, and they received the Holy Ghost.' Such is the account given of the process by S. Luke[2] and afterwards endorsed by S. Paul.[3] On one occasion, indeed, the Apostles were not even consulted, nor invited to co-operate, when the gift was bestowed—that is, on the setting apart of Barnabas and Saul for the work to which the Holy Ghost called them

---

[1] Acts i 8   [2] Ib viii 17   [3] Ib xix 6, and 2 Tim i 6

Himself.[1] And in no case were they permitted to read the hearts of those who received the gift at their hands, or ever to be certain whether it would be turned to account or received in vain. The union of the individual with Christ in each case was to be the work of the Holy Ghost and known only to the Holy Ghost. It had been described by anticipation once for all: 'So is the kingdom of God, as if a man should cast seed into the ground, and should sleep and rise night and day, and the seed should spring and grow up, he knoweth not how.'[2]

The institution of the sacraments of baptism and of the holy Eucharist, as recorded in the Gospels, presents many parallels and some contrasts. The form for administering baptism that has come down to us is supplied only by S. Matthew;[3] the authority[4] for repeated administrations of the holy Eucharist, in remembrance of Him who instituted it, is supplied only by S. Luke, confirmed and amplified by S. Paul. No words accompany the institution of either sacrament explaining, first, what was meant or designed by it; secondly, with what particular forms it was to be accompanied; thirdly, to whom—that is, whether to women as well as men, to infants as well as adults—it was to be administered; and, lastly, who might and who might not administer it. S. John, who passes over the institution of both in complete silence, though he must have been present on each occasion, records two separate discourses of our Lord at the commencement of His ministry, foreshadowing the purpose that would dictate the institution of each and the agency that would be employed for effecting it. Again, the same Evangelist alone reports other discourses uttered by Him at the close of His ministry throwing additional light on both points, which were further supplemented, as well as reiterated, by S. Paul. The Fathers on their part attest the unanimity with which the early Church applied

[1] Acts xiii. 2
[2] S. Mark iv. 26-7
[3] xxviii. 19
[4] S. Luke, xxii. 19; 1 Cor. xi. 24-6

all these passages of the fourth Gospel to the sacraments in question, whatever opinions have been entertained in modern times of their relevancy.¹

A few words from the first and second of these passages, placed in parallel columns, may be well left to speak for themselves.

S. John iii. 3, 5, and 6.	*S. John* vi. 53, 56, and 63.
'Verily, verily, I say unto thee Except a man be born again, he cannot see the kingdom of God. 'Verily, verily, I say unto thee · Except a man be born of water and of the Spirit, he cannot enter into the kingdom of God. 'That which is born of the flesh is flesh; and that which is born of the Spirit is spirit.'	'Verily, verily, I say unto you · Except ye eat the flesh of the Son of man, and drink His blood, ye have no life in you. 'He that eateth My flesh and drinketh My blood, dwelleth in Me, and I in him. 'It is the Spirit that quickeneth, the flesh profiteth nothing: the words that I speak unto you, they are spirit, and they are life'

Two verses of the third set complete the subject with a fulness that leaves nothing to be desired.

'But the Comforter, the Holy Ghost, whom the Father will send in My name, He shall teach you all things, and bring all things to your remembrance, whatsoever I have said unto you.² . . . He shall glorify Me, for He shall take of Mine, and shall declare it unto you.'³

Could the Apostles have been told more plainly than they are told here, what the Holy Ghost would be sent to do for them in preaching the word, which is set forth in the first of these verses, and in administering the sacraments, which is set forth in the last?

But, as the meaning, as well as the rendering of the last has been somewhat obscured, it may save time to settle both points before going further. Our Lord attached so much importance to the declaration made by Him in this verse,

---

¹ Johnson (*Unbloody Sacrifice*, c ii § v pp 382-91, ed 1714) might have doubled his references for the second of these passages
² S John xiv 26   ³ Ib xvi 15

16 INCORRECT RENDERINGS OF S. JOHN XVI. 15.

that He must needs explain, and then reiterate, what He had there said in the next. 'All things that the Father hath are Mine: therefore said I, that He shall take of Mine, and shall shew it unto you.' The A. V. translates the same Greek word 'receive' in v. 14 and 'take' in v. 15. The Revisionists much more correctly translate 'take' in both. 'Take' is what the Greek word means *primarily*; and S. John might have just as easily written δέξεται as λήψεται had he meant 'receive.' The Vulgate renders 'accipiet' in both places. Our A. V. translated from the Latin in one place, and from the Greek in the other. But there is an earlier authority than the Vulgate for 'accipiet' in S. Hilary,[1] and it was he probably who decided that point for the Latin Church. This was unfortunate, as Greek was not his native tongue, nor is it in Greek scholarship that he excels most. S. Jerome follows him, however, in translating the tract of Didymus[2] on the Holy Ghost, whose comment on this verse he then appends. 'Propterea autem ista dicuntur, ut eandem in Trinitate credamus esse naturam Spiritûs Sancti, quæ est Patris et Filii.' Though the Greek of this tract is no longer extant, we have the equivalent of this passage supplied in another work of Didymus on the Trinity,[3] where we get the additional fact that Didymus originated the Greek view, based on this verse, that 'taking of mine' was equivalent to '*taking of me*,'[4]—a view, which as soon as ever the controversy between the two Churches on the Procession commenced, entirely limited the application of this verse by both to the relations of the Holy Ghost to the Son *in the Godhead*—the Greeks describing Him as 'proceeding from the Father,' but 'taking from the Son,' and the Latins insist-

---

[1] *De Trin* viii. 20.
[2] § 37.
[3] III 40
[4] The Holy Ghost was accordingly spoken of in the East as ὃς ἐκ Πατρὸς ἐκπορεύεται, καὶ τοῦ Υἱοῦ λαμβάνει S. Epiph. *Hær* lxii 4,
lxix 52, lxxiv 10, *Ancor.* § 6, S Cyril on S John xvi 14. Hence the true reading is that of the A V and of the Vulgate: λήψεται both in verses 15 and 14—λαμβάνει, the reading of most MSS, being a correction

ing with S. Hilary—though he too followed the Greeks in making 'de meo' synonymous with 'a me'[1]—that 'taking from,' or as they put it, 'receiving from,' and 'proceeding from the Son,' meant the same thing; the consequence being, that attention was entirely diverted from what our Lord meant to impress most on His disciples in these words, as the context proves: namely, what the Holy Ghost would *do for them*; in other words, His relation to the two sacraments that would unite them to Christ. 'He shall take of the *grace attaching to my flesh*, or of the knowledge which I possess, and declare it unto you,' as S. Chrysostom expounds it [2]—the very notion underlying the prayer of invocation, or ἐπίκλησις, as we shall see. Yet even S. Chrysostom fails to point out, and indeed to be conscious of, the remarkable pendant to it in that equally studied expression of our Lord—εἰς τὴν ἐμὴν ἀνάμνησιν—preserved by S. Paul[3] and S. Luke.[4] Here, too, the rendering of our A. V. is a pendant to the inference which has been drawn from its fellow passage, for our rendering is *not* 'in *My* remembrance,' but, following the Roman Missal, '*in memoriam mei*'—that is, in remembrance *of Me*. These two utterances, accordingly, may well be thought to have been designed by our Lord to explain each other.

But again, neither is this the sole, nor yet the clearest, testimony rendered by S. Paul to the record of S. John, on the mission and action of the Holy Ghost in applying the sacraments to the individual Christian, and to the corporate body, twice designated the Church in the first Gospel—and in that alone—by Christ. On this last point, indeed, he devotes a whole chapter to expatiate—the twelfth of the first of Corinthians—as having been previously brought out by none, prefacing it, therefore, by the explicit declaration, that the Holy Spirit is both Lord and God: 'Now there are diversities of gifts, but the same Spirit. And there are differ-

---

[1] 'A Filio igitur accipit, qui et ab eo mittitur,' *De Trin.* viii 20   [2] *Ad loc*   [3] 1 Cor xi. 24
[4] xxii 19

ences of administrations, but the same Lord. And there are diversities of operations, but it is the same God, who worketh all in all.'[1]

Yet even in this chapter he cannot avoid mixing up the work of the Holy Ghost in the individual with His work in the Church. He says at starting,[2] 'I give you to understand that no man can say that Jesus is the Lord, but by the Holy Ghost.' This is tantamount to making all saving faith His gift, His best gift, as demonstrated in the next chapter. We find the two things equally blended in his last Epistle. 'Wherefore I put thee in remembrance, that thou stir up the gift of God, which is in thee by the putting on of my hands.'[3] This was at his ordination. Eight verses on: 'That good thing which was committed unto thee, keep by the Holy Ghost who dwelleth in us': that is, from the day of their baptism onwards till then. As he had told all his Roman converts dogmatically, 'But if the Spirit of Him that raised up Jesus from the dead dwell in you, He that raised up Christ from the dead shall also quicken your mortal bodies by His Spirit that dwelleth in you.' Six verses are occupied in developing the responsibilities laid upon them by this indwelling.[4] Elsewhere this is taken for granted and enlarged upon; 'Know ye not,' he says to the Corinthians,[5] 'that ye are the temple of God, and that the Spirit of God dwelleth in you? If any man defile the temple of God, him shall God destroy, for the temple of God is holy, which temple ye are.' In asking how we become this, we are brought insensibly to the remaining point: namely, to the action of the Holy Ghost in the two sacraments, testified to by Christ Himself previously to their institution, as reported by S. John. On this point S. Paul speaks everywhere with extreme delicacy, limiting himself to fill up, expand, throw together, and present in one consistent view, all that his Lord had traced by snatches, and at

---

[1] Vv. 4-6   [2] V 3   [3] 2 Tim 1 6 and 14
[4] viii 11-17   [5] 1 Cor iii. 16.

ACTION OF THE HOLY GHOST IN THE SACRAMENTS. 19

different times, in broad outline. Baptism was, by His command reported in the first Gospel,[1] to be administered to all converts in the name of the Trinity; but, in discoursing on it previously to Nicodemus, He had described it as a birth 'from above,'[2] or a birth by means 'of water and the Spirit' combined. S. Paul, accordingly, repeats this in different terms, writing to 'his own son Titus,' and calling it 'the washing of regeneration,' and the renewing of the Holy Ghost.'[3] He expounds it, writing to the Corinthians, in plain and positive language, telling them that 'by one Spirit are we baptised all into one body, whether we be Jews or Gentiles, whether we be bond or free . . .'[4] that is to say, 'baptised into Christ,' as he puts it still more definitely, for developing his argument on justification, to the Romans[5] and Galatians.[6] 'For ye are all one in Christ Jesus,' as he tells the latter, borrowing the very words uttered by our Lord in His prayer for unity, given in the last Gospel, and pointing out to them its realisation in their own persons by the action of the Holy Ghost at their baptism. Numerous restatements or amplifications of this fact are found in other passages up and down his Epistles. First, those which speak of that 'sealing' which we call 'confirmation.' As he says in his Epistle to the Ephesians: 'In whom also, after that ye believed, ye were sealed with the Holy Spirit of promise.' And again: 'Grieve not the Holy Spirit of God, whereby ye are sealed unto the day of redemption.'[7] Anciently this formed part of the baptismal rite, reserved to the Apostles. 'Then laid they their hands on them, and they received the Holy Ghost.'[8] Next, those which speak of putting on the new man. As he tells the Corinthians: 'Therefore, if any man be

---

[1] xxviii 19
[2] ἄνωθεν, S John iii 3 The 'anew' of the Revised is as inadequate as 'again' of the A V Then ἐξ in the fifth verse means more than 'of'
[3] iii 5
[4] 1 Cor xii 13
[5] vi 3
[6] iii. 27–8
[7] i 13 and iv. 30 Comp 2 Cor i 22
[8] Acts viii 17

in Christ, he is a new creature; old things are passed away; behold, all things are become new.'[1] And again: 'This I say, therefore, and testify in the Lord . . . that ye put off the old man . . . and that ye put on the new man, which after God is created in righteousness and true holiness.'[2] A third way of putting it is, where he dilates on 'walking after the Spirit' in contradistinction to walking after the flesh;[3] on 'the spiritual' as opposed to the 'natural man';[4] on the 'fruits of the Spirit' as opposed to 'the works of the flesh.'[5] All these passages are corollaries to his declaration of our oneness with Christ and our union with His body, stated in positive terms by the Apostle to be due to the action of the Holy Ghost at the font. Water is the material cause, but the Holy Ghost the real efficient cause, of our new birth. Baptism is administered in the name of the Father, Son, and Holy Ghost because the Three Persons constituting the Godhead are joint parties to it. Our union with Them results from our union with Christ, as our union with Christ results from the operation of the Holy Ghost. It was the Holy Ghost who prepared the body which Christ assumed: it is the Holy Ghost who first cleanses us from the taint inherent in man since the fall, and then at once grafts us into that immaculate body. We are no sooner made members of that body than we become members of each other, collectively forming His Church, truly called for that reason His mystical body.

To particularise the chief points on the sacrament of the Eucharist brought out by the Apostle, we must go back a little. First, as has been previously noticed, it is to him really—for S. Luke drew from him—that we are indebted for those words of our Lord, 'Do this' (twice repeated) 'in remembrance of Me,' which stamp it as a commemorative rite, and warrant its frequent celebrations. Now, in which of his Epistles are these words reported; and in what part of it?

---

[1] 2 Cor v 17 [2] Eph iv 17-24 [3] Rom viii 1
[4] 1 Cor ii 14-15 [5] Gal v 19-23

In his first to the Corinthians, at the end of chap. 11: in other words, on the actual threshold of a chapter dealing exclusively with 'spiritual gifts,' or chap. 12. But, again, this is not his first mention of the Eucharist. His first mention of it occurs in chap. 10. Accordingly, we see there is a clear method in his way of handling it. For the commencement of chap. 10 is much too like an introduction to the general subject not to be taken into account. 'Moreover, brethren,' he says, 'I would not that ye should be ignorant how that all our fathers were under the cloud, and all passed through the sea, and were all baptised unto Moses in the cloud and in the sea; and did all eat the same *spiritual* meat, and did all drink the same *spiritual* drink; for they drank of that *spiritual* rock that followed them, and that rock was Christ.'[1] ... Why this reminder, and what suggested it to him? About to speak to them about the Eucharist, he was himself reminded of the discourse relating to it, preserved by S. John, where these words occur: 'I am that bread of life. Your fathers did eat manna in the wilderness, and are dead. This is the bread which cometh down from heaven, that a man may eat thereof and not die. I am the living bread which came down from heaven. If any man eat of this bread, he shall live for ever; and the bread that I will give is My flesh, which I will give for the life of the world.'[2] He recalled this address as he wrote, but in recalling it, he clenched its *spiritual* import once for all. Even 'our fathers,' who lived under the law—under a carnal dispensation—he tells the Corinthians, were *spiritually* baptised, and *spiritually* fed; and that *spiritual* meat and *spiritual* drink was Christ. *A fortiori*, therefore, they must all, who lived under the Gospel, disabuse themselves of all carnal ideas in approaching the sacraments on which he was about to dilate, particularly that of the Eucharist, of which he treats first, as most important. 'Wherefore, my dearly beloved,' he continues by way of preface to it, 'flee from

[1] Vv. 1-5.   [2] S. John vi. 48-51.

idolatry. I speak as to wise men; judge ye what I say.' Idolatry was the *counterpart* of the Law, viewed as a *carnal system*; its antagonism to the Law consisted in the worship of images and of many gods. It was opposed to the Gospel on all three grounds *equally*. Having delivered himself of this solemn warning, he bursts forth, 'The cup of blessing which we bless . . . the bread which we break,' is neither more nor less than the ' spiritual meat and drink' on which our fathers were fed in their wandering through the wilderness: it is Christ Himself. One is the ' communion of His body,' the other ' of His blood.' A very delicate question here presents itself. Was it, or was it not, intentional on the part of the Apostle, to refrain from ever using the word '*flesh*' in connection with either sacrament. 'Baptised into Christ,' he says, but *not* His flesh; and ' into His body,' *not* His flesh, again. Of 'the cup of blessing' he asks—and asks without hesitation—' is it not the communion of the blood of Christ?' and of the bread: ' is it not the communion of His body?' For having as good as told them that Christ had been the same meat to the Israelites that He was to them, and added that it was *spiritual* food in each case, the Corinthians would understand each question he propounded to them afterwards on the Eucharist to be propounded in that sense. Whereas, had he said of the bread: ' Is it not the communion of His flesh?' it might have perplexed them not a little. For had not our Lord told Nicodemus, 'That which is born of the flesh is flesh; and that which is born of the Spirit is spirit'?[1] Had He not closed the discourse, where He had talked about His flesh to the carnal Jew, in these decisive terms: 'It is the *Spirit that quickeneth*,' or maketh alive; 'the flesh profiteth nothing'? And, in *instituting* the sacrament, had He *ever* employed the word '*flesh*' Himself? The Apostle does no more than repeat his Master, when he tells the Corinthians in his second Epistle: 'The letter killeth, but the *Spirit*

[1] S John iii 6

quickeneth,' or maketh alive.[1] It is his own review of the general position that afterwards causes him to say: 'Wherefore, henceforth, know we no man *after the flesh*: yea, though we have known Christ after the flesh, yet now, henceforth, know we *Him so* no more.'[2] In other words: 'Brethren,' he says in this passage, 'though we are still in the flesh, let us have done with the flesh; let it not be so much as named amongst us. We are living under a new dispensation, opposed to it in every way—a dispensation which the Holy Ghost was sent down from heaven to watch over and impregnate with life—a dispensation for effecting our union with Christ, and incorporating us into the body which He assumed and still wears in glory, by the action of the Holy Ghost in the sacraments, and on our souls, and on the Church at large. His action is entirely veiled from the natural man: it is unseen, undiscoverable by the senses, addressed to our minds alone, *wholly spiritual*, without any carnal admixture or savour of earth. Such is the dispensation under which we live.' 'Therefore, if any man be in Christ, he is a new creature; old things are passed away; behold, all things are become new.' To crown all, as though it were the thing uppermost in his mind, and next to his heart, writing to the Romans from Corinth—to the capital of the Gentile world of that day—and desirous of impressing them deeply with the character of his mission, as 'minister (λειτουργὸς) of Jesus Christ to the Gentiles,' he has employed the identical terms which afterwards became liturgical with S. Cyril of Jerusalem, and the Latin and Greek Fathers generally, for describing the consecration of the Eucharist by the celebrant (ἱερουργῶν), through the hallowing of the oblation by the Holy Ghost[3] (ἡγιασμένην ἐν Πνεύματι ἁγίῳ προσφοράν) and also, by his application of them, recalled vividly the striking testimony given to it in advance by the last of the Prophets.[4]

[1] iii 7
[2] Ib v. 16, Revised V.
[3] Rom xv 16
[4] Malachi iii. 4.

CHAPTER III.

THUS, whichever way we turn, whether to the conception of our Lord, His baptism in the Jordan, His own comments on first appearing as a teacher in the village synagogue where He had been brought up, His own assertion of the power by which He cast out devils, His own declaration of the inner character of the kingdom of heaven which He came to preach—all recorded by SS. Matthew, Mark, and Luke—or to His other discourses recorded by S. John, or to the broad interpretation put upon them all by S. Paul, or to the *consensus Patrum* in expounding the mysteries of the Trinity and the Incarnation from Scripture generally, we find ourselves confronted by the same cardinal truth: namely, that while the Incarnation and its application to man have both been in one sense the work of the whole Godhead, it was exclusively the Son who became incarnate, and exclusively the Holy Ghost by whom His Incarnation was brought about and His Incarnate life made the pattern and earnest of its own effectual communication to redeemed man by the operation of the Holy Ghost through the sacraments. Man had to be sanctified as well as redeemed to be fitted for heaven. The Son undertook his redemption, the Holy Ghost his sanctification, and each had a corresponding dispensation assigned to it in succession. It would be difficult for man to decide which has benefited him most, the Second or the Third Person in the Godhead; in other words, which of Them has been his best 'Comforter.' It is the death upon the cross, so full of pain and shame, with good reason, on which his affections centre; yet that death and those thirty-three years passed in humiliation and preparation for it by Him who endured it were but the climax and foregone conclusion of a long series of affronts and insults offered to Him as God—in breaking, misinterpreting, and perverting His precepts, in worshipping idols in His stead, in slaughtering His prophets, and in profaning His temple—by the very people whose exclusive civilisation, spread, and aggrandisement the dispensation called the Law was designed to promote. And how can we venture to maintain that there have been fewer provocations or less shameful insults offered to the Holy Ghost under the Gospel? By how many millions of souls in all ages and lands has He not been grieved, resisted, and at length ejected, whose defilements He had washed away at the font and then made their hearts His abode previously to their driving Him out? Simony, reprobated by the Apostles themselves as a wicked affront to His Person, because founded on the supposition that His gifts might be bought with gold—when and where has it not been common in the Church? Unlawful tampering with the Creed—on what *other point* has it ever been condoned and upheld, even to the extent of precipitating a rent in the Church, but the article (framed by one General Council and then confirmed solemnly by four in succession, and with the rest of the Creed pronounced unalterable) for defining His procession? Lastly, this unique sacrament of the Eucharist on which we are now engaged, will it not have to be confessed that the prime point in celebrating it, on which the modern Church is at variance with the primitive, consists *in the suppression*, throughout the Western Church, *of all special reference to His action* in its administration?

How much of all this may border on—and really, perhaps, in some cases, involve—sin against the Holy Ghost, and then entail as its penalty that loss of love between Christians which has become chronic and causes so much scandal and scepticism in the world at large, churchmen of all communions would do well to consider. And there is one more point which

I have reserved for notice, before closing this digression, for its special bearings on our immediate subject. Tertullian, the earliest of the Latin Fathers (and also the earliest of any Fathers) whose various and valuable treatises have come down to us in a complete form, has given the Holy Ghost an official title, to which the whole Western Church was virtually pledged by S. Jerome [1] till it was usurped by man; and himself laid so much stress on it that we shall find it repeated again and again in his works, as though forecasting that the day might come when the Latin-speaking Church would need to be reminded of it. 'Christ,' he says, 'was vicar of His Father under the Law; and the Holy Ghost is "*vicar of Christ*" under the Gospel.'[2] Tertullian could have designated the Holy Ghost by no title better calculated to express with equal terseness all that our Lord, and S. Paul after Him, had said, and all that the early Church, in strict conformity with their words, held in common with himself, and had by degrees incorporated into the deepest of her services, on the part assigned to the Holy Ghost under the Gospel. The sum of it has already been stated in the words of Hooker : 'Life, as all other gifts and benefits, groweth originally from the Father, and cometh not to us but by the Son, nor by the Son to any of us in particular but through the Holy Ghost.' Let us now put this back into Greek, as it stands in S. Cyril of Alexandria, whose words they are : Πάντα τοίνυν ὁ Θεὸς καὶ Πατὴρ ζωογονεῖ δι' Υἱοῦ ἐν ἁγίῳ Πνεύματι. And then, in

---

[1] *In Luc* Hom xx ad init 'Quando venit Dominus Jesus, et misit Spiritum Sanctum, Vicarium suum, vallis omnis expleta est'

[2] 'Cùm proptereà Paracletum miserit Dominus, ut quoniam humana mediocritas omnia simul capere non poterat, paulatim dirigeretur, et ordinaretur, et ad perfectum perduceretur disciplina ab illo *Vicario Domini*, Spiritu Sancto' *De Virg Vel* c 1. 'Jesum Christum .. in cœlos ereptum, sedere ad dexteram Patris, misisse *vicariam vim* Spiritûs Sancti, qui credentes agat ' *De Præsc Hær* c 13 ' Spiritus Sanctus . *Christi Vicarius*' Ib c 26 'Christus Dominus, qui ab initio Vicarius Patris in Dei nomine et auditus sit et visus. ' *Adv Marc* iii 6 Most fully, *De Animâ*, c 1 ' Cui veritas comperta sine Deo, cui Deus cognitus sine Christo, cui Christus exploratus sine Spiritu Sancto ?'

HIS EPIKLESIS ALL BUT FORGOTTEN BY US. 27

a passage just before, which Hooker has not quoted entire: Πᾶσα γὰρ χάρις καὶ πᾶν δώρημα τέλειον ἐφ' ἡμᾶς ἔρχεται παρὰ Πατρὸς δι' Υἱοῦ ἐν ἁγίῳ Πνεύματι. Hooker stops at this point; must we say because the reference was lost on him, or because the reference would point to an omission in the ritual of his own day which he could not defend? Anyhow, let us hear the remainder. S. Cyril is commenting, in the sentence last quoted from him, on those words of our Lord: ' He took bread, and gave thanks, and brake, and gave to them, saying, This is my body which is given for you: do this in remembrance of me.' It is *in commenting on this verse* that he says at starting:[1] ' Every grace and every perfect gift comes to us from the Father, through the Son, in ' or ' by the Holy Ghost.' Then he continues: ' Hence what was *done* was a type for ourselves of that *prayer* which we should ever put up when the gift of the mystical and life-giving oblation is about to be made by us; which, accordingly, we are wont to do.' S. Cyril here refers pointedly to the prayer of invocation, or ἐπίκλησις, as it is still called, but which, for the inadequate notion hitherto prevailing of it, we must pause to dwell upon at some length.

Hooker never so much as alludes to it where it would have helped him most,[2] nor elsewhere that I can discover. The reaction towards the first Prayer Book of Edward VI. had not manifested itself in his day. It is not so much as noticed in the Greek Ecclesiastical Thesaurus of Suicer, nor in the modern Greek Lexicon of the Roman and Byzantine periods by E. A. Sophocles; Bingham misrepresents it in one place,[3] and says nothing on the special name given to it by the Greek Fathers in another; Goar is scarcely more precise;[4] Bona regards it only from a controversial point of view;[5] Albertin also, though he calls attention to its

---

[1] *In Luc* xxii 19
[2] *E. P* v 67
[3] *Ant.* XV. 1. 3-4, and ib. 3, 12.
[4] *Euchol* p 140, note 139
[5] *Rer Liturg* II xiii. 4–5, with Sala's notes

universal employment in the early Church.[1] Its controversial bearings were further intensified after the candid avowals of its undoubted import and intention in the ancient liturgies of the West as well as of the East by Renaudot[2] and Le Brun,[3] had drawn down upon them the vehement animadversions of the Dominican Orsi,[4] the Jesuit Benedict,[5] and others of the Ultramontane school, who foresaw instinctively what issues it involved. These were brought out professedly for the first time by Pfaff,[6] a learned Lutheran, in their true character, so far as his subject carried him, and admitted practically by Le Quien[7] in his notes on S. John Damascene, and by the Benedictine Toutée[8] in his dissertations on S. Cyril of Jerusalem; the latter of whom strove to neutralise what he was unable to gainsay by the consoling reflection, 'Totam hanc controversiam ad fidem nihil pertinere.'[8] And this is a position which seems to have been conceded till recently by all who followed—by Johnson,[9] for instance; by Brett,[10] and even by Neale,[11] whom Daniel largely quotes on so many points with such deserved praise, but, on this, remarks curtly, 'Difficillima quæstio omnino non enodata est.'[12] Archdeacon Cheetham[13] under ἐπίκλησις, and Mr. Blunt under 'Invocation,'[14] in their respective Dictionaries, also limit their explanations to its liturgical sense. Mr. Scudamore concludes his cursory treatment of it with this remark,[15] 'We may be disposed to regret that the use of a prayer expressly asking for the action of the Holy Ghost upon the elements was not continued: but it is clearly not necessary.'

Mr. Scudamore pointedly refrains from including among

---

[1] *De Sacram Euch* 1 6
[2] *Lit. Orient* vol 1 diss i c 3
[3] *Explicat de la Messe*, vol iii Diss I art v 26
[4] *Diss de Sp S Invoc*
[5] Zach *Thesaur. Theol* x p 2, p 625
[6] *Diss de Consecratione Euchar*
[7] *De Fide Orthod* iv. 13
[8] Diss iii § 95
[9] *Unbloody Sac* c 2, § 1, subsect 4
[10] *Liturgies*, Diss, § 18
[11] *Eastern Ch* Introd vol 1 diss ix
[12] *Cod Liturg* vol iv note 1 top 69
[13] *Dict of Christ Antiq*
[14] *Theol Dict*
[15] *Not Euchar.* Part II. c vi § 7, p 591

the authorities cited by him in the short section where this remark occurs any reference to the great work of Dr. Neale, whom, indeed, he rarely quotes on any point unconnected with the Armenians, except to find fault with. On the other hand, Dr. Hoppe, whose treatise specially devoted to this subject exhausts it in all senses but one, justly credits Dr. Neale with having been *the first* to clear the ground from which a complete view of it alone was obtainable.[1] And then he himself, having studied it from that standpoint, became so convinced of its intrinsic necessity, that, by way of insuring its ubiquity whenever the sacrament of the Eucharist is celebrated, he rests it in the celebrant, who performs the act of consecration on each occasion in the power of the Holy Ghost received by him at his ordination.[2]

The admission implied in this solution is clearly that of one who has looked all the facts of the case full in the face, done strict justice to them in his own work, and tried hard to reconcile them with existing forms which he is, *ex officio*,[3] bound to defend. Yet even in his solution, interpreted by the remarks with which he has accompanied it, we may detect glimpses of that higher ground which the title of his work, possibly, dispensed him from exploring further, but which my title constrains me never, from first to last, either to lose sight of myself or allow it to pass out of sight with my readers. For what, after all, is ἐπίκλησις but a *de fide* dogma put into prayer? It must have welled from the lips of the Apostles themselves on the day of Pentecost. Its dogmatic expression is simply what has been already twice given in the words of Hooker and of S. Cyril of Alexandria, viz. that 'every good gift, originating with the Father, cometh not to us but by the Son, nor by the Son to any of us in particular but through the Holy Ghost.'

[1] *Die Epiklesis*, p 42, note 93 (Schaffhausen, 1864)
[2] Ib Zweiter Theil, *Absicht und Berechtigung der Epiklese*, pp 263-7
[3] As Rector of the Diocesan Seminary at Braunsberg of Ermland in Prussia

30 CONFOUNDING PERSONS IN THE GODHEAD.

This truth having been accepted everywhere by all as part of the deposit which the Church had received from the Apostles and the Apostles from Christ, was it not a natural consequence—nay, matter of course—that the whole Church should be found at her earliest dawn, invoking the action of the Holy Ghost in every celebration of each sacrament, and with marked emphasis in celebrations of the most august? I shall show that this was the case presently; but first let me press the doctrinal point home. Could His agency cease to be recognised or could any other, human or Divine, be substituted for His, in any single case, *salvâ fide*? That the whole Trinity co-operated in redeeming, as well as in creating, man, is a Catholic doctrine; but, push it too far, and we are precipitated into Sabellianism. Praxeas,[1] and Sabellius, and those who maintained their opinions, were pronounced heretics, and were called Patripassians. They were pronounced heretics because they refused to admit any distinction of Persons in the Godhead. They were called Patripassians, *from confounding Their offices*. The second error in this case sprang from the first, but it is equally pernicious with the first. He who begins with either is sure to end in the other. The offices assigned in Scripture to each member of the Godhead can no more be confused than Their Persons. From the teaching of Praxeas and Sabellius it would follow logically that the Father suffered on the Cross. The Catholic doctrine was that it was neither the Father nor the Holy Ghost who suffered on the Cross, but only the Son—He who became man. Equally false teaching it would have been to have asserted that the Son was conceived in the womb of His mother by the Father or by Himself; equally false to have asserted that it was the Father or the Son who descended on the day of Pentecost upon the Church. Nor can we avoid applying the same rule to

---

[1] As Tertullian, in his terse manner, says of him: 'Unicum Dominum vindicat omnipotentem mundi conditorem, ut de unico hæresim faciat Ipsum dicit Patrem descendisse in virginem '—*Adv Prax.* 1

the sacraments. It would be false teaching to assert that the Father or the Son or Both are received in any laying on of hands, unless, mediately, through the Holy Ghost. He who commanded His Apostles to administer baptism in the name of the Father, and of the Son, and of the Holy Ghost, said not, 'Except a man be born of water and' of the Father, or of the Son, but 'of the Spirit.' He who heard His disciples murmuring over the 'hard saying' with which He had dismissed the Jews, unable to comprehend *how* He could give them His flesh to eat, solved this difficulty for them, as He had that other for Nicodemus, by emphasising the same agent, 'It is the Spirit who quickeneth.' Hence the Fathers apply these words indifferently to prove the action of the Spirit in both sacraments.[1]

'Who does not know,' says Dr. Hoppe, in the following eminently truthful, eminently noble, burst, 'what weighty importance Christ attaches to the sending of the Holy Ghost? It is the Spirit through whom His work of redemption receives accomplishment, as we learn through S. John.[2] To the Holy Ghost *the whole work of the Redeemer is given over*; not only the truth, but also grace—the truth which Christ announces, and grace which Christ obtains. . . . He takes *not* of His own, *but of what Christ is*.[3] According to the ordinance of Christ, He functionates in the sacraments as Priest of the Church; through whom, as His visible organ, He consummates the foundations which Christ laid. It is He who baptises, confirms, forgives sins, anoints for the death-struggle, and knits the marriage-tie. Nobody doubts this. . . . We ask now: "Shall the Eucharist alone be exempted?"'

His answer to this question has been anticipated. He was driven by the necessities of his position to invent one,

---

[1] Notably, S Greg Nyssen, speaking of both in the same breath Τὸ δὲ ζωοποιοῦν τοὺς βαπτιζομένους, τὸ Πνεῦμά ἐστι καθώς φησιν ὁ Κύριος περὶ αὐτοῦ, τοῦτο λέγων τῇ ἰδίᾳ φωνῇ ὅτι τὸ Πνεῦμά ἐστι τὸ ζωοποιοῦν — *Adv Maced* § 19
[2] St John xiv 16 and 26, xv 26, xvi 7–14
[3] Ib xvi 14, specially.

too pious not to command respect, but too unhistoric to pass muster. Yet so travestied has history been on this point, that each disguise must be carefully stripped off and laid bare before we shall find ourselves in a position to determine what *is* history and what is *not*. Fortunate would it have been for me to have been preceded in this arduous task by such a learned and honest enquirer as Dr. Hoppe. I am glad to be able to refer to him at starting in confirmation of my own researches.

Accordingly, the prayer called *epiklesis*, as he writes it, or invocation of the Holy Ghost, as I explain it, was anything but peculiar to the primitive Communion Offices or Liturgies, but entered every service where the special action of the Holy Ghost was required or desired. S. Gregory Nyssen, for instance, quoted in a note by Dr. Hoppe,[1] calls the baptismal formula, supplied by S. Matthew, 'the baptismal epiklesis,' and asks what command of our Lord could be plainer? Firmilian had described it as an 'invocation of the Trinity,' some 150 years earlier.[2] S. Cyril of Jerusalem, midway between them, besides invoking the Holy Ghost himself on his catechumens during their instruction,[3] not only makes express mention of the epiklesis, as being then used at baptism, confirmation, and the Eucharist, but compares the effects produced by it at each;[4] while S. Epiphanius bears out S. Gregory Nyssen in designating the baptismal formula by that name.[5] Siricius, Bishop of Rome, tells Himerius of Tarragona that the canonical way of receiving heretics back into the Church is 'with imposition of hands, *per invocationem solam septiformis Spiritûs.*' S. Jerome, writing against the Luciferians, testifies to the same rule. S. Maximus of Turin, testifies to the unshackled character of His action: 'Notandum est quia Spiritûs Sancti gratia lege non stringitur, necessitatis vinculo non tenetur; sed, sicut ubi vult spirat, sic et quibus vult gratis

---

[1] Hoppe. p 308, note 649   [2] Ib   [3] *Catech* xvii 38
[4] *Catech* xx 3, xxi 3 xxiii 7   [5] *Ancor* § 116

THE EPIKLESIS OF THE GREEK RITUALS.

sua dona dispensat.'[1] If we turn to the Euchologion, or Greek Ritual, by Goar, and avail ourselves of the translation of several of the Offices contained in it by Dr. Littledale, we see forms of epiklesis prescribed, in regular sequence, for the identic occasions on which it was used by S. Cyril, though possibly fuller than they were then. For instance, the last prayer uttered in making a catechumen is:—

'Fill him with the might of Thy Holy Spirit, in the unity of Thy Christ, that he may no more be a child of the body, but a child of Thy Kingdom. . . .'[2]

Four pages on, we have words similar to our own at the font:—

'Thou didst hallow the streams of Jordan, sending down upon them from heaven Thy All-holy Spirit. . . . Be present now also, O merciful King, through the visitation of Thy Holy Spirit, and sanctify this water.'[3]

Previously to anointing the candidate, the oil is thus blessed:—

'Bless this oil with the might, and operation, and visitation of Thy Holy Spirit, that it may be the anointing of incorruption . . . for the removal of all evil from them who anoint with it in faith, and from those who partake of it.'[4]

In anointing the candidate with it, the priest says:—

'The servant of God is anointed with the oil of gladness in the Name of the Father, the Son, and the Holy Ghost.'

Baptism follows in the same form, only with an Amen repeated after each name. After which a second anointing takes place, the priest repeating these words:—

'The seal of the gift of the Holy Ghost: Amen.'[5]

The same form, *mutatis mutandis*, reappears at all ordinations, from the lowest to the highest. For that of a

---

[1] Serm lxi ed Migne
[2] Goar, p 339, Littledale, *Offices of the Eastern Church*, p 137
[3] Goar, 352-3; Littledale, 141
[4] Goar, 354, Littledale, 144
[5] Goar, 356, Littledale, 147

deacon, the bishop, laying his right hand on the candidate, says:—

'The Divine grace, which always healeth that which is sick, and filleth up that which is lacking, advances N. the most pious subdeacon to be deacon. Let us therefore pray for him that the grace of the All-holy Spirit may come upon him.'[1]

The formal epiklesis comes last in what follows; after which the bishop puts the stole on the newly-ordained, over the left shoulder, and his instalment takes place.

Later practice may be conveniently summarised in the words of the Orthodox Confession, submitted by the authorities of the Russian Church to the Eastern patriarchs for approval, and synodically confirmed by them on March 11, A.D. 1643.

Among the requisites to a Sacrament or Mystery, the third is:—

'The formal epiklesis of the Holy Ghost, by which the priest hallows the sacrament, with full intention of hallowing it.'

This extract conducts us appositely to our next question: namely, *To whom* is this Invocation addressed? The Holy Ghost is really the Thing invoked, *not* the Person, as might be inferred from the words as they stand here. But we shall have to notice similar phrases in the Fathers themselves before we have done. In strictness, as well as in general, it was God, or the Trinity, or the Father as representing the Trinity, who was invoked to send the Holy Spirit from heaven, as being the Person whose action was required. I know of but one liturgy where the address is to the Son, and another where the address is to the Holy Ghost; but each is a clear exception, and perhaps only due to the idiosyncrasies of the Church in which it was used. For in the *earliest* Latin Offices the action of the Holy Ghost is invoked in the same form as the Greek.

[1] Goar, 252, Littledale, 148

At the blessing of the font in the Gelasian Sacramentary the prayer is: 'Respice, Domine, in faciem ecclesiæ Tuæ . . . ut Tuæ Majestatis imperio sumat *Unigeniti Tui gratiam de Spiritu Sancto*: Qui hanc aquam regenerandis hominibus præparatam arcanâ Sui luminis admixtione fecundat'[1]—a prayer of singular beauty.

At the blessing of the oil :—[2]

'Emitte, quæsumus, Domine, Spiritum Sanctum Paraclitum de cœlis in hanc pinguedinem olei, quam de viridi ligno producere dignatus es, ad refectionem mentis et corporis.'

In anointing the baptised :—[3]

'Tu, Domine, immitte in eos Spiritum Sanctum Tuum Paraclitum; et da iis Spiritum sapientiæ et intellectûs: Spiritum consilii et fortitudinis: Spiritum scientiæ et pietatis: adimple eos Spiritu timoris Dei, in nomine D. N. Jesu Christi'—from which our own form was borrowed.

At the ordination of deacons :—[4]

'Emitte in eos, Domine, Spiritum Sanctum. . . .'

At the ordination of priests :—[5]

'Exaudi nos, Deus salutaris noster, et super famulos Tuos benedictionem Sancti Spiritûs, et gratiæ sacerdotalis effunde virtutem. . . .'

But a change manifests itself in the final benediction even of this Office,[6] which is not found in the Leonine, further enlarged both in the prayers and ritual of a MS. of the tenth century;[7] and all but completed in a still later Pontifical, where the singing of the beautiful hymn 'Veni, Creator Spiritus,' is prescribed for the first time; but where, to make way for this addition apparently, the important prayer of the older liturgy called '*Consummatio presbyteri*' disappears altogether.[8] With this exception, all the other prayers of the Gelasian are repeated, with merely verbal differences, in the Gregorian Sacramentary,[9] though it is

[1] Muratori, *Liturg* 1 569
[2] Ib p 555.
[3] Ib p 571
[4] Ib p 516
[5] Ib p 513.
[6] Ib p 514 Comp ib p 425.
[7] Ib ii p 411-14.
[8] Ib 427-30
[9] Ib pp 55, 63, 65, 360.

a ninth century MS. which contains them. Farther on, in the same volume, the same change reappears in the 'Missale Francorum' at the final benediction of presbyters, in its earliest form;[1] while the prayers in ordaining deacons and subdeacons remain unaltered in that Missal; and the prayers at blessing the font in the old Gallican Missal[2] and Gallican Sacramentary which follow.[3]

Reserving these changes for future notice, we come to our next point, viz. epiklesis, or invocation of the action of the Holy Ghost at the Eucharist. And here the first question that meets us is: How comes it that, epiklesis having been proved, from the foregoing extracts that have been given of them, to have constituted as it were the soul of all the ancient Offices of the West and East alike for baptising, confirming, and ordaining, and to be still little less even now, it was nevertheless from its employment at the Eucharist, really, that it acquired its distinctive name in olden time, and has been made the subject of so much controversy for the last thousand years or more. The answer to this question must be returned under two heads. In olden time the august character of the Eucharist differentiated it from all other rites. It was raised high on a pinnacle by itself in every mind. It was the crowning act by which both membership in the Church and union with the Head of the Church was consummated. The Apostles themselves had preached, prayed, and baptised, previously to the day of Pentecost; they had never celebrated a Eucharist till after the Holy Ghost had come down. He came down in fire, like the fire that had consumed the sacrifices of the elder dispensation—that was *essential*, more particularly for roasting the Paschal lamb. Hence the hour of His coming down, the third hour, became for ages, all over the Church, the canonical hour for celebrating the Eucharist.

---

[1] Muratori, ii pp 668-9.
[2] Ib p 740
[3] Ib. pp 849-50 Extracts from other Western Sacramentaries may be seen in Martene, *De Ant. Eccl.* *Rit* i art 18 *et seq*

Hence, too, the earliest receptacles in which the Eucharist was reserved for the sick were golden dove-cots or doves.[1] Doves of silver and gold were suspended over altars and fonts alike.[2] As Tertullian says with exquisite beauty: 'Nostræ columbæ domus simplex; in editis semper, et apertis, et ad lucem. *Amat figura Spiritûs Sancti orientem*, Christi figuram.'[3] Similarly, the Eucharistic epiklesis had this distinctive character given to it from the first: viz. that it was moulded as well as grounded on those words of our Lord to which special attention has been already directed: 'He shall glorify Me; for *He shall take of Mine, and shall shew It unto you*;' twice repeated. Certainly not least of those things which our Lord might be supposed to call His own, *at that particular time*, was the body which He had assumed, which within twelve hours He would offer on the cross for man, and whose offering he had just instituted the Eucharist in advance to commemorate. *This*, accordingly, the *Holy Ghost* would afterwards *take, and show to man*. Those words dictated to the Church the prayer with which we are now concerned. It was a twofold action of the Holy Ghost that was suggested by them; and it was a twofold action on His part, in consequence, that was invoked. The Church prayed that the Holy Ghost might descend on the Eucharistic oblation, and convert its elements into the media for incorporating Christ, both God and man, with His people: that is to say, first, by making the bread His body, and the wine His blood, in the true sense contemplated by Him when he set them apart at supper-time for that purpose; and, secondly, by fitting His people for their reception. Thus it was a twofold action of the Holy Ghost that was invoked: the first expressed in liturgical Greek by the verb ποιεῖν (to make); the second by the verbs ἀποφαίνειν or ἀποδεικνύναι (to proclaim or declare). Moderns have gone

---

[1] Du Cange, s. v *Peristeria*; Hoppe, ii, p 261
[2] Mansi, *Concil.* viii. 1040.
[3] *Adv Valent* c 5, quoted by Dr Hoppe, ib. note 566.

far to confuse these words by proving that the two last *may sometimes* do duty for the first. Sometimes, no doubt, they may; but in this particular case the fact seems to have been overlooked that Christ had already settled their meaning by anticipation Himself. In the accurate Greek Lexicons now in general use—to go no further—His own word ἀναγγελεῖ, which our A. V. readers 'show,' and the liturgical words ἀποφαίνειν and ἀποδεικνύναι have the same Latin equivalent assigned them, viz. '*renuntiare*.' But it would be difficult to prove that ἀναγγέλλειν and ποιεῖν could be interchanged. The truth of the matter is, that all three verbs are correlatives to the word used by S. Paul in writing on the same subject to the Corinthians [1]—διακρίνειν, rendered in our A. V. by 'discern.' The Holy Ghost, by declaring Christ present in the Eucharist to the recipient, enables each faithful soul to *discern* what no eye can see.

Latin authorities are still extant that cannot be gainsaid, dispensing us from all further argument on this head. Just the oldest form of the Roman liturgy that has come down to us supplies us with the most perfect model of the epiklesis of primitive times. I should spoil the moral effect of the following extracts by translating them. In the Leonine Sacramentary, then, immediately before the *Vere dignum*, or Preface, we read:—

'Mitte, Domine, quæsumus, Spiritum Sanctum, Qui et hæc munera præsentia nostra *Tuum* nobis *efficiat sacramentum, et ad hoc percipiendum nostra corda purificet.* . . .'[2]

And, again, in the same place,[3] but also the Mass for Christmas Day:—

'Munus populi Tui, Domine, placatus intende : quo non altaribus Tuis ignis alienus, nec irrationabilium cruor effunditur animantum, sed *Sancti Spiritûs operante virtute*, sacrificium jam nostrum *corpus et sanguis est Ipsius Sacerdotis*. . . .'

[1] 1 Cor. xi. 29.   [2] Muratori, *Liturg.* i. 457.
[3] Ib. 469.

Two passages in the Gelasian are to the same effect: the first for Whitsun Eve, but in the same place:—[1]

'Virtute Sancti Spiritûs, Domine, munera nostra continge: ut quod solemnitate praesenti *Suo nomine dedicavit,* et *nobis faciat intelligibile,* et aeternum. . . .'

The other is for the Post-Communion of the same day:—[2]

'Praesta, quaesumus, omnipotens Deus, ut Spiritus adveniens *majestatem nobis Filii Tui manifestando clarificet.* . . .'

And, again, in blessing an altar:—[3]

'Hoc altare *sacrificiis spiritalibus* consecrandum . . . ut in hâc mensâ sint Tibi libamina accepta, sint grata, sint pinguia, et Spiritûs Sancti Tui semper rore perfusa. . . .'

And, again, even in the Gregorian, 'post velatum altare':—[4]

'Descendat, quaesumus, Domine Deus noster, Spiritus Sanctus Tuus super hoc altare: Qui et populi Tui *dona sanctificet,* et *sumentium corda dignanter emundet. . .* '

Passages like these date themselves and cannot be explained away. If it be asked how it has come to pass that there are so few of them, I reply that to answer this exhaustively would plunge me further into modern entanglements than I would fain go now. Positive questions are what I would ask permission to confine myself to elucidate, to the utmost of my power, in what remains of this and in the following chapter. Controversial points will be reserved more advantageously for a separate chapter by themselves, and there dealt with as a whole.

The two points remaining on the positive side to be distinctly brought out are: 1. What was universally supposed to be the effect of the action of the Holy Ghost on the sacrament by those who invoked it? and 2. Was His action invoked universally, and to the exclusion of any other, during the whole period covered by the Church of the Fathers?

The first of these questions will occupy me to the end of

[1] Muratori, *Liturg* i 599   [2] Ib 600   [3] Ib. 610-11.
[4] Ib ii. 241; repeated, 487.

this chapter; the second will be commenced, but probably not finished, in the next, as it must land us in controversy. First, then, as regards the effect attributed universally to His action, anticipated or imparted, the following extracts will need no comment from me to make them plain to my readers. They have been culled indiscriminately from the primitive liturgies of the Eastern Church, edited by Dr. Neale, and of the Western, edited by Muratori. The conception in both is identic and, being of their essence, gives its character to each part alike. From first to last it is on the action of the Holy Ghost that the whole rite turns.

In anticipation of His action the altar is called in the liturgy named after S. Mark 'holy, heavenly, rational, intellectual,' and the oblation prepared for it 'rational and bloodless.'[1] In the liturgy named after S. James[2] the table is called 'spiritual and holy,' the sacrifice 'a sacrifice of praise,' and the gifts offered 'spiritual.' In the liturgy named after S. Chrysostom the altar is called 'heavenly,' the mysteries enacted on it 'divine,' the sacrifices 'bloodless.'[3] In the liturgy named after S. Basil,[4] the mysteries are called 'heavenly,' the sacrifice 'rational and bloodless,' the service 'rational.' After communicating, in the liturgy named after S. Mark the celebrant returns thanks on behalf of all for the 'holy, spotless, immortal, and heavenly mysteries,' that they have received.[5] After consecration, but before communicating, the deacon in the liturgy named after S. James bids the people pray, 'by the hallowed and honourable, heavenly, spotless, ineffable, glorious, awe-inspiring oblation' there made, that God, having received it thence on His 'holy, rational, and spiritual altar on high, for the odour of a sweet-smelling sacrifice, would send down on them His heavenly grace and the gift of His Holy Spirit in return for it.'[6] In the liturgy named after S. Chrysostom this prayer is repeated almost word for word in the

---

[1] Neale, pp 7 and 16 [2] Ib 113, 124 [3] Ib 29
[2] Ib. 39, 40, 50 [4] Ib. 154, 156 [6] Ib. 66–67.

FURTHER ILLUSTRATIONS. 41

same place,[1] to which the celebrant adds: 'Make us worthy to partake of Thy heavenly and terrible mysteries of this holy and spiritual table. . . .' 'Let us bow our heads to the Lord,' says the deacon at the conclusion of the Lord's Prayer. 'Look down from heaven, O Lord,' continues the celebrant, 'upon those who have bowed their heads unto Thee; for they have *not bowed them to flesh and blood*, but to Thee, the terrible God. . . . Hear us, O Lord Jesus Christ,' he concludes. 'Thou, who sittest above with the Father, and art thus invisibly present with us, deign by Thy mighty hand to communicate to us of Thy spotless body and precious blood, and to Thy people through us.'[2] After consecration, the celebrant, in the liturgy named after S. Basil, prays: 'Thou God, who hast received these gifts, cleanse us from pollution both of flesh and spirit, and teach us to perfect holiness in Thy fear: that we, with the pure witness of our conscience, receiving our portion of Thy hallowed things, may be united to the holy body and blood of Thy Christ, and, receiving them worthily, may have Christ dwelling in our hearts, and may become a temple of Thy holy Spirit. . . .'[3] The concluding prayer of the celebrant before communicating[4] is that of the liturgy named after S. Chrysostom. The rubrics of all four liturgies direct the breaking of *the bread* for distribution in administering communion.[5]

We must not, of course, look for the same fulness or precision in the Western liturgies. The earliest specimens given of them are but incomplete portions in each case, not the whole. Was it considered advisable to *print only* portions of them; or were the various MSS. containing them printed entire? Muratori calls attention to several passages in the Sacramentary which he prints as the Leonine[6] favouring his continuance to it of that title.

---

[1] Neale, p 138
[2] Ib pp 139–140.
[3] Ib 168.
[4] Ib 170, comp. 140.
[5] Ib 28, 71, 141 The direction is not repeated in the liturgy named after S Basil
[6] Diss c 3.

We might have liked to know, but we are not told by him, whether the particular part called 'the Canon,' which is wanting in his edition of it, was wanting in the MS. also from which his edition was drawn, dated by him about 1,000 years from his time. No Canon, again, is given by him in his printed edition of the Gelasian Sacramentary proper, in two books, embracing the whole year from Christmas to Christmas. A kind of appendix—a third book, he calls it—follows, exhibiting a Canon in full, a few pages from its commencement: but a Canon which, from its containing an addition we know on the best authority to have been made to the Roman liturgy then in use by S. Gregory the Great, must in any case be later than Pope Gelasius by one hundred years at least. Thus much everybody must admit; but it by no means follows from this testimony that we can infer more. What Venerable Bede records on this point of S. Gregory shall be given in his own words:—[1]

'Sed in ipsâ missarum celebratione tria verba maximæ perfectionis plena superadjecit'—*sentences,* he means—' " Diesque nostros in Tuâ pace disponas, atque ab æternâ damnatione nos eripi, et in electorum Tuorum jubeas grege numerari." '

These graceful sentences have long adorned that part of the Roman liturgy called for one thousand years or more 'the Canon.' But we are not told by Bede what place they occupied in the liturgy when he wrote thus of them. For in his time there was no part of the Office commonly designated by that name. What S. Gregory may have comprehended by that word when it was used by others in corresponding with him is not clear. But when his interlocutor on one occasion had blamed him for having ordered the recital of the Lord's Prayer *mox post canonem,* he corrects him, and says, 'mox post *precem,*' twice repeated, in his reply.[2] In another of his letters where the word

---

[1] *E H* ii 1 [2] *Ep* lib ix 12, ed Ben.

occurs, he merely quotes it without remark, as having been used by his correspondent.¹

Accordingly, what Muratori prints, both at the end of the Gelasian and the commencement of the Gregorian Sacramentaries, as 'the Canon,' exhibits an arrangement and a name historically several hundred years later than the times of Pope Gregory I. and Venerable Bede, though incorporated in it and also placed exactly where those words stand now, is the addition reported by the latter to have been made by the former to the Office for celebrating the Eucharist at Rome, such as it was in his day.

Could a copy be printed entire, should any exist, of the *prayer*, called by S. Augustine the *mystical* prayer,² called by Pope Vigilius 'the canonical prayer,'³ called by Pope Gregory 'the prayer' *par excellence*, when his alterations in the liturgy were challenged—called by him, according to Paul the deacon, his biographer, in describing its effect, the *catholic prayer*⁴—it would, beyond dispute, be found in strict accordance with the now disjointed remains of a liturgy from which the following extracts are taken, and would at once dispel endless false notions that have been propagated with such diligence and so long maintained respecting the origin and intact character of what is now called 'the Canon' of what is now called 'the Mass.'

'God,' then, according to the Leonine Sacramentary, satiates His people with 'heavenly gifts' in the Eucharist.[5] And they, on their part, pray 'ut Divinæ virtutis effectum, quem corporaliter sumpsimus, *spiritaliter sentiamus*;'[6] and again, 'quæ nobis munera dignaris præbere cœlestia, per hæc eadem tribuas nos inhærere cœlestibus.'

They represent themselves 'repleti cœlesti mysterio,' or, as having received 'heavenly sacraments.'[7] They pray 'ut

---

[1] *Ep* lib xiv 2 Thus, both the note to this passage and Menard's note 24 *in Lib Sacram* are simple, but in them unpardonable, misstatements

[2] *De Trin* iii 4
[3] *Ep ad Prof* § 5
[4] § 23.
[5] Muratori, i 294
[6] Ib 296
[7] Ib pp. 302, 305

quæ visibilibus mysteriis celebrando suscepimus, invisibili consequamur effectu.' They ask, 'non terrena sapere, sed amare cœlestia.'[1] On Whitsunday, the prayer of the celebrant, immediately before what would now be called the Preface for the day, is : ' Propitius, Domine, quæsumus hæc dona sanctifica: et hostiæ *spiritalis* oblatione susceptâ, nosmetipsos Tibi perfice munus æternum . . .'[2] In a Preface for ordinary days God is thanked for instructing them with ' *spiritual* institutions.'[3] In a Post-Communion prayer for ordinary days He is asked to protect His people, whom he has been pleased to vivify with *spiritual food*,'[4] or ' *heavenly* meat and drink,' as it is called further on.[5] In the Preface for Christmas Day, these words are put into the mouth of the celebrant : ' *Tuæ laudis* hostiam jugiter immolantes, cujus figuram Abel justus instituit, agnus quoque legalis ostendit . . . Christus implevit.'[6]

Passing from the Leonine to the Gelasian Sacramentary, we find the presbyter, in explaining the Lord's Prayer to the candidates for baptism, observing on its first petition relating to man : ' Hic *spiritalem cibum* intelligere debemus. Christus enim est noster panis.'[7]

In the Post-Communion for Whitsunday, the celebrant says aloud : ' Præsta quæsumus, Domine, ut a nostris mentibus et *carnales amoveat* Spiritus Sanctus *affectus,* et *spiritalia* nobis *dona* potenter infundat.'[8] On the octave of Whitsunday, he says to himself: ' Remotis obumbrationibus carnalium victimarum, *spiritalem* Tibi, summe Pater, *hostiam* supplici servitute deferimus, quæ miro ineffabilique mysterio et immolatur semper, et eadem semper offertur. . .'[9]

At blessing an altar the form runs : ' Altare *sacrificiis spiritalibus* consecrandum . . . ut in hâc mensâ sint Tibi libamina accepta, sint grata, sint pinguia, et Spiritûs Sancti Tui semper rore perfusa. . . .'[10]

[1] Muratori, i 313
[2] Ib 318-20
[3] Ib 350.
[4] Ib 367
[5] Ib 392
[6] Ib 470 ; repeated in the Gelasian, 496.
[7] Ib 544.
[8] Ib 601
[9] Ib 606
[10] Ib 610-11.

In the Post-Communion for Advent we have this strong appeal:—

'Repleti *cibo spiritali alimoniæ*, supplices Te deprecamur, omnipotens Deus, ut *hujus participatione mysterii* doceas nos terrena despicere, et amare cœlestia. . . .'[1]

And in the prayers to be said by the celebrant to himself on ordinary days:—

'Munera, Domine, Tibi dicata quæsumus sanctifica, et per eadem nos placatus intende. . . .'

Or, '*Mystica* nobis prosit *oblatio*; quæ nos et a reatibus nostris expediat, et perpetuâ salvatione confirmet. . . .'[2]

The earliest MS. of the Gregorian Sacramentary from which Muratori prints he considers later by 100 years than those just extracted from—in other words, he considers it a MS. of the middle of the ninth century; it must be therefore scrutinised more closely.

Yet it repeats '*super oblata*' what would seem given a less important place in the Leonine.

'Super has, quæsumus, hostias, Domine, benedictio copiosa descendat, quæ et sanctificationem nobis clementer operetur, et de martyrum solemnitate nos lætificet.'[3]

Farther on, the same position is assigned to the following:—

'Sacrificia, Domine, Tuis oblata conspectibus, ignis ille Divinus assumat, qui discipulorum Christi Tui per Spiritum Sanctum corda succendat.'[4]

Close upon this, and in the same position once more, we have:—

'Munera, Domine, oblata sanctifica, ut Tui nobis Unigeniti corpus et sanguis fiant:'[5] to be repeated on the third Sunday after Pentecost word for word, and its commencement to commence the prayer 'super oblata' time after time. On S. Peter's day it is varied thus: 'Hostias' (*not* hostiam), 'Domine,

---

[1] Muratori, 1 p 681.
[2] Ib 701
[3] Ib ii 83, comp i 457
[4] Ib. ii 93
[5] Ib pp 95 and 165

nomini Tuo sacrandas offerimus, apostolica prosequatur oratio. . . .'[1]

On another occasion, in the same position:—[2]

'Sacrificium Tibi, Domine, *laudis* offerimus . . . hostias laudis,' farther on.

After communicating:—[3]

'Sanctificet nos, Domine, quæsumus Tui perceptio sacramenti.'

Once more 'super oblata':—[4]

'Benedictio Tua, Domine, larga descendat: quæ et munera nostra, deprecantibus Sanctis Tuis, Tibi reddat accepta, et nobis *sacramentum redemptionis efficiat.*'

This brings us to the end of the Christian year for festivals; in those for Sundays the same pronouncements occur again and again, only varied in expression; in those for special occasions, too, there is no perceptible change. In consecrating an altar, for instance, the prayer 'post velatum altare,' though quoted already for a different purpose, being as short as it is conclusive, may well be repeated:—

'Descendat, quæsumus, Domine Deus noster, Spiritus Sanctus Tuus super hoc altare: Qui et populi Tui dona sanctificet, et sumentium corda dignanter emundet.'[5]

With this our extracts from the Vatican MS. of the middle of the ninth century may well end. What Muratori prints as 'in calce Vaticani codicis,'[6] with all that follows in relation to this Sacramentary, may be described as a conglomerate of old and new matter—of old prayers still retained intact, or with new ideas or phrases introduced into them by later pens—in marked contrast to what has hitherto been printed by him. Two extracts of each kind may suffice to bear out this assertion. Of the first kind an excellent specimen occurs at the end of his latest MS.

'Propitius, Domine, quæsumus hæc dona per *virtutem*

[1] Muratori, ii 102
[2] Ib pp 116 and 125
[3] Ib 120
[4] Ib 128
[5] Ib 211
[6] Ib 274, and from that to p 507

NEW WORDS INTRODUCED. 47

Sancti Spiritûs sanctifica: et, *hostiæ spiritalis* oblatione susceptâ, nosmetipsos Tibi perfice munus æternum: per,' &c. No language could be more primitive than this; and it is to be said 'super oblata'—that is, in consecrating the oblation, as we see from a preceding extract of the same page, where the well-known formula 'Hanc igitur oblationem,' &c., identifies their place; but then the occasion, which is quite special, explains their being retained.[1]

Our second extract of the first kind is given as a Preface for the fifth Sunday after Epiphany, and runs thus:—[2]

'Vere dignum, &c, æterne Deus, et Tibi hanc immolationis hostiam offerre, quæ est salutifera, et ineffabile Divinæ gratiæ sacramentum. Quæ offertur a plurimis, et unum corpus Christi *sancti Spiritûs infusione* perficitur. Singuli accipiunt Christum Dominum, et in singulis portionibus totus est; nec per singulos minuitur, sed integrum se præbet in singulis. Propterea ipsi, qui sumimus communionem hujus sancti Panis et calicis, unum corpus Christi efficimur.'

Parts of this are couched in language which is certainly new; but, so far as concerns teaching, the old lines are maintained, and it is perfectly sound.

The first specimen of the second kind is also part of a Preface:—

'Per Christum Dominum nostrum, Cujus . . . . crux salvificat, sanguis emaculat, *caro saginat*. . . .'[3]

In the next the celebrant prays after communicating:—

'Misericordiam Tuam suppliciter deprecor, omnipotens Deus, ut me famulum Tuum, quem divinis sacramentis, carne et sanguine Domini nostri Jesu Christi Filii Tui, satiasti, ab omnibus inimicorum incursibus liberare, et carnis immunditiâ. . . .'[4]

What shall we say of these two passages? We have

---

[1] Muratori, ii 390, under this heading 'Missa pro gratiâ Sancti Spiritûs' [2] Ib 298. [3] Ib 276, repeated, word for word, p 310, and virtually, p 301. [4] Ib 390.

48 WORDS BANISHED FROM PRIMITIVE LITURGIES.

become too much habituated to their language to think of criticising it at first sight; yet, as matter of fact, it marks an era—an era to which, while they form a preface, they will be said by some to lend a colour.

Muratori tells us candidly [1] that our last extract occurs among a number of additions at the end of another of his MSS. written in a hand of about the eleventh century: which I can well believe, both of it and of its immediate predecessor; for, to the best of my belief, after diligent examination, it may be stated as a fact that *no such expressions can be found in any liturgy*, Western or Eastern, *before that time*. My thesis has been, what the foregoing extracts have been selected to prove, that the whole character of the primitive liturgies, being based on the action of the Holy Ghost, was *spiritual exclusively* throughout, allowing no carnal conception of any kind to intermingle with it except to be deprecated and cast forth. It is thus a simple fact, which no human ingenuity can set aside or explain away, that the words σὰρξ and σαρκικὸς, *caro* and *carnalis*, with their cognates, are banished from them absolutely to that degree that no such expression as even '*flesh of Christ*' is ever used in the prayers for consecrating or communicating of any single liturgy dating from primitive times; nor, again, *will any citation be found* in other portions, either after communion or before the Preface, *from that part of the sixth chapter of S. John which records His own emphatic words about His flesh to the carnal Jew*, though at the same time those liturgies themselves were *built upon* the *single sentence* by which the purport of those words was afterwards explained to His disciples: 'It is the *Spirit* who quickeneth.' They employ no words that are not strict congeners of His acts. Christ Himself, in instituting the sacrament which they commemorate, said, 'This is my body,' *not* my flesh. Even here, though they never fail to repeat His words, 'Take, eat, this is my body,' &c., they refrain from using the words

[1] Muratori, ii 381-2

THE OLD CHARGE BROUGHT AGAINST CHRISTIANS. 49

'eat' and 'drink' themselves, except when quoting Scripture or explaining it. 'Eat of this *bread* and drink of this *cup*' is freely quoted in six out of the eight liturgies given in parallel columns by Dr. Neale.[1] 'Broken and not divided: eaten, or distributed to the faithful, and not consumed,' is an explanation of the words of institution given by three.[2] 'Take,' 'partake,' 'receive' were the expressions for describing the act of communicating most in use; but in giving communion the celebrant said no more than this, 'The body of Christ' and 'The blood of Christ'; nor the recipient of each more than 'Amen.'[3]

Now, let me not be misunderstood on this point. I am simply stating the fact, which anybody may verify for himself, and a remarkable fact it is surely: that neither in consecrating nor in communicating is this expression 'the *flesh* of Christ' to be found in a single primitive liturgy, nor any reference to *those words of His to the carnal Jew* on that head recorded by S. John. Those words were just as constantly quoted and paraphrased and dilated upon lovingly by the Fathers in their own writings as by ourselves; which only makes their absence from the liturgies all the more pointed. Hence what explanation of their absence from the liturgies can be given but this, that in celebrating this august mystery the collective Church with one mind determined to know nothing *after the flesh* under any guise; yea, though it knew Christ well enough after the flesh in professing its faith, it would only know Him after the Spirit in partaking of Him?

Possibly there may have been another reason also that weighed with them—namely, the old charge brought against Christians of feeding on human flesh, of celebrating Thyes-

[1] Neale, ii 559-61
[2] Ib pp 650 and 667 '*Eat* of the *body and blood*' is an expression common to the Mozarabic and Armenian, when not quoting Scripture, but to no others Ib pp 641, 646, 689 The Armenian alone quotes S John vi 56-7 Ib pp 658 and 662 The Mozarabic 'Ave in ævum sanctissima caro Christi' (Lesley, *Missal* p 7) is 'a late insertion'; Neale, ib p. 669, note 9
[3] Bingham, xv 5, 8

E

tean orgies by night.¹ S. Augustine states openly that at first sight the words of our Lord to the carnal Jew might appear to enjoin a crime.² S. Cyril says the Jews who surrounded our Lord after the miracle of the loaves and fishes, and listened to what He said of it, thought He was inviting them to a horrible repast at which they would have to eat flesh and drink blood like savages.³

It was animated too by the same thought, in maintaining a studied reserve from expressions calculated to foster the idea that it was by carnal manducation that Christ and His elect were united in one. Eating with the mouth assimilated the outward elements to the material frame: caused the amalgamation, in other words, of one body with another. The union between Christ and His elect was of another kind, and fell under another category. It was *the union of their souls with His body*. No other union is so much as hinted at or shadowed forth in these liturgies; and it is their strength as well as their charm that they send us back to old times. When God created man He formed his body first and then united that body to a soul. The laws of their union are still unfathomable by us: chemical analysis will experiment upon them in vain to the end of time. Yet each of us accepts their union as a fact, lives on the strength of it, acts upon it day and night through life, and shrinks from everything calculated to bring about its dissolution. To us it is a much more *real* union in every sense than the assimilation of what we eat or drink to our frames, or even the acquisition of what we learn by our minds. For both our minds and our frames are, separately, the victims of a constant flux between gain and loss; but on *their union* all our interest in this life depends. When, therefore, the Son of God was about to redeem man, He decreed that the benefits of His redemption should be applied to individuals in every case by the union of each soul with the body which

¹ Theoph *ad Autol* iii 4, Athenag *Apol* c 3
² *De Doct Christiana*, iii 16
³ *In Johann* vi 62–3

He was about to offer in sacrifice for all. And that union it was which the Holy Ghost was sent down from heaven to effect: which is, in point of fact, merely the old process reversed. For *earth* our bodies were first formed, and then our souls. For *heaven* our souls are re-formed first, and then our bodies. The first Adam brought death into the world through his body; the second Adam brought life through His. Now the union of our souls with that Divine body that was offered for them ought to present no greater difficulty to our understandings than the union of our souls with our own bodies. It is but the same principle, differently carried out, in the hands of the same agent. The Holy Ghost descended the first time from heaven to prepare that body for God; He descended for the second time to communicate that body, no longer on earth, to man. His omnipresence supplies the electric cable down which currents of grace speed from that body to our souls—bridges over the distance between Christ in glory and His elect on earth. The union of our souls with His body now will ensure the complete regeneration of our whole man hereafter.

Such is the doctrine which all the Fathers who have left any definite teaching on the subject behind them *uno ore* proclaim; no other doctrine was either known or taught in the Church besides this in their time. The Church saw in her daily celebrations, all the world over, a lively realisation of those words of our Lord respecting that other Paraclete who would be with her when He was gone. 'He shall take of Mine, and shall show it unto you'[1]—a wonderful accomplishment of the night- and day-dream of her great Apostle, that by 'ministering ($\iota\epsilon\rho o \upsilon \rho \gamma o \hat{\upsilon} \nu \tau \alpha$) the gospel of God' in his way, 'the offering ($\pi \rho o \sigma \phi o \rho \grave{\alpha}$) of the Gentiles might *become* acceptable, being *sanctified by the Holy Ghost*.'[2]

It is to substantiate this *uno ore* that I must devote my next chapter.

[1] S John xvi 15   [2] Rom xv 16.

CHAPTER IV.

I MEAN this chapter to be exhaustive; but human infirmity stands often in the way of human intentions, however laboriously worked out. I have gone through, with special reference to the Eucharistic epiklesis, every piece *seriatim* in the invaluable 'Patrologia,' Greek and Latin, of the late Abbé Migne down to the end of the ninth century; and I trust in the extracts which follow to have omitted nothing that any writer has said on that subject in explicit and intelligible language within that date, and to have given his words at sufficient length to place their meaning beyond dispute; reserving for separate consideration in a subsequent chapter every piece savouring of another doctrine, but supposed to belong to the same period. Writings containing nothing to the point, or nothing authentic or in plain, unmystic terms, will be passed over in silence; under this last head I include such writers as Origen, Isychius, and the fabled Areopagite. Plain statements of the Real Presence will not always be noticed, on account of their number; but seeming contradictions to it will not fail to be pointed out where they occur. It may be premised, indeed, at starting, that the Fathers are just as distinct and just as unanimous in upholding an outward as well as an inward part of the sacrament after consecration, as in upholding the human and Divine natures of our Lord subsequently to their hypostatical union in Him. Hence they designate the sacrament at one time by the names of the outward part, never intending to imply that the inward was not there too; at another time they mention the inward alone, but are far from implying that the outward was any less than what it had been before. The liturgies themselves dispense with all further proof on that head. 'Sir, break the *holy bread*,' says the deacon to the celebrant before they communicate; which done, the celebrant, in communicating himself, 'takes a particle of the *holy bread*' and says, ' The blessed and most holy body of our Lord and God and Saviour Jesus Christ is communicated to me.'[1] This is from the liturgy named after S. Chrysostom. Amalarius,[2] with the Roman Office-book open before him in the ninth century, still mentions the 'fractio *panis*' at the same point.

1. It is common enough for a catena to begin with the honoured name of S. Justin Martyr, who may have been born before the last of the Apostles died, and who must, anyhow, have conversed with their immediate successors; but it is by no means common for the earliest authority quoted in a catena to be both the clearest and the fullest. Yet this is what S. Justin, rightly construed, is on the subject of the *epiklesis*, as it was called then, as it was used then and ever afterwards. But to be rightly construed, his times and his personal history must be fully weighed. He was a Samaritan by birth, but his ancestors were Greek, and he was taught neither the religion of the Samaritans nor their language. His opinions in early life were moulded on the writings of Plato, whose cosmogony, when he became Christian himself, he strove to harmonise with that of Moses, and whose theology with that of the Gospels. With the books of the Old Testament he was well acquainted in their Greek version, whose history he recounts, as it was told him, with great unction, professing to have verified it on the spot. Both Josephus and Philo were writers held in high esteem by him. The Gospels, he tells us, then bore that name; but his own name for them (and it is the next best

---

[1] Neale, ii pp 642 and 663, and so the rest
[2] *De Eccl Off* iii 31. 'Rumpit oblatam' is the expression of Ord Rom I in Muratori, ii 984. No earlier rubric is given by him.

that has yet been given them) is 'Memoirs.' Further, we learn from his own writings that he must have passed a considerable time at Rome; that he visited localities at Alexandria, and in towns of Italy—that he explored the rock at Cumæ, for instance, whereon the Sibyl raved; that he could have been no stranger to Jerusalem, from what he says of its actual state then; and that he disputed in the porticoes of a gymnasium somewhere [1] with Trypho the Jew. Thus we must not avoid making account of his travels, as well as of his acquaintance with books, in estimating his testimony. For had he found a different ritual at Rome from what he had found at other places visited by him, as Alexandria: and, above all, from what he remembered in Palestine, his observant mind would have certainly led him to notice those variations in some form or other, instead of leaving us to infer from his account of the ritual he describes that it was everywhere the same. Moreover, we must not forget that in describing a thing of this kind for the first time, when of special terminology there was none to select from; nor a canon of Scripture settled; nor a definite Creed formulated; nor the principle of obedience to authority taught and enforced as a duty; each writer must coin expressions for himself, which his own writings also must interpret in future, should his own terms not become current, or more precise take their place?

To apply these remarks beforehand to a passage which will occur afterwards in the context of which it forms a part: S. Justin tells us,[2] that as 'Jesus Christ our Saviour was incarnate by the Word of God, and assumed flesh and blood for our salvation, so we have been taught that the food from which our flesh and blood derive nourishment by assimilation, *having been made the Eucharist* ($εὐχαριστηθεῖσαν$) by invocation ($δι'$ $εὐχῆς$) of the Word that is from Him ($Λόγου$

---

[1] Eusebius says, at Ephesus (*E H* iv 18); but had it been there, must he not have told us something about S. Paul, and a good deal more about S John? It must have been at some considerable place, no doubt.

[2] *Apol.* i. 66.

HIS LOGOS THE HOLY GHOST.

τοῦ παρ' Αὐτοῦ), is both the flesh and blood of that same Jesus who was made flesh.' In a writer of the fourth or fifth century this passage would be difficult to explain; in S. Justin, taken by itself, it is not. S. Justin quotes the Apostles rather as credible witnesses than defers to their language. Besides he shows little or no acquaintance with the Gospel of S. John, and never once names S. Paul. But he was full of the twofold idea, that the Jehovah of the Old Testament was the Second Person of the Trinity;[1] that He who 'spake by the prophets'—or, which comes to the same thing, inspired them—was the Third. Hence their constant phrase ' *The word of God* ' or ' of the Lord ' or ' *from the Lord* '[2]—the very phrases employed by him in this passage —must have been associated in his mind with the Third Person, till he heard Christians designate the Second Person by that name. Further, his argument is, that He who brought about the conception of our Lord is He who makes the Eucharist what it is; and this, he particularly says, is what he had been *taught*, though he expresses it in terms derived from the Greek version of the Old Testament prophets, as was only natural in his case. The most, therefore, that is open to criticism *in this passage* is, that it misapplies names: that is to say, assigns a title to the Third Person of the Trinity that was henceforth reserved to the Second. Yet the Old Testament Scriptures still form part of the Christian Bible, and the Greek version of them is still in use. True, there is another passage, thirty-three chapters earlier, of the same work, in which S. Justin has been understood, and at first sight may certainly seem, to

---

[1] Almost all the early Fathers agreed with him in this opinion, says Bishop Bull, *Fid Nic* i 1, 3 *et seq*, and iv 3, 2 It is expressed most clearly *Dial c Tryph* c 126-9, while c 56 1b says it was ' by *the Holy Ghost*,' that Christ in all those passages of the O. T was called ' Lord.' Canon Swainson in Dr. Smith's *Christ Biog Dict*, art. 'Holy Ghost,' p 115, might have found this fact of assistance to him

[2] All three forms occur in Jeremiah the first in i 2 ; the second in i 4 and *passim* ; the third in xviii. 1 —all in the LXX version.

attribute the conception of our Lord as man to the action of the Second Person of the Trinity: that is, of Him who is called 'the Word' in our sense—that is, of Himself as God. Yet in that same chapter S. Justin quotes the express words of the Gospel attributing it to the action of the Holy Ghost—of the Holy Ghost by whom, according to S. Justin himself, Moses and the prophets were inspired to call Christ Lord all through the Old Testament.[1] What can be clearer than that his object in this formal statement is to identify 'the Holy Ghost' of the Gospel with 'the Word' by whom the prophets of the Old Testament were inspired? Commentators have been puzzled to know (and Otto's '*si quid video*' shows that he is still in doubt himself[2]) where 'Moses *has indicated Him*'—which S. Justin affirms he has—as 'the first-born,' *not* of, but '*to God*.[3]

Perhaps he may be referring to the verse which he credits Plato[4] with having read: 'The Spirit of God moved upon the face of the waters,' which is the *first* explicit *indication* in the books of Moses of the existence of a Divine Personality distinct from the Creator, who was, according to S. Justin, Jehovah or God the Son.[5]

If we consider that the distinctive titles now attributed, of 'the Holy Ghost' to the Third Person of the Trinity, and of 'the Word' to the Second, only date, the former from the Gospel of S. Matthew (supposing it to have been written

---

[1] See note 1 to the preceding page I had worked all this out before reading the learned work of Semisch, and am only too pleased to find how much he agrees with me—B iv 4, 2, *Doctrine of the Logos* (Ryland's Tr ii 211) Bishop Bull, among others, classes him with Tertullian and several early Fathers who confuse the titles and offices of the Son and Holy Ghost (*Def Nic* ii 4, 11, and iii 10, 13 Comp the remarks of the Benedictine editor of S Hilary, Praef § 58-68, and of S Irenæus, on iv 7, where the Holy Ghost is called 'the εἰκὼν of the Son')

[2] *Apol* i 33, note 12.

[3] Υἱὸς τῷ Πατρί could not be mistaken (ib 63), but πρώτοκος τοῦ Θεοῦ follows even there, and in all other cases where the Son is clearly meant

[4] Ib c 60

[5] ὁ μόνος λεγόμενος κυρίως υἱός, ὁ λόγος πρὸ τῶν ποιημάτων καὶ συνὼν, καὶ γεννώμενος, ὅτε τὴν ἀρχὴν δι' Αὐτοῦ πάντα ἔκτισε καὶ ἐκόσμησε — *Apol* ii 6

first), and the latter from the Gospel of S. John (supposing it to have been written last); and further, that we have literally no proof of the last Gospel having been seen by S. Justin;[1] we can hardly wonder that he should have taken such pains, at a time when all terminology was unformed or indistinct, to identify 'the Holy Ghost' of the Gospels with 'the Word' of the Old Testament prophets, thereby making Him the Announcer of Christ to the faithful both anterior to His coming in the flesh and after His ascension, as well as the prime Co-operator in His Incarnation.

Should this solution be accepted of a crucial question which has employed so many pens as yet to no purpose,[2] but which has never hitherto been argued on the same grounds as now, the remaining point—'by invocation of' ($\delta\iota'$ $\epsilon\dot{v}\chi\hat{\eta}s$)—is solved by anticipation. For $\epsilon\dot{v}\chi\hat{\eta}s$ is merely the Latin '*precis*' translated into Greek; and 'precis' sometimes alone,[3] or with adjuncts, as 'canonical' or 'mystical,' is, in liturgical language, the Latin equivalent of the Greek epiklesis. Now, as I have explained before,[4] the Greeks frequently called their prayer 'Epiklesis of the Holy Ghost'; by which they meant, *not* that the Holy Ghost was prayed to, but that He was prayed *for*. 'Invocation' or 'prayer *of* the Word,' therefore, would here mean the same, viz. prayer *for* the Word.' Nobody could have stumbled at this phrase had *epiklesis* and its history been familiar to those who merely tried to discover what explanation could be given of it compatible with good Greek—a consideration not always uppermost in the minds of the framers of liturgies.

Thus interpreted, this celebrated passage will be found

---

[1] The single reference, 'Christ said, " Except ye be born again, ye cannot enter into the kingdom of heaven '' (*Apol* 1 61), he may have heard said at the font, when he was baptised himself, just as with us

[2] See Semisch (Ryland's Tr),
vol 11 338-43, and Otto's note 4, *ad loc*

[3] Innocent I *Ep* xxv 2 'Antequam precem sacerdos faciat' S. Gregory I., already quoted, 'Orationem Dominicam idcirco mox post precem dicimus'

[4] Above, p. 34

to fall in so completely with all that follow as to leave no room for doubt that, however peculiar its language, it must mean what they mean; otherwise, its divergence must have been remarked and pointed out in ancient times, when few writers were more studied.

This, then, is the account which he gives us of the whole ceremony.[1]

'Our prayers ended, we salute each other with a kiss'— since called the kiss of peace. 'Then is brought to the president of the brethren bread and a cup of water and wine mixed, which having taken, he renders praise and glory to the Father of all things, through the name of the Son and of the Holy Ghost, with much thanksgiving for these blessings accorded to us by Him. And when the president has finished the prayers and the thanksgiving, the whole congregation present testify their assent by a loud "Amen," which in Hebrew means "may it be." The president having finished his thanksgiving, and the people said "Amen" to it, those called by us deacons administer to each of those present a portion of the bread and of the water and wine that has been made the Eucharist, taking away portions also for those who are absent.

'And this food we call the Eucharist, which nobody may share but a believer in the truth of our doctrines, and who has been washed in the laver of regeneration and for the putting away of sins, besides living as Christ has handed down. For these things are not received by us as common bread or common beverage. For, just as our Saviour Jesus Christ was incarnate by the Word of God, and assumed flesh and blood for our salvation, so we have been taught that the food from which our flesh and blood derive nourishment by assimilation, having been made the Eucharist by invocation of the Word that is from Him, is both the flesh and blood of that same Jesus who was incarnate.

'For thus the Apostles, in those memoirs called the

[1] *Apol* i 65-66.

S. IRENÆUS AGREES WITH HIM.

Gospels, drawn up by them, have handed down, as having been commanded them, that Jesus, having taken bread and given thanks, said: "Do this for remembrance of Me. This is My body." Then having taken the cup, and given thanks similarly, that He said: "This is My blood," and gave to them alone.'

It will be observed that he quotes the words of institution in a separate paragraph, *after describing* the rite, both as being contained in the Gospels and as embodying the precept on which the rite was founded. He makes frequent reference to the Eucharist in other parts of his works, showing how he valued it as an institution; but this is the only formal account given by him of the manner of celebrating it in his day, and of what he had been taught respecting it himself.

2. S. Irenæus, whom I quote next, came likewise from the East to sojourn in the West and, for aught we know, may have met him at Rome with his master, Polycarp. At any rate, from the manner in which he twice quotes him in his own work against heresies,[1] and also records his martyrdom, we must infer that S. Justin could have been no stranger to S. Irenæus (though his senior by perhaps twenty years), nor his writings either.

S. Irenæus, we know from his own statement,[2] grew up under S. Polycarp at Smyrna, and whether he accompanied him in his journey to the West or not, he tells us that Anicetus, who was Bishop of Rome then, allowed his old master to consecrate the Eucharist in the episcopal church there—plain proof that there was no difference then in their respective liturgies. And S. Irenæus himself was also sent thither with a letter, when presbyter of the Church of Lyons, from the Lyonnese martyrs, recommending him to Eleutherus, Bishop of Rome, some twenty years later;[3] so that he too must have observed the difference, had there been any, between the Gallican and Roman liturgies of that age.

---

[1] Lib iv 6, v. 26, and i. 28, all preserved by Eusebius
[2] *Frag* 2–3, ed Stieren.　　　　　[3] Euseb *E H* v 4.

Now the first passage that I shall adduce from him has a double clue to its meaning, as it has come down to us in a Greek dress as well as in the Latin of his translator. And he might be supposed to have written it with the passage from S. Justin in his mind, only put into plainer and more ecclesiastical language, such as we might expect from a bishop He says, then:—

'As the bread, which is from the earth, after receiving the *invocation of God* on it is no longer common bread, *but the Eucharist,* consisting of two things, an earthly and a heavenly; so our bodies, after partaking of the Eucharist, are no longer destructible, having hope of the resurrection that is for ever.' [1]

In this passage, the Greek, as it stands, is a quotation preserved by S. John Damascene, so that no objection can be taken to it on the score that, instead of *epiklesis*, the word has been mis-copied 'ekklesis.' The Latin word 'invocatio' shows plainly which word it was translated from; and in the remaining passage from his work against heresies, where the Greek has been preserved, it is twice, *not* 'ekklesis,' but 'epiklesis.' Here, therefore, practically, we have the formal title for this prayer in Greek, by which it has ever since been known, shortened or varied in expression, for convenience, or at the will of the writer. At one time we find it called 'the epiklesis' by itself; at another with the *genitivus objecti* following—' epiklesis of the Holy Ghost'; at another, with the *genitivus subjecti*—' of God, of the Father, of the Trinity,' the thing intended by it in all cases being, that God is invoked in it to send down the Holy Ghost on the elements, to *make* them the sacrament, and then to *declare* Christ present to the receiver. This twofold purpose is not always expressed, but it is always presupposed. The very next instance that will be adduced from S. Irenæus is of the declaratory kind. But there is yet another twofold question of great interest suggested by this passage,

[1] Hær. iv. 18, 5,

to which precedence must be given. As it contains the first extant mention of the Greek name given to this prayer, can it have been his own invention? Certainly not, or some explanation of it would have been given, or at least some account of the prayer. Instead of which it is introduced by him as a familiar title for a well-known prayer, too long current for anybody to mistake. How, then, had it first become known to him? It had descended to him, mediately through S. Polycarp, from 'the beloved disciple'—from S. John, who records those sayings of Jesus: 'It is the Spirit who quickeneth . . . He shall glorify Me; for He shall take of Mine and show it unto you.' Consequently, S. Basil was not indulging in any mere flowers of rhetoric, but actually speaking from book, when, apostrophising its origin as lost in antiquity, he says: 'Which of the saints has left us in writing the words of the epiklesis, declaratory both of the bread of the Eucharist and of the cup of blessing?'[1] The other point is, could there have been a current name for this prayer in Greek carried to France by S. Irenæus, and to Rome by S. Polycarp, and no Latin equivalent for it where Latin was spoken? That Latin equivalent, it has been pointed out already, dates from S. Justin—translated into Greek only, because his work was in Greek—but employed by him on grounds very natural in his case, resident as he was then at Rome, and preparing a memorial for presentation to the Emperor and finding in the Latin term 'precem' a word certain to be understood in both languages by Christians and pagans alike—without discovering to pagans the secret meaning which it had in the liturgy for Christians.

These reasons explain his using that word instinctively for his own purposes; but the *fact of his using* it supplies the last link of the proof—first, that both S. Irenæus and he speak of the same prayer; and, secondly, that this prayer was then as current in the West as in the East, and had a special name for it current in both.

[1] *De Spir S* § 66, ed. Ben., with the note.

I quoted S. Basil out of his turn for another purpose, the more readily for the countenance given by him to the following from S. Irenæus—the Pfaffian fragment, as it is called, but which, having been accepted and reprinted by Harvey[1] and Stieren,[2] his latest editors, needs no further discussion of its genuineness from me, though I beg to disclaim vouching for it myself.

'They who have given their attention to the deuteronomic constitutions of the Apostles, know that the Lord in the New Testament instituted a new offering in accordance with the words of the prophet Malachi.... Wherefore, the oblation of the Eucharist is also not carnal, but spiritual, and thereby pure. For we offer to God the bread and the cup of blessing, giving thanks to Him that He bade the earth bring forth these fruits for our food; and then, having finished the offering of them, we invoke the Holy Ghost to declare this sacrifice, both the bread the body and the cup the blood of Christ, that they who receive these antitypes may obtain remission of sins and everlasting life.'

Pfaff himself says he cannot determine to what work of S. Irenæus this fragment belongs. It was copied by him from a medieval common-place book, which has since disappeared, given as from S. Irenæus. In the phrase 'we invoke the Holy Ghost,' the Holy Ghost is *the object* of the prayer, as has been said before; and by 'antitypes' the outward part of the sacrament, as with us. The Holy Ghost makes the inward part present, and then enables us to discern it. There is no reference throughout the writings of S. Irenæus that have come down to us and speak of the Eucharist, to any factor in its consecration but this prayer,[3] and His agency; and, for both, the evidence both widens

---

[1] *Fragm*. 36
[2] *Fragm* 38
[3] He need not have been thinking of S Justin when he twice calls it τὸν λόγον τοῦ Θεοῦ—lib. v 2, 3, in a passage too long to quote, but where the meaning is identic, for his own τὸν λόγον τῆς ἐπικλήσεως in the next passage makes him consistent with himself We must bear this in mind when we meet with similar expressions in later writers

and gets more explicit as we proceed. More valuable than the witness of S. Irenæus himself is the singular testimony, which he mentions incidentally, rendered to them by the heretics of his day. Of one Marcus, founder of the Marcosians in France, and afterwards in Asia Minor, he reports that—

'Pretending to consecrate the Eucharist with chalices of water and wine mixed, and making the address of the invocation unusually long, he contrived they should appear purple and red, as though the Grace, which is from the Powers on high, dropped its own blood into those chalices at his invocation.'[1]

Thus heretics, as well as Fathers, representing the West and East at that date, testified to the consecration of the Eucharist by the prayer called epiklesis, and by that alone ; and, in order to prove the efficaciousness of that prayer in their hands, actually furnished a precedent for the blasphemous deceits of a later age. More than this : S. Hippolytus[2] and S. Epiphanius,[3] by quoting this passage with marked adhesion as it stands, testify to the continuance of the same teaching on that subject in the Churches and ages to which they severally belonged.

3. Origen, again (or whoever wrote the Dialogue given to him as Adamantius and ascribed to him in their 'Philocalia' by S. Basil and S. Gregory), makes the Marcionist say of the Holy Ghost : 'He comes down upon the Eucharist.'[4] In his acknowledged works he is either too mystical to be precise or too reserved to be clear. 'Touching the Eucharist,' he says in one place, 'who would find either the manner of receiving it or the ritual observed in celebrating it easy to explain ? Such mysteries are best left to the discretion of the sons of Aaron, their appointed ministers, to reveal or to keep secret as occasion may require.'[5] Yet there is one passage (misapplied, as will be pointed out later, in the

[1] *Adv Hær* 1 13, with Harvey's notes on 1 8, 17, and 1 7, 2
[2] *Philos* vi 39.
[3] *Hær* xxxiv 1
[4] § 2, with Wetsten's note
[5] *Hom* v 1.

Catechism of the Council of Trent) which shows clearly that the special sense claimed for the word εὐχὴν in S. Justin was familiar to him and his countrymen at that time; for he says:—

'Let Celsus, then, as an Agnostic, tender his thanks to demons; while we, giving thanks to the Maker of the universe, eat also, with prayer and giving of thanks for blessings received, our oblations of bread, which *through prayer* becomes a certain holy body, that also makes holy those partaking of it with right dispositions.'

He is thus in strict accord with S. Justin and S. Irenæus. Farther on he is still more explicit as to what bread he means. 'The bread,' he says, 'which is called the Eucharist is a symbol of our thanksgiving to God.'[1]

Like Tertullian, Origen calls the Holy Ghost 'Vicar of Christ,' in his commentaries on S. Luke;[2] which S. Jerome by translating with approval adopts. Hence this expression is circulated among the works of both. All that S. Justin and S. Irenæus wrote must have been well known to Tertullian, as he speaks of them both with admiration. In particular he says of S. Irenæus that he was 'a profound inquirer into doctrines of every kind.'[3] Tertullian, though he has left us no precise statement of his own on the point relating to the Eucharist which concerns us here, says of the sacrament of baptism: 'Dehinc manus imponitur, *per benedictionem* advocans et invitans Spiritum Sanctum.'[4] We shall find S. Cyril of Alexandria calling the prayer invoking the descent of the Holy Ghost 'a benediction' farther on.

Christian literature was as yet confined to a small circle and to two languages at most; and ritual was of the simplest kind everywhere, leaving but little scope for diversities. And the only questions relating to the Eucharist to which attention was directed in early times were confined to the

---

[1] *Contra Cels.* viii 33 and 57.
[2] *Hom* xxii in Luc iii 4.
[3] *Adv Valent.* c 5
[4] *De Bapt.* c 8

character of the oblation: namely, that it should include nothing else 'but what the Lord had commanded'—that is, bread and wine mingled with water.¹ Distinctions, therefore, began to be made very soon between the Eucharistic oblation and all others; not so the prayer by which it was held to be consecrated. It was only by degrees that it came to be regarded as '*the* prayer' *par excellence* by Latins, '*the* invocation' by the Greeks. A statement of Tertullian having been misconstrued, we shall be brought back to him again.

4. Midway in the third century we find S. Firmilian, a well-known occupant of the see rendered afterwards so famous by S. Basil in Cappadocia, confirming the statement quoted in advance from him in a letter translated and preserved by S. Cyprian among his own letters, where the doings of a fanatic woman are recorded, who went about his diocese 'both pretending by a by no means despicable *invocation* to consecrate bread and celebrate the Eucharist, and offering the sacrifice to God without the customary sacramental predication; baptising, too, numbers, with interrogatories put into such usual and legitimate terms as to seem in no respect to differ from the formularies of the Church Would Stephen,' asks Firmilian, 'and those who agree with him approve this, especially since neither profession of the Trinity nor the usual questions put in church were omitted by her.'² If no prayer of invocation in consecrating the Eucharist was then current at Rome, Stephen, the Roman bishop to whom Firmilian appeals, must have been at a loss to comprehend the drift of his argument.

It is a pity S. Cyprian should not have preserved the original Greek of this letter besides translating it; but there can be little doubt of the Greek word, translated by him 'invocatio,' being '*epiklesis*,' as the old translator of S. Irenæus has translated it by the same word where we have the Greek. Accordingly, what S. Firmilian means is that this woman invented a counterfeit 'epiklesis' for conse-

¹ Bingham, *Ant.* xv. 2, 3. ² *Ep* lxxv ed Ben

ciating the Eucharist in appearance so nearly resembling what he used himself in church as to be mistaken for it, but lacking all the customary sacramental terms of his own form. In administering baptism her imitation of the formularies of the Church, as might be supposed, was closer still.

Hence S. Firmilian, while testifying to the counterfeit practices of heretics in Asia Minor at that date, makes his own ritual plain. *His* 'epiklesis' and what S. Irenæus imported into France were the same; and S. Cyprian, by translating and upholding his letter in hot controversy with the Bishop of Rome for what it lays down on baptism, must have exposed himself to a fierce retort had there been the smallest discrepancy between what is stated in it on the subject of the Eucharist and his own teaching and practice. The fact is, the very question that was then argued hinged on the presence or absence of the Holy Ghost.

5. S. Cyprian and those who held with him affirmed that there could be no consecration of the chrism nor of the Eucharist by a heretic because, having lost the Holy Ghost, he could perform no spiritual ministrations.[1] Again, 'where the Holy Ghost is wanting,' as he says in another place,[2] 'there can be no sanctification of the oblation.' Could any language be plainer? It follows, accordingly, that, in the opinion of S. Cyprian and of all his African and Eastern friends, the bestowal of the inward part or thing signified in the administration of baptism and confirmation, of holy orders and the Eucharist, was so entirely dependent on the action of the Holy Ghost in each case that, where this was wanting or not forthcoming, nothing beyond the outward or elementary part was ever given or received. Yet loudly as Stephen proclaimed his dissent from their extreme views on baptism, it is nowhere so much as hinted that their views on the Eucharist were not his also.

I shall come back to S. Cyprian later, on another topic, which it would only complicate matters to dwell on now;

[1] *Ep.* lxx.   [2] *Ep.* lxiv.

S. CYRIL OF JERUSALEM. 67

and to Africa later, after additional light has been elicited from other quarters, beginning with Jerusalem.

6. There S. Cyril delivered his Catechetical Lectures A. D. 348, as presbyter of that Church, over which he subsequently presided as bishop. Of his Catechetical Lectures it may be said at once, that they illumine this subject with the fulness of the sun at mid-day, and of themselves establish his orthodoxy. But he was consecrated bishop A. D. 350 by the pupil and successor of Eusebius the Church historian at Cæsarea, and thus his lawful metropolitan, Acacius: one of the ablest of the Arians belonging to the Court party, who thought to have gained him over to their side. Disappointed in this, he was persecuted by them with a virulence that only ceased with their downfall, and drove him three different times into exile. Yet his exile has this special interest attaching to it, that it brought him into repeated contact with other dioceses and Churches besides his own: with Tarsus, where he soon acquired great distinction as a preacher; with Seleucia, where he succeeded in getting his embittered metropolitan deposed, and himself restored, at the Council held there A.D. 359; with Antioch, where he was cordially welcomed by S. Meletius; with Constantinople, where he sat in, and was highly complimented by, the Œcumenical Council held there A.D. 381. Had he noticed anything peculiar in their way of celebrating the Eucharist, or their authorities noticed anything peculiar in his, would it not have been wellnigh certain, in those days of lynx-eyed criticism, to have provoked remark and entailed dispute?

Reverting to his lectures, let us note that exactly ninety years had intervened between the death of S. Cyprian and their delivery—years of fierce persecution in their earlier portion; of State patronage in their next; and of fierce controversies in their last—abundant room surely for change, both in ritual and in teaching. But it is on antiquity that S. Cyril takes his stand throughout these lectures for both. At the same time, while constantly referring in them to

S. James, 'brother of our Lord,' as first bishop of his Church, he never attributes the Offices then in use, which he was commenting upon, to his authorship. Prescription and their own agreement with Scripture constitute the grounds on which he bases his recommendation of them to his catechumens. In instructing them on baptism, confirmation, and holy communion, in succession, he explains to them step by step the ritual and ceremonies in detail of each; devoting two lectures to baptism, one to confirmation, and two to the Eucharist;[1] but adjourning his explanation of the ceremonies of baptism and confirmation till his hearers had been recipients of both, in order that he might speak without reserve to them of the last and most august.

Coming to this, in a preliminary lecture,[2] before describing its ceremonies, he appeals, like both S. Justin and S. Irenæus, to the authority for its institution; quoting, first, the words of our Lord at full length; then referring to the water at Cana turned into wine; next, to the conversation recorded by S. John after the miracle of the five loaves; and in conclusion, at greater length, to the types and prophecies foreshadowing it under the law. These form his introduction to the ritual explained in his fifth and last lecture.

Now this, on account of its altogether exceptional character, must be carefully gone through.

A running comment, of whose authorship and date there can be no reasonable doubt—written also by one who subsequently became bishop, who sat in the second Œcumenical Council, and is classed among the Fathers of that early period—on the liturgy which he was then using in the Church he served, and that Church Jerusalem, is absolutely without parallel in patristic literature; the nearest approach to it, yet in a great measure borrowed from the lectures preceding it, being Rufinus on the Creed.

It is a point on which opinions may vary, whether, from

[1] The five called his '*Catecheses mystagogicæ*'   [2] *Mystag* iv

his not reciting the prayers he describes, they had as yet been committed to writing or not; but whichever opinion we adopt, we must admit he would not have been dealing fairly with his audience if their subject-matter had not always been the same, or if he had omitted any that could be considered a *sine quâ non* to the rite.

The scene opens with the deacon offering water to the celebrant and presbyters encircling the altar (on which the elements had previously been deposited), to wash their hands. S. Cyril unfolds the spiritual meaning of each of these ceremonies as he proceeds. The kiss of peace follows, on the invitation of the deacon. Here we must pause for a few moments, for here we have positive proof how keenly the slightest deviation in ritual was noticed and remarked upon, even in those days, by every Church from its own. In the East the kiss of peace preceded, in the Roman and African Churches it followed, consecration. Both sides were conscious of this divergence. Within half a century from this, Innocent I. of Rome animadverts upon it;[1] while S. Augustine points out to his catechumens the place given to it in his liturgy, with as marked stress as S. Cyril to his.[2] Hence the inference before proof, that no greater ritualistic differences existed in these three Churches at that time, or they would have been challenged and explanations of them demanded. The prescriptive rule laid down by S. Irenæus, and so tersely developed by Tertullian, and so unflinchingly maintained against the world in high theology by S. Athanasius, was everywhere then in full force. ‘Nobis nihil ex nostro arbitrio inducere licet, sed nec eligere quod aliquis de arbitrio suo induxerit,'[3] was the cry that went up from all. Τὰ ἀρχαῖα ἔθη κρατείτω stereotyped it with œcumenical obligation in the sixth Nicene canon. Innovations in doctrine, ritual, or Church government had no

[1] *Ep (ad Decent)* xxv 1
[2] 'Ecce ubi *peracta est sanctificatio*, dicimus Dominicam orationem..., *Post ipsam* dicitur, Pax vobiscum; et osculantur se Christiani in osculo sancto '—*Serm* ccxxvii. ed Ben
[3] Tert. *De Præscr.* c 6.

quarter given them: the Church in which they were found was called upon to account for them, and to state the authority that first licensed their use. When S. Vincentius put that rule into the language with which we are most familiar, it was fast sinking into decay, like the Church of the Fathers itself; but now it was paramount.

'After this,' proceeds S. Cyril, the celebrant exclaims aloud: "Lift up your hearts:" and you answer: "We lift them up unto the Lord." He continues: " Let us give thanks unto the Lord:" and you answer: " It is meet and just so to do."

These versicles and responses are quoted word for word by S. Augustine to his catechumens from his own liturgy, just where they are quoted by S. Cyril from his. But S. Augustine takes a leap from this point to the Lord's Prayer. S. Cyril fills up the whole chasm, thus:—

'After this we make mention of heaven, and earth, and sea; sun, moon, and stars; and the whole creation, rational and irrational, visible and invisible; angels, archangels, powers, dignities, dominions, principalities, thrones, cherubim with their many countenances, saying virtually with David: " O magnify the Lord with me." We make mention of the Seraphim also, that Esaias beheld in the Holy Ghost encircling the throne of God, and covering his face with two wings, and his feet with two, and flying with the remaining two, and saying: "Holy, holy, holy, is the Lord of hosts." For we repeat this divine song of the Seraphim that has been handed down to us, in order to be sharers in the vocal melodies of the host on high.' Such are the topics composing his Preface.

'Then, after *having sanctified ourselves with these spiritual hymns*, we beseech *the merciful God to send down the Holy Ghost upon the elements ready laid out, that He may make the bread the body and the wine the blood of Christ*. For universally whatsoever may have been brought into contact with the Holy Ghost at once becomes hallowed and changed.'

Here the statement is so full and so plain, that 'he that runneth may read.' The transition from the hymns to the '*epiklesis*' is immediate; nothing in prose or verse intervenes: *God is invoked*, to *send down the Holy Ghost*, that *He*—the Holy Ghost—may make the elements in each case what Christ called them in each case when He instituted this sacrament: in other words, to *eucharise them*, as the earliest Father who describes its celebration has expressed it—to make Christ '*really present*,' as it has since been called.

This done, S. Cyril passes at once to describe the grand intercessory prayer following, with Christ really present, to intercede, then and there *with His people*, for the whole Church and all its members, living or departed.

'Then, after the spiritual sacrifice, the bloodless and divine service, has been consummated, we beseech God, by the propitiation of that sacrifice which we represent, for the common peace of the Churches, and for the well-being of the world; for emperors, armies and allies; for the sick and afflicted; and generally, for all in need of any kind, we make common prayer, and present this sacrifice.

'Then we make mention of those who have previously gone to their rest: first, patriarchs, prophets, apostles, martyrs, that God by their prayers and good offices would deign favourably to entertain our request; then also for all holy fathers and bishops who have fallen asleep; and, in a word, for all who have fallen asleep amongst ourselves, believing it to be of the greatest profit to those souls for whom petition is made, with the sacred and thrilling sacrifice still celebrating.

'After this, we recite that prayer which the Saviour gave to His own disciples to hand down ; . . . which ended, the celebrant says: "Holy things for holy persons."'

This short sentence, consisting of two words in Latin, and four in Greek, forms a pendant to the epiklesis, and implies that its full effects had been realised: in other words, that the Holy Ghost has both sanctified the oblation, and all who are to be partakers of it—another proof how everything was held to be centred in that prayer.

Thus S. Cyril himself explains it: 'Holy is the oblation on which the Holy Ghost has descended, and holy are ye that have been vouchsafed the gift of the Holy Ghost. *Sanctis, igitur, sancta conveniunt.* They reply with becoming meekness: "One is holy; the one Lord Jesus Christ." Then one sings those divine words of the thirty-fourth Psalm, inviting them to communion—"Oh! taste and see how gracious the Lord is." . . .'

His directions to communicants in concluding this lecture are not the least interesting of the whole.

'Going up, then, not with the hollow of your hands spread out, nor with your fingers disjoined, but letting your left hand serve for a throne to your right—as about to be used for receiving a king—receive, with its palm made concave, "the body of Christ" and answer, "Amen." Next, having been admitted to communion of His body, present yourself for the chalice of His blood, not extending your hands, but bending low, adoringly and reverentially, say "Amen, be thou sanctified," as you receive.

'Finally, wait for the prayer that follows, and thank God for having deigned to make you partakers of such high mysteries.'

Thus in this lecture we possess a complete key of the most authentic, most unexceptionable kind, to all the passages already quoted or about to follow from the Fathers, supplied by one of themselves, and supplied, not from scattered extracts taken out of their context, some from commentaries, some from sermons, and some from controversial pieces, but solely from one discourse, taking the entire liturgy then in use for its text, and explaining each part of it in order to catechumens preparing for communion; delivered, too, by the presbyter of their church, who was then catechist and afterwards their bishop. Surely this was a case where the truth, the whole truth, and nothing but the truth would be told, and in which an author, on becoming bishop, was bound to have rectified all incorrect or imperfect statements of his, had it contained any.

How much is opened, accordingly, by the key thus put into our hands, it will be well to point out distinctly before going further.

(1) With the exception of the kiss of peace, which as we have seen, was given everywhere, but not in all Churches at the same time, we must conclude that the description given by S. Cyril of the liturgy then used in his Church would be, so far as essentials are concerned, a correct description of the liturgies of every Church in that age.

(2) Applying the same key to what is now printed as the liturgy of S. James, we find a way opened to us of ascertaining how much of it is old and how much new. First, then, 'the washing of hands' is thrown back indefinitely by the new matter introduced. Secondly, 'the kiss of peace' is thrown back to follow the Creed. Now, the Creed entered into no Communion Office till the fifth century. It was first introduced at Antioch by Peter the Fuller, A.D. 471, and at Constantinople by Timotheus, A.D. 511.[1] On the other hand, 'the versicles and responses' preceding the *Tersanctus* are word for word with those given by S. Cyril. The 'Eucharistic Preface,' too, corresponds so fully with the summary given of it by S. Cyril, that we can hardly doubt its being identic in words with his. But of the four prayers margined by Mr. Hammond as 'Recital of the work of Redemption, Words of Institution, Confession of Faith, and the Great Oblation,'[2] not a trace occurs in S. Cyril. The 'Invocation' may be longer here than what is described as such by S. Cyril, but it is in form the same prayer. The 'intercessory prayer,' too, must be substantially what S. Cyril used, to judge from his description, though longer, those parts excepted only which Mr. Hammond brackets. 'The 'preface to the Lord's Prayer and the *embolismus*'

[1] Bingham, *Ant* x 4, 17. [2] *Ancient Liturgies*, p 40-2.

after it are wanting in S. Cyril: as are likewise the 'prayer of humble access and elevation.' The *Sancta sanctis* with its response are word for word with S. Cyril. But of the 'fraction and commixture, consignation and intinction,' he drops no hint. All these additions are clearly moulded after the liturgies of S. Basil and S. Chrysostom, though their counterparts even there may have been additions themselves. The beautiful anthem, 'O taste and see,' sung whilst all were communicating, is identic in the existing S. James and S. Cyril, and peculiar to both.

(3) Returning to S. Cyril, on the crucial point of importance, we must conclude that in all Churches alike the elements were then considered to be made the sacrament— *eucharised*, as S. Justin puts it; consecrated, as we say ourselves—by the prayer then and still known to the Greeks as *epiklesis*, and to the Latins, down to the days of S. Gregory the Great, if no further, as *precis*, which S. Cyril epitomises in a way to leave no reasonable doubt of all it contained— namely, that it was a formal petition addressed to the Godhead[1] for the descent of the Holy Ghost, to make Christ really present—as the inward part of the sacrament—in the *body that was slain* and the *blood that was shed for man*; and then to reveal, exhibit, declare that inward part, in all its reality, to each faithful communicant, whose heart He had also prepared for its reception. If S. Cyril, in explaining all this, has employed any terms or phrases open to misconception, especially when interpreted by controversies that have occurred since, we must again remember that, having no terminology to direct him, he had to coin phrases for himself. It is therefore to his general meaning that we must refer for their explanation. And here the

---

[1] Yet also called 'Epiklesis of the Holy Ghost' (*Cat* xxi 3), and 'of the adorable Trinity' (*Cat* xix 7), by S Cyril himself, as Toutée points out (*ad l* note 2) His *Diss.* in § 92-97, learned and candid as it is, has this defect that it measures authentic treatises of the Fathers by liturgical fragments of uncertain date, and thus assumes omissions in them without proof

point, indisputably, that stands out in fullest relief is, that he refers everything to the action of the Holy Ghost. His epithets are 'spiritual,' 'bloodless,' 'holy,' 'heavenly,' throughout. It is abundantly clear that nothing carnal ever crossed his mind in connection with the ritual he describes. The word 'flesh' never occurs so much as once in his lecture any more than in his liturgy. 'The supersubstantial Bread,' he says, in commenting on the Lord's Prayer, 'is co-ordinate with the substance of the soul. . . . It passes not into the draught.' It is touched neither by the hand nor by the lips of man. The Holy Ghost makes It present in the sacrament, but enshrouds It from view; carries It straight to the heart of the receiver whose sins are purged, and unites It to his soul, as soul and body were first united, when the first Adam was formed; but preserves It from profanation by those whose souls steeped in sin block the way. Christ Himself, speaking of the Holy Ghost, said, 'He,' *not* man, ' shall glorify Me ; for He,' *not* man, ' shall take of Mine '—to wit, of the body which you now see—' and shall show It unto you.' *It*, not the soul of Christ nor His Divinity, was sacrificed for man. Our Lord, accordingly, chose that part of Him which was nailed to the cross for man, to be the medium for incorporating each of us with Himself in the Eucharist, and for applying that sacrifice to each of us at the same moment. *It*, once sacrificed for man, carries with It the extension and application of that sacrifice to every soul forming one with It. And hence that sacrifice is *perpetuated*, in being pleaded for every soul incorporated with It, at every celebration of the Eucharist, to the end of time. Nevertheless, as is the Presence, so is the Sacrifice. Both are spiritual, while both are realities in the strictest sense; being due to the action of the Holy Ghost, which equally transcends time and space, making the past contemporary with the present in its application, and spanning the distance between that Body radiant in heaven, and the mystical body petitioning for incorporation with It on earth.

Such is unquestionably the full meaning of S Cyril in this lecture, and such the teaching of the whole Church for eight centuries at least. Our Lord, being present, in the body that was slain for man, by the operation of the Holy Ghost in the Eucharist, was held to be the foundation of its propitiatory character before God and of its healing effects on man; while the operation of the Holy Ghost, determining the manner of His presence, necessarily prevented any carnal associations from gathering round its application in either respect. This will be made doubly patent as we proceed. Meanwhile, before we quit S. Cyril, let it be pointed out how completely the teaching here laid down by him on the relation of the Holy Ghost to the Eucharist accords with that of S. Cyprian and the Africans and of his own previous lectures on baptism and confirmation, viz. that the consecration and administration of the inward part of each sacrament belong to the Holy Ghost alone.

'If you play the hypocrite when you approach the font,' he says,[1] 'men indeed baptise you there, but the Holy Ghost will not baptise you. If you approach in faith, men indeed minister to you, so far as appears to the senses, but the Holy Ghost gives you that which is not seen.

Further on :—

'As the bread of the Eucharist is no longer mere bread, but the body of Christ after the invocation of the Holy Ghost, so likewise this holy chrism is no longer the bare thing it was, nor could anybody call it common *after the epiklesis*, but a gift of Christ and of the Holy Ghost . . . . for while the body is anointed with the visible chrism, the soul is sanctified by the holy, life-giving Spirit.'[2]

Once more, regard these passages from another point of view, and let the question be put, 'Is not the high doctrine maintained in these passages on the mission and official prerogatives of the Holy Ghost in relation to the sacraments of the Church inconsistent with any fancied leanings on

[1] *Cat.* xvii. 36.   [2] *Cat.* xxi. 3.

the part of the writer of them towards semi-Arianism, out of which sprang Macedonianism? Does it not answer itself?

To advert, in conclusion, to some minor points. As S. Cyril begins by informing his catechumens with what rite the liturgy commences, what ministers take part in it, and what place they occupy; then recounts what is said by the deacon and by the celebrant at each point, and what responses are made by the people where their parts are separate, the inference must be that where no such distinction is drawn, and he uses the plural 'we,' what follows concerns them all equally and unites all in spirit at least, if not in voice. All are found, accordingly, to join, 1, in the Preface; 2, in the epiklesis; 3, in the intercessory prayer after consecration; and 4, in the Lord's Prayer, at the end of which the people are directed to say 'Amen,' thus testifying their heartfelt assent to all that has preceded, besides which each communicant is directed how to arrange both hands for receiving communion and to say 'Amen' on its being administered to him in the words 'Corpus Christi' by the celebrant, the same formula virtually that was used by Christ Himself *in administering* to His Apostles, viz. 'This is My body.' On posture not a word is said; it was dictated plainly by custom *then* as now. No Church in the East but those which have been Europeanised contains sitting accommodation of any kind; all stand, when not kneeling or prostrate. By the twenty-first Nicene canon all are required to remain standing on all Sundays in the year, and between Easter and Pentecost on all week days too.

Quitting Jerusalem, where the memories of the day of Pentecost were likely to be preserved freshest, let us go forth into the world of contemporaries on all sides of S. Cyril and their immediate successors, and see what support is given to his teaching on this subject, and to his practice, by theirs.

7. S. Ephrem may well speak for the far East—the

'prophet of the Syrians' as he was called—with Nisibis and Edessa for his headquarters at different periods of his life, which was a long one, from about A.D. 308 to about A.D. 378. He would be thus forty years old or so when S. Cyril delivered his lectures. He might be thought to be commenting on them in what follows, and with a fulness that leaves nothing to be desired. As translated in the 'Library of the Fathers,' he says,[1] on Ezek. x. 2 :—

'These coals and the man that is clothed in fine linen, that bringeth and casteth them upon the people, are a type of the priest, by whose mediatorship the living coals of the life-giving body of our Lord are given away. But see, there is another cherub that reacheth forth and placeth them in his fists. This is a type to show that it is *not* the priest who is able to make the body of the bread, but another—to wit, the Holy Ghost. The priest, therefore, doth but lend his hands as a mediator, and his lips offer prayers with supplications, as a servant suing for mercy. . . .'

This is tolerably plain speaking on the part assigned by him to the priest. But the 'locus classicus' of this period is contained in a sermon of his translated from the Slavonic by Kohl A.D. 1729,[2] though its genuineness, as might have been expected, has been warmly contested.[3] Of this hereafter: of the sermon now. The key to its contents is supplied in this short sentence near the opening: '*Precibus* sacerdotis, Sanctique Spiritus adventu, panis fit corpus, vinum sanguis.' And for the present only that part of it will be given which specially concerns us here.

'The adorable Word of God,' he asks, 'who wished above all things to be made man, how should He be supposed unable to make bread His body and wine His blood? In the beginning He made the earth bring forth grass, which, therefore, to this hour, rain descending on it from heaven,

---

[1] Vol xli p 146, note d (S Ephrem), and as below, *Op* Tom Syr et Lat. tom iii p 175

[2] *Op.* vol iii 608, Greek and Latin (Rome, 1746)

[3] Ib Præf p lv, with the Antirrhetic of Peter Benedict, S J., ib. vol. i. ad init

produces grass, in virtue of the divine command it then received. Now, on the other hand, God says similarly, 'This is My body . . . . this is My blood,' and 'Do this in remembrance of Me.' Since, then, all things take place by His almighty command until He comes Himself—in His own words literally, ' Till I come '—as also the grass is renewed by rain falling on the earth; so, too, this spiritual rain—in other words, the Holy Ghost coming down at the prayers of the priest and by His own power—straightway makes this bread the body and this wine the blood. For as God in the beginning, when creating all things, brought them forth by the power of the Holy Ghost; so likewise to this day He makes all things in a supernatural way by the power of the Holy Ghost: which is what none may understand but by faith. For, as the Holy Virgin said to the archangel, ' How shall this be, seeing I know not a man? ' and received answer from Gabriel: ' The Holy Ghost shall come upon thee, and the power of the Highest shall overshadow thee '; so you may in like manner ask now, ' How can the bread become Christ's body? ' and lo! here is your answer: ' The Holy Ghost by His advent effects what the human mind cannot grasp.'

Nothing could be plainer or more explicit. The words pronounced by our Lord at the last supper, and His words in creating the world are compared. Men pray for rain to come down, to give effect to the one: the priest prays for the Holy Ghost to descend, to give effect to the other. The Holy Ghost prepared the body which the Saviour assumed at His Incarnation: the Holy Ghost makes that body present in the Eucharist; and then by making us worthy partakers of it, effects our incorporation with Him. This last is not brought out with equal fulness here; but it is implied, and it is the point on which his friend S. Basil loved to dwell most.

8. Another charming assertion of the same doctrine meets us in a short tract of another Eastern of the same

period, but less known to fame, the Greek Jerome.¹ 'Many Christians living in the world,' he says, 'experience the workings of such grace of the Holy Ghost: as, for instance, those who assist at the altar, and those who approach thither to partake of the Christian mysteries. For both overflow suddenly with tears of joy and delight; convincing every Christian thoroughly that it is not mere bread and wine that he receives then, but, in very truth, the body and blood of the Son of God *sanctified by the Holy Ghost.* For we never experience the same effects, nor ever the same grace, life, sweetness, or emotion, when we consume plain bread and wine at our own table, although the bread supplied there to us may be purer, and the wine older and of a better quality, than the bread and wine offered at the altar.'

The unassuming character of this little piece makes its testimony the more striking.

9. Egypt is just as explicit in the Alexandrian Eusebius, though who he was and when he lived may not be clear: 'Many presbyters make the oblation who are living in sin; yet God is not alienated from it on that account, but sanctifies it with the Holy Ghost; and the bread becomes the body, and the chalice becomes the blood, of our Lord Jesus Christ.'² This is from his fifth sermon.

S. Athanasius is not only too reserved, but where more explicit would require too much explanation to be quoted with effect, so far as his acknowledged works are concerned. The alleged fragment from a sermon of his to the newly-baptised, which Cardinal Mai prints,³ is not at all in keeping with his style; nor is it more than mere conjecture which makes the Eutychius who quotes it patriarch of Constantinople.⁴

10. Peter II., the successor of S. Athanasius, has a casual

---

¹ Ap Galland *Bibl Vet Pat.* vii 529.
² Mai, *Spicil Rom* ix 659-60
³ Ib *Nov Biblioth* ii 584.
⁴ Ib *Script Vet* ix 623, *note*

expression in his encyclic describing the excesses committed by the civil governor, Palladius, at his church, which is decisive both as to the ritual then in use there and to his own teaching which accompanied it. 'They got a boy of infamous character,' he says, 'dressed him in female clothes, and set him to profane, by dancing on it, the holy altar, *where we invoke the descent of the Holy Ghost.*' This letter is given at full length by Theodoret, and with full approval of its contents.[1]

Peter was succeeded at Alexandria by his brother Timothy; after whom came S. Theophilus, too well known, unfortunately, for his opposition to S. John Chrysostom for his statements to command general acceptance. But his encyclic about to be quoted comes to us in the Latin dress made for it by S. Jerome, whose approbation it must be allowed, therefore, to carry with it, testifying also to its acceptance by the West.

11. 'Origen,' he there says, 'could not have reflected that the mystic waters in baptism are consecrated by the advent of the Holy Ghost; or that the Lord's bread for exhibiting the body of the Saviour, which we break for our sanctification, with the holy chalice which we set on the table of the church, being both inanimate, are both sanctified by the invocation and advent of the Holy Ghost. . . .'[2] Had this not been the customary manner of consecrating the Eucharist in all Churches at that time, could S. Jerome have let it pass unchallenged, in bespeaking the attention of the Latin-speaking Churches to the epistle, dogmatically converting it into conclusive proof against Origen?

12. S. Isidore of Pelusium was the loving pupil of S. Chrysostom, who owed his deposition to S. Theophilus. Yet he condemns the heterodox views of a monk of his named Marathonius, on precisely the same grounds as his metropolitan had condemned Origen a few years before.

'As our Lord and Saviour, when He became man, Him-

---

[1] *E. H.* iv 19. [2] *Ep* xcviii § 13.

self taught that the Holy Ghost is the complement of the Divine Trinity, and is joined with the Father and the Son in the baptismal form, as freeing us from sin, and also declares the common bread on the mystic table to be His incarnate body, how can you presume to teach of the Holy Ghost that He is a creature?'[1]

The letters of the monk and his metropolitan thus between them show what importance was then attached by all schools and in all parts of the Church to the prayer invoking the action of the Holy Ghost to make the Eucharist what Christ had designed it to be.

13. Conformably with this, Didymus, appointed by S. Athanasius catechist of Alexandria—whose work on the Holy Ghost his pupil S. Jerome translated, and for whose Catholicity, he tells Rufinus[2] he will vouch, so far as concerns the Trinity—styles the Holy Ghost 'the Spirit of sanctification and the sanctifier';[3] adding that, although we must consider each Person in the Trinity just as competent to effect all things as the other Two, nevertheless it pleased the Father that all should be made by the Son, and have sanctification and power imparted to them by the Holy Ghost.'

Didymus imitates the reserve of his great predecessor in the catechetical school, Origen; but we must not forget that he lost his sight when a boy, and therefore could never have ministered at the altar in mature years. He has been understood to say that there were those who communicated at each hour of the day in his time at Alexandria: for he adds immediately, 'partakers of that august mystery know what I mean.'[4] Yet it is also possible that, being blind, he delighted in making spiritual communions himself and encouraged others to do the same, till the practice became popular. There is in a tract of his countryman and contemporary S. Macarius a glowing passage which points that

[1] *Ep* i 109
[2] *Adv Ruf* ii. 16
[3] *De Trin* ii 3-5, and i 36.
[4] Ib iii 21

way.¹ Anyhow this is about all the reference made by him to the Eucharist in his masterly work on the Trinity; and in his special tract on the Holy Ghost, where we might have expected more, there is none whatever. So much so, that S. Ambrose, who borrowed largely from it in his own treatise, supplements it on the very point with which we are concerned here most; investing his own statement thereby with enhanced interest, as will be remarked again in dealing with it.

14. S. Nilus, though brought up by S. Chrysostom at Constantinople, may speak also for Egypt, whither he retired later in life to found a monastery. Writing to his friend Philip, he says, in a letter remarkable for its clearness and terseness alike:—²

'A charter, with reference merely to its material parts, would be called a simple compound of papyrus and glue: but after it has received the subscription of the emperor, it is called, as everybody knows, a *Sacra*. Let me beg of you to understand our Divine mysteries in the same way. Previously to the prayer of the celebrant, and the descent of the Holy Ghost, the oblation is only simple bread and wine. But subsequently to that awful invocation, and the advent of the adorable, life-giving, and gracious Spirit, the elements deposited on the holy table are no longer simple bread and common wine, but the immaculate body and precious blood of Christ the Lord of all, cleansing each devout and earnest communicant from defilement of every kind.'

S. Nilus here reproduces the teaching of two patriarchates at different times in his life.

15. S. Cyril of Alexandria was quoted almost at starting for the dogma translated by Hooker, to the effect that 'Life groweth originally from the Father; and cometh not unto us but by the Son; nor by the Son to any of us in particular but by the Holy Ghost.' Yet in his application of it he will require careful analysis, and full explanations, to

¹ *De Carit.* c. 29.   ² *Ep* lib i. 44.

be understood now and then. A very delicate controversy disturbed his episcopate; and it originated with the bishop of a see that had long been in violent antagonism to his own, with grave faults committed on both sides. Circumstances of this kind should have put him on his guard; but his own temper was impetuous, and not the least likely to be mollified by the conceit of the man whose crude teaching he had to expose. Yet, when he carried his temper with him into the subtler dogmas which he had to expound, he obscured his undoubted greatness as a theologian. For now and then he pushed his conclusions too far, and had to retract. We must begin, then, by recalling the plain statements of his predecessors on the point which concerns us most.

His own uncle, S. Theophilus, had condemned Origen for teaching doctrines incompatible with the action of the Holy Ghost on the Eucharistic oblation, which was held to be sanctified by His descent thereon. And S. Peter, the successor of S. Athanasius, in a glowing encyclic had informed the world of the foul outrage recently perpetrated in his church by the desecration of the altar whereon he and his were wont to invoke the descent of the Holy Ghost.

Now, in commenting on the institution of the Eucharist as described by S. Luke, S. Cyril both applies his own dogma to the letter and repeats his predecessors.[1]

'The Saviour,' he says, 'gives thanks: that is, He discourses in prayer, as it were, with God the Father, by way of declaring Him a joint author and approver of the vivific blessing about to be imparted to us. For every grace and every perfect gift comes to us from the Father through the Son by the Holy Ghost. Accordingly, what was done was *a type to ourselves of the prayer which should always ascend from us*'—'typum nobis exhibebat *precis ejus*, quam proferre deberemus,' as the received Latin version has it[2]—

[1] *In Lucam*, xxii. 19
[2] Mai, *Pat Nov. Bibl* ii 414, gives it as it stands in Migne.

'in presenting that oblation of mystical and vivifying grace, which has therefore become customary with us. For, having offered up our thanksgivings and ascribed glory to the Father, Son, and Holy Ghost in a common doxology, we thus draw near to the holy table, believing that we are blest and vivified by what we receive there. For we receive within us the Word of the Father, incarnate for our sakes, and both life and life-giving.'

Nothing could be plainer or fuller than this, except in one single particular. He not only testifies to the habitual use by his Church of the prayer for the descent of the Holy Ghost on the bread and wine, called *epiklesis* by his predecessors, but makes the act of our Lord in giving thanks *its type*. Yet, it will be observed, he gives no name to it in this passage. And all through his other writings his own name for it is not theirs, but 'mystical eulogia': that is to say, he calls it by one name peculiar to himself, yet authorised in the Gospels, and S. Justin by another. S. Justin speaks of the *eucharised*, S. Cyril of the *eulogised*, oblation: one founds his name for that prayer on the act of our Lord in giving thanks; the other on the act of our Lord in blessing. But as it is the act of our Lord in giving thanks *only* which is recorded by S. Luke, S. Cyril, in commenting on S. Luke, pronounces that act its type there, though he prefers elsewhere naming it from the act of blessing which S. Luke omits. That such is his name for that prayer is plain from the following.

(1) 'It is no lamb from the flock which sanctifies those that are in Christ, but Christ Himself, *holily consecrated through the mystical eulogia*, by favour of which we are blest and quickened.'[1]

(2) 'To the true worshippers of God, there will be, *by means of the spiritual eulogia*, participation in the mysteries of Christ and in the grace which is supplied in holy baptism.'[2]

(3) 'God formerly descended on the sacrifices offered to

[1] *In Luc.* xxii. 14.   [2] *De Ador. in Sp. et Ver.* vi. p. 177.

Him in the form of fire and consumed them . . . but on the spiritual sacrifice now presented to Him, He comes down invisibly by the Holy Ghost, declaring its life-giving character to those who desire to be partakers of it. And we receive the veritable Thing in faith.'[1]

(4) The liturgy that he used, whether what is now called S. Mark's or not, contained the usual proclamation to intending communicants in the usual place—'Sancta sanctis'—on which his namesake of Jerusalem had commented a century before : ' Sancta sunt, quæ proposita sunt, recepto Spiritûs Sancti superventu.' The Alexandrian Cyril expounds the other member of the sentence thus :—[2]

'Though the Magdalen may not touch Christ, nothing hinders all who have been made partakers of the Holy Ghost from touching Him. Hence to those desiring to receive *the mystical eulogia*'—giving his name, not to the prayer here, but to the effect of that prayer—' the ministers of the holy mysteries in a loud voice say, *Sancta sanctis*: indicating that to remain to communicate is most befitting such as have been sanctified by the Spirit.'

'The eulogia,' Bingham observes, 'in the more ancient writers *is the very same with the Eucharist,* . . . but in after ages it was distinguished from the Eucharist as something that after a sort supplied the room of it. The Council of Nantes, A.D. 890, ordered the presbyters to keep some part of the people's oblations till after the service, that such as were not prepared to communicate might on every festival and Lord's day receive *this eulogia,* when blessed with a proper benediction.'[3] This is perfectly true, so far as it goes: there is a form for blessing it, which is still used in France, where it is called '*pain béni*,' and handed round during High Mass indiscriminately to all who put out their hands for it.

But neither Bingham, nor Suicer, to whom he refers, nor

---

[1] *De Ador in Sp et Ver* xi p 404   [2] *In Joh* xx 17.
[3] *Ant* xv 4, 3.

any writers of that period, appear to have been acquainted with the prayer called ' Epiklesis,' and consequently fail to notice that by the *mystical eulogia* S. Cyril constantly means this prayer as well as its effect, which we call ' the Real Presence'; and that by the epithets 'mystical' and ' spiritual ' which he applies to it he proclaims its identity with the ' mystical prayer ' of S. Augustine, the ' canonical prayer' of Vigilius,' and the ' catholic prayer ' of S. Gregory the Great. And this fact, unearthed, discloses another fact, further still from the surface.

One of the writings of S. Cyril in which this prayer is so designated by him is his celebrated encylic with its twelve anathemas against Nestorius, which instantly became standard at Rome from the extraordinary confidence reposed in its author and his teaching by Pope Celestine. Dionysius Exiguus accordingly translated it from the Greek to go with his Latin version of the Canons. Its seventh section runs thus:—

' Of necessity we should add this too. For declaring the death according to the flesh of the only-begotten Son of God, that is of Jesus Christ, and confessing His resurrection from the dead, and His ascension into heaven, we celebrate the bloodless sacrifice in our churches. *And thus we proceed to the " mystical eulogia," and are sanctified*: having been made partakers of the holy flesh and the precious blood of Christ the Saviour of us all. . . .'

' Sic etiam ad mysticas benedictiones accedimus, et sanctificamur,' is the rendering of the italicised words by Dionysius,[1] and in the ' Prisca Versio ' which preceded his,[2] on which we shall dwell presently: but first let us try to do full justice to the unique character of this all-important passage, on which apparently not a word has been expended hitherto. For S. Cyril is here literally giving us the order for consecrating the oblation then observed in the Alexandrian liturgy, so that by comparing it with that of S. Mark as

[1] Mansi, iv. 1090.   [2] Ib v. 507.

now printed, we may discover at a glance what he omits.[1] For he quotes its *ipsissima verba* from the point at which he starts. He begins, then, *not* with the words of institution, like that of S. Mark, but, passing them over in silence, like his namesake of Jerusalem, he recites the commemoration of the death, resurrection, and ascension of the Saviour, *which is made to follow them* in that of S. Mark now; and so comes to the prayer, *just as* it is still given there, for the action of the Holy Ghost *on the elements* and in *the hearts of intending communicants*,[2] and which he therefore designates in the plural number, 'mystical benedictions': as Dionysius both translates and interprets him at the same time. We shall find a great deal more to elicit from this unusually distinct statement as we proceed; it only remains to notice the decisive rendering of it by Dionysius. Dionysius was bringing out his Latin version of the Canons about the time, or just before the time, when Gelasius became Pope (A.D. 492), whereby general interest was awakened at once to the subject in the West: the firstfruits of which are still to be seen in the Gelasian Sacramentary, and may with absolute confidence be set down to Pope Gelasius. For that Pope, being an African, must have been well acquainted with what S. Augustine and his own contemporary S. Fulgentius had written on' the part assigned to the Holy Ghost in consecrating the oblation, and with the epiklesis of the African liturgy then in use: for which they will both be cited in evidence further on, and, indeed, Gelasius himself. In the Leonine Sacramentary, then, the Office for ordaining presbyters ends with their 'consecration.'[3] In the Gelasian this is repeated word for word, after which follow (1) their 'Consummation' and (2) their 'Benediction.' In this last the petition of the latter part runs thus:—

'Ut purum atque immaculatum ministerii Tui donum

---

[1] Liturgies by Neale and Littledale, pp. 22-24; Hammond, pp 186-7

[2] Ἔτι δὲ ἐφ' ἡμᾶς, καὶ ἐπὶ τοὺς ἄρτους, καὶ ἐπὶ τὰ ποτήρια ταῦτα Τὸ Πνεῦμά Σου τὸ Ἅγιον κατάπεμψον, ἵνα αὐτὰ ἁγιάσῃ καὶ τελειώσῃ

[3] Muratori, *Liturg Rom*. i. 425.

custodiant: et, *per obsequium plebis Tuæ*, corpus et sanguinem Filii Tui *immaculatâ benedictione* transforment.'[1]

That this last expression owes its origin to the celebrated encyclic of S. Cyril there can scarce be so much as a shadow of doubt; but further discussion of it now would be premature for anything beyond the light which it throws on the prayer there so designated by S. Cyril, which is that the name given to it by him indicates in the clearest way the intention of the Church in formulating it: viz. that it expressed the deep sense she felt of the need of a prayer equal in efficacy to those words of her Divine Head in both blessing and giving thanks which are *not* recorded, and which, had they been recorded, could never have served her children as they served Him, the Holy Ghost being ἴδιον Αὐτοῦ (consubstantial with Him), which to beings created in time He could not possibly be. She therefore prayed for the very help which He had Himself, on leaving her, promised to send her from above, that her children might be certain to obtain in each sacrament, on receiving it in due form, all that it was intended to supply. Such, then, was the intention with which (in times coeval with the Apostles themselves, in the opinion of S. Basil) this prayer was framed, in the opinion of S. Cyril.

In parting from the latter, it may be well to recall the fact that his controversy with Nestorius betrayed him into statements and expressions which were severely criticised at the time, and will always require to be explained. One of the sharpest rebukes administered to him in his own day was from his aged master S. Isidore, quoted in one of the noblest defences made for him in modern times, and probably the last thing penned by the revered leader of the Oxford movement.[2] Yet there are some passages equally calling for remark that have not yet been remarked upon, in which

---

[1] Muratori, *Liturg Rom* i 514
[2] *Library of the Fathers: S Cyril* *of Alexandria*, Preface, xciv. (Parker and Rivingtons, 1881)

S. Cyril seems to confound, not, indeed, the Persons of the Son and the Holy Ghost, but their respective functions.

First, however, let us give precedence to the explanations wrung from him by Thodoret on a deeper question still. Commenting on his ninth anathema, Theodoret says that if, in contending that Christ was glorified by the Holy Ghost as being *His own*, he means that the Holy Ghost is of the same substance with Him and proceeds from the Father, all will agree with him and accept his statement as consistent with orthodoxy. But if his meaning be that the Holy Ghost is from the Son as from a cause, or has His existence through the Son, his statement will be rejected as heterodox and impious : for all believe the Lord when He says, 'the Holy Ghost, who proceeds from the Father. . . .'

S. Cyril, in reply, says it was quite true that our Lord cast out devils by the operation of the Holy Ghost, but it was not as one of the saints, to whom the Holy Ghost had imparted a power not their own. 'For the Holy Ghost both was and is the Spirit of Christ, as He was beyond any doubt of the Father too. . . . So that, although He proceeds from the Father, as the Saviour said, yet was He *not alien* from the Son.'[1] . . .

Passing to their functions : of course what either of Them is said to have done, we may not doubt might have been done by the other equally. The sole question is, to which of Them Holy Scripture, interpreted by the Church, ascribes the act. To take the clearest instance which presents itself and will of itself explain others. In his sermon against those who refused to confess that the Blessed Virgin was mother of God, printed by Mai, we have the following account given of the Incarnation :—

'At no time was Jesus ever a simple man prior to the union and communion of God with Him. But the Word Himself, present in the Blessed Virgin herself, took to Himself a temple of His own from her substance and came forth

[1] Mansi, v 123

from her, a man in outward appearance, but within very God.'[1]

Throughout this sermon the Holy Ghost has no part assigned Him in it. In the dialogue with Nestorius which follows, the verse from S. Luke declaring His action in the Incarnation is quoted, and this afterwards is twice maintained.[2] The commentary on S. Luke given to us in the same volume contains no more than fragments on the first chapter; but the statement of the Evangelist is explained on verse 5 of the second chapter, by alleging as what S. Paul says of the second Adam, γεννητὸς γέγονε πνεύματος— which seems strange. Throughout the five tomes against Nestorius, translated in the volume of the 'Library of the Fathers' to which attention has been already called, we find S. Cyril himself exclaiming:[3] 'As I have repeatedly said, He made His own the body which was taken from forth the holy Virgin;' but not a hint occurs in any part of this treatise that the Holy Ghost had been a party to its production.

Accordingly, the question is, why S. Cyril should have referred so seldom, and even then so cursorily, to the action of the Holy Ghost in bringing about the Incarnation. And this question immediately suggests another, belonging to Church history. Why was the Creed in the enlarged form given to it at the second Œcumenical Council (that of Constantinople) never quoted or even noticed at the third Œcumenical Council (that of Ephesus), over which S. Cyril presided? The only Creed recited there was the Nicene Creed, as it issued forth from the Nicene Council; and in this form the words 'by the Holy Ghost of the Virgin Mary' were wanting. But this is not all. Astounding as it may seem to us, S. Cyril, after quoting it at full length in this same treatise, turns round upon Nestorius and says:[4] 'Come now, therefore, noble sir, where, tell me, have they put of the Son, "Incarnate of the Holy Ghost and the Virgin

[1] *Nov. Bibl Pat* ii 77   [2] Ib pp 102–3.   [3] P 60   [4] P 31

Mary"?' As the revered author of the note appended to this startling appeal replies: 'Nestorius, being Archbishop of Constantinople, was not unnaturally quoting' from the Creed of Constantinople in its enlarged form.

We cannot answer either question in a few words satisfactorily by itself, but, looking at the facts generally which suggested both, we may say they prove that, during his controversy with Nestorius, S. Cyril studiously kept out of sight all passages in Holy Scripture that could be misinterpreted adversely to the perfect Godhead of the Son: not by any means that he ever failed himself to estimate them at their true value, writing as a theologian in his own closet for the edification of his flock. The controversy raised by Nestorius dealt exclusively with the union of the human and Divine natures in the Second Person of the Trinity, and S. Cyril resolved it should be rigidly confined to this point, and not extended to the relations borne by the Second Person of the Trinity to the Third by anything that fell from him. As, then, in the Council of Ephesus he took his stand on the old Nicene Creed, where the Holy Ghost was barely named, so he excluded as much as possible from his controversial tracts and letters all passages of Holy Scripture where great delicacy was required to harmonise the action of the Holy Ghost with that of the Son.

Whether S. Cyril pushed his economy—or, as it would now be called, his diplomacy—too far in any given case, we can hardly be competent at this distance of time to pronounce. What *really concerns* us is to recognise that in every such case S. Cyril must be read, as we should say, between the lines, and given full credit for everything that is in accordance with his own dogmatic teaching in other works, and with that of his orthodox contemporaries, though he makes no reference to it on this occasion. In general, if we look for them, we shall find hints thrown out, even where he speaks with most caution, of what we desiderate most.

Take, for instance, this statement in the third section of his synodical letter with the twelve anathemas appended to it.

'He through whom all things were made . . . was made man: that is, having taken of the flesh of the holy Virgin, and made it His own from the womb, He underwent birth as we. . . .'

In deference to the Orientals, he explained subsequently, that when he said 'the Virgin brought forth according to the flesh, his meaning was not to deny the supernatural part of that birth, or to subvert the operation of the Holy Ghost by which *He* formed that which was conceived in her womb.'[1]

Again, there are passages where S. Cyril seems to confound the Holy Ghost with the spirit of Christ as man, and thus to savour of Apollinarianism. For the human nature which the Son of God assumed had a body, soul, and spirit of its own—all equally sinless, and all of course centring in Christ, yet each as much a constituent part of His manhood as the other. Hence there was a 'spirit of Christ,' that was human, and as essentially distinct therefore from the Holy Ghost as man from God. Yet the Holy Ghost might in another sense be called 'the Spirit of Christ' as being consubstantial with His Divine nature, and as being in the economy of grace sent by Him. In all such cases, the context must be carefully noted. For instance, what he says in commenting on those words of our Lord, 'He [the Holy Ghost] shall glorify me.'[2] Now Estius, in his comments on the Sentences,[3] actually claims all these miracles for the soul or spirit of Christ through union with the Word. This is in plain contradiction to those many passages in the Gospels attributing them to the Holy Ghost, as S. Cyril does here. The functions assigned in Holy Scripture to the Son and Holy Ghost are not to be confounded, any more than their Persons.

---

[1] *Apol ad Anath* 1, Mansi, v. 23.
[2] John xvi 14.
[3] Lib. III dist xiv. 4 *ad fin*

16. We pass from the Egyptian to the North-African, from a Greek-speaking to a Latin-speaking Church. S. Augustine died the year before the Council of Ephesus, which, had he lived, he was to have attended. But there had been some friendly correspondence between his Church and that of S. Cyril a few years before respecting the Nicene canons, in which both of them took part, and Celestine, Bishop of Rome, whom S. Cyril represented at Ephesus, was concerned; so that they could have been no strangers to each other. Accordingly, their agreement might almost suffice for that of the entire West and East of the age in which they lived and were confessedly the foremost figures. Here, then, are some passages from S. Augustine, which in spite of his studied reserve on the subject, attest how completely both in ritual and in teaching he was at one with S. Cyril. In the most dogmatic of all his works he says:—

'We call that the body of Christ, which taken from the fruits of the earth, and duly *consecrated by the mystical prayer*, we receive for our spiritual health, in remembrance of His dying for us, and which invested with its visible form by the hand of man, *is not sanctified* to be so great a sacrament *but by the unseen* action of the Holy Ghost.'[1]

In these last words he stereotypes the character of what he calls 'the mystical prayer,' and S. Cyril in some cases, as we have seen, 'the mystical eulogia,' by making the action of the Holy Ghost the one thing needful for sacramental consecration.

Here is another passage,[2] which had best be given in his own words:—

'Norunt fideles corpus Christi, si corpus Christi esse non negligant. Fiant corpus Christi si volunt vivere de Spiritu Christi. De Spiritu Christi non vivit, nisi corpus Christi. Intelligite, fratres mei, quid dixerim. . . . Meum (corpus) vivit de spiritu meo, et tuum de tuo. *Non potest vivere corpus Christi nisi de Spiritu Christi.* . . . Hujus rei

[1] *De Trin* iii. 4, *ad fin.*   [2] *In Johan Ev* c 6, Tract xxvi § 13.

sacramentum, id est, unitatis corporis et sanguinis Christi alicubi quotidie, alicubi certis intervallis dierum, in Dominicâ mensâ præparatur, et de mensâ Dominicâ sumitur, quibusdam ad vitam, quibusdam ad exitium. Res vero ipsa, cujus sacramentum est, omni homini ad vitam, nulli ad exitium, quicunque ejus particeps fuerit. . . .'

His meaning is clear enough, though his words are somewhat involved. The Holy Ghost by His action procures the *res sacramenti* for all, and then enables all to become partakers of it with profit in whose hearts He dwells: but prevents its profanation by those from whose hearts He has been expelled by sin. This is not, indeed, the passage on which our twenty-ninth Article reposes, but it proceeds on the same lines. Unassailed by Nestorianism to the same extent as S. Cyril by Pelagianism, S. Augustine not only discusses the conception of our Lord by the Holy Ghost and the Blessed Virgin with a lucidity which makes everything clear in a didactic work,[1] but boldly forces the Arian Maximinus in a controversial work to acknowledge the Holy Ghost 'Creator of the fesh assumed by the Son.'[2] Afterwards, applying this teaching with equal boldness to the Eucharist, he maintains a twofold position in this passage: (1) that without the Holy Ghost—or Spirit of Christ, as he styles Him here—the flesh of Christ can be neither on the altar nor in the heart; and then (2) adds this magnificent corollary, that in no case can the *Saviour*, the '*res sacramenti*,' be received by any soul '*ad exitium*.' It may exist on the altar, it may exist in the hand of the celebrant, it may be proffered by him to all comers, but on being proffered to a soul steeped in sin or hypocrisy, the Holy Ghost—$\dot{o}$ $\kappa\alpha\rho\delta\iota$- $\gamma\nu\omega\sigma\tau\eta s$ [3]—blocks the way, and the principle '*sancta sanctis*,' which is the intention of the Church, is not infringed, though carried out unknown to the celebrant, and in a way that no eye can see.

[1] *Enchirid* § 11-12.   [2] *C Maxim. Ar.* ii. 17.
[3] Acts i. 24 and xv 8

Two more passages from his sermons shall be given combined in one, both for their liturgical value, and for their intrinsic beauty:—

'Tenetis sacramenta ordine suo. Primo, post orationem' (he is using this word here loosely, as we shall see further on) 'admonemini sursum habere cor . . . respondetis: "Habemus ad Dominum" . . . sequitur episcopus, vel presbyter qui offert: " Gratias agamus Domino Deo nostro." . . . Et vos attestamini, " Dignum et justum est." . . . Deinde post sanctificationem sacrificii Dei, quia nos ipsos voluit esse sacrificium Suum, quod demonstratum est, ubi impositum est primum illud—sacrificium Dei, et nos: id est, signum Rei quod sumus—ecce ubi peracta est sanctificatio, dicimus orationem Dominicam . . . post ipsam dicitur, " Pax vobiscum "; et osculantur se Christiani in osculo sancto . . ."[1]

What follows is then briefly summarised.[2]

'Mysterium vestrum in mensâ Dominicâ positum est: mysterium vestrum accipitis. . . . Audis enim: " Corpus Christi." Et respondes " Amen." Esto membrum corporis Christi ut verum sit Amen. . . . Quando Spiritûs Sancti ignem accepistis, quasi cocti estis. Estote quod videtis, et accipite quod estis. . . .'

In each of these particulars he explains, or is explained by, S. Cyril of Jerusalem. In both liturgies consecration of the elements consists in their *sanctification* by the Holy Ghost.

From what follows we learn what specific names the different prayers in each liturgy then bore.[3] He is referring to 1 Tim. ii. 1.

'Eligo in his verbis hoc intelligere, quod omnis vel pæne omnis frequentat ecclesia: ut precationes accipiamus dictas, quas facimus in celebratione sacramentorum, antequam illud quod est in Domini mensâ incipiat benedici: orationes, cum benedicitur et sanctificatur, et ad distribuendum com-

---

[1] *Serm* ccxxvii, in die Pasch iv, ed Ben
[2] *Serm* cclxxi., in die Pent. postrem
[3] *Ep ad Paul* cxlix 16

S. AUGUSTINE MISINTERPRETED.

minuitur : quam totam petitionem fere omnis ecclesia Dominicâ oratione concludit. . . .'

One more specimen shall be given in conclusion. It has been misinterpreted by Gieseler[1] to show that by the transformation recognised by the early Church after consecration was *only* meant a figurative transformation. He says in his well-known letter to Boniface :—[2]

'Nempe sæpe ita loquimur ut Pascha propinquante dicamus crastinam vel perendinam Domini passionem : cùm Ille ante tam multos annos passus sit, nec omnino, nisi semel, illa passio facta sit. . . . Nonne *semel* immolatus est Christus *in Se Ipso*, et tamen in sacramento non solùm per omnes Paschæ solemnitates, sed omni die populis immolatur : nec utique mentitur, qui interrogatus Eum responderit immolari. Si enim sacramenta quandam similitudinem earum rerum, quarum sacramenta sunt, non haberent, omnino sacramenta non essent. Ex hac autem similitudine plerumque etiam ipsarum rerum nomina accipiunt. Sicut ergo secundum quendam modum sacramentum corporis Christi corpus Christi est, sacramentum sanguinis Christi sanguis Christi est, ita sacramentum fidei fides est.' Gieseler interprets this by what he finds in another place : 'Non enim Dominus dubitavit dicere, " Hoc est corpus Meum," cum signum daret corporis Sui.'[3]

This is no doubt plain enough ; but not in the sense put upon it by Gieseler. S. Augustine never meant for one moment that the bread, which he truly calls a sign, was the sign of an *absent* thing ; he meant, on the contrary, that whereas, before consecration, the bread had been no sign at all, it became by consecration, without ceasing to be bread, the sign of a Thing spiritually and really present : and none the less really from Its being, by means of the bread, concealed from view.

17. Vol. ix. of the Benedictine edition of S. Augustine's

---

[1] Per ii div. 1 § 101, note 15.   [2] *Ip.* xcviii. § 9, ed. Ben
[3] *Cont Manich* c 12.

works is filled with his controversial pieces against the Donatists, and vol. x. with a similar collection against the Pelagians. Of these, the Donatists had encountered other antagonists long before S. Augustine was born; but there were so many points of contact and contrast between him and S. Cyril of Alexandria, that it seemed advisable to pass from one to the other without a break, and then go back to the single passage producible from a North-African of earlier date: namely, from S. Optatus, Bishop of Milevis, author of a work in seven books against the Donatist Bishop of Carthage, Parmenian, and contemporary with S. Cyril of Jerusalem. It is the unity of the Church which is set forth in this work; and it is not wanting in references to the Eucharist on that head. But the passage which concerns us now is of the kind that speaks volumes, as being incidental, drawn from the writer, like that of Peter of Alexandria, by events that could not be passed over in silence, and necessitated explicitness on his part in exposing their enormity.

'What can be more sacrilegious,' he asks his opponent, 'than to break, raze, and remove the altars of God, where you yourselves offered formerly; where the prayers of the people and members of Christ are deposited; whither Almighty God is invoked; whither the Holy Ghost, having been petitioned for, descends? . . . For what is an altar but the place where Christ is wont for a time to dwell in His flesh and blood? . . . What offence have you committed against yourselves that you should destroy those altars, on which, long before our time, you made your oblations, as you thought holily? . . .'[1]

No passage could bear stronger testimony to the ritual of the African Church than this, besides making it clear by implication that the ritual of the Donatists themselves was the same.

18. S. Fulgentius was removed by about two generations from S. Augustine, coming into notice some sixty years from

[1] Lib vi 1, with the two next chapters.

his death. His grandfather had been a senator of Carthage when it was captured by the Vandals under Genseric. He himself was born and bred at Telepte, where no expense was spared on his education. His Latin speaks for itself; but Greek he learnt also so well as to be taken for a Greek by his excellent accent. He was chosen in early life to be procurator of his native town. Later, his travels took him to Sicily and then to Rome; A.D. 507 he became bishop of Ruspe, from which he was at one time banished into Sardinia, but eventually died there. He must, however, have seen a good deal of other Latin-speaking Churches besides his own, previously to his episcopate. He was also profoundly versed in the writings of S. Augustine; and his reply to Peter the deacon and others, forming a deputation from the East to Rome on questions relating to the faith, shows that he was in entire accordance with the rulings of the third and fourth Councils, and with the letters of S. Cyril of Alexandria and S. Leo, to which that deputation had pledged their adherence.[1]

When we find him, therefore, discussing the question, 'Cur in sacrificiis solius Spiritûs missio postuletur?' we must take for granted, surely, that this was the custom of his own Church at that time, and of all other Churches that he had ever visited, of which Rome was one. For in discussing this question he argues on the supposition that it concerned all Churches alike. The question, he says, must be put in this form: 'How comes it that, the sacrifice being offered to the whole Trinity, prayer is made for the descent of the Holy Ghost only, to sanctify the oblation; as though, so to speak, God the Father, from whom the Holy Ghost proceeds, could not sanctify the sacrifice offered to Himself; nor the Son Himself sanctify the sacrifice of His own body which we represent, when He sanctified Himself the body which He offered for our redemption; or, as though the

---

[1] *Ep* xvi and xvii

Holy Ghost had therefore to be sent because the Father or the Son were wanting to us the celebrants?'[1]

No less than six chapters are gravely devoted to explain the principles underlying this practice, amid repeated testimonies to its universality. Here are four specimens.

(1) 'That as often as the Holy Ghost is asked of the Father for consecrating the oblation, the first salutary caution to be observed *by all Christians* is, that no local descent of the Holy Ghost should be supposed or imagined.[2]

(2) 'That when the descent of the Holy Ghost is invoked to sanctify the oblation of the *whole Church*, what is asked virtually seems to me to be, that by the grace of the Spirit the bond of love should be maintained intact in the body of Christ, which is the Church.[3]

(3) 'That when *the Church* asks for the Holy Ghost to be sent down to her from heaven, she asks for the gift of charity and unanimity to be bestowed on her by God. Now, when could the Church, which is the body of Christ, ask more befittingly for the descent of the Holy Ghost than to consecrate the oblation of the body of Christ?[4]

(4) 'Lest any should think that we, when the *Church* asks for the descent of the Holy Ghost *in the prayer of the sacrifice,* by the words "Holy Ghost" understand improperly that love which is shed abroad in our hearts by the Holy Ghost, who is given to us, we must refer to what has been said by the Fathers in support of our view. . . .'[5]

Quotations are then adduced from S. Augustine dwelling on the action of the Holy Ghost in the Church. One more passage shall be given where the same teaching is reiterated in controversy with the heretic Fabian.

'*Holy Church*, then, when in the sacrament of the body and blood of Christ she prays that the Holy Ghost may be sent down to her, supplicates more particularly for the gift of charity, that she may be able to maintain the unity of the

---

[1] *Ad Lomm* ii 6.   [2] C 7   [3] C 9.
[4] C 10   [5] C 12.

Spirit in the bond of peace. . . . The Holy Ghost, accordingly, sanctifies the oblation of the Catholic Church.'[1]

Now, whatever we may think of his explanations, both his character and his statements are transparent enough. He was himself the first theologian of his times, as celebrated in his particular school as Boethius and Cassiodorus in theirs. Further, his orthodoxy, knowledge, and piety went hand in hand. He was master of three languages— Latin, Greek, and his native tongue Punic. He had travelled quite sufficiently to let him into the practices of other Churches besides his own. Unless his statements, therefore, can be shown inaccurate or wanting in good faith, they amount to this—(1) that the Holy Ghost was invoked in the whole Church, when he wrote, to consecrate the Eucharistic oblation; (2) that the prayer employed for that purpose was called in his day 'the prayer of the sacrifice,' being what S. Augustine called in his 'the mystical prayer'; (3) he puts all Christians on their guard against importing into the subject of that prayer any 'local' or 'corporal' or 'temporal' considerations.

Unfortunately, the African Church came to an end within a very short time from this; had it remained till now, there would have been one Latin-speaking Church in all probability still true to his teaching. As it is, he, 'being dead, yet speaketh.'

19. Passing from Africa to Spain, the furthest limit contemplated by S. Paul in his travels,[2] we find his prayer that 'the oblation of the Gentiles (ἡ προσφορὰ τῶν ἐθνῶν) might be acceptable, being sanctified by the Holy Ghost,'[3] liturgically fulfilled there to the letter no less than in Africa. It is true that extant testimonies are scarce—though there is no saying what Spanish archives may yet disgorge— practically confined to one man, S. Isidore, though he must be considered a host in himself. The single fact that he succeeded his brother Leander in the see of Seville, who

[1] *Frag.* 28.   [2] Rom. xv. 28   [3] Ib verse 16.

contracted a lasting friendship at Constantinople with S. Gregory the Great, 'between the years 575 and 585, when Gregory was acting as apocrisiarius of Pelagius II. at the East-Roman Court,'[1] added to his own encyclopædic writings, in which 'it may be fairly said that he represented and gathered in himself all the science of his time.'[2] His intimate acquaintance with the classic and sacred languages— Latin, Greek, and Hebrew—with ritual and Church history, his high character and position, entitles everything that falls from him to the fullest credence, particularly where he merely confirms what had been said by others, as implicitly to be trusted as himself.

One of his works—and the fullest of its kind as yet published under an authentic name—is dedicated to a bishop Fulgentius (Cave says, of Carthage; but Arevalus, of Spain). He had a brother named Fulgentius, Bishop of Astigi, to whom the dedicatory letter prefixed to it would apply; otherwise he speaks of S. Fulgentius of Ruspe and his writings with unqualified praise.[3] In this work 'On the Offices of the Church,' 'the Spanish liturgy,' says Sir. W. Palmer[4]—which he nevertheless wrongly confounds with the Mozarabic, as will be presently shown—'is minutely described.' On account, then, of its crucial importance, which, strange to say, has hitherto been either overlooked or misinterpreted, I give this description of it entire, supplementing it with a further kindred extract from the same work, which is, however, not liturgical, but dogmatic; and begging especial attention to what is italicised in both.

'The order of the Mass and of the prayers by which the sacrifices offered to God are consecrated was *first instituted* by S. Peter, *and it is celebrated all over the world in the same form.*'

'The first of these prayers consists of an admonition to the people to excite them to be instant in prayer to God.

[1] Smith's *Christ Biog Dict* iii. 639.
[2] Ib. p. 307
[3] *De Vir. Illust.* c 27.
[4] *Orig. Liturg.* i. 172 *et seq.*

The second, of an invocation to God that He would of His clemency receive the prayers of the faithful and their oblations. The third is poured forth for the offerers, or for the faithful departed, that they may, through the same sacrifice, obtain pardon. The fourth is introduced after these to accompany the kiss of peace, that all, reconciled to each other in love, may be joined together worthily of *the sacrament of the body and blood of Christ*, His indivisible body being incompatible with disunion of any kind. The fifth is introduced next, by way of preface (*illatio*[1]) to the sanctifying of the oblation, when all creatures in heaven and earth are invited to join in praising God; and "Hosanna in the highest" is sung, because the salvation that ensued to the world on the birth of a Saviour of the house of David was shared on high. The sixth in succession after this is the *conformation of the sacrament*,[2] that the oblation then offered to God, *having been sanctified by the Holy Ghost*, may be conformed to the body and blood of Christ. The last of these prayers is the Lord's Prayer.' Such is his account of the ritual.

Three chapters on a dogmatic account of the Christian sacrifice follow, where, first of its origin, he says:—

'The sacrifice which Christians offer to God was first instituted by Christ our Lord and Master, in commending to His Apostles His body and blood previously to His betrayal: as we read in the Gospel, which states that Jesus took bread and the cup . . . and gave to them. . . Bread, *because it strengthens the body*, is therefore called the body of Christ; and wine, *because it puts blood into the system*,

---

[1] 'Illatio,' in missâ Mozarabicâ, est id quod in missâ Romanâ præfationem vocant, quæ in singulis missis propria est' Du Cange, *s v.* The explanation given of it by Grial belongs to the second prayer, not to this.

[2] This is the reading of Arevalus, which even Hittorp was quite prepared to admit (*De Divin Off* p 1439, ed Paris, 1624), had he not been misled by the Ordo Romanus, printed by him, on a point quite foreign to this, and which a kindred expression in S Gregory of Tours, ' Dominici corporis conformatione' (*De Gloriâ Confess* c. 52), bears out.

is therefore likened to the blood of Christ. But these, visible while they are, pass, on being sanctified by the Holy Ghost, into the sacrament of the Divine body . . .'[1]

These two statements of S. Isidore merely require to be brought into juxtaposition to render his meaning in both plain. His dogmatic statement is as conclusive testimony to his own personal teaching as his 'account of the Mass' is to the ritual then observed in the Church of his day. What he calls the sixth prayer was the prayer invoking the action of the Holy Ghost on the elements. And the result of His action was, from a liturgical point of view, 'the conformation of the sacrament'; while, from a dogmatic point of view, it was the passing of the elements into the sacrament of the Divine body and blood. Further, when he states that the order of the Mass described by him was 'first instituted by S. Peter,' he merely means that it was essentially that of the Church of Rome, as well as of all other Churches at that time—precisely what S. Fulgentius had testified on behalf of the Latin-speaking, and S. Cyril of Jerusalem on behalf of the Greek, Churches in times past. S. Isidore never would have ventured to say this of a revised or newly-constructed liturgy, like the Mozarabic. His own work, he tells his brother in dedicating it to him, was drawn up ' *ex scriptis vetustissimis auctorum*'; and from what he tells us of the works of his brother Leander,[2] it is highly probable that it was taken in hand by him to complete what his predecessor had not lived to finish. Grial says of it accordingly with perfect truth: 'Isidorus ordinem, qui ætate suâ in concilio Toletano quarto jussus est per omnem Hispaniam et Galliciam observari, tantum refert. Qui tamen ordo non idem prorsus retinetur in Mozarabo missali, quod advertit

---

[1] Suggested probably by S. Aug. *C Faust.* xx 13 'Noster autem panis et calix, non quilibet · sed certâ consecratione fit nobis, non nascitur Proinde, *quod non* ita fit, quamvis sit panis et calix, alimentum est refectionis, non sacramentum religionis'; quoted also by Hincmar of Rheims, *Fero Salom* c 10

[2] *De Vir. Illust.* c. 41

etiam Jacobus Pamelius.'[1] S. Isidore was president of the fourth Council of Toledo, whose second canon alone negatives any variation having been contemplated or effected in the public offices of the Church of Spain in his day.[2] One more passage must be quoted from him, occurring in his principal work, which must apologise for its length.

'Sacrifice, so-called as being made sacred: consecrated as it is by *the mystical prayer*, in memory of the Passion of our Lord for us. Whence we call it, in obedience to His command, the body and blood of Christ; because, while consisting of the fruits of the earth, it is sanctified and becomes a sacrament by the Spirit of God operating upon it invisibly; which sacrament of the bread and chalice the Greeks call Eucharist, or, interpreted in Latin, best grace; for could anything be better than the body and blood of the anointed One? . . . Now, the sacraments are baptism and chrism; the body and blood of Christ; called sacraments in each case, because under cover of visible things Divine grace works saving effects through the same, and by its secret and sacred virtue causes them to be thus named. Again, they are received in the Church with profit; because the Holy Spirit abiding in it works out their effect in a hidden way, whether they who administer them in the Church are good or bad. For, since it is the Holy Spirit who vivifies them unseen—in Apostolic times manifested by apparent signs—they are neither amplified by the good deserts, nor diminished by the ill deserts, of those who dispense them . . .'[3]

Passages like these could not easily be glossed over, or pass out of mind. They are repeated word for word by Rabanus Maurus, who was brought up under Alcuin in France, became Abbot of Fulda, and died Archbishop of Mayence, A.D. 856:[4] by Paschasius Radbertus, but altered in

[1] *Ad l*, *Op* p 925, ed Paris, 1601.
[2] Smith's *Dict. of Christian Ant.* ii. 1969.
[3] *Etym.* vi. 19, 38-42.
[4] *De Univ* v. 11, and *De Off* i. 18, 4.

some respects:[1] and by Ratramn or Bertram,[2] both of them monks at Corbey on the Somme in France, but opponents.

20. S. Ildefonse, who sat at the feet of S. Isidore in early life, and afterwards became Bishop of Toledo, bursts forth in a fervid address to the Virgin, illustrating their hold on him.

'I beseech thee, holy Virgin, I beseech thee that I may have Jesus of that Spirit of whom He came to be born of thee. By that Spirit may my soul receive Jesus, by whom thy flesh conceived Him. From that Spirit may it be mine to know Jesus, from whom it was thine to know, to have, and to bring forth Jesus . . .'[3]

Of France nothing is recorded at all tending to show that the teaching and ritual inaugurated at Lyons by S. Irenæus, had undergone any change down to the days of S. Hilary: and his history, for many reasons, forbids us to suppose that he would have countenanced any departure from it. Though separated by two centuries from each other, their sees, occupying central positions in France, were not far apart; and that of Poitiers, being junior to that of Lyons by nearly the same number of years that separated their two bishops,[4] would naturally look to Lyons for traditions. But S. Hilary was doomed, in 'contending for the faith once delivered to the saints,' to visit many countries and Churches besides his own: and the same year that saw him banished from France, not only saw S. Cyril of Jerusalem driven from his see, but actually brought them both into the same provinces of Asia Minor which, after a joint residence of three years (A.D. 356-9), they each quitted for the Council of Seleucia, where S. Cyril triumphed over the Acacians, and was restored to his see; while S. Hilary was ordered back into France by the Emperor. Sufferers both in the same cause, they could hardly fail to become well acquainted and often exchanged ideas. And thus in S.

[1] *De Corp et Sang Dom* c 3
[2] Ib c 40 *et seq*
[3] *De Perp Virg S Mar* c 12.
[4] *Gall Christ.* ii 1137

Cyril, as well as in Asia Minor generally, S. Hilary would find ample confirmation of the teaching and ritual which S. Irenæus had brought with him in his day from those very provinces into France. Now, by a singular coincidence, S. Cyril in his twenty-third catechetical lecture refers to the divine music of psalms sung, inviting people to communion in his Church;[1] and, according to the Benedictine editors of S. Hilary, it was when he returned home finally to rest from controversy that he composed his hymnal and book 'On the Mysteries,' mentioned by S. Jerome, but now lost: 'as though to register his own approval of the chants and other pious usages in celebrating the Eucharist observed in the East, and commend them to his flock in the West for imitation.'[2] A warm approval was given to his hymns in the thirteenth canon of the fourth Council of Toledo, where S. Isidore presided; and their employment at public services is not merely defended, but authorised in future, so far as regards Spain. Further, the only liturgical allusion which escapes S. Hilary in his extant works is where, commenting on the Psalms, he says: 'Let anybody standing outside the church listen to the voice of the people praying within, and be spectator of the hearty singing of hymns, and hear amid the offices of the Divine sacraments, the devout responses of the congregation confessing their faith.'[3] If we knew when these comments on the Psalms were penned, we might be able to decide whether he was describing what went on in his own Church after his return, or in the Churches of the East during his stay there. But S. Hilary, like S. Athanasius, was too much absorbed in upholding orthodoxy respecting the Godhead of the Son,[4] ever to dwell at any length

---

[1] § 20

[2] *Vit* § 111 According to Gennadius, both Musæus and Salvianus, presbyters of Marseilles in the next century, wrote Sacramentaries, no longer extant, and S Gregory of Tours composed a preface to another by Sidonius, Bishop of Auvergne, which has shared the same fate —Palmer, *Orig Lit* 1 144.

[3] *In Psalm* lxv 4

[4] He was one of several early Fathers, also, who confused, *not* the Persons, but the functions assigned in Scripture to the Son and Holy Ghost *Præf Gen.* § 57-68, ed Ben

upon points on which all were agreed. Besides, in speaking of the sacraments, he thought it was his bounden duty to be reserved. 'Horum igitur sacramenta et virtutes neque in gentes efferre, neque cum hæreticis conferre, permittimur,' as he remarks on those words of our Lord cautioning His disciples against casting their 'pearls before swine.'[1] All he permits himself to say of the Last Supper is confined to two points:[2] first, that Judas was absent when 'the Passover was celebrated in taking the cup and breaking the bread'; and, secondly, that 'all the marvels of the Divine mysteries were brought to a conclusion in heavenly songs of joy.' All he permits himself to say of 'the table of the Lord,' in commenting on the Psalms, is that it is 'one from which we receive food—namely, that of the living bread, which, as it is living, has also the power of imparting life to its recipients.'[3] There is just one passage where greater explicitness is forced upon him, in dogmatising upon the Trinity,[4] where the union between Christ and the faithful in the Eucharist is adduced to illustrate the union between Christ and His Father in heaven. Yet, even there the union between Christ and the faithful is repeatedly characterised as brought about '*sub mysterio*,' or '*sub sacramento nobis communicandæ carnis*'—expressions on which it will be more convenient to remark presently. For public attention having been speedily diverted from this work of S. Hilary by the more lucid, and in every respect more masterly, work on the same subject by S. Augustine, there is not a genuine treatise by any French writer for several centuries, in which the reserve practised by him in alluding to the Eucharist in his other works has not been followed; so that no notice was taken of what he had said about it in his work on the Trinity during that time. The tract that first quotes it is a sermon on the Passover, attributed to S. Eligius, Bishop of Noyons, in the seventh century; but, as

[1] S Matt vii 6
[2] Ib xxvi. 17 *et seq*
[3] xxvii 3, ed Migne, § 10.
[4] *De Trin*. viii. 13-15

the manner in which it is quoted deserves at least as much attention as what S. Hilary wrote, I give the extract as it stands in this sermon, italicising each clause that has been interpolated by the preacher.

'Sicut enim vere carnem corporis nostri Christus assumpsit; et vere homo, Qui ex Mariâ Virgine natus est, Jesus Dei Filius est—*non quemadmodum alii homines per gratiam, sed naturâ Filius ex substantiâ Patris*—*ita vera est caro et verus est sanguis Ejus quem ad manducandum et potandum in mysterio sumimus, sicut Ipse testatur;* et nos qui vere sub mysterio carnem et sanguinem corporis Ejus sumimus, *per ea naturaliter unum cum Illo efficimur, in quibus manet post consecrationem similitudo panis et vini, ne sit quidam horror cruoris, sed manet in vis gratia redemptionis.* De naturali enim in nobis Christi veritate Ipse ait : " Caro Mea vere est esca, et sanguis Meus vere est potus ; qui edit carnem Meam et bibit sanguinem Meum, in Me manet et Ego in eo." De veritate carnis et sanguinis Ejus nullus relictus est ambigendi locus : nunc enim et ipsius Domini professione, et fide nostrâ, vere caro est et vere sanguis est ; et hæc accepta et hausta id efficiunt, ut nos in Christo et Christus in nobis sit. . . .'[1]

Of the italicised there is not a word in the passage as it stands in S. Hilary, but the liberties here taken with it show how the Fathers were beginning to be quoted. Passages were quoted loosely, detached from their context, and altered to suit the views of the writer or the subject he had in hand. No objection of course could be taken to the first interpolated clause, nor to the second either, as it borrows '*in mysterio*' from S. Hilary ; but clause 3, whether by design or accident, paves the way for a new interpretation of the whole. One word requires explanation, even of those found in S. Hilary. He talks of Christ, in an earlier part of the same chapter, 'abiding in us *naturaliter*' through 'the

[1] Hom. viii ap Migne, *Pat. Lat* lxxxvii 624-5

sacrament of His body.' By 'abiding *in us*' thus he means 'abides in our souls.'

Quitting S. Hilary, then, where he is most outspoken, and reserving the Gallican liturgy for separate consideration among other liturgies of uncertain date, we must actually descend to the ninth century for the first authentic and explicit testimony to the continued agreement in celebrating and expounding the sacrament of the Eucharist between the French Church of those times and the same Church represented by S. Irenæus. Yet the testimony, when once we arrive there, could not well be more decisive.

21. S. Agobard, who became Bishop of Lyons some 650 years after S. Irenæus and for thirty years adorned it by his great learning and high principle—'canonum imprimis perpetuus et constans defensor,' as Baluze says of him—in a tract 'On the Privileges and Rights of Priesthood,' inscribed to his friend and colleague, S. Bernard, Archbishop of Vienne, thus excites the faithful of their respective sees to increased zeal in frequenting the sacraments of the Church, no matter by whom they are administered. 'For the Divine sacraments,' he tells them—'that is to say, baptism and the consecration of the body and blood of the Lord, and all other appointed channels of grace and life to the faithful—are too great and holy to be improved by the merits of the good or spoiled by the perverseness of the bad, as it is not by any power of man, but on invocation of the Supreme Priest that they are consummated by the majestic and ineffable working of the Holy Ghost.'[1]

What more could S. Agobard have stated on this point had he been asked at the time? And it is important to remark of these words that they are not copied from S. Isidore, though their teaching is identic with his.[2] Further, as S. Agobard and S. Bernard are found acting together harmoniously through life,[3] it is only natural to conclude

[1] C 15, ap Migne, *Pat Lat* civ 142-3
[2] Above p 105
[3] *Gall Christ* xvi 41-44

that what was laid down thus positively by S. Agobard was endorsed in every respect by his friend.

22. But, again, Theodulph was senior to S Bernard by fifteen, and to S. Agobard by twenty, years as Bishop of Orleans, carrying us back, in short, to the last decade of the preceding century. Now this is his description of the Eucharist, at the end of a tract on baptism written at the request of Magnus, Bishop of Sens, and dedicated to him.

'This mystery of a sacrifice, for which the victims of the Law were abandoned as having served their purpose, the Church celebrates, offering bread on account of the living bread that came down from heaven, and wine on account of Him who said, "I am the true Vine," that, by the visible oblation of her priests and the invisible consecration of the Holy Ghost, the bread and wine may pass into the honour of the body and blood of our Lord.'[1]

This again is a twofold testimony composed by one bishop for use by another, and, as such, a complete pendant to that of the two metropolitans: in other words, four considerable sees offering concurrent proof of the doctrinal and liturgical agreement of their national Church, in the manner of consecrating the Eucharist, with the Churches of Spain and North Africa, Egypt and Jerusalem up to that time.

23. One more passage shall be given from the Caroline divines, occurring in a letter addressed to Charlemagne by Maxentius, Bishop of Aquileia, in dedicating to him a tract on baptism, only part of which seems to have been preserved. The letter, anyhow, goes further than the tract, and, in referring to the Eucharist, reproduces a favourite phrase of S. Ambrose, quite alien from the teaching of those spurious works afterwards ascribed to him, which could not have been in existence when these words were penned.

'As regards the body and blood of our Lord Jesus Christ nothing more can be said than what the Lord Himself in the Gospel condescended to say: "I am the living bread which

[1] C 18, ap Migne, *Pat. Lat* cv 240.

came down from heaven," &c. This, then, is to eat that flesh and to drink that blood, to abide through faith in Christ, and to have Christ abiding in oneself through grace; because what is offered by many becomes Christ's one body by infusion of the Holy Ghost, and to each recipient of the body and blood of our Lord Jesus is made remission of all their sins.'[1]

We shall have to call upon these ninth-century divines again to assist in elucidating matters of equal importance further on. Meanwhile their explicitness on this point will throw light on numerous passages that will be presented to us in retracing our steps. Of these the first, and in some respects the most important, occurs in the Caroline Books, which, if not inspired personally by Charlemagne, were composed by his order, and sanctioned by him at the Council of Frankfort, A.D. 794, in refutation of the rulings of the second Nicene Council on images, and, as such, answered by the Roman pontiff, Adrian I., who had pledged his adhesion to that Council. In reply to a parallel sought to be established by the Council between the Eucharist and any representative works of art, the author of this treatise denies indignantly that 'the sacrament of the body and blood of Christ, in commemoration of His Passion, being consummated by the hand of the priest and the invocation of the Divine Name,' will admit of any such comparison.

24. ' Since *this sacrament* is, forsooth, *made what it is by the Spirit of God working invisibly*: these works of art are made what they are by the visible hand of the artist; this is consecrated by invocation of the Divine Name: these painted by one who has learnt his art from man. . . .'[2]

Here the author of this controversial piece gives us plainly to understand that every time there was a celebration of the Eucharist in his church at that date the descent of the Holy Ghost was invoked to consecrate the sacrament by operating

---

[1] § 5, Migne, *Pat Lat* cvi 53
[2] Lib i. 27, ap Migne, *Lat. Lat* cxi 1093-96

upon the elements invisibly that had been set apart on the altar for that purpose by the priest. The chapter in which we meet with this passage will have to be quoted again on other points.

25. Alcuin has been supposed, with most probability, says Cave, to have been the penman of the Caroline books: at all events, in common with all present, he subscribed to them at Frankfort. His allusion is therefore clear enough when he says of the Holy Ghost, in his work on the Trinity —for this is no quotation, but his own exegesis—[1]

'He is called the Paraclete—that is, the Comforter— because, *in distributing the gifts of the sacraments*, He ministers true comfort to the soul: the love of God being thereby shed abroad in our hearts, and the indwelling of the whole Trinity within us assured.'

What he writes to his Lyonnese brethren is to the same effect:—

'In the grains of wheat, whence flour is got for making bread, we have the unification of the whole Church delineated, which by the fire of the Holy Ghost is consolidated into one body, that the members may be made fast to their Head.'[2]

Here the context alone would shew what was passing in his mind. In a letter to Charlemagne, he calls the Last Supper 'the mystical supper'; and speaks of 'the consecration of the bread and chalice' that took place there.[3] In the letter which follows he refers again to the same subject, but his extracts from the Fathers are designed rather to illustrate the character of the atonement generally, which was the point on which he had been consulted by his imperial master.

It is needless to repeat quotations from Latin Fathers bearing on the same subject in other parts of his works, but his constant extracts from S. Chrysostom (whom he translates himself apparently, but never once names), in commenting on the Epistle to the Hebrews, will afford matter for discussion

[1] II 19.   [2] *Ep.* xc ap Migne, *Pat Lat* c 289   [3] *Ep.* clxiv

in a future chapter, where the liturgical works ascribed to him, truly or falsely, will be considered.[1]

26. From him the transition is easy to a countryman, and, though not residing in France, thought by some to have been his master in early life—Venerable Bede, to whom likewise we shall have to return in connection with liturgies farther on, but who is much too striking a witness to the point on which we are now engaged in collecting evidence to be passed over here; for it is not only to ritual and dogma, but historical incident that he will be found to depose.

First, then, in a homily for the third Sunday after the Epiphany, whose genuineness is not disputed, he says:—

'Christ not only washed us from our sins in His blood, when He shed His blood for us on the cross, or when each of us is washed in the water of baptism, mystically representing His passion; but He likewise takes away the sins of the world day by day. In other words, He washes us daily from our sins in His blood, when the memory of His passion is recalled on the altar, when the creatures of bread and wine, by the ineffable sanctification of the Spirit, are translated into the sacrament of His flesh and blood. And so neither is His body slain, nor His blood spilt by the hands of the wicked to their destruction; while they pass through the mouth of the faithful to their salvation. . . .'[2]

Secondly, we read in another work of his this interesting incident recorded of the sixth General Council, held A. D. 680 at Constantinople, when he was himself a boy:—[3]

'Such was the favour accorded to the legates of the general peace, that John, Bishop of Porto, who was one of them, celebrated the Eucharist in Latin on Low Sunday publicly before the Emperor and the patriarch, in the Church of S. Sophia.'

---

[1] The 'Homiliarium' or collection of homilies for the Christian year ordered by Charlemagne and commenced by Paul Winfrid, but continued by later hands, contains a good many by S Chrysostom

[2] *Hom Genuin* i 14, ap Migne, *Pat Lat* xciv 75

[3] *De Temp Rat* (A D 688)

Thirdly, we are told, further on in the same work,[1] that Pope Constantine, being at Constantinople, celebrated before Justinian II. and that the Emperor also received communion at his hands.

The first passage leaves us under no doubt that, whether the liturgy then used in the Anglo-Saxon Church was the Gallican or the Roman, it contained a prayer for the descent of the Holy Ghost upon the creatures of bread and wine to translate them into the sacrament ordained by Christ of His flesh and blood. As a theologian of the highest eminence, and an historian of the utmost probity, Bede testifies here, in terms that cannot be explained away, to the ritual and the teaching of the Church in which he ministered and preached himself. Paschasius Radbertus[2] and Hincmar of Rheims[3] both testify to his meaning, in reproducing this passage.

The second and third passages must be taken to imply that Bede means us to gather from it that the ritual of Rome and Constantinople was then the same, so far at least as this point was concerned. For otherwise the legate, beyond doubt, in quenching one fire would have kindled another, and his errand of peace ministered only to fresh war: a result which a truthful historian could never have passed over in silence, had it ensued—still less recorded, without further explanation, the fact of a Greek Emperor receiving communion from a later Pope. As we shall be brought back to this topic presently, it need not be pursued here further than to remark that John the legate was himself a native of Antioch, and was the first of seven Easterns who became successively Bishops of Rome.

27. From Bede we may be not unnaturally brought to S. Gregory the Great of Rome, whom he lovingly calls the apostle of his countrymen, and then go backwards from him—

---

[1] A D 714
[2] *De Corp et Sang Dom* c ix. 2
[3] *In Ferc Salom* p 765, ap

Migne, *Pat Lat* cxxv ; and *De Car Vit* c 9

for his predecessors are by no means as explicit as he was. And we may begin with a characteristic anecdote told of that apostle by his biographer, Paul Winfrid as he is called, also the historian of the Lombards, whose Homiliarium shows his acquaintance with earlier times than his own.

S. Gregory was administering communion one day according to the solemn form then, as now, in use: ' Corpus Domini ' &c., when he saw a woman among the intending communicants smile. Passing her over, accordingly, till all was over, he sent for and called upon her to explain her conduct. She excused herself on the ground that she happened to have made the bread with her own hands that day which she saw him use. S. Gregory begged his people to join him in prayer that her incredulity might be removed,[1] but addressed her himself in these words:—

'Learn, I say, to believe the Truth, who has testified: "The bread which I give is My flesh. . . ." But our Maker, conscious of our infirmities, by the same power with which He created all things out of nothing, and fabricated a body for Himself by the operation of the Holy Ghost out of the flesh of the Blessed Virgin, converts bread and wine mixed with water, their species remaining unchanged, by the sanctification of His Spirit at the Catholic prayer, for our sakes, into His own flesh and blood. . . .'[2]

S. Gregory would have said 'into the *sacrament* of His own flesh and blood,' agreeably with all previous Fathers, and with Venerable Bede whom we have just left. Indeed, his biographer himself would be searched in vain for any stronger expression in his other works, including even the ' Homiliarium,' or collection of Homilies for the Christian year,

---

[1] This is said to have been removed by a miracle, to which as well as to the word '*species*' we shall be brought back hereafter The first is of a piece with those recorded of S Benedict in the second book of the Dialogues attributed to S Gregory, and supplemented in verse by Paul himself, *De Gest Langob* 1 26 The second may compare with the *similitudo panis et vini*, mixed up with a quotation from S Hilary, but not sanctioned by him

[2] *Vit* § 23.

drawn up by him at the request of Charlemagne. The probability, then, is, that we owe the expression, 'into His own flesh and blood,' to the pen of a later scribe. S. Gregory says himself, anyhow, in the plainest terms:—

'The Lamb is eaten at night, because it is *under a sacrament* now (or, *only* [1]) that we receive the Lord's body, when as yet our own consciences are, in their turn, hid from our eyes. . . . He, therefore, who would celebrate the Paschal solemnity with joy, should neither eat his Lamb raw, nor sodden at all with water, as though desirous of fathoming the depths of His Incarnation with human wisdom, or believing Him to be mere man; but should eat of His flesh roast with fire, as knowing the dispensation of the whole thing to be vested in the power of the Holy Ghost. . . . Again: 'Whatever remains of the Lamb *we burn with fire* when we hand over humbly to the power of the Holy Ghost everything that we find ourselves unable to understand or discern in His Incarnation.' [2]

Again, on the sixth of the Penitential Psalms:—

'Who can express the mercy that condescended to redeem mankind by the shedding of His precious blood, and to impart to his members *the most sacred mystery* of His own life-giving body and blood, by receiving which His body, which is the Church, is both fed and given to drink: is both washed and sanctified?' [1]

One more passage shall be given, on account of its liturgical import:—

'On these grounds, then, let us reflect what manner of sacrifice for us this is, *which is always imitating* for our forgiveness the passion of the only-begotten Son. For which of the faithful can doubt that at the moment of its being offered, heaven is opened at the voice of the celebrant, choirs of angels are present at *this mystery* of Jesus Christ, things below are brought into communion with things above, things

---

[1] The Latin word is 'modo,' which may mean either.
[2] *In Evan II*, Hom xxii. 7-8.
[3] § 11 ed. Ben.

of earth with things of heaven, oneness established between things visible and things invisible.'[1]

When he says 'at the voice of the celebrant,' he means of course what he said in the story related of him by his biographer, 'at the Catholic prayer': the prayer his predecessor Vigilius had half a century before called 'the canonical prayer,' but which he himself, in writing to John, Bishop of Syracuse, prefers calling 'the prayer' *par excellence*, as it had been called by a Roman prelate two hundred years earlier, Innocent I., adopting its previous designation in Greek by S. Justin,[2] when Greek, not Latin, was the language most spoken, or at any rate best understood, by Christians at Rome.

S. Gregory, by going back to the old name of this prayer, testifies to his own sense of its importance.

28. S. Gelasius, one hundred years earlier, argues on the effect produced by it in a way that would be quite past understanding on the supposition that the Roman liturgy contained no such prayer in his time; doubly so, when it is considered that his country was Africa, where everything turned on this prayer in the liturgy then, as we have seen. In short, the inference suggested by both facts together is surely, that either he found this prayer in the Roman liturgy when he became Pope, or inserted it there before writing this tract. For in this tract he distinctly follows Theodoret (who will be quoted further on) in developing an argument against Eutychianism from what he testifies, equally with Theodoret, was then the received teaching of the Church on the Eucharist. It is observable that this tract was quoted in several extracts with high approval by S. Fulgentius in Africa, who was contemporary with him,[3] and by John II.,[4] who succeeded him in the next generation at Rome; a further proof that the ritual and teaching of both Churches

---

[1] *Dial* iv 58 [2] See below, pp 122-3.
[3] *Ep* xiv 19, ap Migne, *Pat Lat* lxv 409.
[4] *Ep.* ii. ib. lxvi. 23

was then identic so far, besides being in accord with Theodoret, and, through him, with the East. This, accordingly, was the teaching of the Roman Church under Pope Gelasius:—

'Certainly the sacraments of the body and blood of Christ which we receive are divine things; as it is owing to them, and through them, that we are made partakers of the Divine nature; although the substance or nature of the bread and wine ceases not to exist. And beyond doubt it is the image and the likeness of the body and blood of Christ that are celebrated in the performance of the mysteries. We say therefore, with good reason, that we must not think of Christ Himself differently from what we profess, celebrate, and receive in those representations of Him: to wit, that as the elements there pass into that substance which is Divine, *by the operation of the Holy Ghost,* without, however, departing from their proper nature; so they likewise demonstrate that prime mystery, whose power and efficacy they truly represent, to be for ever one Christ because both real and entire; the properties of its components remaining intact.'[1]

Gelasius and Gregory were separated from each other by a hundred years, as has been said; and both are credited with Sacramentaries into which we shall have to look critically later, as now printed, on this point. Meanwhile that fact alone suggests a reason for enlarging on some phenomena presented to us in history, during the interval separating between them, and during the ages preceding the earlier of them, likely to assist us in forming an estimate of that liturgy which they are said to have revised in turn.

The late Dean Milman was the first to awaken and arouse public attention to the broad fact, which others have since developed and applied in detail, that for about the first three centuries the Christians of Rome formed practically, not so much a Latin, as a Greek-speaking Church. 'And many vestiges and traditions,' he adds, 'show that their ritual,

[1] *Max Bibl Pat* viii 700–7, where Labbe frankly concedes its genuineness, which had till then been disputed. It is printed in Routh, *Script. Eccl.* ii. 493, with notes.

their liturgy, was Greek.'[1] This opens a page that had never been cut before. Certainly, the letter addressed to the Christian brotherhood of his day at Rome by S. Paul was written, not in Latin, but in Greek; and if S. Mark subsequently composed his Gospel, as tradition says,[2] for the special benefit of those to whom S. Peter had preached, S. Peter cannot possibly be supposed to have preached in a different language from what S. Mark employed for his Gospel. But if S. Peter preached to the Roman Christians in Greek, the liturgy which he used himself and delivered to them for use must have been in Greek also. Now, in whose Church was the Eucharist first celebrated, and a liturgy, therefore, first used? In that of Jerusalem,[3] in that of S. James—the first Church that had a bishop appointed to it: and appointed to it by Christ, (if we may believe tradition[4]) whose cousin he was. Whether the first Eucharist was celebrated by him or by S. Peter, it matters not:[5] Jerusalem was the see—the Church—in which it took place; and the liturgy then used must have remained a fixture there, to whatever other Churches it may have been imported from thence: and its language Greek, however soon afterwards translated into other tongues. S. Peter, it is clear, could have carried no other liturgy with him to Rome than this; nor used it in any language but Greek while there. The liturgy, then, of the Church of Rome would be thus identic with that of the Church of Jerusalem at its commencement. How far will this assumed fact harmonise with the following recorded facts? Of the thirty bishops of Rome from S. Peter

---

[1] *Latin Christianity*, c i
[2] Euseb *E H.* ii 15
[3] Acts ii 42 and 46
[4] Ib vii 19, and Vales *ad l*
[5] Durand *Rat* iv 1, 7, says the first Mass was celebrated at Jerusalem by S James; while S Peter was the first to celebrate Mass at Antioch, and S Mark at Alexandria. He goes a step further (§ 10), and declares that the Eucharist was celebrated in *Hebrew* by the primitive Church, and that it was not celebrated in Greek even, till the reign of Adrian, by the Eastern Church. He omits to state when it was first celebrated in Latin by the Western Church or by Rome Nor can Bona tell (*Rer Liturg* i 5, 4). Martene, quoted further on, supplies some suggestive data.

to Melchiades inclusive, the names of at least half are Greek names. One of them, S. Anicetus, was bishop when S. Polycarp visited Rome; and, although at issue with him on the Easter question, S. Irenæus tells us, as a mark of respect, he let S. Polycarp celebrate the Eucharist at his church in his presence.[1] Had consecration been performed in one way according to the Roman liturgy, and in another according to that of the Church of Smyrna then, how could S. Anicetus have conceded, or S. Polycarp accepted, this privilege? But if S. John carried with him to the seven Churches of Asia the identic liturgy that S. Peter carried with him to Rome, and it was still used at both places in Greek, S. Polycarp would have celebrated for S. Anicetus, as for his own flock at home. Twenty-five years more bring us to the first outburst on the question which they had discussed amicably— that of keeping Easter. Now this whole controversy between Victor and the Churches sympathising with him in the East on one side, and the Churches of Asia Minor on the other, seems to have been carried on by all in Greek: and S. Irenæus in moderating between them writes to Victor in the same tongue. Fifty years later, when the question of rebaptising arose, we find Dionysius of Alexandria writing his first letter on baptism in Greek to Stephen of Rome: his second to Xystus the successor of Stephen; his third to Philemon, his fourth to Dionysius, both presbyters of the same Church; and his fifth to Xystus, who was still their bishop.[2] Dionysius, to whom his fourth letter was addressed, as Bishop of Rome published a work in Greek against Sabellius himself.[3] It is as though prelates and presbyters of the Roman Church alike were Greeks just then; and that Greek was the language which they employed in all cases where they could. Positively, but for a few stray letters in Latin from Cornelius and Lucius, and now and then from

---

[1] 'Hunc honorem Anicetus pontifex Romanus habuit venerabili seni Polycarpo, ut illum in ecclesiâ sacra facere sineret, et quidem præsente se, quod in primis notandum est'— Vales *ad Euseb E H* v 24

[2] Euseb. *E H.* vii. 5.

[3] S. Ath *De Dec. Nic. Syn* § 26.

the Roman clergy to S. Cyprian, and a sorry treatise (now given to the Roman presbyter Novatian) on the Trinity, we should be without ecclesiastical proof that Latin was really current in the Church of Rome till the Roman empire became Christian. And even later, during the whole time passed at Rome by S. Athanasius, not a single letter in Latin of his host Julius, then bishop, has come down to us having the least claim to be genuine. All his genuine letters are written in Greek; the Creed submitted to him by Marcellus, the letters addressed to him by the Eusebians, in the same tongue. The first decretal epistle written in Latin by a Bishop of Rome, now allowed to be genuine, was addressed to Himerius, Bishop of Tarragona, by Siricius, A.D. 385. This epistle treats at starting of baptism. The next immediately following it in the collection of Dionysius Exiguus[1] is the first of Innocent I. addressed to Decentius, Bishop of Eugubium in Umbria, A.D. 405, and dealing, at starting, with questions relating to the Eucharist.

29. Innocent tells his correspondent that, as he made no doubt of his having often visited Rome, and attended church there with him, and been cognisant of the *manner of consecrating the mysteries* there, together with other esoteric practices, he need do no more than answer the queries which had been put to him. Only two queries had been put to him on the Eucharist: and it is to his decision on the first, and his own manner of re-stating the second, that particular attention should be paid.

Both questions referred only to a similar point of order in the ritual: (1) Was the kiss of peace to be given before consecration, or after? (2) Were the names of those who supplied bread and wine for the oblation to be recited before consecration of the oblation, or after? According to his correspondent, the kiss of peace was, in some Churches, ordered to be given *ante confecta mysteria*—'before consecration of the mysteries.' Innocent will not go further into that

[1] Migne, *Pat Lat* lxvii. 238.

point than to answer peremptorily, 'cum *post omnia*, quæ aperire non debeo, *pax* sit necessario indicenda.' In other words, it could only be given after consecration. The extreme relevancy borne by this decision to the problem we have to solve can scarce be exaggerated, especially coupled with what follows—' De nominibus recitandis,' says Innocent, '*antequam precem sacerdos faciat* . . .'[1]—that is, 'As to reciting the names before the celebrant makes the prayer.' To this phrase '*the prayer*' *par excellence*, detached from its context, attention has already been called. In the connection in which it stands here, with the decision of Innocent preceding it on the kiss of peace, it may serve to open a door that has hitherto been kept locked. Down to the first years of the fifth century not a word had been breathed on the Roman liturgy by friend or foe. For aught we know to the contrary, Greek might have been its language till then. Innocent is the first to break silence respecting any part of it—Innocent, the correspondent of S. Augustine and the heads of the Latin Church of North Africa. His manner of speaking of it is precisely theirs. ' Ante confecta mysteria ' finds its pendant in ' antequam illud, quod est in Domini mensâ, incipiat benedici ' of S. Augustine: [2] 'quæ aperire non debeo,' in his ' norunt fideles.'[3] But when he rules that the kiss of peace should always be given after consecration, he then and thus identifies his liturgy with that of the African Church as against that of Jerusalem under S. Cyril. When he uses the phrase ' antequam precem sacerdos faciat,' he further identifies his liturgy with that of the Church of Jerusalem under S. Cyril, through that of the African Church. The single difference between the North African liturgy commented upon by S.

---

[1] Palmer, in giving this passage (*Orig Lit* i 119, note), 'antequam preces sacerdos,' &c, has copied a simple misprint, negatived by *suâ oratione* two lines on *Precem* is the reading of Gallandius and Migne, and they notice no other

[2] *Ep ad Paul* cxlix 16

[3] *In Johan. Evang* c vi, tract. xxvi 13

Augustine and that of Jerusalem by S. Cyril, consists in the place given to the kiss of peace. 'Consecration having been effected,' says S. Augustine, 'we repeat the Lord's Prayer: after which is said, "Peace be with you." Whereupon Christians salute each other with a holy kiss.' At Jerusalem the very first words put into the mouth of the deacon are, 'Receive one another: let us embrace one another,' in commencing the liturgy. Innocent testifies to both usages, in pronouncing for that of a Latin-speaking Church, though, had he looked farther west, he would have found Spain in agreement with Jerusalem on that head. On the other hand, in the Churches of both Jerusalem and North Africa, consecration of the Eucharist was held to be effected by the action of the Holy Ghost; only the prayer invoking His action was called 'epiklesis' at Jerusalem, in North Africa 'the prayer'—*the prayer of the sacrifice*, by S. Fulgentius: *the mystical prayer*, by S. Augustine. Innocent is again at one with the Latin-speaking Church as regards the name; while by employing the phrase 'before the celebrant makes the prayer' to express before consecration, he shows that he is at one with both Churches as regards the thing. Could his meaning be disputed, it would be fixed indisputably by the explicit statement of his successor Gelasius, within the same century, that the transformation of the elements into the sacrament is due to the operation of the Holy Ghost, —agreeably with the teaching of S. Augustine, contemporary with Innocent; and of S. Fulgentius, contemporary with Gelasius. Finally, let it be pointed out also that, in answer to a subsequent question Innocent has been understood to establish another item of agreement between his Church and the East—viz. in testifying that the bread used by him in consecrating the Eucharist was leavened.[2] All, therefore, that has been adduced from this decretal epistle, the first of

---

[1] *Serm* ccxxvii ed Ben
[2] 'Fermentum *a nobis confectum*'. § 5 Comp Bona, *Rer. Liturg.* i. 23 8.

TESTIMONIES OF S. LEO NOT SPECIFIC. 125

its kind, so far as it treats of the Eucharist, points all in one direction, proving clearly that the Church of Rome was at one then with all the other Churches of the West and East hitherto gone through, in having a formal prayer in her liturgy for the descent of the Holy Ghost, and in ascribing consecration of the sacrament exclusively to His action. If the Bishops of Rome between Innocent and Gelasius have been reticent on this subject in their extant works, at least they cannot be quoted for any different teaching or practice.

30. S. Leo, from whom of all others, we might have expected most definite support to their testimony, being himself credited with a Sacramentary prior in time to theirs, has but one liturgical allusion in his extant sermons, and that calling for remark upon other grounds. Addressing those who dallied with Eutychianism, he says:—

'You ought to come to the holy table to communicate nothing doubting in the truth of the body and blood of Christ. For what is taken with the mouth is believed by faith, and "Amen" is answered in vain by those who reason against what they receive.'[1]

The interest of this passage lies in the fact that it is clearly borrowed from Tertullian, with a new application. Eutyches asserted that the body which Christ assumed had ceased to exist: Marcion, ages before, denied that it ever had a real existence. The answer of Tertullian[2] to Marcion was, that Christ, in instituting the sacrament, said: 'This *is* My body.' The answer of S. Leo to the Eutychian is, that each communicant, in receiving the same, says 'Amen.' A letter addressed to him by the Church of Constantinople supplies another instance of the same kind. Alluding to the custom of communicating infants, he says:—

'In that mystical distribution of spiritual alimentation, what is given and taken amounts to this: that, by virtue of the heavenly food thus received, we pass into the flesh of Him who became our flesh.'[3]

[1] *Serm.* xci 3, ed. Migne [2] *C Marc* iv 40 [3] *Ep* lix 2, ed Migne

This is as clearly borrowed from S. Augustine [1] as the other from Tertullian. S. Leo was evidently no stranger to the sacramental teaching of the African Church. And of the 'sanctifying grace' which it appertained to the Holy Ghost to bestow, he says in a third passage:—

'Sine hâc gratiâ *nulla* unquam *instituta sacramenta, nulla* sunt *celebrata mysteria*: ut *eadem semper fuerit virtus* charismatum, quamvis non eadem fuerit mensura donorum.'[2] On this point he expressed the current sentiments of the whole Catholic world.

Between S. Gelasius and S. Gregory we have still clearer indications of the continuance of the same ritual and teaching at Rome.

31. Of Agapetus (the only Bishop of Rome that was ever allowed to pronounce the deposition of a Bishop of Constantinople in a Constantinopolitan synod, and then to have the honour of consecrating his successor) a curious anecdote was told fifty or sixty years after his death by a Roman abbot named Theodore, to this effect:—

Agapetus had the bishop of a small town near Rome, called Rumelli, delated to him for misconduct, and the Pope, without further inquiry, sent him to prison unheard; but on the Saturday night following, Agapetus, to his surprise, was ordered in a vision, not merely to release, but to let the culprit celebrate the Eucharist in his own stead on Sunday. The bishop accordingly took his place that morning at the altar, where a number of Roman clergy were collected round the Pope. But when he came to the prayer for the descent of the Holy Ghost he paused and, after several vain efforts, was unable to proceed. 'He could go no further,' he said, 'till an unworthy deacon then present was removed.' The Pope forthwith ordered the deacon to withdraw, the prayer

---

[1] 'Mysterium vestrum in mensâ Dominicâ positum est, mysterium vestrum accipitis . Audis enim, "Corpus Christi"; et respondes "Amen" Esto membrum corporis Christi ut verum sit Amen '—*Serm* cclxxxi. in die Pentecost postrem, ed Ben

[2] *Serm* lxxvi. 3, ed. Migne

was gone through, and all present, including the Pope, witnessed a visible descent of the Holy Ghost.

This anecdote was neither told nor recorded for any controversial or party purpose, but as details of conversation between a host and his guests.[1] Divested of all its accessories, therefore, the liturgical fact underlying it stands out in high relief and proclaims itself. The liturgy which was used on that occasion must have been the Roman, and its prayer for the descent of the Holy Ghost on the elements its consecration-prayer.

A.D. 536 was the year in which Agapetus consecrated Mennas to the see of Constantinople in the room of Anthimus, having been sent thither himself on a mission from the Gothic king Theodatus. He died there the same year.

32. Vigilius, who succeeded him, saw more perhaps of Constantinople than any Bishop of Rome before or since, and during all the seven weary years of his detention there must have been jealously watched in everything that he did or said by the Emperor Justinian, whose prisoner he virtually was, and by whom he was constantly taken to task for his theological utterances. Had he left nothing behind him on the Eucharist to testify to his practice, could we suppose that, had there been anything different in his manner of celebrating it from the ritual then observed in every Constantinopolitan church without exception, he would not sooner or later have been detected by the lynx-eyed Emperor and made to render account of each act? But the fact is, what he has said himself on the subject both confirms the truth of the story told of his immediate predecessor and leaves us in no doubt that the Emperor might have watched him celebrate the Eucharist every day of his enforced stay without discovering any perceptible difference between the consecration-prayer then used in the Church of Rome and his own. For in a letter addressed by Vigilius, two years

---

[1] The guests were John Moschus, who records it (*Prat Spirit* c 150, ap Migne, *Pat Gr* lxxxvii 3015, and S Sophronius his friend and fellow-traveller, who became patriarch of Jerusalem, A D. 629

after he became Pope, to Profuturus, Bishop of Braga, fresh and important light is thrown upon the Roman liturgy by him in acquainting his correspondent that it consisted, as it still consists, of two parts, the first part varying with the festivals, the second part admitting of no change. This distinction had never been drawn before ; and this division holds good still. We must not, however, by any means jump from hence to the conclusion, either that the existing names of those parts were the names by which they were distinguished *then,* or that the contents of either part were the same then as now. Vigilius himself assigns no name to the first part, but merely notes that for Easter and Ascension, Pentecost and Epiphany, with other festivals, special commemorations, suitable to the occasion, were appointed ; accordingly these changed with the season—and, he might have added, with the country too. For we must not fail to notice the *possible* bearing of this distinction on the well-known query put to S. Gregory by our Anglo-Saxon apostle respecting ' consuetudo missarum,'[1] nor the still earlier, if authentic,[2] statement of John III. about ' officia missarum ' in reply to Edald, Archbishop of Vienne. Granting that the ' missæ ' mentioned in both letters *include* celebrations of what is now popularly called the Mass—which is far from certain, for in ancient times ' missa ' was a general name for every part of divine service, as Bingham conclusively shows—Vigilius as good as tells us that the queries in each case relate to the first half of the liturgy and to

[1] Ap Bede, *E H* i 27

[2] No such a name as Edald occurs among the archbishops of Vienne till the eighth century (*Gall Christian* xvi 4 and 35), and the only other letter attributed to this Pope has long been pronounced spurious Migne, *Pat Lat* lxxii 13–18 This letter, which is given also by Mansi, follows it, and is made to say ' De officiis missarum, de quibus in literis vestris requisistis, sciat charitas vestra, quia varie apud diversas ecclesias fiant aliter enim Alexandrina ecclesia, aliter Hierosolymitana, aliter Ephesina, aliter Romana facit, cujus morem et instituta debet servare ecclesia tua, quæ fundamenta sancti habitus ab illâ sumpsit ' If genuine, this letter must have been written by John VII, who was a Greek, became Pope A D 707, and wrote to King Ethelred in favour of Wilfrid of York

that alone. 'The *tenor* observed by us in consecrating the gifts offered to God,' says Vigilius, 'is *always the same*. . . . Wherefore we have sent you the text of the *canonical prayer*, which, by the blessing of God, we received from apostolic tradition, appended below.'[1]

The context alone shows that by the 'canonical prayer' he means the prayer by which he 'consecrated the gifts offered to God,' and whose 'tenor was always the same'—in other words, the prayer invoking the action of the Holy Ghost on the offerings of bread and wine. To this prayer, it cannot be repeated too often, S. Gregory refuses pointedly to endorse the application of the novel term 'Canon' by his Sicilian interrogator. Rather he will go back himself to the days of the first Innocent and call it once and again '*the prayer*.'[2] Yet in the next breath he seems to derogate from it by attributing its composition to 'a scholastic' or learned man, instead of deriving it from 'apostolic tradition' with Vigilius. What explanation can be given of this apparent contradiction? The simplest possible. If S. Peter brought a liturgy to Rome with him, it must have been in Greek. Being in Greek, it must have been, in process of time, translated into Latin. Mere bilinguists were then employed to translate. S. Gregory, with his eyes fixed on the uncouth dress in which it had come down to him, naturally decided that it could not have been the work of an Apostle, and assigned it on that account solely to the scholastic, *a Greek perhaps*, whose translation it was; while testifying, at the same time, to those traces of its original— the *Kyrie eleisons* and *Alleluias*—which that scholastic had shrunk from meddling with, and which it therefore to this day retains. In the Office for Baptism of the Gelasian Sacramentary we have the Greek of the Niceno-Constantinopolitan Creed given at full length in Latin characters, and a rubric

---

[1] Ap. Migne, *Pat Lat.* lxix. 18.   [2] *Ep* lib ix. ep 12, ed Ben

directs that Creed to be recited on all occasions in both tongues.[1]

One remark more before quitting this celebrated letter.

S. Gregory declares in it that some friends of his Sicilian interviewer—Greeks or Latins, he could not say which—had murmured at his arrangements, asking how he could expect to succeed in keeping down the Church of Constantinople when he followed its customs in every particular.[2] After such a sweeping accusation, the points actually pressed against him in the discussion that ensued must appear to the reader so surprisingly few, and so much more surprisingly trivial, as to suggest that either S. Gregory found the Constantinopolitan liturgy so like the Roman that there were no other items to be borrowed from it; or else that he deliberately passed over all the changes then being imported into the Roman from it of real importance without a word. Which alternative seems more probable of the two we shall have to consider and decide later. Meanwhile let attention be renewed generally to the Eastern influences still dominating at Rome through constant intercourse—broken off, indeed, now and then, but only to be found more and more indispensable when resumed—with the capital to which the seat of empire had been transferred. It was not merely that the secular post of apocrisiarius at Constantinople was often a stepping-stone to the spiritual post of pontiff at Rome (as it had proved in the three cases of Vigilius, Pelagius I. and Gregory I. himself) or that during the 150 years immediately succeeding Gregory no fewer of his successors than ten were Greeks by race; but it was really that all the Councils received as œcumenical up to the seventh had been held in the East; the Creed and all the canons

---

[1] Muratori, *Lit Rom* i 540-2 According to the 'Turonensis Anonymus,' quoted by Martene (*De Ant Eccl Rit* lib i part ii, c 3, art 2, § 6 11), with other writers, not only the 'Gloria in excelsis,' but even the Epistles and Gospels, and Lections from the prophets, used to follow the same custom at times

[2] 'Qui ejus consuetudinem *per omnia* sequitur'

binding on the whole Church framed there too; and Greek, not Latin, the official text of their publication.

All these broad historical facts go far, indeed, to corroborate the proof, supplied by direct evidence, that the consecration-prayer of the Roman liturgy was then identic, and had been identic from the earliest age, with that of Jerusalem and the far East, of Egypt and North Africa, Spain, England and France, together with other Churches not yet investigated, besides explaining the preference shown by S Gregory for its old name, his warmth in defending himself when charged with having borrowed everything from Constantinople, his generous and truly Catholic decision on the whole matter—so like the advice given by him to our first Archbishop of Canterbury—that he felt himself just as much bound to copy from his subordinates, when he could copy from them with profit, as to correct their errors when they went astray. All is clear up to this point in the ritual of the Church of Rome. To advance further would necessitate discussing the merits of the Leonine, Gelasian, and Gregorian Sacramentaries in their existing state, and would land us in anachronisms by dealing with questions at which we have not arrived.

From Rome, then, our next halting-place will be North Italy.

33. Here S. Ambrose, who first meets us, is a host in himself, quoted only from his acknowledged works. Pieces confessedly spurious that have been ascribed to him, and sentences interpolated in his genuine works to give colour to them, will be considered with others of the same kind in a separate chapter further on.

Now, of all the works of S. Ambrose, his treatise 'De Spiritu Sancto,' which is in three books, is certainly the best authenticated; for S. Jerome was attacked by Rufinus [1] for having maligned it during his lifetime, as having been copied from the work of Didymus on the same subject,

[1] *Invect* ii 24, ed Vallars.

already noticed. Nor can the Benedictine editors deny the charge to have been well founded.[1] But Didymus, as I pointed out and tried to explain,[2] makes no reference throughout his work to the invocation of the Holy Ghost, which we know from other sources the Alexandrian liturgy then contained. S. Ambrose not merely draws attention to it, but enumerates it among the proofs of His Divinity.

'How then,' he asks, 'has He not all things which belong to God, Who is named with the Father and the Son by the priest in baptising; Who is *invoked at the oblations*; Who is extolled with the Father and the Son by the Seraphim in heavenly places; Who dwells with the Father and the Son in the saints; Who is infused into the just, and inspired into the prophets? All Scripture for the same reason is said to have been inspired by God, because God inspires whatever the Spirit has spoken.'[3]

Nor is this an isolated passage by any means. He commences his treatise by a comment on the cry raised by the children of Israel, 'Who shall give us flesh to eat?' viewed in connection with the offering presented by Gideon to the angel,[4] as follows:—

'Now, when the angel stretched forth his rod and touched the rock, out of which fire uprose and consumed the flesh, he showed that the flesh of the Saviour, fired by the Divine Spirit, should burn up all sins committed by man.'[5]

Further on, he says:—

'There can be no plenary benediction except by infusion of the Holy Ghost.'[6]

In the next section he adds:—

'It is God, remember, who bestows the Holy Ghost. For this is no work of man, nor can He be given by man.

---

[1] Vol ii 598, in Præf
[2] Above, p 83
[3] III. § 112
[4] Numbers xi 4, and Judges vi 21.
[5] I 3
[6] Ib § 19

But He Who is invoked by the priest, is imparted by God: it is God Who gives; the priest ministers.'

'The treatise 'De Fide' by S. Ambrose was written at the special request of the Emperor Gratian, and written, therefore, with more than ordinary care. In this work he says:—

'We, then, as often as we receive the sacraments, which by the *mysterious action of the sacred prayer are transfigured into the body and blood*, announce the death of the Saviour.'[1]

Here, by 'the sacred prayer' he means the consecration-prayer invoking the action of the Holy Ghost upon the bread and wine—'Who is invoked at the oblations,' as he had said himself.

Again, in his 'Apology for David,'[2] dedicated to the Emperor Theodosius:—

'This is what he referred to when he said, "Offer the sacrifice of righteousness and put your trust in the Lord." This is that spiritual offering of righteousness, and holocaust of fervent devotion, and of the infusion of the Holy Ghost, which he says is in store, when the souls of the faithful shall have commenced coming to that spiritual altar of the Lord, with hearts purged from pleasures and enjoyments, and seeking only to bring forth the fruits of a holy life.'

Again, in his comments on S. Luke,[3] a work cited by S. Augustine:—

'The heavenly bread is the word of God. Hence, too, that Wisdom Who makes the holy altars abound with the food of the Divine body and blood, exclaims: "Come, eat of my bread and drink of the wine that I have mixed."'

Finally, the Appendix to the second volume of the Benedictine edition of S. Ambrose contains two prayers to be said before celebrating the Eucharist, 'hactenus Ambrosio attributæ,' say the editors, who might, nevertheless, have

[1] IV § 124   [2] I. § 84.   [3] C. vi. § 63

seen, had they examined the first of them more critically, that it embodies his own teaching on the Eucharist many times more closely than several pieces printed in their edition as his. S. Ambrose constantly shows that he was well acquainted with Greek, and Durandus is frank enough to admit that he borrowed numbers of things from the Greek rite.[1] But an Englishman may go further than this; and with the precedent of the prayer of S. Chrysostom, which he hears morning and evening every time he attends church, and knows to be contained word for word in the third antiphon of the prothesis in the liturgy called after that Father,[2] he may hold it quite possible that S. Ambrose was indebted for the first half of the following, in his private devotions, to his own liturgy.

'Grant, O God, of Thy clemency that Thy benediction in all its fulness, and Thy sanctification in all its Divinity, may descend upon this oblation. Let Thy Holy Spirit in His invisible and incomprehensible Majesty likewise descend, O Lord, as He descended on the sacrifices of the Fathers in olden time: and both make our offerings of bread and wine Thy body and blood, and also teach me, unworthy minister that I am, to celebrate so great a mystery with such pureness of heart and tears of devotion, with such awe and reverence, that Thou mayest graciously and favourably receive this sacrifice at my hands to the profit of all, whether living or departed.'[3]

It lends additional interest to this prayer, that it is given entire—with merely trivial changes—among the prayers used by S. Anselm;[4] and that it accords so completely with his own doctrine that, had the teaching of this prayer entered into discussion at the Bari conference,[5] he must have held a brief for those whom he opposed on the Procession, as will be shown in due course from his writings.

---

[1] *Rat* v 2, 5
[2] Neale's *Primitive Greek Liturgies*, ed Littledale, p. 116.
[3] App p. 491.
[4] *Orat* xxix, ap Migne, *Pat Lat* clviii 924.
[5] Collier, *E H*., A D. 1098

S. GAUDENTIUS OF BRESCIA.

34. Travelling eastwards from S. Ambrose, we come to S. Gaudentius, whose suffragan he was, and by whom he was nominated to the see of Brescia, which he held. Their teaching was identic on the point with which we are now engaged. Explaining it to his neophytes, S. Gaudentius says:—

'It is the Passover of the Lord: that is, the passage of the Lord: lest you should esteem that earthly which was made heavenly by Him who passes into the same, making it His body and blood. For what we have expounded in general terms previously, respecting the manner of eating the flesh of the lamb, we must specially remember in touching upon the same mysteries in the Passion of our Lord, that you may not for a moment think of raw flesh and clotted blood with the Jew, and ask with horror, "How can this man give us his flesh to eat?" nor again attempt in the weak and carnal spirit of this world to depreciate this sacrament, as being a common thing of earth. But that you may believe that what is announced has been accomplished by the fire of the Divine Spirit; since what you receive is His body who is the bread from heaven, and His blood who is the true Vine. For when He administered the consecrated bread and wine to His disciples, He said thus: "This is My body; this is My blood." Let us trust Him on whom we have believed. Truth can never speak false. Hence, when He spoke to the multitudes about eating His flesh and drinking His blood, and they murmured and said, "This is a hard saying, who can hear it?" in order to evaporate those thoughts, against which I have cautioned you, by fire from heaven, He rejoined at once: "It is the Spirit who quickeneth; the flesh profiteth nothing. The words which I have spoken to you, they are spirit and they are life."'[1]

This extract may suffice from S. Gaudentius, whose extant works are so few; but his two journeys to the East should not be forgotten in connection with it. He was at Cæsarea in Cappadocia, where the memories of S. Basil were

[1] *Serm.* ii., ap. Migne, *Pat. Lat.* xx. 858.

still fresh (A.D. 387) when the news that he was elected bishop reached him. He would have gladly remained where he was, he tells us himself pointedly, could he have done so 'without detriment to his soul.' For he received such letters from S. Ambrose and his suffragans insisting on his return, that the Eastern bishops actually said he should be *refused communion* if he delayed going.[1] This is conclusive proof that he had no more distaste for 'the Greek rite' than his master: and that not his teaching merely, but his own ritual was in agreement with it. His second journey was some twenty years later, when he formed part of a deputation from the West to intercede with the Emperor Arcadius for S. John Chrysostom, whose letter of thanks to him for his good offices is still extant.[2] That brought him to Constantinople, and reopened the Eastern Churches to him once more.

35. S. Jerome—whose birthplace, Stridon, in the neighbourhood of Aquileia, takes us still further East—may be said to have perfected his theological studies at Constantinople, where no less a personage than S. Gregory, 'Theologus dictus,' of Nazianzum, was his instructor, and where the Œcumenical Council was then sitting (A.D. 381) which formulated and appended that article to the Nicene Creed where belief in the Holy Ghost is professed. He was thus in the thick of the discussions that took place respecting His Godhead and His prerogatives. No wonder, therefore, that he should take such pains to translate the work of Didymus of Alexandria for the edification of his Latin-speaking brethren on the first head, and the letter of S. Theophilus of Alexandria for their edification on the second. Anyhow, by translating them, he has identified himself with both so fully that, having quoted them elsewhere, we might be dispensed from quoting him here. But there is just one passage which combines in a few words so well all the influences derived from their works and from the Creed of Constantinople conjointly,

[1] *Serm* xvi. ib p 956 [2] In Præf ib. pp 803-4.

S. JEROME AT CONSTANTINOPLE.

that it deserves bringing out. He is commenting on Zeph. iii, 4, and he says:—

'The priests also, who administer baptism, and at the Eucharist *imprecate the advent of the Lord*;[1] who compound the chrism, lay on hands, instruct catechumens, ordain Levites and other priests, must not be indignant with us for expounding these prophecies, but must rather entreat the Lord, and take care themselves, that they be not of the number of those priests who profane the holy things of the Lord.'[2]

Here the full meaning of those words '*ad Eucharistiam Domini imprecantur adventum*' is of the last importance. By the word 'Domini,' S. Jerome most certainly means the *Holy Ghost*, who had just had that title formally given to Him by the 150 Constantinople Fathers in their new article—'The Lord and Giver of Life.'[3] And by the word 'imprecantur,' he most certainly refers to the 'precem,' or consecration-prayer, as it was called by the Latin-speaking Churches, in which the descent of the Holy Ghost was invoked.

He had pushed the case too far in what he had previously said:—

'The priests who minister at the Eucharist, and distribute the blood of the Lord to the people, wickedly contravene the law of Christ if they think that the words of him who recites the prayer make the Eucharist, apart from his life; and that the solemn invocation is alone necessary, without reference to what the celebrants may be themselves.'[4]

The Council of Constantinople was still sitting when S. Jerome was carried off to Rome the year following by SS.

---

[1] Comp S Fulgent *Ad Mon* ii 12 'Dum ecclesia, in sacrificii prece, Spiritûs Sancti deposcit adventum'
[2] *Op* vi 721, ed Vallars
[3] Κύριον Αὐτὸ, καὶ Θεὸν ἀποφαίνοντες, as the Fathers of the fourth Council say of them in their letter to the Emperor Marcian; Mansi, *Conc* vii 460
[4] *Op* ib p 718. S Cyprian, quoted above, with Agobard, quoted above, between them state the Catholic doctrine, which S Jerome cannot have meant to infringe Comp too, the Alexandrian Eusebius, quoted above.

Epiphanius and Paulinus, who had been summoned thither by the Emperor Theodosius; and he remained there three years, on terms of the closest intimacy with Pope Damasus, till Damasus was no more, viz. A.D. 385. Damasus, therefore, must have consulted[1] him when his own synodical letter, preserved by Theodoret, was penned, in which all persons are anathematised 'who, while they maintained right opinions about the Father and the Son, entertained wrong opinions about the Holy Ghost.'[2] Anyhow their intimate relations must have suffered had there been the least disagreement between them then on this point.

The Constantinopolitan Fathers, on the other hand, in their synodical epistle to Pope Damasus and the West in general (also preserved by Theodoret) inform them, in concluding their letter, that, in spite of all he had endured from the Arians, they considered S. Cyril to be the rightful Bishop of Jerusalem—mother of all the Churches, as they call his see—with whose lectures on the liturgy then in use there we commenced at starting: another proof, surely, that all other liturgies, including the Roman, were then in full agreement with it on fundamentals.

The Churches of Asia Minor, of Syria, and Constantinople, still remain to be questioned on that head.

36. Let us begin with S. Basil, whose desire to find himself at one with Egypt and the West was very great, and whose standard treatise (dedicated to Amphilochius, author of a similar work, now lost) on the Holy Ghost, entitles him to precedence.

First, then, he is never tired of reiterating the dogma translated by Hooker from S. Cyril of Alexandria, that it is from the Holy Ghost that 'all good things gush forth in exuberance to the world of creatures,' as he puts it in his letter to his brother Gregory;[3] or as he plies it against Eunomius: ' Take away the Son from the universe, and you take away Him who created it; take away the Holy Ghost,

[1] *E H* v 11. [2] Ib c 9 [3] *Ep* xxxiii 4, ed Ben.

and you take away Him who perfects it;'[1] or as he sums it up formally for Amphilochius: 'Consider the Father the first Cause of all things that are made; the Son, their Framer; the Holy Ghost, their Finisher.'[2]

But it is in attesting the application of this doctrine to the Eucharist from time immemorial by the Church at large that he is most explicit, and, in point of fact, unique. Thus he states it :—

'Of the dogmatic teaching and preaching committed to the Church to keep, one portion is secured to us in written documents; another is handed down to us by tradition in mystery from the Apostles. Edification is equally promoted by both, nor are the claims of either disputed by any possessed of the slightest acquaintance with the laws of the Church. For were we to attempt to reject unwritten usages as being devoid of any binding power, we should, without intending it, damage the Gospel in many particulars of vital importance, or rather, bring down its preaching to an empty name. Who told us in writing, for instance—that I may first mention what is commonest, and actually comes first— to sign with the sign of the cross those who have hoped in our Lord Jesus Christ? What Scripture bids us turn to the east when we pray? Which of the saints has bequeathed to us in writing the words of the *epiklesis* at consecrating[3] both the bread of the Eucharist, and the cup of blessing? For, far from contenting ourselves with those things which the Apostle or the Gospel record, we say other things—after as well as before; fraught with great effect on the mystery— which have descended to us by tradition.'

These words may well be left for the present to speak for themselves, though there is one point on which they will have to be re-examined hereafter.

37. To quote S. Gregory (brother of S. Basil, and Bishop

---

[1] Lib v p 307
[2] *De Spir. S* § 38.
[3] Ibid § 66, ἐπὶ τῇ ἀναδείξει on which the Benedictines have a long note, but meanwhile their rendering is 'cùm conficitur' Its meaning has been anticipated.

of Nyssa) for what he says on the Trinity, would be to quote S. Basil over again. But this is what he says of the part assigned to the Holy Ghost in the sacraments. First, of baptism :—[1]

'The giver of life to the baptised is the Holy Ghost, as our Lord himself says of Him: "It is the Spirit who quickeneth."'

Then of the Eucharist and confirmation in the same breath :—[2]

'The bread, again, is in the first instance common, but after the mystery of its consecration it is both called and is the body of Christ. Similarly the mystical chrism; similarly the wine. Both are worth little previously to their benediction, but by the sanctification of the Holy Ghost each operates with signal effect.'

S. Cyril of Jerusalem, from whom it is borrowed, must interpret this passage for us.

S. Gregory, the friend of S. Basil and of his brother, though he speaks often of the Eucharist, speaks always under great reserve, like S. Epiphanius, of whom Petavius says: 'On the sacraments and interior mysteries he never drops a remark but with caution and circumspection . . . on the Eucharist his words at times are timid and obscure.' Just in one place casual mention escapes him of the *epiklesis* at baptism;[3] but where we might have most expected fuller information, he pulls up abruptly, and says :—[4]

'The other mysteries connected with baptism, and the inner mysteries, are performed agreeably with the tradition of the Gospel and of the Apostles.'

38. Theodore, Bishop of Mopsuestia, though his writings generally shared condemnation with him at the fifth Council, deserves to be quoted for one passage, which in a few words represents the effect of the consecration-prayer of his liturgy

---

[1] *Adv Maced* § 19, ed Migne
[2] *In Bapt Christi*, § 2, ib *Pat Gr* xlvi 582
[3] *Ancor* c 117
[4] *Expos de Fide*, c 23, and Petav *ad l*

from a novel point of view. Commenting on 1 Cor. x, 3-5, he says:—

'In other words, the rock was to them what Christ is to us: whose blood is drunk by us the faithful, *spiritually changed* at the mysteries.'[1]

39. An Egyptian eremite, named Mark, had preceded him in commenting on Melchisedec:—

'Melchisedec brought out bread and wine for the refreshment of those who were returning from the war: and so Christ the great High Priest supplies consecrated bread and wine to those who come back to Him from the spiritual conflict, bidding them all take and eat thereof. . . .'[2]

40. Passing from Asia Minor to Syria, the first thing that meets us is a well-known *locus classicus* in the learned bishop of Cyrus, in the patriarchate of Antioch, and Church-historian, Theodoret. It has often been quoted for another —that is, a theological—purpose, but it will be quoted here for its liturgical bearings as well. To include both, we must quote from two dialogues out of three, instead of only from one. The interlocutors in all are the same: Eranistes, or the eclectic, and Orthodoxus, or the sound churchman. In the first of these dialogues we have the following:—[3]

'*Orth*. In the institution of the mysteries, He called the bread His body, and the wine mixed with water His blood.

'*Eran*. He did.

'*O*. But our Saviour, you see, changed the names, and gave to His body the name belonging to the symbol, and to the symbol that of His body. In the same way, having called Himself the vine, He called the symbol blood.

'*E*. Quite true; but I should like to know the reason of this change of names.

[1] Ap Migne, *Pat Gr* lxv 887 It should be read side by side with a characteristic story told of a Sciote by Abbot Arsenius in the Append ad Pallad ap Migne, ib pp 155- 159; and the closing remark of the Sciote more particularly
[2] Ib p 1132
[3] Ap Migne, *Pat Gr* lxxxiii 55

'*O.* The object of it is clear enough to all initiated in Divine things. He wished all partakers of the Divine mysteries, instead of fixing their attention on the nature of the things they saw, to be led by this change of names to believe in the change wrought by grace. For He who called that which is by nature body, corn and bread, and again Himself the vine, bestowed honour on the visible symbols in styling them the body and blood; yet not by changing their nature, but by joining to their nature grace.

'*E.* Thus mystical things were described mystically, and things not patent to all were made plain. . . .'

He returns to the same topic in his second dialogue :—[1]

'*O.* Tell me now, symbols of what are those mystical symbols offered to God by the celebrant?

'*E.* Symbols of the body and blood of the Lord.

'*O.* Of a real body, or of an unreal?

'*E.* Of a real.

'*O.* Quite right. For there must be an archetype where there is an image. Painters themselves imitate nature, and copy likenesses of things that are seen.

'*E.* Certainly.

'*O.* Then, the Divine mysteries being antitypes of a real body, the body of the Lord is a body still, unabsorbed by His Divine nature, though replete with glory.

'*E.* You have reverted to the Divine mysteries opportunely for I will prove to you from thence the transformation of the body of the Lord into a different nature. Reply, therefore, to my questions.

'*O.* I will.

'*E.* What do you call the oblation previously to the sacerdotal epiklesis?

'*O.* I must not answer too clearly, for fear any not initiated should be within hearing.

'*E.* Answer, then, enigmatically.

'*O.* Food from such and such grain.

[1] Ap Migne, *Pat Gr* lxxxiii, 165–70

'*E.* And the other symbol, how is it called?

'*O.* It has a common name likewise, signifying a kind of drink.

'*E.* After sanctification, pray, what do you call them?

'*O.* The body of Christ, and the blood of Christ.

'*E.* And you believe, then, that you partake of the body and blood of Christ?

'*O.* I do.

'*E.* As, therefore, the symbols of the Lord's body and blood are one thing before the sacerdotal epiklesis, but are changed after the epiklesis and become another, so the Lord's body and blood passed, after His Ascension into the Divine substance.

'*O.* You are taken in the net you have woven yourself. For the mystical symbols, after their sanctification, are not divested of their own proper nature, but remain in their former substance, form, and appearance, just as visible, just as tangible as before; yet they are believed and recognised mentally to be what they have become, and adored as being what they are believed to be. Place, then, the image side by side with the archetype, and you will see their resemblance, for the type must be like the reality. That body retains its former appearance, form and, in a word, its bodily substance; but it became immortal after its resurrection, and incorruptible, and has been honoured with a seat on the right hand, and is adored by the whole creation, as being the body of the Lord of all.

'*E.* Yet the mystical symbol changes its former name. For it is no longer called what it was called before, but is called *body*. It is necessary, therefore, that the reality should be called God, and *not* body.

'*O.* You seem ignorant on this point. For it is called not only body, but also bread of life. Thus our Lord called it Himself. In the same way we call His actual body divine, life-giving, the Christ's, the Lord's body: teaching, that it is not common to any man whatsoever, but belongs exclusively to our Lord Jesus Christ, both God and Man—Jesus Christ, the same yesterday, to-day, and for ever.'

He could not have spoken more distinctly than he has on both points. His sound churchman maintains against the eclectic, that it is the action of the Holy Ghost, invoked in the *epiklesis*, which makes Christ present in the Eucharist, yet without affecting the condition of the elements in any way whatsoever, except that it conceals Christ beneath them.

40–41. From Theodoret, about midway in the fifth century, we pass to Leontius and Anastasius, about midway in the sixth, though the identity, perhaps, of both admits of doubt. Anastasius seems to have been a presbyter and monk of Jerusalem, but, from the length of time spent by him in a convent on Mount Sinai, surnamed Sinaita, who became Patriarch of Antioch A.D. 561. Leontius, on the other hand, a Byzantine lawyer in early life, ended his days in a convent near Jerusalem. Migne places Leontius in his eighty-sixth volume and Anastasius in his eighty-ninth,[1] but the common account makes Anastasius senior of the two by three decades. Both composed treatises against the same sects as Theodoret; and both argue from the Eucharist in terms resembling his.[2] Anastasius, for instance, maintains that the Monophysite necessarily denies the truth of the Eucharist in administering it to the people with the received formula. For instead of those words, 'The body and blood of our Lord,' he ought rather to say to each communicant in turn, 'The Godhead of our Lord Jesus Christ alone.'[3] Then, in discoursing on the Eucharist itself, he bursts forth in a strain too like S. Chrysostom not to have been inspired by him:—[4]

'What art thou doing, O man, while the ministering

---

[1] *Pat Gr*
[2] Anastasius, indeed, notices in one place, that our Lord said, 'This is My body,' *not* this is an antitype of My body,' seemingly considering antitype and type synonyms, *Viæ Dux*, ib p 297
[3] Ib p 209
[4] Ib p 840

angels are covering the mystical table with their sixfold wings, and the Cherubim standing by, chanting the Trisagion with resplendent voice, and the High Priest interceding for you, and all present in a tremor between fear and awe, while the offering of the Lamb of God is in the act of being exhibited, and the Holy Ghost in the act of coming down on the oblation?'

This sermon is well worth a careful perusal, both for its comments on the liturgy then used at Antioch and for the spirit of deep piety that runs through it. In one respect alone could we maintain that the liturgy then used in the patriarchal Church had advanced a step beyond the liturgy described by S. Cyril of Jerusalem in his catechetical lectures two hundred years before—namely,[1] that at Antioch it was customary for the celebrant, after consecration, 'to raise the bread of life aloft, and exhibit it to all.' There is not a hint of any further divergence between the two liturgies in this sermon.

Leontius in one place charges the Nestorians with having extemporised an '*anaphora*' different from that received by the Churches from the Fathers, and paid no respect to that of the Apostles, nor judged that to be worth any notice which had been compiled in the same spirit by the great Basil.'[2]

He makes, in another place, this threefold distinction:—[3]

'According to our belief the Church, and the holy bread, and that which was crucified, is each of them a body; but we do not, on that account, attribute to Christ three bodies. For it is clear that Christ has neither two nor three bodies. But because each of them participates in the same Spirit, who anointed the crucified, who sanctifies this bread, who makes the whole Church holy by partaking thereof, all are considered the body of Christ—one, regarded as belonging

[1] *Viæ Dux*, p 841 [2] *Adv Incorr et Nest* iii 19.
[3] *Adv Nest* iii 12.

to Christ, but regarded as bodies in the abstract, three—to wit, one peculiar to Christ Himself, then the bread, and then the Church.'

In other words, the natural, the sacramental, and the mystical bodies, as they have since been called. It is his distinct recognition of the action of the Holy Ghost in each that concerns us here. The exact statement of the first passage will be pointed out later.

We shall find nothing more to dwell upon at either Antioch or Jerusalem with any profit. Either there are two or more writers of the same name, but of different ages, undistinguishable from each other; or, the writings ascribed to them are doubtful, or else not explicit, or else not to the point. Consequently, the youngest of the five patriarchates of antiquity remains alone to be examined; and a single witness will amply suffice for that purpose. Christian Constantinople to this day holds to the teaching of S. John Chrysostom, and uses the liturgy bearing his name. More than this, the rest of the East follows suit.

42. But the writings of S. Chrysostom, voluminous as they are, will, for reasons that will appear as we proceed, have to be subjected to the most searching scrutiny; and in this scrutiny not the least important element will be the dates of their composition. Extracts, therefore, will only now be made from those whose dates can be fixed with tolerable precision, and at no greater length than will suffice for present purposes. We shall find ourselves thus limited to the earlier part of his career, when he preached at Antioch—before the distractions of a Court and the cares of a diocese weighed upon him. His noble work 'On the Priesthood' is generally believed to have been composed when he was still a deacon—some time, that is, between A.D. 381–86.

In this work, after a graphic reference to the prophet Elijah and his great sacrifice on Mount Carmel, he proceeds:—[1]

[1] iii 4

'Transfer yourself from thence to what is now being enacted, and you will not only behold marvels, but things exceeding amazement of every sort. For there stands the celebrant, not bringing down fire, but the Holy Ghost: and making long supplication, not that a flame sent forth from on high should consume the oblation, but that grace, descending on the sacrifice should, by means of it, impart glowing radiance to the souls of all, and exhibit them in greater brilliancy than molten silver fresh from the furnace.'

And again, farther on in the same work :—[1]

'It is necessary that he [the celebrant] should excel all for whom he pleads, about as much as it is reasonable that a general should excel his host. But when he invokes the Holy Ghost, when he consummates the awful sacrifice, when he holds in his hand the Lord of all, I pray you, tell me where shall we rank him? and what is the extent of the discretion and purity that we should require of him?'

Again, in a well-known sermon, either preached by him as a deacon, or during the first lustrum of his priesthood, a passage which doubtless has been often copied : [2]

'What is it you are doing, O man, when the celebrant stands before the table, with hands outstretched towards heaven, invoking the Holy Ghost to come down upon the oblation, and all is silent and still; when the Holy Ghost is in the act of bestowing grace; when He has come down and is operating on the elements; when you behold the immolation of the lamb represented and in its completion—is that the time which you choose for tumult and disturbance, for invective and strife?'

Once more: in the first of his sermons on Whitsunday (and a Whitsunday on which Flavian, then Bishop of Antioch, officiated, as the opening sentence shows, though the exact year cannot be fixed) we have the following—[3]

[1] Ib vi 4
[2] *Hom de Cemet et de Cruce*, § 3
[3] *De Pentec Hom* i 4

'Had not the Holy Ghost been in our common father here, when but a short time since, going up into this holy sanctuary, he prayed that peace might be with you all, you would not all have responded, "And with thy spirit." Accordingly, not merely when he goes up thither, and addresses you, and prays for you, do you make that response; but when standing by this sacred table, he prepares to offer that tremendous sacrifice—the initiated know what I say—he never so much as touches the oblation till he has first imprecated grace from the Lord on you, and you replied, "And with thy spirit," reminding yourselves in the very words of that answer that the celebrant effects nothing by his mere presence, and human nature nothing towards speeding the oblation; but that it is the grace of the Spirit, present, and coming down upon all present, which perfects that mystical sacrifice. For, though it is a man who is present, it is God, nevertheless, who works through him. Regard not, therefore, the nature of the things which you see; but regard the gift of the Unseen. Not one of the things which take place within this holy sanctuary is human. If the Spirit were not there, the Church could not hold together; but if the Church holds together, it is plain the Spirit is present.'

Could any teaching be more fervent, unequivocal, or outspoken on the subject to which it relates than the teaching of these four passages on Eucharistic consecration? Is is not identic also with that of S. Cyril of Jerusalem—the Church first examined on that head, and from which we set out? We have now completed our circle. We have gone the round of all the Churches existing in the time of the Fathers, and competent to speak from authentic records, asking the same question of each in turn, and all have returned us the same answer exactly, though some with twice the fulness of others. Not a single dissentient has appeared in sight or crossed our path, either in teaching or practice, and we assert confidently that, with a single exception, no trace can be shown of any teaching or practice conflicting with it, or even put side by side with it, in authentic documents. Consecration in those primitive times was understood everywhere to be brought about by a prayer of the celebrant addressed to the Godhead invoking the action of the Holy Ghost upon the material oblation, to sanctify—that is, to set it apart solemnly—for sacramental purposes ordained by Christ, and then, under cover of it, to effect the incorporation of individual souls with Christ incarnate, by grafting them into spiritual union with that body which was slain for man. The Holy Ghost being the accredited agent of this union, the whole process of its accomplishment was of a spiritual kind, immaterial and unseen. Still it ought to have been comprehended readily by those for whose benefit it was ordained. For it was but a new application of a principle coeval with themselves, individual souls being thus united, in this sacrament of their redemption, to a *life-giving body*: just as the soul of each man is, at his birth, united to his own body, that must one day die.

Such is the case for the positive side, and it is clear enough. Unfortunately, there is a negative side, to which we must address ourselves without flinching, however intricate.

CHAPTER V.

DOCTRINE, Catholic doctrine, stereotyped in Catholic ritual, on the sacramental application of the Incarnation to the baptised Christian, is the subject to which our inquiries have been confined hitherto, and a pleasant labour of love it has been to collect all the unequivocal evidences of its true character and of the glorious unanimity with which it was professed by the whole Christian world from its earliest age till darkness set in.

Controversy must now be faced, with all its pitfalls and entanglements, with all its animosities, its spurious authorities, its false conclusions, its degrading practices; enveloping everything in mist and fog, and darkening a path too thickly bestrewed with briars and thorns to allow of any satisfaction in threading it, even with a goal in sight.

Meanwhile, before grappling with its mazes, there are some facts—distinct matters of history—that require thorough setting out in advance, that we may be able to appeal to them as we proceed.

I. Authentic evidence—doubtless many will be surprised to hear—is wholly wanting that the early Church was in the habit of reciting what are called 'the words of institution' in consecrating the Eucharist, or was conscious of having received any command of our Lord or tradition of His Apostles to recite them for that purpose. I have carefully gone through every genuine work of every writer of the

Latin Church for eight centuries and a quarter, and of the Greek Church for about the same time, without finding a single passage from which their employment in any liturgy for that purpose during that period could reasonably be inferred, except in one conspicuous case, which it will take some time to unravel when we are brought face to face with it. Testimony to the employment at baptism of the baptismal formula still in use meets us at every turn. The words of our Lord in instituting the Eucharist and in discoursing on it are quoted at every turn for enforcing its frequent celebration by the clergy and its frequent reception by all. But of their recital at consecration of the elements in any liturgy, or of any precept committing the Church to their recital at that particular time, the genuine writings of antiquity that have come down to us will be searched in vain for any proof or even hint.

For *distribution*, indeed, contradistinguished from consecration, it will be seen at a glance, the case stands very differently: and the contrast can escape nobody when it has once been pointed out. The words used in distributing the consecrated elements to communicants in every Christian Church from the earliest times invariably were, 'The body of Christ' and 'The blood of Christ' in the vernacular of the country: to which the invariable reply was 'Amen.' Church history records no better authenticated fact than this. As regards consecration, this is the utmost that can be said with truth. The teaching of the Roman Catholic Church of our own days, making the recital of the words of institution by the celebrant essential to it, is founded on a tradition, asserted and maintained certainly for upwards of 1,000 years in the West, that from the times of the Apostles themselves the Eucharist was never consecrated in any Church without those words. But if such was really the tradition of the Church of Christ, what becomes of the fact that historical evidence for it is wholly wanting all through patristic times, and in the West suddenly breaks off at the ninth century, and cannot be carried up a peg higher? Witnesses to it *from that time* till now are numerous, continuous, and authoritative, such as must have inspired increased confidence the older it grew; while the reverence that seemed to be implied in it for the words of our Lord procured immunity from hostile criticism for it at the Reformation. Had it been attacked then, its history would have been laid bare long since, and all the passages from the Fathers supposed to favour it silently withdrawn one by one, throwing it back in future for support on its own echo. We have seen what the tradition of the whole Catholic world for upwards of eight centuries was on the subject of consecration, illustrated from primitive liturgies, and expounded in the genuine works of the Fathers in every part of the Christian Church with a fulness and a clearness that leave nothing to be desired. Two of them in particular—the two Cyrils, of Jerusalem and Alexandria—separated by half a century from each other, and in quite different works: one explaining the liturgy that he was using daily, step by step to his catechumens; the other, in an encyclic addressed to the whole Church, reciting the very words of the order for consecrating the Eucharist then observed at Alexandria: yet neither of them making any mention of or reference to the words of institution in their respective statements—certainly may be taken to settle this question, each in the negative, for his particular Church. Yet has not a 'consensus Patrum' been incontrovertibly shown, both for what they omit, and for what they state? What are the passages in their writings that have been adduced to make them contradict themselves and favour a theory that obtained a footing solely by causing their genuine works to be forgotten, or by interpolating them, and giving their time-honoured names to fictitious works brought out by the inventors of it in its support?

Tertullian is the earliest writer whose words have been thus misused. Writing against Marcion, he says of our

Lord in one place:[1] 'Acceptum panem, et *distributum discipulis*, corpus illum Suum fecit, "Hoc est corpus Meum," dicendo.' There the quotation generally stops: but what are the very next words? 'id est, "*figura* corporis Mei." Figura autem non fuisset, nisi veritatis esset corpus.' Nobody can tell what Tertullian means as well as Tertullian himself. In the first place, he is speaking, *not* of consecration, but of *distribution*. In the next, he is commenting on what is recorded in the Gospels to have been said by our Lord: not testifying to what was said by the celebrant in the liturgy. In the next, he gives us to understand his meaning is, that Jesus, in saying 'Hoc est corpus Meum,' made the bread 'a figure of His body'—*not* His actual body —and that, being 'a figure of His body,' it proved that His body was no phantom, but the real thing which Christians held it to be. By 'the figure' Tertullian of course meant 'the sacrament.'

After all, this passage should be read side by side with one directed against the *followers* of Marcion in the fourth book of the work of S. Irenæus against heresies, from which it was evidently borrowed. 'How could the Lord,' he asks them, 'if born of another father, of the same condition as ourselves, taking bread confess it to be His body with truth, or declare the mixed chalice to be His blood?'[2] Here S. Irenæus implies distinctly that consecration had preceded distribution.

Similar liberties have been taken with a well-known letter of S. Cyprian on the mixed chalice,[3] which Sir W. Palmer, instead of accepting the stock quotation from it without examination, ought to have been the first to expose. It stops short at precisely the same point as that from

---

[1] Lib iv 40
[2] C 33
[3] 'De Sacramento Dominici Calicis,' is the Latin title *Ep* lxiii ed Ben On this particular head his words are 'Unde apparet, sanguinem Christi non offerri, si vinum desit calici, nec sacrificium Dominicum *legitimâ sanctificatione celebrari*, nisi *oblatio et sacrificium* nostrum *responderit passioni*'

Tertullian: though S. Cyprian, like Tertullian, explains himself in the very next sentence. This is the quotation:

'Passionis Ejus mentionem in sacrificiis omnibus facimus.'

And everybody stops there, Sir W. Palmer included,[1] who would have been saved several inaccuracies had he looked further. For what are the words of the parenthesis which *immediately* follows? *Passio est enim Domini, sacrificium quod offerimus*,' demonstrating what S. Cyprian meant by the word 'Passio.' The celebration of the Eucharist *was* the 'passion of the Saviour,' which it commemorated—without a word more: '*doing*' (as our Lord had commanded) 'in His remembrance' what He had done: *not* saying what He had said. Or, as S. Cyprian expresses it himself in another place, ' Nihil aliud, quàm quod Ille *fecit*, facere debemus.'[2] The argument of the whole letter turns upon this.

Another passage, less frequently quoted, because confessedly corrupt, and having all the marks of an interpolation, is from the 'Ancoratus' of S. Epiphanius: but, anyhow, his reference is solely to Scripture—' ut in Evangelio legitur'—where the words of institution are quoted as spoken by Christ Himself: not as forming any part of the liturgy then used in his Church.[3]

This closes the list of passages from acknowledged sources, and a short list it is. Martene, conscious of their paucity, strives to add another, by misquoting—let us hope, from oversight—words from a sermon of S. Augustine, that bear a meaning quite different in the edition of his Benedictine brethren to which he refers, and where no other reading is named.

'Panis ille, quem videtis in altari, *sanctificatus per verbum Dei*, corpus est Christi.'[4]

The italicised will at once be recognised by English

---

[1] *Orig Lit* i 139, note *x*
[2] P 109, line 33, ed Baluze.
[3] C 57, ed Migne
[4] *Serm* ccxxvii. ed Ben.

readers as a quotation from S. Paul.[1] Martene[2] changes it into 'per verbum *Christi*.'

Mr. Maskell, whom few would suspect of quoting second-hand without verifying, bids us in his Preface[3] 'hear *S. Augustine*,' and then follows a quotation from what is described in his note as 'Serm. xxvii. tom. v.' So it stood in the older editions, though even there it is Serm. 28, not 27. But, having since been discovered[4] identic with Lib. v. 4 of the 'De Sacram.' of the pseudo-Ambrose, it has been placed among the spurious sermons at the end of tom. v. of his works: 84th in the Benedictine edition.

The Catechism of the Council of Trent makes a number of statements on the 'form of the Eucharist, as regards the bread,' derived wholly from spurious works: in the first place misinterpreting the Gospels, as though our Lord had in consecrating the elements used those words, 'Take, eat, this is My body' (which we are *not* told), instead of having used them in distributing His own body to the disciples (which we *are* told). In asserting, secondly, that infinite passages might be quoted to that effect from the Fathers: the fact being that S. Chrysostom is the only Father who connects those words ever with consecration; and in his earlier and more standard works not even he.

Lastly, the passage from S. Chrysostom on Judas is the *only* passage which, *if genuine*, is from a *genuine source* bearing on the subject of all the passages appended in a note to this section. The spuriousness of the tract 'De Sacramentis' will be demonstrated further on. The passages from S. Irenæus and Tertullian have just been disposed of. The passages from S. Augustine, S. Cyril, Origen, and the Greek Jerome, not only make no mention of the words of institution, but in explicit terms testify to the prayer of invocation, as may be seen in the preceding chapter, where

---

[1] 1 Tim iv 5
[2] *De Ant Rit* 1 4, art. viii. § 20
[3] *Ancient Lit* p civ.
[4] To Oudin belongs the merit of this discovery. See the *Notit* in Migne, *Pat. Lat* clxxxix 1508

they are quoted at length to that effect. The passage from Isychius, whose identity still has to be proved, is confined to the fulfilment of the types of the Old Testament by Christ in His own person, without going further.[1]

Surely the positive and deliberate statements of the great founder of our Anglo-Saxon Church, S. Gregory, may be placed in the scales against the *self-supporting tradition of all the divines* of the ninth century put together, on the point which concerns us now. He says of the Lord's Prayer emphatically that 'the Apostles themselves were wont to consecrate the Eucharistic oblation to the recital of that prayer alone.'[2] He says of the most solemn part of his own liturgy, which he was revising or had just revised, that it was 'composed by a scholastic.' Then, fresh from these words, let us inquire whether the words of our Lord may not have been a hundred times better understood by the Fathers in invariably repeating them at the distribution of the consecrated elements than by the ninth-century divines, who were the first to make consecration depend on their recital in the place which they occupy to this day in the Roman Canon. Now, apart from the ingrained prepossession of 1,000 years which has accustomed us all in the West to regard them exclusively from this point of view, that question could not be so much as put with any colour either in the abstract or the concrete. Not in the abstract: for the custom of the Fathers is made fast to an unbroken chain of evidence from Apostolic times; while for the tradition of the divines of the ninth century not a scrap of historic evidence can be produced. Not in the concrete: as a reverential consideration of the words and acts of our Lord at His last supper with His disciples must make plain to everybody but those who deliberately refuse to construe them in their obvious acceptation.

---

[1] Part ii c iv § 20, and the note
[2] 'Mos fuit Apostolorum, ad ipsam solummodo orationem, oblationis hostiam consecrare' *Ep* lib ix ep 12, ed Ben

For His outspoken words, recorded in the Gospel or by S. Paul, were threefold—two speeches on administering communion in each kind, both of which were seized upon and appropriated at once by the early Church in giving communion to her children, as has been said; and a third enunciating this command, ' Do '—*not* say, *not* recite, but ' *Do* this in My remembrance.' Do what? ' Having taken bread, and given thanks over it, and blessed it, as you have seen Me do, break and distribute portions of it to others, as I have done to you. Then, having taken the cup and given thanks over it, present it to all, that all may drink of the fruit of the vine which it contains, as you have seen Me do to you likewise.'

Now it is evident that neither the first two nor the last of these recorded speeches of our Lord contain any formula for consecration; and yet the first two cannot *but* imply that consecration of the elements had preceded them. Either, therefore, the elements must have been consecrated by His previous acts alone, or some words joined to His previous acts, which had the effect of consecrating them, must have been left out. To which of His acts may we reasonably conclude words to have been joined? The question is no sooner asked than it is answered. To His acts of blessing and of giving thanks. Why, then, have the words that accompanied them been omitted? As even S. Paul was not authorised to supply them, the omission was plainly not accidental, whether we can fathom the design that prompted their omission or not. As we have no report given us of the words of our Lord in blessing and giving thanks over the bread and chalice, we can only conclude that He would not allow any record of them to be preserved, either by pronouncing them inaudibly or by forbidding them to be handed down. Yet is it possible that no lesson was intended in this, or that such marked conduct on His part, when they had leisure to reflect upon it, could have been lost upon His Apostles? Besides, was it not all of a piece with

His own parting injunction to them that 'they should not depart from Jerusalem, but wait for the promise of the Father'? of which He had told them in these words: 'Ye shall receive power after that the Holy Ghost is come upon you . . .' and 'He shall teach you all things and bring all things to your remembrance whatsoever I have said unto you . . .' and 'He shall take of Mine and show it unto you' (twice repeated). Our Lord purposely left blanks, as it were, for the Holy Ghost to fill in. The Eucharist that was not allowed to be celebrated for ten days after His departure— the new sacrament of the new Dispensation—He willed should exhibit a prime instance of this, unprovided with a formula for consecration. The Holy Ghost had no sooner descended than the blank was filled in, and the 'breaking of bread' commenced. The Church that started into consciousness at His touch did not require to be told further what to do. She turned to Him for assistance, to whom she owed her new life. Her *epiklesis* supplied her at once with a formula for consecration and with a Consecrator in Him.

This is the explanation of both the antiquity and the universality proved to belong to it in the preceding chapter, and till its disuse by the West the bond of union between the Churches of Christendom was never rent, nor communion denied to any that sincerely professed their common creed and adorned the faith of Christ by their lives. It was worthy of the darkest ages of Europe to have remained passive when this sublime prayer was being expunged from her liturgies, and the words of Christ in *distributing communion* travestied with a non-natural meaning in the mouths of her celebrants, and diverted to a purpose not intended by Him whose words they were, to the sowing of discord in His Church, to the official dethronement of Him whom the Fathers of the Western Church had pointedly styled His Vicar, and Christ Himself declared His successor in designating Him 'another Paraclete.'

DETHRONEMENT OF THE HOLY GHOST.

But we must deal tenderly with good men in disastrous times, who were taken in themselves, and never conscious of the mischief which they helped to spread, and whose age was formed by events that were none of their making, and far beyond their control. We must deal tenderly, too, with good men in the best of times, wedded to a tradition more than 1,000 years old—however unsound at the core—which they will feel bound on conscientious grounds to defend to the last, until its true character has been established on evidence which they cannot dispute.

The 'mystery of iniquity' that was at work in Apostolic times, never had a wider field for operations than when three-parts of the East had struck colours to the soldiers of Mahomet, and three-parts of the West to barbarians that had not as yet been won to the Gospel. And the diseases which escape notice longest are those which are deepest-seated in the constitution, and require to be unravelled with patience, to be surely removed. It is on this account that the point on which we are now engaged has never been probed hitherto, and, if taken in hand at all, must be probed to the roots.

II. To whom, then, was this change due: when and where was it contrived? I trust to be able to show conclusively that it originated with the Arians, and that it won its way on false pretences, stealthily but slowly, from East to West, destined under cover of night to succeed at last.

But again we must commence with established facts, before plunging into debateable ground.

Of all the heresies in early times there were none to be compared with the Arian for its untiring machinations and deliberate purpose to subvert belief in Christ as God. It employed all the arts of Satan—force, fraud, and artifice—to this end; and when foiled and decisively worsted in this fell design, it employed its expiring energies in depreciating the Holy Ghost, and making Him out the creature that it would have made Christ Himself. We have merely to go to the larger work against Marcellus of Eusebius the historian, written some time between A.D. 336–40, for proof of this,[1] a work which no doubt served Macedonius for a text-book when he got made patriarch of Constantinople some few years later. It was he who developed this new heresy, while patriarch, and his disciples who propagated it after his death, which happened in the first year of the emperor Julian, A.D. 361. Pope Liberius, therefore, who survived him five years, must have been well acquainted with his false teaching. It has thus been a grand mistake with most hitherto to suppose the worst sin committed by Pope Liberius to have been his having subscribed under pressure to a semi-Arian creed; and to ignore the latest act of his official life, when, being his own master, and in full possession of his see, and claiming to speak on behalf of the whole West, he admitted the Macedonian leaders, and among them the actual framers of the heterodox formula, signed by him—we are told, against his will—to full communion on their own terms,[2] without demanding from them any formal

---

[1] *Eccl Theol* ii 6, on which Bishop Mountague says 'Aperte Spiritum Sanctum in albo reponit creaturarum Eumque a Filio perinde atque cætera productum, disertis verbis repetit, quod et blasphemus statim repetit' (ap Migne, *Pat Gr* xxiv 1013)

[2] I avail myself of the French of M Rohrbacher (*Hist de l'E* vii 28), who translates Socrates quite correctly so far (*E H* iv 12)· 'D'abord le Pape ne voulait pas les recevoir, les regardant comme des Ariens, qui avaient aboli la foi de Nicée Ils répondirent qu'ils étaient revenus de l'erreur et qu'ils avaient rejeté depuis longtemps la créance des Anoméans, et confessé le Fils *semblable au Père en toutes choses* qu'il *n'y avait point de différence entre le semblable et le consubstantiel*' M Rohrbacher has no comment on this; but to what does it amount?

It amounts to telling the Pope that, if he would allow their semi-Arian interpretation of it, they were prepared to put their names to the Nicene Creed Liberius, *without another word*, 'leur demanda leur confession de foi par écrit' and they handed him the Nicene Creed in writing, with their names affixed to it—of course suppressing their own interpretation of it, accepted in advance, and *suppressing also* from the list of heresies condemned by them the *Macedonian*—that is, their own—which the Nicene Creed, as it ended with the simple words 'and in the Holy Ghost,' could not touch

Thus Liberius actually received them into full communion *on the very terms* of the semi-Arian creed which he was said to have signed under pressure, and without requiring them to recant their Mace-

abjuration of their own fell tenet, for which they got called *Pneumatomachi*—fighters against the Holy Ghost—or even questioning them on that head. Of this heretical act of Liberius, in thus officially condoning their fresh attack upon the faith, S. Basil had bitter cause to complain to the day of his death, for the troubles it occasioned in the East, and for the power of doing mischief which it put into the hands of Eustathius of Sebaste, the arch-contriver of it. Well might he, cut to the quick, exclaim: 'Certainly faith with us is not one thing at Seleucia, another at Constantinople, another at Zele, another at Lampsacus, and another at Rome; nor yet is it that which is carried about now, diverse from its predecessors, but it is always one and the same.'[1]

Nor was it in the East alone that its effects were felt. Eustathius and his friends started triumphant from Rome, and went about everywhere boasting of their success; having with them the letter of Liberius in their favour addressed to a number of bishops by name, and to the Easterns in general. Where they could, they stopped on their way back, as in Sicily, and got a synod assembled to hear the good news, so that before they reached home they were practically restored. 'What proposals were made by Liberius of happy memory to Eustathius,' says S. Basil, 'and what engagements were entered into by him, I know not. I only know he brought back a letter for restoring him, on exhibiting which to the Synod of Tyana, he was put back in his place. That faith on

---

donianism But to the semi-Arian view, Sozomen tells us, he declared his assent *unasked at Milan*, hoping of course that it would have softened the emperor, and prevented his exile (*E H* iv 11) So that he may have experienced as little difficulty in *re-*accepting semi-Arianism as in condoning Macedonianism

[1] *Ep* ccli 4, ed Ben And there are numbers more to the same effect,

in reference to this man whom Liberius had sent back with honour Abbé Rohrbacher merely refers to *Ep* cclxiii 3, as though it stood alone, and takes care we shall hear no more of what even it contains than gives colour to his remark Had he quoted it entire, he must have commented on it in another strain A specimen is given in the next page

which he was received he now destroys, siding with those who anathematise the consubstantial, and occupying the post of leader of the Pneumatomachians.'

This letter, it is true, was written ten years after the Synod of Tyana, but Eustathius had only worn the mask as long as it suited his purpose, and S. Basil is describing the overt acts, not of one year, but of many.

I submit, therefore, that should the problem be forced on us further on, how Macedonianism came to obtain a footing in the West, the historical answer will have been supplied in advance—through Liberius.

Another point connected with the Arians of all grades is still clearer: their affected regard for Scriptural terms and expressions. The term *Homoousion*, consubstantial, encountered their opposition from the first on that ground, and retained it to the last. Eusebius, the historian, not daring to controvert its insertion in the Creed after its acceptance by Constantine, loudly testified his disapprobation of it, in the praise lavished by him on the anathema tacked to the Creed for prohibiting the unscriptural phrases condemned in it, adding that almost all the dissensions and perplexities ever experienced in the Church had arisen from the employment of terms unknown to the inspired Scriptures.[1] The Acacians, long afterwards, condemned the Homoousians, the Homoiousians and the Anomeans in one lot for the same reason.[2] But to what purpose was Scripture turned by the Arians? They served themselves of it to disprove the Divinity, first of the Son, and then of the Holy Ghost. They saw that by quoting passages detached from their context, or with their own text interpolated or corrupted, or with their meaning distorted or perverted, they could obtain specious support for all the false teaching advanced by them, and having for its object to deceive the unwary. This was no secret to their orthodox contem-

---

[1] Soc. *E. H.* i. 8   [2] Ib. ii. 40

poraries. Didymus, the Alexandrian catechist, in his masterly work on the Trinity, devotes the last book entirely to the rectification of a long list of their stock passages, thus perverted, by submitting each to the test of one or more of his dogmatic positions, carefully worked out from Scripture, and laid down by him in advance. His logic is as trenchant as his method is admirable. Their exposure is most instructive.[1]

That honesty was not more respected by the Arians, as a body, than Scripture, these few instances extracted from Socrates will suffice to shew. (1) Threatened at one time by Constans, then ruler of the West, for deposing S. Athanasius, they manufactured a Creed expressly for him, differing from their own which they had just published at Antioch.[2] (2) Starting from Rimini, with the Creed they had just put out there, they republished it at Nice in Thrace, calling it after that town, and then passed it off as the Nicene Creed.[3] (3) On the accession of the emperor Jovian, a number of them, representing all shades of opinion, subscribed to the Nicene Creed itself, declaring beforehand that there was no real difference between it and their own semi-Arian formula: like the Macedonians who were subsequently received by Liberius.[4] (4) Their groundless calumnies against S. Athanasius are well-known. But the worst of all is told so naively by Socrates[5]—and it was a story that would long survive where the scene was enacted—that it may be given in his words. Arsenius, a schismatic bishop in Egypt, was said to have been punished by S. Athanasius with the loss of one of his hands. The hand was carried about and displayed, and at length taken to Tyre, where there was a council sitting in judgment on S. Athanasius: but Arsenius was said to have died of the injuries he had received. All of a sudden S. Athanasius was informed by a friendly magistrate that Arsenius was at that moment in Tyre, behind the scenes.

[1] Migne, *Pat Gr* xxxix 769–992   [2] *E H* ii 18
[3] Ib ii 37   [4] Ib iii 25   [5] Ib i 32

He was dragged out and exhibited to the council with both hands entire, S. Athanasius asking triumphantly to which part of him the third hand belonged. The emperor was informed by S. Athanasius himself of what had taken place: but the council, notwithstanding, with singular effrontery voted him deposed from his see. And, 'wonderful to say,' adds Socrates, 'he who had been reported slain by S. Athanasius, voted alive for his deposition.'

S. Athanasius himself mentions that on another occasion they concocted and sent letters in his name to the Emperor, that he had neither written nor ever intended to write.[1]

Among the letters ascribed to S. Basil are four that, to judge from their titles, passed between him and Apollinarius. The judgment expressed by Coteler (who brought them to light) on their origin is to this effect—that they were forged either by the Arians or Apollinarians, to establish his complicity with the errors of both. He says further: 'Cæterum, etsi suppositiciæ, *magni faciendæ sunt epistolæ*: per quas nimirum cernere est veterum hereticorum malitiam, fraudem, errores.'[2]

The Benedictine Garnier similarly points out how interlarded the comments of S. Basil on the Psalms and on Isaiah have come down to us with the comments of Eusebius the historian on the same books;[3] while the Lutheran Augusti draws attention to the close resemblance between the sermons of S. Chrysostom and Eusebius, Bishop of Emesa ('factionis Arianæ signifer,' as S. Jerome calls him[4]), on Judas Iscariot, but thinks, because S. Chrysostom wrote last, it was simple copying on his part.[5] Most of us know how the 'Filioque' got into the Niceno-Constantinopolitan Creed. It was not by copying, nor by translating, but inter-

---

[1] *Apol ad Imp* § 11 et seq
[2] *Eccl Gr Monum* ii 553-4
[3] *Præf ad S Basil* §§ vi and x
ed Ben
[4] *Chron* A D 348
[5] *Euseb Em. Opusc* p 144

INTERPOLATIONS OF THE FATHERS.

polating. Reccared, the Gothic king, whose deed it was, had been brought up an Arian, and the Council which received his abjuration (A.D. 589), accepted his version of the Creed, and all his anathemas appended to it, without a word. It won its way in the dark, 'while men slept,' slowly and silently from that time, scarcely noticed and unopposed, till it might seem to have established for itself a prescriptive title; till a well-known maxim in law, ' *Quod fieri non debet, factum valet*,' might be thought by many to be the simplest settlement of a fine-drawn question of religion; till, all of a sudden, it was seized upon with avidity by the founder of a new empire and converted into the means of attacking the last œcumenical Council held in the old, for upholding the Creed which three previous œcumenical Councils had decreed under pains and penalties should ever remain intact. And then, gradually, by successors of Pope Liberius, though bound by the oath which all Bishops of Rome formerly took at their consecration, to uphold the Creed of those Councils— *usque ad unum apicem*, without changing a syllable—first sacrificed it to secure their temporalities, and at length adopted themselves the interpolation decreed by two crowned heads, as a stepping-stone for making their see superior to the rulings of œcumenical Councils, even when confirmed by their predecessors, and thus establishing a complete dictatorship over the whole Church for each successive Bishop of Rome during his lifetime.

To such colossal effects has a single interpolation of a a word of four syllables in the Creed of the Church ministered. As a very parallel case will soon occur, it seemed desirable to recal its prototype, whose tortuous history some may have forgotten, and others hear for the first time summarised.

Reccared, the Gothic king who introduced it, had been brought up an Arian, as has been pointed out; and, as it was his first act in abjuring Arianism, it is not a little singular that it should have passed unchallenged on that account alone.

But a surprise still more extraordinary meets us on getting to the bottom of the parallel case, and dragging into daylight its connection with avowed Arianism. For here the Catechism of the Council of Trent steps in to our amazement,[1] and for *primitive testimony to the institution of the Eucharist* appeals absolutely to the very man—Eusebius of Emesa. But who was he? Why, the same whom S. Jerome, thirty-two years old when he died, designates 'standard-bearer of the Arians.' It is only too true! He was infinitely better known in his own age than he has been since. Cardinal Newman [2] passes him over in silence. Socrates and Sozomen both state that his parents were well-born citizens of Edessa, in Mesopotamia, where he was brought up himself, and studied Greek under a Greek master then residing there. This shows, of course, that Greek was not his native tongue, any more than it was of S. Ephrem the Syrian, his compatriot and contemporary. He had two masters who taught him the Scriptures, of whom Eusebius, the historian and his namesake, was one. Being at Antioch about the time when Eustathius was deposed by the Arians (A.D. 331), he, to avoid being installed there bishop, hurried away to Alexandria, where he studied philosophy. Ten years after, he was offered that see, too, by the Council of Antioch, from which S. Athanasius had been expelled, but he declined it. Later he became Bishop of Emesa, which he continued to be till his death. His Life was written by a devoted admirer of his, an ex-presbyter of Alexandria, named George, subsequently Bishop of Laodicea, called by S. Athanasius the worst heretic of the whole party. S. Jerome speaks in his biographical notices of Eusebius as

---

[1] Part II c iv § 3, where the pseudo-Cyprian and pseudo-Ambrose are quoted further on

[2] *Arians*, p 158, ed 1854 His biographer is named, who believed him a much greater man than himself.

a writer 'elegant and rhetorical in his style, who wrote innumerable works amazingly popular, and read with avidity by those who studied declamation . . .' and besides other works, 'short, but exceedingly numerous homilies on the Gospels.' Unfortunately, S. Jerome fails to tell us in what language they were written. S. Ephrem composed all his works in Syriac; though they were, during his own lifetime, translated into Greek, and since then into Latin. The two fragments preserved of Eusebius by Theodoret are written in good Greek. But Theodoret may have turned them into Greek himself. He quotes Eusebius only to show that he was orthodox where the Monophysites erred. Yet in the second of the passages quoted from his book, annihilation of the soul is represented as though the writer himself believed it. The fragments brought out for the first time by Augusti may or may not have been composed in Greek, but that they got mixed up with the sermons of a certain Eusebius of Alexandria, 'about whom Gallandius hesitates not to say that all is uncertain, and nothing can be affirmed on good grounds as to his age, or as to his bishopric,'[1] is only due to the fact that Eusebius of Emesa was resident at Alexandria for some time, and may have composed them there, and also that his Life was written by an ex-Alexandrian presbyter. They are much too like the description given of his works in general by S. Jerome, and for other reasons, which will appear presently, to be transferred to another, of whom and of whose writings nothing certain is known. One of them, for Good Friday, can have scarcely been preached as a sermon, though it might have supplied hints for the wondrous dialogue between Sin, Death, and Satan in 'Paradise Lost.' Another is the one from which Augusti thinks S. Chrysostom borrowed—a point to which we shall be

[1] Dr Smith's *Christ Biog Dict* vol. ii. 305, with 307 and 358. It might turn out that Eusebius of Emesa was the real author of all the sermons ascribed to the Alexandrian, and that his having been offered that see may have been the foundation of the alleged bishopric of the latter.

brought back shortly. But first, the patchwork collection of homilies, upwards of two hundred in number, in Latin, ascribed to Eusebius of Emesa, requires sifting; for, though they cannot all be 'the short but exceedingly numerous homilies on the Gospels' attributed to him by S. Jerome, it is just as likely that Syriac homilies by Eusebius of Emesa, thus noticed by S. Jerome, should have been translated into Latin after having been circulated in Greek (as Syriac homilies by S. Ephrem then formed the groundwork of, and gave name to, a collection like the present), and then, in process of time, got interlarded with casual remarks by those who used them, compromising their antiquity. Oudin, who has reviewed them at great length, and been thought by later writers, as Augusti,[1] to have left nothing unsaid, not only fails to account for the name given to this collection, but also to see that the extracts quoted by Theodoret are quoted for a purpose that completely meets his objections to particular homilies, which on all other grounds Eusebius might be supposed to have written. I select his first instance:[2] 'How can a writer,' he asks, 'who died A.D. 361, be credited with a homily which notices the Pelagian heresy? Thus it speaks: "Which testimony supplies a most evident and cogent argument against the blasphemies of Pelagius, who presumes to assert that baptism is not to be administered to infants with a view to life, but with a view to the kingdom of heaven."' The homily where this sentence occurs found a place for ages among the homilies of S. Jerome, and of S. Cæsarius of Arles, probably from having been preached by both; and from either of them this remark may have proceeded. Just in the same way, Theodoret, in his Dialogue, tells the Monophysite that Eusebius had supplied strong arguments against his heresy by anticipation.

According to the last arrangement of these homilies,

---

[1] *Euseb Emes Opusc* pp 93-4   [2] *Script Eccl* tom. i 396.

which is that of the *Maxima Bibliotheca Veterum Patrum*, from which I quote,[1] we have two separate batches, the first and last, on the Gospels of the Sundays and Festivals of the year. Of them all, only two concern us now: the fifth, in the first batch, of those entitled ' *De Pascha*,' with the remark about Pelagius interwoven in it;[2] and another, in the second batch, headed '*Dominica in Ramis Palmarum*.'[3] These titles, by whomsoever affixed to them, are not such as to discredit their antiquity. S. Gregory Nazianzen has a long oration '*In Sanctum Pascha*': and S. Gregory Nyssen five with the same title, and that of the 'Resurrection of Christ' appended to it. Bingham shows that the seven days before and the seven days after Easter, besides Easter Day itself, were comprehended under this title.[4] The other title is shared by sermons doubtfully given by Montfaucon to S. Athanasius,[5] and by Petavius to S. Epiphanius.[6] But the writer of the homily 'De Pascha' declares it himself to be for the day on which the Eucharist was instituted – called by us Maundy Thursday, but which was in strictness the first evening of Good Friday, or the Parasceve: and of course the evening of the betrayal too. Consistently with this, it deals with the Eucharist exclusively. The other homily, though its heading is 'Palm Sunday,' has nothing at all to do with Palm Sunday, but is wholly taken up with the Passion— a title, by the way, given to a sermon by S. Ephrem. Thus it might be headed 'for the Parasceve,' like the other. The Eucharist comes on for treatment in it, as might have been expected: only not at anything like the length of the other. Both are beyond doubt by the same writer; and there is nothing in either, with the exception of what has been already noticed in the first, to discredit—but a good deal, on the contrary, to suggest—their being by Eusebius of Emesa: or at least, by one of his school. In short, the sermon of S.

---

[1] Lugdun, 1677, vol vi 618-822
[2] Ib p 636
[3] Ib 746
[4] *Ant.* xx. 5, 1, and xxi 1, 31
[5] *Collect Nov Pat et Script Gr* ii 63.
[6] Ap. Migne, *Pat. Gr* xliii 427

Ephrem, already quoted,[1] heard when the writer was at Edessa with his family, may have suggested both. Now, their true character is brought out most clearly by being placed in parallel columns with kindred extracts from two sermons on the betrayal of Judas—or rather, two recensions of one sermon preached on different occasions, and at a considerable interval one from the other—by S. Chrysostom, as they stand in the edition of Montfaucon,[2] which, whatever opinion may be formed of them, have too much by far in common with these Latin homilies to have been the effect of chance. The question, therefore, that their juxtaposition must raise will be: how to account for their similarity? Observe, though Montfaucon thinks the sermon which he has placed first must have been preached some years before the other, he confesses he can date neither, nor say where they were preached. On the other hand, it is in these sermons that Augusti finds clear tokens of S. Chrysostom having borrowed not a little from the sermon, short as it is, which he has printed in Greek on the betrayal of Judas, and by Eusebius of Emesa too.[3] But all that Eusebius says in this sermon about the Eucharist is that Judas partook of it: an opinion which S. Chrysostom certainly shares and expresses in each of these sermons. Still, in this he is not half so singular as in his agreement with the Latin homilies; which, as will be seen, involves a clear departure from his own teaching already quoted. Eucharistic consecration is the subject handled in both.

[1] Above. p 78.
[2] Tom ii 376-96.
[3] This sermon is also printed, among those supposed to be by the Alexandrian Eusebius, by Mai, Spicileg Rom ix. 693, from a MS. at Grotta Ferrata.

'HOMIL. V DE PASCHA' says:—

'Hence, because He was about to remove from our gaze, and to carry to heaven the body which He had assumed, it was necessary that He should consecrate for us *on this day* the sacrament of His body and blood, that what was once offered in expiation should be worshipped ever afterwards in mystery; and since redemption goes on uninterruptedly from day to day, that the oblation of it also might be perpetual, and the eternal Victim ever live in remembrance, as well as always be present in grace, a Victim verily both perfect and unique: to be appreciated, not from what is patent to sense; to be realised, not by the sight of the outer, but by the affections of the inner man. Hence, too, the authority confirming it to us is Divine: "For My flesh is meat indeed, and My blood is drink indeed, as He says"'

So far, nothing could have been better said, or in greater harmony with the teaching of the Church of the Fathers He goes on:—

'Away, then, with every doubt and misgiving. The Author of the gift is witness to its truth. *For the invisible Priest, by the secret power of His word, converts the visible elements into the substance of His body and blood, on saying:* "*Take, eat; this is My body;*" *and again, in repeating the consecration*· "*Take, drink; this is My blood.*" Thus, *as at the nod and*

S. CHRYSOSTOM 'DE PRODITIONE JUDÆ,' &c.

Before quoting the sermon placed first by Montfaucon, it may be remarked that both sermons occupy the same number of pages in his edition, and that the Eucharist has the same place and the same number of sections assigned to it in both—namely, the two last. Yet it cannot be denied that this subject forms an integral part of both sermons; though what is said is not identic in both. Strange to say, their discrepancies partake, to no small extent, of the discrepancies between the two Latin Homilies. But, again, the whole of the bracketed portion of both sermons, corresponding to the italicised portion of both homilies, might be away, without spoiling their sense; or might have been penned by S Chrysostom with those homilies in Greek at his side.

In the first he opens the subject thus·—

Sermon I.

'Formerly the Passover was a Jewish feast. It has ceased to be this; and is a spiritual Passover, which Jesus then instituted. For, as they were eating and drinking, says the Gospel, Jesus having taken bread, brake it and said : "This is My body, which is being broken for you for remission of sins" The initiated know what words were said. And again the cup,

command of the Lord were created out of nothing the heaven of heavens, the depths of the sea, and expanse of earth, so with equal power in spiritual sacraments, what a word orders in might is instantly produced in fact...'

What immediately follows is beside the point It will be observed that there has been as yet no distinct assertion of the presence of the words of institution in the liturgy. After a while he illustrates his position by the baptismal formula (which, be it remembered, *is* enjoined in Scripture by Christ Himself), much as S. Cyril of Jerusalem illustrates his by reference to the chrism (but had nothing in Scripture to show for it). 'The candidate for baptism,' he says, 'before those words are pronounced, is still held in the bond of original sin. Those words are no sooner pronounced, than he is loosed from it. Similarly, when the elements are placed on the altar, to be blessed by the Divine words, before they are consecrated by invocation of the Supreme Name, it is the substance of bread and wine that is there, but after the words of Christ it is the body and blood of Christ. And why should we wonder at His being able to change with a word what He made with a word? He is surely credited with a less miracle, when affirmed able to change for the better what He is acknowledged to have created out of nothing.' The reasoning is close; but no such command of Christ can be shown for repeating saying: "This is My blood, which is being poured out for many, for remission of sins" And Judas was present when Christ said all this,' &c Further on.—

'It is now time for us to approach this awful board. Let us approach it with becoming gravity and sobriety... Christ is even now present. He who prepared that table, the same prepares this now. For it is not man who causes the elements to become the body and blood of Christ, but Christ Himself, who was crucified for us. [The priest who stands formally ministering says those words, but the power of the grace is of God. " This is My body," says he. That word transforms what lie there. And, as that word which says, "Increase, and multiply, and replenish the earth," once spoken, becomes effective for all time, enabling our nature to be prolific in offspring, so this word, once spoken also, perfects the sacrifice from then till now; and from now till His coming again, on every table, in every church']

This passage marks by a well-known phrase, not found in the other, the reserve maintained habitually by S. Chrysostom on these subjects elsewhere. 'The initiated know what is said.' Again, it opens with the assertion that this is 'a *spiritual* Passover,' which the other only supplies at the end. Yet the other, again, supplies things wholly wanting in this.

His words in administering this sacrament, as for using the formula with which He enjoined baptism to be conferred. The writer is evidently pleading here for something he wants, and hopes soon to have, while testifying to another that was still in force viz. 'the invocation of the Supreme Name': but will not add for what.

EUSEBIUS, DOM. IN RAMIS PALMARUM.

'"As they were supping, Jesus took bread," &c The Lord expounds in this passage what He meant when He said on another occasion, "Except ye eat the flesh of the Son of Man and drink His blood ye have no life in you." Lo! *the Priest for ever after the order of Melchisedeck converts bread and wine, by power ineffable, into the substance of His body and blood* For as He then both lived and talked, and still was eaten and drunk by His disciples, so He remains still intact and entire, and is daily drunk and eaten by His faithful ones in the sacrament of bread and wine Indeed, unless the bread and wine were turned into His flesh and blood, He could not ever be eaten and drunk corporally. For those things are changed into these things. How, indeed, this takes place He only knows who both knows all things and can do them Further, *what He said then by Himself He says now by His servants. "This is My body"* And such is the efficacy and force of that word, that the

S CHRYSOSTOM.
Sermon II

Sermon II, then, opens the subject, like the first. 'Formerly the Passover was a Jewish feast; but it has ceased to be this. Then, says the Gospel, Jesus having taken bread [into His holy and immaculate hands] and given thanks, and broken it, said to His disciples: "Take, eat; this is My body, which is being broken for you and for many, for remission of sins And again, having taken the cup, He gave to them, saying: 'This is My blood, which is being poured out for you, for remission of sins" And Judas was present when the Lord said this,' &c.

Further on: 'It is now time to draw near to this awful and fearful board Let us all, then, approach it with a pure conscience. Christ is now here and preparing the table For it is not man who causes the elements to become the body and blood of Christ. [The priest only stands formally ministering and offering a petition, but it is the grace and the power of God that works all things. "This is My body,' says he; that word thing is done as soon as said *Just in the same way, when He says, " This is My blood," the wine straightway becomes His blood " He took the cup and gave thanks, and gave to them saying · Drink ye all of it This is My blood of the New Testament, which will be shed for many for the remission of sins"* This, He says, is " My blood which is to be shed · " not one portion of it then, and another now : but one and the same in each case—to-morrow flowing out of His side ; to-day seen in the chalice and drunk by you . . .'

The author of both passages is plainly the same His way of quoting the words of institution, separately and consecutively, shows this. And his argument is identic in both. But in this last passage there is no mention of the ' invocation of the Supreme Name ', and the words of institution are quoted, *as they stand now in most liturgies*, more resembling the Roman, indeed, than any other, as having been preached in Latin, or turned into Latin at all events. And he distinctly tells us that these words are ' said now by the servants of Christ.'

transforms what lie there. And as that voice which said " Increase, and multiply, and replenish the earth," was a word that became fact, enabling human nature to become prolific, so this word spoken, for ever causes worthy communicants to grow in grace ']

This passage, besides laying down nothing at starting on the spiritual character of the Christian Passover, departs from the reserve of the first by quoting epithets applied to the hands of Christ, it may be then in the liturgy, but not in Scripture On the other hand, it specifies a petition offered up by the celebrant, probably what the Homilist has called ' the invocation of the Supreme Name,' and then instead of referring to the sacrifice, dwells on the effects of the sacrament for good in all worthy communicants.

I have bracketed as much of these sermons, *not* as I would pronounce *spurious*, but as much as might have been imported from the Latin homilies, and is unlike what S. Chrysostom uniformly lays down in all his best pieces that we possess. For in these bracketed portions we have two things asserted. First, the presence of the words of institution in the consecration prayer of the liturgy then used in his Church, which is stated as a fact ; and then his own teaching, founded on it, that those words have no sooner been pronounced by the celebrant than the real Presence takes place.

So far as I have been able to discover, in making either assertion S. Chrysostom absolutely stands alone. Far from supporting his teaching, no other Father of the Eastern or the Western Church testifies even to what he reports as fact. I make this statement on historical grounds *solely*, believing it will be found in that sense quite correct: and challenging further inquiry by others who may doubt its accuracy.

But it will not take me long to show that in making his second assertion S. Chrysostom departed from the emphatic teaching of his earlier and more finished works. For all of these, which contain anything on the subject, bear unequivocal testimony to the teaching of the whole Catholic world round him then, which declares consecration to be the effect of that prayer whereby the action of the Holy Ghost was secured. Nor is there to be found in any of these the slightest reference to the words of institution, except as contained in the Gospels.

Two passages from his noblest work, 'On the Priesthood,' and two from among the most striking of his sermons, having been already quoted, it is needless to repeat. His Commentaries have not yet been adduced. In the eighty-first and eighty-second, as Montfaucon numbers them, of his Homilies on S. Matthew he traverses the whole ground covered by these sermons on the betrayal of Judas; and in the fifth section of the eighty-second, just where the bracketed portion of those sermons would have been most apposite to the context, it is conspicuous by its absence. In commenting on those words in S. John, 'And I knew Him not,' he asks, 'How then didst thou know Him? By the descent of the Spirit, replies the Baptist. Thou seest, then, that this was the work of the Spirit—namely, to show Christ.'[1]

Hom. xvii 2

Further on,[1] commenting on those words, 'I am the bread of life,' he says, ' He will come presently to the tradition of the mysteries. But He first speaks of His Divinity. For in those words, " I am the bread of life," nothing is said about His body. Towards the end He says of this too, " The bread that I shall give is My flesh." Now it is of His Divinity that He is speaking. For as God the Word He is bread, just as that other bread that He was about to give becomes heavenly bread by the descent on it of the Spirit.'

On the first Epistle to the Corinthians,[2] speaking of the visit of the wise men to Bethlehem, he says: 'Thou lookest not on a manger, but on an altar: not on a woman holding a babe, but on a priest standing by and the Spirit profusely descending on the elements.'

Again, on the second Epistle: 'This altar you may see lying everywhere, both in byways and in the markets, and sacrifices offered on it at all hours: for here, too, sacrifice is performed. And as the priest stands invoking the Spirit, so dost thou—not indeed by voice, but by deeds—invoke the Spirit too.'[3]

And again, on the Epistle to the Ephesians: 'It is not on account of the elements only that the Spirit descends, but He descends at all times for those chants.'[4]

These two last references are the more noteworthy from being casual. Literally, then, we can find nothing in his choicest homilies which is not to this effect; and we may even search through his homilies whose date cannot be verified, but whose matter by common consent places them among the least esteemed of any delivered by him, without finding more than one pendant to the bracketed portion of these sermons. To the best of my belief there is but one: namely, the fourth section of the second homily on Chapter I. of the second Epistle to Timothy:—

'No man ever differed from another man as much as Christ from the Baptist; yet the Spirit descended on Christ

[1] Hom. xlv 2. [2] Hom xxiv 5 [3] Hom xx 3 [4] Hom iii 5.

to teach us that God worketh everything, that God does everything. It may sound paradoxical what I say, but do not be surprised or excited. The oblation is the same, whoever offers it. Whether Peter or Paul, it is the same what Christ gave to His disciples and what the priests offer now—the one not inferior to the other, because it is not men who sanctify this, but He who sanctified that. For as the words which God spake are the same which the priest also says now, so likewise the offering is the same and the baptism which He gave. Thus the whole thing is of faith. The Spirit at once fell on Cornelius, because he had previously fulfilled his part and contributed his faith. This, then, is His body, as was that. He who thinks one less than the other is not aware that Christ is even now present and acts. . . .'

The genuineness of this passage has never, I believe, been disputed, and it attests that 'the words which God spake are the same which the priest also says now'—meaning, I presume, that the words of institution entered into the consecration-prayer of the liturgy then used in his Church. And the action of the Holy Ghost, if it is implied, is certainly not expressed.

But, again, let us remember, it is on the historical problem solely that we are now engaged, and it is not with a view of representing S. Chrysostom in the light of an innovator on primitive doctrine that his writings have been thus closely scrutinised. On the contrary, the passages quoted from him show indisputably that he is so much fuller and stronger than any of his contemporaries on two special points as to suggest that he must have been impelled thereto by some reason in the background, which we must try to get at: his first point being that the Eucharist is essentially throughout a spiritual ordinance, removed both in thought and act from everything carnal or of earth; and his second that it is God, not man, who consecrates the sacrament: one of the Trinity, not of the hierarchy, by whose operation Christ is made present at each celebration of it in the body which was offered on the cross for man. We have, therefore, this threefold problem to solve before quitting S. Chrysostom. How comes it that he is of all those designated Fathers by the collective Church the *only* Father who (1) distinctly testifies, once or twice, to the presence of the words of institution in the liturgy then used by himself; who (2) teaches, once or twice, with the same distinctness that consecration follows on their being pronounced by the celebrant; and who (3) protests in unusually strong terms, as though arguing against an opponent, that it is not man, but God, who consecrates, and that the whole design of the Christian Passover is *to make men spiritual*?[1]

Now I believe that a complete solution of this problem is obtainable through the medium of a short tract, or rather fragment of a tract, ascribed till recently by common consent to the youthful amanuensis and ever afterwards devoted admirer of S. Chrysostom, and who likewise succeeded him, after a short interval, in his see, S. Proclus, but in which, apart from its authorship, I trust to have found the right key to a portion of history that has hitherto been given up in despair or misread. If it states what is fact it is of secondary consequence by whom it was penned. If it states what is fact, people may some day be grateful to Providence for having preserved it to us. Nevertheless, no solid reasons have yet been advanced in disproof of its authorship; while there are several in its favour that have not hitherto been considered. But for Dionysius Exiguus, who translated them into Latin, several interesting letters of Proclus might never have been as well known as they are. So far as matter and style go there is little to choose between them and this piece. It greatly tends to confirm its genuineness that it has come down to us in its original Greek, as well as in a Latin translation, which is of course later. The objection specially pressed against it by Sir W. Palmer[2] rather

[1] *Hom in S Matt.* lxxxii 1   [2] *Orig Lit* i 19, note

ITS AUTHENTICITY CONFIRMED.

confirms its authenticity likewise than invalidates it. For it no doubt *suggests* the title subsequently given to S. Chrysostom of the 'golden mouth'; yet by whom could it have been more *naturally* suggested than by his second self, Proclus? Again, the hint was no sooner thrown out than it was adopted by common consent. For within a hundred years of his death [1] Cassiodorus, in the far-distant Gothic kingdom of Italy, decorates 'the saintly John,' as he calls him in another place, with that title full-blown, '*John Chrysostom.*' [2]

The Greek title prefixed to this piece runs thus:— 'Of the same Proclus: a discourse respecting the tradition of the holy Liturgy;' proving that it occupied a place then amongst his other works, besides being itself founded on an expression of S. Chrysostom, 'the tradition of the mysteries,' above quoted, in commenting on S. Matthew.

It begins by stating: 'That many other divine teachers and pastors of the Church, among those who had succeeded the Apostles, had left editions behind them in writing of the mystical liturgy to the Church: first and foremost of them all, the blessed Clement, disciple and successor of the coryphæus of the Apostles—the Apostles themselves having dictated his to him—and the divine James. appointed first Bishop of Jerusalem by Christ Himself. . . . For the Apostles, after the Ascension of the Saviour into heaven, having assembled daily for prayer before setting forth on their missions, and experienced consolation in the mystical consecration of the Lord's body, ever mindful of those words of His, "This is My body," and "Do this in My remembrance," and "He that eateth My flesh and drinketh My blood dwelleth in Me, and I in him," . . . took to celebrating its performance with many prayers and hymns at great length, as being also the most important of all things

[1] Le Brun (*De la Messe*, III 7) is thus *two centuries* out in his objection
[2] *Inst Div Lit* c 8-9

for them to teach. . . . Approaching God, therefore, with such earnest supplications, they waited for the descent of the Holy Ghost, to *exhibit* and *declare*[1] by His divine Presence the bread and the wine mixed with water, set out for consecration, the body and blood of our Saviour Jesus Christ, all which takes place no less still up to now, and will take place to the end of the world. Nevertheless the length of this liturgy was, in process of time, so much increased by constant additions, that it had to be recast in a more compendious form by S. Basil, and to have more things taken out of it by S. Chrysostom—*our own father of the golden mouth,*' as the writer lovingly calls him—' in order to be adapted to the changed habits of their age.'

I have condensed and re-arranged parts of this, with a view of making it more intelligible, but have added nothing of my own, and subtracted nothing, beyond repetition, of the original. If S. Proclus was the author of this tract, he was then using the liturgy which he describes as having been recast by S. Basil, and revised and further abridged by his old master and predecessor in the see of Constantinople. If S. Proclus was not the author of this tract, what is recorded in it was nevertheless a fact in his history, to which another deposes. For the liturgy now used in the Church of Constantinople is substantially the same liturgy that received its final shape from S. Chrysostom, was used in that form by himself, as his own writings testify, and has ever since been called by his name. There are doubtless accretions in it, as now used, of much later date; but all these, tested by his writings, could be made patent at any moment, and their removal would only restore this liturgy to what it was in his day. Different recensions of it prove nothing against its identity. There would of course be no means of preventing their spread, after it had superseded all other liturgies in Churches ecclesiastically dependent on Constantinople when it was introduced, but afterwards wrested from the

[1] ὅπως... ἀποφήνῃ τε καὶ ἀναδείξῃ, ap Migne, *Pat Gr* lxv 849-52

LITURGIES OF S. JAMES AND S. CLEMENT. 181

empire whose capital remained the same, though its emperor was no longer theirs.

Further, the materials used by S. Chrysostom and S. Basil in their joint work are stated in this tract to have been, first and foremost, the liturgy called after S. Clement of Rome, and, subordinately to this, the liturgy called after S. James of Jerusalem. Now this is a fact which each may verify for himself. Only first it is necessary to show that these liturgies existed then, and that each compiler was aware of their existence.

By the liturgy called after S. James of Jerusalem, is clearly meant the liturgy which S. Cyril of Jerusalem describes so well in his catechetical lectures that we can almost assist at each part of its celebration; and which S. Anastasius, Patriarch of Antioch in the sixth century, leaves us to infer from his glowing oration, already noticed, was used still, in all Churches of his patriarchate, unchanged in every respect, except the one particularised by him with so much unction that it might be supposed to have commenced with himself. S. Cyril tells us expressly that S. James, the Lord's brother, was the founder and the first bishop of his own see, Jerusalem: he makes no such assertion respecting the liturgy which he was then expounding there, but he says nothing, on the other hand, to the contrary.

By the liturgy called after S. Clement of Rome, is clearly meant the liturgy now found in the eighth book of the Apostolical Constitutions.

So much depends on this liturgy, that we must endeavour to get to the bottom of it, discarding all extraneous questions respecting the collection in whose last book it appears. Coteler's was once the standard edition of the Apostolical Constitutions, and he gives us the opinions of the best commentators up to his time. Ultzen's is the last and best edition of them (published 1853), and he, too, gives us the opinions of the learned about them up to then, besides the readings of three Bodleian MSS. as far as they go, which he considers mere excerpts.[1]

Now, the first question that meets us in connection with this liturgy concerns its name. By whom was that name given to it, and when? The ordinary title given to the Apostolical Constitutions[2] belies their contents. Ultzen abandons it. Their publication is nowhere confided in them to Clement. He is never mentioned but in connection with others, and on a par with them. He figures in a list of bishops ordained by the Apostles, as having been ordained by S. Peter;[3] but midway in the list, not at their head. He is prayed for in public by the faithful,[4] but after S. James, and in company with him and S. Euodius. His prominence reveals itself nowhere but in the title. What authority can we find for the title? Bishop Hefele says: 'About A. D. 500, Dionysius Exiguus translated a collection of Canons from Greek into Latin for Stephen, Bishop of Salona, at the head of which he placed fifty Canons which, according to him, *proceeded from the Apostles*, and *had been arranged and collected* by their disciple, Clement of Rome.'[5] It is strange Bishop Hefele should have lent his name to such a mis-statement. Dionysius makes no such assertion. It has been made for him in the title prefixed to his collection.[6] What Dionysius says is, that he translated from Greek Canons 'qui dicuntur Apostolorum,' and there stops. Fifty years later, John Scholasticus, a presbyter of Antioch, who became subsequently Bishop of Constantinople, published a collection of Greek Canons which included eighty-five Canons attributed to the Apostles. As this number has never since been increased, it was the same probably when Dionysius translated what prove to be practically the first fifty. And it is in the eighty-fifth and last of them that we

---

[1] Præf xxv note 7
[2] 'Constitutiones Sanctorum Apostolorum per Clementem episcopum et civem Romanum'
[3] VII 46.
[4] VIII. 9.
[5] *Councils*, Eng Tr p 449
[6] 'Regulæ ecclesiasticæ Sanctorum Apostolorum prolatæ per Clementem Ecclesiæ Romanæ pontificem.'

THE EIGHTY-FIFTH APOSTOLICAL CANON. 183

find a statement, which doubtless gave rise to both titles, prefixed to the Constitutions and Canons.

It commences with a list of the books of Holy Scripture then accounted canonical, and it ends as follows:—

'*Two Epistles of Clement*: and Constitutions in eight books addressed to you bishops *by me Clement*: which ought not to be divulged to all, on account of the mystical things contained in them: and our Acts of the Apostles.'

Appended to this is a short exhortation, which, as it is anything but irrelevant to our present inquiry, shall be given also:—

'Let these things, O bishops, have been appointed to you by us in the way of canons. Abiding in them, you will be saved and have peace. Unfaithful to them, you will be punished, and have endless war amongst yourselves, paying the penalty due to disobedience. May the *alone God, the alone Eternal, the Maker of all things,* unite you all *through peace in the Holy Spirit,* fit you for every good work— unmoveable, unblameable, irreproachable—and judge you worthy of eternal life with us, through *the mediation of His beloved Child Jesus Christ the God and Saviour of us,* with whom be glory *to Him the God and Father of all in the Holy Spirit, the Paraclete,* now and ever and throughout all ages, Amen.'

The italicised portions of each are reserved for comment in bringing to light all the decisive marks of Arianism hitherto not noticed in this liturgy. But first let us trace back the name it has so long borne to the earliest date that can be claimed for it.[1]

S. Epiphanius is the earliest writer who quotes definite passages from the Constitutions. He quotes seven words of their opening sentence; makes another slight reference to the third chapter of the first, and a slighter but possible reference to the twenty-third chapter of the seventh book.

---

[1] Ültzen, pp. 253-4 Coteler, *Pat Apost* 1. 454, places it at the end of the Canons too, but separating them from the Constitutions.

But all his other references are confined to the fifth book, which deals principally with festivals known to all, and which, according to him, contains nothing anyway contrary to the faith, or to the canons and rules of the Church. But he particularly there limits his remark to this one book.[1] How comes it that he never quotes from the other books? He as good as tells us himself. Without referring to them in any way, he designates the twelve Apostles, coupling them with ' James, the Lord's brother, and first Bishop of Jerusalem,' in a remarkable passage,[2] '*celebrants of the Gospel, and founders of mysteries,*' thus unmistakeably betraying his acquaintance with the eighth book of the Constitutions and with the liturgy contained in it. His acquaintance with that of S. James needs no comment, as it was probably that of his own Church, then under Antioch. But when he calls the twelve Apostles themselves 'celebrants of the Gospel, and founders of mysteries,' he merely repeats the words of the eighth book of the Constitutions in concluding its liturgy :—

'These things we, the Apostles, appoint to you bishops and presbyters and deacons, respecting *the mystical Service.*'[3]

Then, further, the subject-matter of the eighth book is stated, in the Greek inscription prefixed to it, to be, 'Concerning spiritual gifts, ordinations, and ecclesiastical canons,' bearing out Ultzen entirely, who appends the Canons to the Constitutions. Accordingly, the reticence of S. Epiphanius, apart from the extreme reserve that was habitual to him on such subjects, finds its natural explanation in the last of these Canons, where Clement, as we have seen, adjures the bishops whom he addresses in it not to divulge these Constitutions to all, on account of the *mystical things* contained in them.

That the liturgy forms an integral part of the subject-matter of the eighth book is self-evident, from the position assigned to it there, midway between the ordinations

[1] *Hær* lxx 10   [2] *Hær* lxxix 3, ed. Migne.   [3] C 15 *ad fin.*

of bishops and presbyters. The Bodleian Baroc. MS. 26 omits it, simply because foreign to its purpose. It omits a host of other portions of the eighth book on the same grounds.

The name, therefore, commonly given to this liturgy must needs be coeval with the eighty-fifth Apostolical Canon, and the eighty-fifth Apostolical Canon was, in all probability, coeval with S. Epiphanius. Anyhow, the first collector of Greek Canons, a learned patriarch of Constantinople, named John, who flourished in the sixth century, while fixing the number of Apostolical Canons at eighty-five, recites the eighty-fifth at full length in the form it still bears.[1] And hence that other name, founded on the declaration appended to it, which is given to this liturgy by Leontius, of Byzantium, at the end of the sixth century,[2] viz. that ' of the Apostles'; on which a good deal hangs that must be discussed later, when it will also be pointed out that the name really designed for it by its compiler never became current, but was stillborn.

Proof has yet to be given that S. Chrysostom and S. Basil were cognisant of its existence. What proof of this is common to both is singularly precise and strikingly similar. But proof of this peculiar to S. Chrysostom is of unusual interest and much earlier. The first Christmas-day sermon preached by him, on being ordained priest at Antioch some months before, was devoted in a great measure to justify the change which he seems to have been the means[3] of bringing about in keeping it, thereby giving his discourse somewhat of a sensational turn. According to Montfaucon, it was delivered on December 25, A.D. 386.[4] The exact day and

---

[1] *In fin* ed Instell *Bibl Jur Can* p 601
[2] *Adv Nest et Eutych* III 19
[3] *Op* vol II p 354, ed Montf His use of the plural number, ' us ' and ' we,' tends to keep this fact out of sight But now and then ' you ' comes in, opposed to both
[4] The sermon of S Gregory Nyssen, to which he refers at the end of his preface, is a ·doubtful' one, according to Migne (*Pat Gr* xlvi 1127), and has no specific reference to the date of the festival.

month of that festival, he tells his audience, were far from easy to discover; and, in short, had not been known in the East till quite recently. Ten years ago he was ignorant of them himself. But its true date must have been always known to those who had access to the public archives at Rome. From such he had derived his information—from actual inhabitants of that city. The twenty-fifth day of the ninth month, according to them, was the right day. He would prove them to be correct. April was the first month of the Conception, and December the ninth. Now, from whom did his information come? He will not name them further than that they were Romans. But information of the exact day and month of that festival is supplied in his own words by the supposed Clement in the fifth book of the Constitutions;[1] and in the eighth book we have S. Peter and S. Paul ordaining[2] that on that festival no work shall be done.

S. Chrysostom, therefore, must have been cognisant of the fifth and eighth books of the Constitutions in the year in which he became priest, if not before. And he attests that an innovation in respect of the day on which Christmas was to be kept in the East was brought about by their means.

The proof common to him and S. Basil, though of another kind, is scarcely less cogent. Both of them seem taken aback and perplexed at something that had transpired or been done: as though called upon to justify their conduct on some point or points affecting the Eucharist. S. Chrysostom all of a sudden concentrates attention on the words of institution occurring in the liturgy, and on the effect produced by them in the mouth of the celebrant; passing over in complete silence the action of the Holy Ghost, which, till then, in connection with consecration of the oblation

---

[1] C 13 'Let the festival of the Nativity be kept on the twenty-fifth day of the ninth month by you'

[2] C 33 'I Peter, and I Paul ordain On the festival of the Nativity let there be no work done.'

had been his all but exclusive theme. S. Basil, as though accused of having subordinated Scripture to tradition, devotes a whole chapter[1] of his work on the Holy Ghost to show that, although part of the doctrines taught and received by the Church had undoubtedly come down to her in writing, still there was another part also which she had received in mystery by tradition from the Apostles; and foremost in this class he mentions the prayer for the descent of the Holy Ghost to consecrate the oblation, called epiklesis, as though it had been for the Apostolic origin of this prayer mainly that he was contending. He himself characterises this prayer as being for the *exhibition* ($\dot{a}\nu a\delta\epsilon i\xi\epsilon\iota$) of the bread of the Eucharist and of the cup of blessing, which is a further and still more cogent proof, as we shall see. The nearest approach to this in S. Chrysostom is where, commenting on S. John, already quoted, he says that the sole purpose for which the Holy Ghost descended on our Lord at His baptism was to manifest Him to man: to prove to man that He was the Christ.

Having thus recalled these peculiarities in their acknowledged writings, let us proceed to verify the statement of the tract ascribed to S. Proclus, as far as it can be verified at this day in the liturgies still bearing their names. Their relative length to each other *now*, cannot assist us possibly to a correct opinion of their relative length to each other when they were first put into shape: nor, again, to the overgrown liturgies of that date, which it is said they were drawn up to supersede. But let us assume—what we are quite justified in assuming—that the liturgy called after S. Clement has come down to us stereotyped in the eighth book of the Constitutions, and the liturgy called after S. James in the comments of S. Cyril of Jerusalem on it, as it stood in his day, and we shall find ourselves in a position to estimate generally to what extent the existing liturgies of S. Chrysostom and S. Basil have been, in point of fact, indebted to

[1] C 27, already quoted

both. The author of the tract ascribed to S. Proclus attributes precedence to the liturgy called after S. Clement naturally for two reasons: because, first, it was believed to have come direct from the Apostles through S. Clement; and, secondly, because the liturgy called after S. James, being not merely that of Jerusalem, but of the whole patriarchate within which the sees of S. Chrysostom and S. Basil anciently lay, it was in fact their own liturgy which they revised by that of the supposed Clement.

Starting accordingly from this assumption, we find that what S. Chrysostom and S. Basil copied principally from the Clementine was the form of its consecration-prayer, which proceeded on a new principle, or differed at all events materially from what they had used hitherto, but to which, coming, as it professed to come to them, direct from the Apostles through S. Clement of Rome, and recapitulating so many words and acts of our Lord recorded in the Gospels or by S. Paul, they could not but have deferred. Still they must have felt that in adopting it they were departing from the lines of their predecessors somewhat; while from their having borrowed comparatively little else from that liturgy without corrections, and from their having pointedly retained the Lord's Prayer, which it omitted, we seem warranted in concluding that they were not without misgivings even in what they borrowed, and absolutely could not persuade themselves of its genuineness or of its soundness in those parts which they declined transplanting into their own.

To save time, and to facilitate conclusions at each stage of this important enquiry, we may do well to study the consecration-prayers, as they now stand in the liturgies of S. Chrysostom and S. Basil, side by side with that of the Clementine: remembering at the same time that the correspondence between them may have grown considerably fainter from alterations than it was when S. Chrysostom and S. Basil brought about their revisions.

THE WORDS OF INSTITUTION. 189

St. Basil.

'He hath left us memorials of His saving Passion, these which we have set forth according to His behests For being about to depart to his renowned life-giving and voluntary death, on the night in which He gave Himself up for the life of the world, having taken bread into His holy and undefiled hands, and exhibited it to Thee, the God and Father, and given thanks, blessed, sanctified, and broken, He gave to His holy disciples and apostles, saying: "Take, eat this is My body, which is being broken for you, for remission of sins" In like manner also the cup of the fruit of the vine · having taken, mixed, given thanks, blessed, sanctified, He gave to His holy disciples and apostles, saying: "Drink ye all of it: This is My blood of the New Testament, which is being shed for you and many for the remission of sins. Do this in My remembrance. For as often as ye may eat this bread and drink this cup, ye show forth My death and confess My resurrection."

Clementine.

'Mindful, then, of what He endured for us, we give thanks to Thee, God Omnipotent, not as much as we ought, but as much as we can, and fulfil His ordinance. For, on the night in which He was betrayed, having taken bread into His holy and blameless hands, and having looked up to Thee, His God and Father, and broken, He gave to His disciples, saying: "This is the mystery of the New Testament. Take of it, eat · this is my body, which is being broken for many for remission of sins." In like manner also the cup : having mixed it with water and wine, and sanctified, He gave it to them also, saying. "Drink ye all of it. This is my blood, which is being shed for many for remission of sins. Do this in My remembrance. For as often as ye may eat this bread and drink this cup ye do show forth My death, till I come."

St. Chrysostom.

'Who having come and fulfilled His whole mission for us, on the night in which He was betrayed, or rather delivered Himself up for the life of the world, having taken bread in His holy, blameless and undefiled hands, and having given thanks, and blessed, sanctified, broken, gave to His holy disciples and apostles, saying: "Take, eat: this is My body, which is being broken for you for remission of sins." In like manner the cup, after having supped, saying "Drink ye all of it This is My blood, which is being shed for you and many for remission of sins."

St. Basil.	*Clementine*	*St. Chrysostom*
'Mindful, then, O Master, of His saving Passion, life-giving Cross, three days' burial, resurrection from the dead, return to heaven, sitting on the right hand of Thee, the God and Father, and His glorious and terrible second presence, we offer to Thee Thine own of Thine own in all and through all things. Wherefore most holy Master, we sinners and unworthy servants of Thine, who have been counted worthy to minister at Thy holy altar, not for our righteousness—for we have done nothing good on earth—but for Thy mercies and consolations which Thou hast shed abundantly on us, approach with confidence Thine altar, and having placed thereon the antitypes of the holy body and blood of Thy Christ, we beseech Thee, Holy of holies, by the favour of Thy goodness, let Thy Holy Spirit come on us and on these gifts lying here, and bless, sanctify, and exhibit them, this bread the very precious body of our Lord, God and	'Wherefore, mindful of His Passion and death, resurrection from the dead and return back to heaven, and second and future presence, wherein He comes with power and glory to judge the living and dead, and to requite everyone according to his works, we offer to Thee King and God according to Thine ordinance this bread and this cup, giving thanks to Thee through Him for that Thou hast granted to us to stand before Thee and minister to Thee And we beseech Thee that Thou wouldest look favourably on these gifts lying before Thee, Thou God who needest nothing: and that Thou wouldest look propitiously on us for honour of Thy Christ and send down Thy Holy Spirit on this sacrifice, the witness of the sufferings of the Lord Jesus, that He may declare this bread the body of Thy Christ, and this cup the blood of Thy Christ, that all who partake thereof may be confirmed in holiness, obtain remission of sins, be delivered	'Therefore, mindful of this salutary command, and of all that has taken place for us— the cross, the tomb, the three days' resurrection, the reascent into heaven, the seat on the right hand, the second and glorious presence again —we offer to Thee Thine own of Thine own, in all and through all things 'Moreover we offer to Thee this bloodless and reasonable service, beseeching, entreating, and supplicating, that Thou wouldest send down Thy Holy Spirit on us and on these gifts lying before Thee, and make this bread the precious body of Thy Christ, and what is in this cup the precious blood of Thy Christ, having changed them by thy Holy Spirit. so as to become to those who partake of them for sobriety of soul, for remission of sins, for communion of Thy Holy Spirit, for accomplishment of the kingdom of heaven, for freedom of speech with Thee, not for judgment or condemnation.'

COMPLETENESS OF THE PARALLEL.

St. Basil.	*Clementine.*
Saviour Jesus Christ, and this cup the very precious blood of our Lord God and Saviour Jesus Christ, which has been shed for the life of the world, having changed them by Thy Holy Spirit, and that all of us who partake of the one bread and cup Thou wouldest unite with each other in communion of Thy one Holy Spirit, so that none of us may partake of the holy body and blood of Thy Christ for judgment or condemnation'	from the devil and his snare, become worthy of Thy Christ, obtain eternal life, Thou being reconciled to them, Omnipotent Master'

By way of finishing one subject before commencing another, it should here be noticed how completely these parallels accord with the statement of the Proclean tract. The author of that tract, whoever he may have been, was persuaded that the Apostle '*dictated*' to S. Clement the liturgy bearing his name. Then he lays stress on the *words of institution* and on the ' consolation derived by the Apostles *from remembering them in consecrating the Eucharist*'; and then speaks of their 'approaching God with earnest supplications, while waiting for the descent of the Holy Ghost to *exhibit* ($\dot{\alpha}\nu\alpha\delta\epsilon\hat{\iota}\xi\alpha\iota$)—the word used by S. Basil—'*and declare*' ($\dot{\alpha}\pi o\phi\hat{\eta}\nu\alpha\iota$)—the word used in the Clementine—'by His Divine Presence the bread and the wine *mixed with water*'—particularly specified in the Clementine—'set out for consecration, *the body and blood of our Saviour Jesus Christ*,' the exact expression of S. Basil once more. Such are the points to which he makes emphatic and exclusive reference. Further, there is not a word in his statement of either which is not seen to be verified in these parallels. Now, as nobody would maintain, or at all events has ever maintained, that the consecration-prayer of the Clementine was borrowed from the liturgies of either S. Basil or S. Chrysostom, the statement of this author is at least entitled to credit until distinct evidence to the contrary can be shown, that S. Basil set the precedent of borrowing his from the Clementine, which S. Chrysostom afterwards followed—a very natural way of explaining their similarity.

But, again, let us take this further fact into consideration. Leontius of *Byzantium*, writing against the Nestorians and Eutychians[1] in the sixth century, tells us that Theodore, Bishop of Mopsuestia, the friend of S. Chrysostom, and master of Nestorius, 'improvised a new consecration-prayer (anaphora)' for his followers: neither 'respecting that of the Apostles' (certainly the Clementine) 'nor that of the great Basil compiled in the same spirit.' Now, in what was his 'anaphora' most removed from that of S. Chrysostom and of S. Basil? Here lies the clue to what the late Dr. Neale confessed he could not explain:[2] viz. in the absence from it of the words of institution, which to this day, he adds, in all the purest Nestorian liturgies are wanting. This is a fact of sovereign importance both to the authorship and the statement of this tract; for as a short interval of only two years and five months elapsed between the deposition of Nestorius and the election of S. Proclus to that see, S. Proclus had in all probability the honour of restoring the liturgy that he had used himself under his old master, and may well have written this tract, for circulation among *his suffragans only*, to convince them of its superior claims. This would account naturally for the fragmentary condition in which it has come down to us, as well as for its having lain unnoticed so long. A confidential communication to bishops from their metropolitan might sleep for centuries in their archives undisturbed, especially when there was any

---

[1] Lib III 19, ap Migne
[2] *H E Ch.* Gen Introd pp 323 and 483, note, comp Renaud. *Lit*

Or II 566–648, and *The Nestorians and their Rituals*, by the late Mr. Badger, II 241

cause for its concealment, such as was afterwards supplied in this case by the censure passed on the eight books of the Constitutions and their contents by the second Trullan canon, A.D. 692.[1]

Taking these facts and probabilities into consideration, it seems to me no person could be named *so* likely to have written this tract *as Proclus*, among whose works it has always consistently figured. And it is additional proof of his authorship surely that he should have shown his independence by emphasising his preference for the subjective operation of the Holy Ghost in the heart of the receiver (ἀναδεῖξαι) with S. Basil, instead of the effect of His descent on the elements (ποιῆσαι) with his old master. It will be remembered that S. Isidore of Pelusium, as loving a pupil of S. Chrysostom as S. Proclus himself, manifests the same preference, though the term employed in the passage quoted from him is that of the Clementine, not of S. Basil.

But, again, if this tract had never been written, or at any rate never come down to us, it would still have to be explained how S. Basil and S. Chrysostom came to adopt into their respective liturgies the words of institution in the exact form given to them in the Clementine. For it cannot for one moment be credited that, had the liturgy commented on by S. Cyril of Jerusalem contained them in that form, or, indeed, in any form at all, he would have passed them over unnoticed. He quotes them at starting as his authority for celebrating the sacrament to which they relate, but he nowhere refers to them in expounding the liturgy then used by him in detail to his catechumens. Equally without reference to them, again, is the sermon of S. Anastasius, Patriarch of Antioch, three centuries later on the same liturgy. So that Nestorius, in introducing a liturgy without them at Constantinople when he became patriarch, might say he had merely fallen back upon that of the patriarchate in which he had been brought up; though

[1] Ultzen, Præf p ix , Johnson *Vade Mecum*, vol ii. 265

Leontius, having as a Byzantine been accustomed from childhood to that of S. Chrysostom, charges Theodore with having departed from the liturgy received from the Fathers, as well as having cast a slur upon that of the Apostles and of S. Basil.

It is a fact, therefore, substantiated historically by strong positive and unvarying negative evidence, which their juxtaposition doubly confirms, that S. Basil and S. Chrysostom revised the consecration-prayer, as it now stands in their respective liturgies, on the model of the Clementine, commencing with the words of institution, not included in their own previously, but retaining the invocation of the Holy Ghost at its close, though only to *declare*, not to *make*, Christ present; and S. Basil following it practically throughout and at greater length of the two; S. Chrysostom, on the other hand, rigidly continuing to invoke the action of the Holy Ghost on the elements for making Christ present.

So far we have the teaching of their own writings with us. When we attempt to go further they fail us, or their meaning is open to doubt. Nor could it be thought surprising if their consecration-prayers, as now printed, exhibit undeniable marks of having been retouched since their day. These two clauses, for instance, may well have been inserted to assimilate them to each other in later times when their joint use commenced, the first where petition is made for the Holy Ghost to descend '*on us and on* the oblation'; the second where petition is made for the Holy Ghost to *transmute the elements*. The train of ideas in connection with each will be found to be foreign to the writings of S. Chrysostom and S. Basil. But this by the way. It is on the broad fact of their revision that we are now engaged. And we want to know why they should have remodelled their consecration-prayer only by the Clementine Liturgy and borrowed next to nothing else from it. Did other portions of it excite their misgivings? Were they not both unanimous in *not* imitating its omission of the Lord's

Prayer? Hence forebodings are multiplied upon us as we proceed, at each stage, that there must be something radically wrong in this liturgy: something which has not yet been fathomed: something which must have escaped those more particularly to whose researches we are most indebted, and in whose judgment we should ordinarily repose the most implicit confidence.

For English divines, whose writings have deservedly become standard on these subjects, seem to vie with each other on all occasions in speaking well of this liturgy. Bingham translates it entire with as little questioning as if it had indisputably proceeded from the Apostles themselves.[1] Mr. Brett follows his example, but calls it in addition [2] 'the best exemplar extant of the old traditional form.' Dr. Hickes: 'the standard and test by which all others are to be tried.'[3] Sir W. Palmer is more cautious:[4] 'an author who affixed to this liturgy a title *which could not have been rightly given to it* would not have felt any scruples in altering or improving the liturgy which he published; and, indeed, he bears witness to the fact of his having made some alteration by giving the name of a foreign bishop to that liturgy.... In its order, its substance, and many of its expressions, *it is identical with that of S. James.* But its author has permitted his learning and devotion to enrich the common formularies with numerous ideas full of piety and beauty!'

A writer in the 'Church Quarterly,' who writes with the best intentions and much earnestness, goes furthest of all. He tries to recover all the heresies which this liturgy was drawn up to refute, from expressions in it. But he forgot to ascertain first what heresy it may have been designed *to support.* For is it a rare thing in ecclesiastical history to find one heresy refuting every known error *but its own*? Even the archangel Uriel was outwitted once.

[1] *Ant* b xv c 3, § 1
[2] *Liturgies*, Diss p 205
[3] Ib p 30
[4] *Orig Lit* 1 8-9

' For neither man nor angel can discern
Hypocrisy—the only evil that walks
Invisible, except to God alone . . .
And oft, though wisdom wake, suspicion sleeps
A't wisdom's gate, and to simplicity
Resigns her charge: while goodness thinks no ill,
Where no ill seems . . .'

Englishmen are slow to remember evil where they see good. Foreigners have never forgotten the bad things asserted of the Apostolical Constitutions in the second canon of the Trullan Council; nor has it escaped some that a slur was designedly cast upon their liturgy by leaving it out in the thirty-second canon of the same council, where the liturgies of S. James and of S. Basil are mentioned for praise. But the judgment passed upon them by Le Clerc was formed on internal evidence [1] and is to this effect—that they ' were composed, just as we have them, by a learned Arian towards the end of the fourth century, but not allowed to be divulged at first—as the eighty-fifth Apostolic Canon already quoted directs—in order that they might serve the Arian ' cause later all the more effectually when they got into circulation.' Proofs of the Arianism contained in them are given in the notes bearing his name, published by Coteler in his edition of the 'Apostolical Fathers' with his own, at the foot of each page wherever it occurs; but they cannot often have been studied in England, where the demerits of the Clementine liturgy seem as yet to have struck nobody whose attention it has engaged. Le Brun cannot have looked at them himself seriously to be able to say: [2] ' Il est visible en effet, que des Ariens y ont inséré leurs erreurs en quelques endroits; quoiqu'ils en aient laissé plusieurs, qui leur sont contraires.'

As though any falsehood would be tolerated or could obtain credence for a moment, except in exact proportion to the amount of truth combined with it. Through truth it is

[1] *Diss. de Const* cs 5 and 32, in Coteler's *Pat Apost.* II. 493. His Notes on their text are in vol 1 ed. 1724, fol [2] *De la Messe*, III 21

that falsehood ever attracts or obtains assent; and the most dangerous untruth is plainly that which contains most truth. It is believed all the more readily, because so much that it propounds is known to be true; it is also the more difficult to expose when it has been concocted with such artifice that few can guess where falsehood begins or where truth ends.

The false Decretal Epistles of the pseudo-Isidore—which Pope Pius VI., too late for the credit of his see that had profited by them so long, would have willingly seen committed to the flames at last [1]—even they bore testimony to many particulars of Church discipline which we know from other sources existed when they were penned. The Clementine liturgy bears out the comments of S. Cyril of Jerusalem on his own liturgy, and likewise the remarks of most of the Fathers in other lands who have spoken of theirs. It has this further advantage, that it would seem never to have received additions, or had alterations inserted in it, since the day on which it was first put into writing. Other observations of a more pertinent nature must be made before stripping it of the disguise that it has so long worn. Of these the most trivial, still not the least pertinent, may come first—Arian tricks, the only phrase that will describe them aright. They have been touched on before.[2] The trick by which that party tried to get their creed republished at Nice in Thrace mistaken for the Nicene Creed was described there. A kindred trick may be noticed in the underlined ending of the eighty-fifth Apostolical Canon, by which the learned and deeply-pious Bishop Beveridge was taken in.[3] 'Two epistles of Clement, and Constitutions in eight books addressed to you bishops by me Clement'—in order that the Epistles and Constitutions might be supposed to have emanated from the same pen—just as the Creed of Nicæa

---

[1] *Pii Sexti Resp ad Metrop Mogunt Trevirens Coloniens et Salisburg* Ed. alt. Romæ, 4to, MDCCXC, n. 100. Now very scarce, and not published elsewhere
[2] Above, p 163
[3] *Synod* ii. Annot. p. 40.

from Nice. Beveridge would fain have attributed this in his charity to S. Clement of Alexandria, that the speaker might have been a real Clement—such artifice being quite foreign to his mind. Yet it stopped short of the coarser forgeries of a later age; for it would not *assert* that both the epistles and constitutions were by the same Clement, though it left others free to draw that conclusion if they pleased.

A third trick of the same kind brings us to our immediate subject. For the author of this liturgy, by putting it into the mouth of S. James the Greater, who dictates it, evidently meant it should be mistaken for that of S. James the Less, which it was designed to supersede. He must have been mortified at the result, if he meant his trick to succeed, for it signally failed. People never called his liturgy by the name he thought they would, nor mistook it for the rival Communion Office of S. James the Less. But in the main it had a success far beyond anything its author could have conceived or hoped. For, through the medium of S. Basil and S. Chrysostom, the first to be deluded by it, the liturgies of the whole world sooner or later, one by one, submitted to have their consecration-prayer recast in its mould. And why was this? Because, pursuant to another Arian device, it incorporated so much Scripture into the very marrow of its formula—' In the same night that He was betrayed took bread '—a touch of poetry comes next : His holy and spotless hands, and upward look ; then, finally, Scripture again : ' brake, and gave to His disciples, saying, &c.' After this, and at a sufficient interval, is introduced the old traditional Invocation, by which the whole Church' had, till then, exclusively consecrated, as has been proved in detail. By this artifice the old order was discredited and at last broken through ; the prerogatives of the Holy Ghost obscured in one part of the Church, and altogether forgotten, as far as this application of the Incarnation was concerned, in another ; the Church rent in twain not on His procession merely, but on the sacrament of love too, wherein till then He had knit Christians to Christ.

But now what had preceded this attractive formula, this angel of light, by which even Uriel might have been beguiled? The Preface to it shall be estimated by no words of mine. It contains its own sentence within itself. Three parallel columns will expound it to us; but this time S. Basil and S. Chrysoston are removed far away. S. Chrysostom will have none of it; S. Basil, bits of the last part only, which he revised himself. It is Arius who is there made to lead us to Christ.

By way of preparing ourselves for this discovery, let us hear the tenets of Arius expounded by one whose felicity of language and lucidity of style combined have become proverbial during his lifetime, and who cannot certainly be supposed to have been biassed in describing them by the question on which we are now engaged. It is Cardinal Newman, accordingly, who, when Vicar of the church of S. Mary the Virgin, said:—[1]

'The Arians attempted to draw their conclusion of the dissimilarity of the Father and the Son from the $ἀγέννητον$, which was acknowledged on all sides to be the peculiar attribute of the Father, while it had been the philosophical as well as the Valentinian appellation of the supreme God . . . Their argument has been expressed in the following form: the essence of the Father is $ἀγέννητον$, that of the Son, $γεννητόν$; but $ἀγέννητον$ and $γεννητὸν$ cannot be the same . . . It was incumbent on them next to explain in what sense our Lord was the $μονογενὴς$, since they refused to understand that word according to the Catholic comment of the $ὁμοούσιον$. Accordingly, they pronounced the $γέννησις$ to be a kind of creation; and then they at once proceeded to hide the offensiveness of this dogma by the variety and dignity of the titles by which they distinguished

[1] *Arians*, p. 120, ed. 1854.

the Son from all other creatures. They declared that He was, strictly speaking, the only creature of God, as alone made immediately by Him, and hence called μονογενὴς, as γεννηθεὶς μόνος ἐκ μόνου; whereas all others were created through Him as the instrument of Divine Power, and that in consequence he was κτίσμα, ἀλλ' οὐχ ὡς ἓν τῶν κτισμάτων· γέννημα, ἀλλ' οὐχ ὡς ἓν τῶν γεγεννημένων· or, to express it with something of the ambiguity of the Greek, that He was not a creature like other creatures. Another ambiguity of expression followed. The idea of time depending on that of creation, they were able to grant that He who was employed in forming the worlds, therefore existed before all time, πρὸ χρόνων καὶ αἰώνων, not granting thereby that He was from everlasting, but that he was brought into existence ἀχρόνως—independent of that succession of second causes . . . to the laws of which creation itself may be considered as subjected . . .

'This account of the Arian system may suitably be illustrated by some of the original documents of the controversy.'

Arius himself, for instance, writes of his own bishop Alexander to Eusebius bishop of Nicomedia thus:—

'He has driven us out of the city (Alexandria) as impious men (ἀθέους), merely for dissenting from his public declarations: that "as God is eternal, so is His Son—when the Father, then the Son—the Son is present in God without a birth (ἀγεννήτως), ever-begotten (ἀειγενής) an unbegotten-begotten—neither in thought nor by an instant of time is God anterior to the Son: an eternal God, an eternal Son—the Son is from God Himself (ἐξ αὐτοῦ τοῦ θεοῦ)."'

In the three columns which follow, the letter of Arius to Bishop Alexander of Alexandria forms the first, and extracts from Arian Creeds the last; with so much of the Clementine Liturgy as may suffice for comparison, in the centre. The texts of each are given underneath each as notes.

EPITHETS RESERVED TO THE FATHER.

Letter of Arius, translated by Cardinal Newman: 'Arians,' p. 122.[1]	Clementine Liturgy. for the most part from Bingham, 'Ant.' xv 3, 1.[2]	Extracts from Arian Creeds translated.[3]
'Our faith ... is this. We believe in one God, alone without birth, alone everlasting, alone unoriginate, alone truly God, alone immortal, alone wise, alone good, alone sovereign, alone judge of all, ordainer and dispenser: unchangeable and unalterable; just and good: of the Law and the Prophets, and of the New Testament We believe that this God gave birth to the only-begotten Son before eternal periods: through whom He hath	'It is very meet and right, before all, to praise Thee, the really existent God, existent before the originated, of whom all paternity in heaven and upon earth is named; the alone unbegotten, unoriginate, without either king or master; the independent, the furnisher of every good thing, the superior to all cause and origination, the abiding always the same and in the same way, of whom all things issued forth into being as from a	They say they 'believe in one God, the God of the universe, fabricator and caretaker of all things cognisable by mind or sense (a). Of whom all paternity in heaven and upon earth is named, (b) . . recognising the Father as alone unoriginate, and unapproachable, with a birth unapproachable and incomprehensible by all, but the Son as having been born before the ages, and not Himself unbegotten too, similarly with the Father, but as

[1] *Letter of Arius to Alexander, Bishop of Alexandria, in S Ath 'De Synod'* § 16, *and S Epiph 'Hær.'* lxix § 7

Ἡ πίστις ἡμῶν .
ἔστιν αὕτη· Οἴδαμεν ἕνα
Θεὸν μόνον ἀγέννητον,
μόνον ἀΐδιον, μόνον ἄναρχον, μόνον ἀληθινὸν, ἀθανασίαν ἔχοντα μόνον σόφον, μόνον ἀγαθὸν, μόνον δυναστὴν, μόνον κριτὴν πάντων, διοικητὴν, οἰκονόμον ἄτρεπτον καὶ ἀναλλοίωτον· δίκαιον καὶ ἀγαθὸν· Νόμου, καὶ προφητῶν, καὶ Καινῆς Διαθήκης τοῦτον Θεὸν γεννήσαντα Υἱὸν μονογενῆ πρὸ χρόνων

[2] *Clementine Liturgy— Eucharistic Preface —Mr Hammond's 'Ancient Liturgies,' p* 12

Ἄξιον ὡς ἀληθῶς καὶ δίκαιον πρὸ πάντων ἀνυμνεῖν Σε τὸν ὄντως ὄντα Θεόν, τὸν πρὸ τῶν γεννητῶν ὄντα, ἐξ οὗ πᾶσα πατριὰ ἐν οὐρανῷ καὶ ἐπὶ γῆς ὀνομάζεται, τὸν μόνον ἀγέννητον καὶ ἄναρχον καὶ ἀβασίλευτον καὶ ἀδέσποτον τὸν ἀνενδεῆ, τὸν παντὸς ἀγαθοῦ χορηγὸν, τὸν πάσης αἰτίας καὶ γενέσεως κρείττονα, τὸν πάντοτε κατὰ τὰ αὐτὰ καὶ ὡσαύτως ἔχοντα ἐξ οὗ τὰ πάντα,

[3] *Extracts from Arian Creeds of Antioch and Sirmium and Constantinople in Soc.* 'E H' b 11

First, as to what they say of the Father —

Εἰς ἕνα τὸν τῶν ὅλων Θεὸν πιστεύειν τῶν πάντων νοητῶν τε καὶ αἰσθητῶν δημιουργόν τε καὶ προνοητήν . Ἐξ οὗ πᾶσα πατριὰ ἐν οὐρανοῖς καὶ ἐπὶ γῆς ὀνομάζεται . Τὸν μὲν Πατέρα μόνον ἄναρχον ὄντα καὶ ἀνέφικτον, γεγεννηκέναι ἀνεφίκτως καὶ πᾶσιν ἀκαταλήπτως οἴδαμεν Τὸν δὲ Υἱὸν γεγεν-

(a) First Creed of Antioch, A D 341, Soc *E H* 11 10
(b) Ib 18, third Creed of Antioch.

202 NOT TO BE GIVEN TO THE SON.

Letter of Arius.

made those periods themselves, and all things else. That He gave birth to Him not in semblance but in truth, giving Him a real existence at His own will, so as to be unchangeable and unalterable. God's perfect creature, but not as other creatures; His making, but not as if made—not, as Valentinian maintained, a development, nor again, as Manichæus, a consubstantial part; nor as Sabellius, Son and Father at once Nor as Hieracas, a light from light, or torch divided in two—nor as if He was in being previously, and afterwards begotten, created again to

αἰωνίων, δι' οὗ καὶ τοὺς αἰῶνας καὶ τὰ λοιπὰ πεποίηκε γεννήσαντα δε οὐ δοκήσει, ἀλλὰ ἀληθείᾳ ὑποστήσαντα δὲ ἰδίου θελήματι, ἄτρεπτον καὶ ἀναλλοίωτον κτίσμα τοῦ Θεοῦ τέλειον, ἀλλ' οὐχ ὡς ἓν τῶν κτισμάτων γεννήματα, ἀλλ' οὐχ ὡς ἓν τῶν γεννημάτων οὐδ' ὡς Οὐαλαντῖνος προβολὴν τὸ γέννημα τοῦ Πατρὸς ἐδογμάτισεν· οὐδ' ὡς Μανιχαῖος μέρος ὁμοούσιον τοῦ Πατρὸς τὸ γέννημα εἰσηγήσατο οὐδ' ὡς Σαβέλλιος ὁ τὴν μονάδα διαιρῶν υἱοπάτορα εἶπεν οὐδ' ὡς Ἱεράκας λύχνον ἀπὸ λύχνου,

Clementine Liturgy.

starting-point. For Thou art the unoriginate knowledge, the everlasting vision, the unborn hearing, the untaught wisdom; the first by nature, and alone by existence, and superior to all number, who broughtest all things from non-existence into existence through Thine only begotten Son; having begotten Him too before all ages, by will, and power, and goodness, immediately; sole-begotten Son, Word-God, living wisdom, first-born of every creature; angel of Thy great counsel, Thy highpriest, king and lord of every nature cognisable by mind or sense, who is before all, and

καθάπερ ἔκ τινος ἀφετηρίας εἰς τὸ εἶναι παρῆλθεν. Σὺ γὰρ εἶ ἡ ἄναρχος γνῶσις, ἡ ἀΐδιος ὅρασις, ἡ ἀγέννητος ἀκοὴ, ἡ ἀδίδακτος σοφία ὁ πρῶτος τῇ φύσει, καὶ μόνος τῷ εἶναι καὶ κρείττων παντὸς ἀριθμοῦ ὁ τὰ πάντα ἐκ τοῦ μὴ ὄντος εἰς τὸ εἶναι παραγαγὼν διὰ τοῦ μονογενοῦς Σου Υἱοῦ αὐτὸν δὲ πρὸ πάντων αἰώνων γεννήσας βουλήσει, καὶ δυνάμει, καὶ ἀγαθότητι, ἀμεσιτεύτως, Υἱὸν μονογενῆ, Λόγον Θεόν, σοφίαν ζῶσαν, πρωτότοκον πάσης κτίσεως, ἄγγελον τῆς μεγάλης βουλῆς Σου, ἀρχιερέα Σὸν,

Arian Creeds.

having origin in the Father who begat Him. For God is head of Christ. . . . Since we recognise the God and Father of the only-begotten, as the alone self-subsisting and unbegotten, unoriginate and invisible God, who alone has being of Himself, and alone bestows being without stint upon all others. (c) . . . If any dare to say that the unbegotten, or a part of Him, was born of Mary, let Him be anathema . . . If any, calling Him who was born of Mary, God and man, considers Him the unbegotten, let him be anathema .. If any call the Son unbegotten and unoriginate, as mean-

νῆσθαι πρὸ τῶν αἰώνων, καὶ μηκέτι ὁμοίως τῷ Πατρὶ ἀγέννητον εἶναι καὶ αὐτόν, ἀλλ' ἀρχὴν ἔχειν τὸν γεννήσαντα Πατέρα Κεφαλὴ γὰρ Χριστοῦ ὁ Θεὸς ' Ἐπειδὴ τὸν αὐτοτελῆ καὶ ἀγέννητον, ἄναρχόν τε καὶ ἀόρατον Θεὸν, ἕνα μόνον οἴδαμεν τὸν Θεὸν καὶ Πατέρα τοῦ μονογενοῦς, τὸν μόνον μὲν ἐξ Ἑαυτοῦ τὸ εἶναι ἔχοντα, μόνον δὲ τοῖς ἄλλοις πᾶσιν ἀφθόνως τὸ εἶναι παρεχόμενον Εἴ τις τὸν ἀγέννητον, ἢ μέρος αὐτοῦ ἐκ Μαρίας λέγειν γεγεννῆσθαι τολμᾷ, ἀνάθεμα ἔστω Εἴ τις

(c) Soc E H c 19, fourth Creed of Antioch.

THE ONLY-BEGOTTEN GOD.

Letter of Arius

be a son... But as we affirm, created by the will of God before times and before periods; and having life and existence from the Father, who at the same time gave to share His glorious perfections 'For when the Father gave to Him the inheritance of all things, He did not thereby deprive Himself of attributes which are His without origination, being the source of all things.

'So there are three Persons. and whereas God is the source of all things, and therefore unoriginate and altogether separate from all, the Son on the other hand, begotten by the Father time-apart, and

ἢ ὡς λαμπάδα εἰς δύο οὐδὲ τὸν ὄντα πρότερον, ὕστερον γεννηθέντα, ἢ ἐπικτισθέντα εἰς Υἱὸν . ἀλλ' ὡς φαμὲν, θελήματι τοῦ Θεοῦ, πρὸ χρόνων καὶ πρὸ αἰώνων κτισθέντα, καὶ τὸ ζῆν καὶ τὸ εἶναι παρὰ τοῦ Πατρὸς εἰληφότα καὶ τὰς δόξας συνυποστήσαντος τοῦ Πατρὸς Οὐ γὰρ ὁ Πατηρ, δοὺς αὐτῷ πάντων κληρονομίαν, ἐστέρησεν ἑαυτὸν ὧν ἀγεννήτως ἔχει ἐν ἑαυτῷ Πηγή γάρ ἐστι πάντων

"Ωστε τρεῖς εἰσιν ὑποστάσεις, καὶ ὁ μὲν Θεὸς, αἴτιος τῶν πάντων τυγ-

Clementine Liturgy.

through whom are all things For Thou, eternal God, hast made all things through Him, and through Him vouchsafest to the whole universe all the care that it requires. For through whom Thou didst grant being, by Him also didst Thou bestow well-being. The God and Father of Thy sole-begotten Son, who before all through Him didst make the Cherubims and Seraphims, ages and hosts, dominions and powers, principalities and thrones, archangels and angels, and after these things didst make through him this visible world and all things in it. For Thou art

βασιλέα δὲ καὶ Κύριον πάσης νοητῆς καὶ αἰσθητῆς φύσεως, τὸν πρὸ πάντων, δι' οὗ τὰ πάντα Σὺ γὰρ, Θεὲ αἰώνιε, δι' αὐτοῦ τὰ πάντα πεποίηκας, καὶ δι' αὐτοῦ τῆς προσηκούσης προνοίας τὰ ὅλα ἀξιοῖς Δι' οὗ γὰρ τὸ εἶναι ἐχαρίσω, δι' αὐτοῦ καὶ τὸ εὖ εἶναι ἐδωρήσω· ὁ Θεὸς καὶ Πατὴρ τοῦ μονογένους Υἱοῦ Σου ὁ δι' αὐτοῦ πρὸ πάντων ποιήσας τὰ Χερουβὶμ καὶ τὰ Σεραφὶμ, αἰῶνούς τε καὶ θρόνους, ἀρχαγγέλους τε καὶ ἀγγέλους καὶ μετὰ ταῦτα πάντα ποιήσας δι' αὐτοῦ τὸν φαι-

Arian Creeds.

ing two unoriginates and two unbegottens, and making two Gods, let him be anathema. For the Son is head and origin of all things, but God is head of Christ (d) . . And none are ignorant of this Catholic truth, that Father and Son are two Persons. of whom the Father is greater, while the Son is subject, in common with all whom the Father has put in subjection to Him, (e) . . . the Father Almighty, of whom are all things. (f) . . .'

Of the Son they say :
' And in one Lord Jesus Christ His Son, the only-begotten God, through whom all things were born; who

Θεὸν καὶ ἄνθρωπον τὸν ἐκ Μαρίας λέγων, τὸν ἀγέννητον αὐτὸν νοεῖ, ἀνάθεμα ἔστω Εἴ τις ἀγέννητον καὶ ἄναρχον λέγοι τὸν Υἱὸν, ὡς δύο ἄναρχα καὶ δύο ἀγέννητα λέγων, καὶ δύο ποιῶν Θεοὺς, ἀνάθεμα ἔστω Κεφαλὴ γάρ ἐστι καὶ ἀρχὴ πάντων ὁ Υἱὸς, κεφαλὴ δέ ἐστι τοῦ Χριστοῦ ὁ Θεός Καὶ τοῦτο δὲ καθολικὸν εἶναι οὐδεὶς ἀγνοεῖ, δύο πρόσωπα εἶναι Πατρὸς καὶ Υἱοῦ καὶ τὸν μὲν Πατέρα μείζονα τὸν δὲ Υἱὸν ὑποτεταγμένον μετὰ πάντων ὧν αὐτῷ ὁ Πατὴρ ὑπέταξεν .

(d) Soc E H c. 30, first Creed of Sirmium, A D. 351 (e) Ib. third Creed of Sirmium, A.D. 358.
(f) Ib c 41, Acacian, at Constantinople, A.D 360

THE WORD-GOD.

Letter of Arius.

created and set forth before all periods, did not exist before He was begotten; but being begotten by the Father time-apart, was brought into being the one production of the one Father. For He is not eternal, or co-eternal, or co-begotten with the Father: nor hath an existence collateral with the Father, as if there were two unbegotten principles; but God is before all things, as being individual, and the principle of all, and therefore before Christ also . . Inasmuch, then, as He hath His being from God, and His glorious perfections, and His life . and is entrusted with all things

Clementine Liturgy

He that established the heaven as a vault, and extended it as a parchment, and based it on nothing by a sole fiat, and fixed the firmament; and formed day and night; and begirt with rivers the world made by Thee through Christ. And not only didst Thou fabricate the world, but thou madest in it the cosmopolitan man: having proclaimed him its ornament For Thou saidst to Thy Wisdom: Let us make man in our image and likeness; and let them have dominion over the fish of the sea, and fowl of the heaven. For Thou, God Almighty, didst through Christ plant in Eden

Arian Creeds.

was begotten of the Father before all the ages, God of God, whole of whole, alone of alone, perfect of perfect, King of king, Lord of lord, a living word, wisdom, life, true light, way of truth, resurrection, shepherd, door, inconvertible, and unalterable, the unchangeable image of the Godhead, substance, power, and counsel and glory of the Father; first-born of every creature, who was in the beginning with God, Word-God, according to what is said in the Gospel, "The Word was God," . . . mediator between God and man, apostle of the faith that is ours and founder of the life,

---

χάνων, ἔστιν ἄναρχος μονώτατος· ὁ δὲ Υἱὸς ἀχρόνως γεννηθεὶς ὑπὸ τοῦ Πατρός, καὶ πρὸ αἰώνων κτισθεὶς καὶ θεμελιωθεὶς, οὐκ ἦν πρὸ τοῦ γεννηθῆναι, ἀλλ' ἀχρόνως πρὸ πάντων γεννηθεὶς, μόνος ὑπὸ τοῦ Πατρὸς ὑπέστη Οὐδὲ γάρ ἐστιν ἀΐδιος, ἢ συναΐδιος, ἢ συναγέννητος τῷ Πατρί· οὐδὲ ἅμα τῷ Πατρὶ τὸ εἶναι ἔχει, ὥς τινες λέγουσι τὰ πρός τι, δύο ἀγεννήτους ἀρχὰς εἰσηγούμενοι· 'Αλλ' ὡς μονὰς καὶ ἀρχὴ πάντων, οὕτως ὁ Θεὸς πρὸ πάντων ἐστί. Διὸ καὶ πρὸ τοῦ Υἱοῦ ἐστιν . Καθὸ οὖν παρὰ τοῦ Θεοῦ τὸ εἶναι

νόμενον τοῦτον κόσμον, καὶ πάντα τὰ ἐν αὐτῷ. Σὺ γὰρ εἶ ὁ τὸν οὐρανὸν ὡς καμάραν στήσας, καὶ ὡς δέῤῥιν ἐκτείνας, καὶ τὴν γῆν ἐπ' οὐδενὸς ἱδρύσας γνώμῃ μόνῃ· ὁ πήξας στερέωμα, καὶ νύκτα καὶ ἡμέραν κατασκεύασας· ὁ ποταμοῖς διαζώσας τὸν ὑπὸ Σοῦ διὰ Χριστοῦ γενόμενον κόσμον Καὶ οὐ μόνον τὸν κόσμον ἐδημιούργησας, ἀλλὰ καὶ τὸν κοσμοπολίτην ἄνθρωπον ἐν αὐτῷ ἐποίησας, κόσμου κόσμον αὐτὸν ἀναδείξας· Εἶπας γὰρ τῇ Σῇ σοφίᾳ, Ποιήσωμεν ἄνθρωπον κατ' εἰκόνα ἡμετέραν, καὶ καθ' ὁμοίωσιν· καὶ ἀρχέτωσαν τῶν

Πατέρα Παντοκράτορα, ἐξ οὗ τὰ πάντα.

Next, as to what they say of the Son —

Καὶ εἰς ἕνα Κύριον Ἰησοῦν Χριστόν, τὸν Υἱὸν Αὐτοῦ, τὸν μονογενῆ Θεὸν δι' οὗ τὰ πάντα ἐγένετο τὸν γεννηθέντα πρὸ πάντων τῶν αἰώνων ἐκ τοῦ Πατρός, Θεὸν ἐκ Θεοῦ, ὅλον ἐξ ὅλου, μόνον ἐκ μόνου, τέλειον ἐκ τελείου, βασιλέα ἐκ βασιλέως, Κύριον ἀπὸ Κυρίου λόγον ζῶντα σοφίαν, ζωήν, φῶς ἀληθινὸν, ὁδὸν ἀληθείας ἀνάστασιν, ποιμένα, θύραν ἄτρεπτόν τε καὶ ἀναλλοίωτον τὴν τῆς Θεότητος

THE SON NOT EVEN THE DEMIURGE.

Letter of Arius.

—for this reason God has sovereignty over Him, as being His God and before Him. And such phrases as "from Him," and "from the womb," and "issued forth from the Father," and "am come"; if they are understood, as they are by some, to denote a part of one and the same substance, and a development: then the Father will be of a compound nature, and divisible, and changeable, and corporeal, and thus far, as far as their words go, the incorporeal God will be subjected to the properties of matter'

ἔχει, καὶ τὰς δόξας, καὶ τὸ ζῆν, καὶ πάντα αὐτῷ παρεδόθη, κατὰ τοῦτο ἀρχὴ αὐτοῦ ἐστιν ὁ Θεὸς. Ἄρχει γὰρ αὐτοῦ, ὡς Θεὸς αὐτοῦ καὶ πρὸ αὐτοῦ ὤν. Εἰ δὲ τὸ ἐξ αὐτοῦ, καὶ τὸ ἐκ γαστρὸς, καὶ τὸ ἐκ τοῦ Πατρὸς ἐξῆλθον, καὶ ἥκω, ὡς μέρος αὐτοῦ ὁμοουσίου καὶ ὡς προβολὴ ὑπό τινων νοεῖται σύνθετος ἔσται ὁ Πατὴρ, καὶ διαίρετος, καὶ τρεπτὸς, καὶ σῶμα κατ' αὐτοὺς, καὶ τὸ ὅσον ἐπ' αὐτοῖς, τὰ ἀκόλουθα σώματι πάσχων, ὁ ἀσώματος Θεός.

(g) First Creed of Antioch

Clementine Liturgy.

towards the east a paradise adorned with all kinds of plants meet for food, and inducted him into it, as into a well furnished house. ... For all these things glory be to Thee, Almighty Master. ... 'For Thou art holy truly, and most holy, and exalted on high for ever. Holy, too, is Thy sole-begotten Son, our Lord and God, Jesus the Christ, who in all things having ministered to Thee His God and Father, both in fabricating different things and taking care of them as they required, did not overlook the race of mankind when lost, but ... appeased Thee

ἰχθύων τῆς θαλάσσης καὶ τῶν πετεινῶν τοῦ οὐρανοῦ . . Σὺ γὰρ, Θεὲ παντοκράτορ, διὰ Χριστοῦ παρὰ δεῖσον ἐν 'Εδὲμ κατὰ ἀνατολὰς ἐφύτευσας, παντοίων φυτῶν ἐδωδίμων κόσμῳ, καὶ ἐν αὐτῷ ὡς ἂν ἐν ἑστίᾳ πολυτελεῖ εἰσήγαγες αὐτόν Ὑπὲρ ἁπάντων Σοὶ ἡ δόξα, Δέσποτα παντοκράτορ . . .

"Αγιος γὰρ εἶ ὡς ἀληθῶς καὶ πανάγιος, ὕψιστος καὶ ὑπερυφούμενος εἰς τοὺς αἰῶνας "Αγιος δὲ καὶ ὁ μονογενὴς Σου Υἱὸς ὁ Κύριος ἡμῶν καὶ Θεὸς 'Ιησοῦς ὁ Χριστὸς, ὃς εἰς πάντα ὑπηρετησάμενός Σοι τῷ Θεῷ αὐτοῦ

(h) Fourth Creed of Antioch

Arian Creeds.

as He says: "I came down from heaven, not to do my own will but the will of Him that sent me." (g) ... Not that in calling the Father of our Lord Jesus Christ one God, the only-unbegotten, we therefore deny the Christ to be a God before ages, like the followers of Paul of Samosata (h) ...

'If any calling the Christ God before ages should not confess that the Son of God assisted the Father in the fabrication of the universe, let him be anathema.

If any should call the Son of God internal or external Word, let him be anathema. (i) ...

οὐσίας τε καὶ δυνάμεως καὶ βουλῆς, καὶ δόξης τοῦ Πατρὸς ἀπαράλλακτον εἰκόνα, τὸν πρωτότοκον πάσης κτίσεως, τὸν ὄντα ἐν ἀρχῇ πρὸς τὸν Θεόν, λόγον Θεόν, κατὰ τὸ εἰρημένον ἐν τῷ εὐαγγελίῳ, Καὶ Θεὸς ἦν ὁ Λόγος . μεσίτην Θεοῦ καὶ ἀνθρώπων, ἀπόστολόν τε τῆς πίστεως ἡμῶν, καὶ ἀρχηγὸν τῆς ζωῆς ὥς φησι, ὅτι καταβέβηκα ἐκ τοῦ οὐρανοῦ, οὐχ ἵνα ποιῶ τὸ θέλημα τὸ ἐμὸν, ἀλλὰ τὸ θέλημα τοῦ πέμψαντός με

Οὔτε μὴν ἕνα Θεὸν λέγοντες εἶναι τὸν τοῦ Κυρίου 'Ιησοῦ Χριστοῦ Πα-

(i) First Sirmian Creed

BUT ONLY THE ASSISTANT.

Clementine Liturgy	Arian Creeds.
His God and Father, reconciling Thee to the world, and freed all from the wrath impending them; born of a virgin, born in flesh, the God-Word, the beloved Son, the first-born of every creature, according to the prophecies foretold by Him of Himself, of the seed of David and Abraham, and of the tribe of Judah Thus He who moulds all that are born, was born in the womb of a virgin. the fleshless was made flesh; He who was born outside time, was born in time '	' Whose generation nobody knows, or He only who begat Him. . . We say that the Son is like the Father in all respects, as the Holy Scriptures affirm and teach ' (k)

καὶ Πατρί, εἷς τε δημιουργίαν διάφορον, καὶ πρό νοιαν κατάλληλον, οὐ περιεῖδε τὸ γένος τῶν ἀνθρώπων ἀπολλύμενον, ἀλλὰ . . καὶ ἐξευμενίσατό Σε τὸν αὐτοῦ Θεὸν καὶ Πατέρα καὶ τῷ κόσμῳ κατήλλαξε, καὶ τῆς ἐπικειμένης ὀργῆς τοὺς πάντας ἠλευθέρωσε, γενόμενος ἐκ παρθένου, γενόμενος ἐν σαρκί, ὁ Θεὸς Λόγος, ὁ ἀγαπητὸς Υἱὸς, ὁ πρωτότοκος πάσης κτίσεως, κατὰ τὰς περὶ αὐτοῦ ὑπ᾿ αὐτοῦ προρρηθείσας προφητείας ἐκ σπέρματος Δαβὶδ καὶ Ἀβραὰμ καὶ φυλῆς Ἰούδα καὶ γέγονεν ἐν μήτρᾳ παρθένου ὁ διαπλάσσων πάντας τοὺς γεννωμένους, καὶ ἐσαρκώθη ὁ ἄσαρκος, ὁ ἀχρόνως γεννηθεὶς ἐν χρόνῳ γεγεννήται . .

τέρα, τὸν μόνον ἀγέννητον, διὰ τοῦτο ἀρνούμεθα τὸν Χριστὸν Θεὸν εἶναι προαιώνιον, ὁποῖοι εἰσὶν οἱ ἀπὸ Παύλου τοῦ Σαμοσατέως

Εἴ τις λέγων Θεὸν τὸν Χριστὸν πρὸ αἰώνων Υἱὸν τοῦ Θεοῦ ὑπουργηκότα τῷ Πατρὶ εἰς τὴν τῶν ὅλων δημιουργίαν μὴ ὁμολογοίη, ἀνάθεμα ἔστω Εἴ τις ἐνδιάθετον ἢ προφορικὸν λόγον λέγοι τὸν Υἱὸν τοῦ Θεοῦ, ἀνάθεμα ἔστω

Οὗ τὴν γέννησιν οὐδεὶς ἐπίσταται, ἢ μόνος ὁ γεννήσας αὐτὸν Πατήρ "Ομοιον δὲ λέγομεν τὸν Υἱὸν τῷ Πατρὶ κατὰ πάντα, ὡς αἱ ἅγιαι γραφαὶ λέγουσί τε καὶ διδάσκουσιν.

(k) Creed of Rimini, A D 359 Soc E H. ii. 37.

The only question that could ensue from a careful and dispassionate comparison of these three columns is surely which of them contains most Arianism. His own letter, though written on behalf of others besides himself, who shared his opinions during his lifetime, and the Creeds formulated after his death by his partisans, of course speak for themselves; but in all three columns there is the same fathomless chasm, or radical inequality, maintained throughout, in spite of all the specious phrases and imagery devised for concealing it from view, between Him who is called the Father, with all the fullest attributes of Divinity stated to be peculiar to Himself, and Him who is called the only-begotten Son, but amid such qualifications as, while they serve to secure for Him what may be called the fact and the rights of primogeniture over beings and systems of every kind called into being subsequently through Him, disclaim for Him in the same breath all title to be considered either co-eternal or co-equal in any single respect with Him who is not only called his Father, but again and again his God. And the excessive length at which, in a liturgy professing to be Christian, the prerogatives and attributes claimed for the Father alone are rehearsed, and the multiplication of fine words and phrases to gloss over the very subordinate part even in the creation of the material world assigned to the Son, is surely calculated to excite the gravest suspicions that some other purpose was intended to be subserved by this Preface than appears on the surface: for believers in Christ and intending communicants at His holiest ordinance were not exactly the class of persons requiring to be admonished at such length and at such a time that there is but one God! Every Church that had a liturgy shrank as by instinct from assimilating its own Preface to that of the Clementine, which to this day stands alone. Providentially, so far as we know, the liturgy containing such a preface never came to be used in any Church.

Let us animadvert on a few of the passages in it that

call most for notice and contain pregnant hints of its authorship. The first and second Creeds of Antioch, which were formulated more particularly for the East, style the Father the 'demiurge'—that is, the *fabricator*—of the universe: the second and fourth, put into shape for transmission to the West, call Him 'creator' (κτίστην). By the last word is meant creating out of nothing; by the first fabricating out of existing materials, as Deans Liddell and Scott tell us.[1] Accordingly, when the Father is styled 'Creator,' the part of 'demiurge' may be supposed to have been reserved for the Son; but when the Father is styled 'demiurge,' there can be no post but that of *assistant* left for the Son. This is, therefore, the standpoint of the first two Creeds; and we have the first Creed of Sirmium, in accordance with them, anathematising those who deny that the Son *assisted* the Father in *fabricating* the universe.

Now it is just this part which is allotted to the Son in the Clementine Preface, wherever He is named, in going through the different stages of the creation, the part of 'demiurge' being reserved all through them to the Father. The second Creed of Antioch and this liturgy further correspond in what Cardinal Newman calls 'the variety and dignity of the titles by which they distinguish the Son to hide the offensiveness of their dogma,'[2] making Him a creature, though not like the others. A third point is their agreement in styling the Son 'God-Word,' or 'Word-God,' which the author of the second Creed of Antioch had the assurance to justify by reference to the well-known verse: 'The Word was God.' As though the omission of both article and copula—which Bingham in his translation supplies without authority—made no difference to their interpretation of it, exposed at the time by Bishop Alexander in his encyclic.[3]

Again, the second Sirmian Creed[4] reminds us that our

[1] S v Δημιουργός
[2] *Arians*, p 120
[3] Given at length by Socrates, *E H* 1 6.
[4] Ib 11 30.

Lord had said of Himself on earth : 'I go to My Father and your Father, and to My God and your God,' as if anybody doubted that He who was His Father as God was His God as man. By distorting a frequent interlacing expression of S. Paul—'Blessed be the God and Father of our Lord Jesus Christ'—and then giving it a different application, this Preface maintains again and again, on the strength of it similarly, that the Father was not only Father, but also God of the Son before as well as after the Son became man.[1]

Evidently this Preface must have been composed when Arianism was at its height, and by no mean hand. It is eloquent enough, no doubt; but eloquent in what?—in asserting all through a radical, essential inequality between the Father and the Son. Could it be proved here and there to be directed against other heresies, may it not be shown *without proof* that the letter of Arius, which has been placed side by side with it, expressly repudiates several heresies by name? But, again, if its Arianism is of the most pronounced kind, is not its Macedonianism in every way much worse? Let us go back to the prayer for Catechumens, attributed to S. Andrew, and headed as though this liturgy commenced with it; and there, by the newly consecrated bishop in blessing them, the 'unbegotten and unapproachable God—the only God, the God and Father of His Christ, His only begotten Son'—is at last styled 'God of the Paraclete' and 'Lord of the universe,' which is just the *blasphemy* perpetrated, as Bishop Mountague shows,[2] by Eusebius the historian in Chapter VI. of Book III. of his 'Ecclesiastical Theology,' where we find it stated with amazing assurance as a part of the traditionary teaching of the Church that the Holy Ghost holds exactly the same intermediate position between the Son and the universe that the Son holds be-

---

[1] This, it will have been seen, was what Arius distinctly professed on logical grounds.

[2] Hammond, p 4, without remark, Introd. p xli.

tween the Holy Ghost and the Father. This is also the teaching of the work against Sabellius 'De Fide,' printed by Sirmond as a work of Eusebius the historian,[1] but since given to Eusebius of Emesa.[2] It is also the teaching of the Apostolical Constitutions themselves all through—'One God, Father of one Son, not more: of one Paraclete through Christ,' as it is distinctly laid down in Chapter XI. of Book VI.

But, again, the Eucharistic Preface contains a still more flagrant insult to the Holy Ghost than the baptismal blessing; for neither in connection with the work of creation nor of redemption is He so much as named. And even when the seraphic hymn, 'Holy, holy, holy, Lord God of Sabaoth,' is expanded by the celebrant, he characterises the Father as being 'the All-holy, the highest, and exalted over all for ever,' and His only-begotten Jesus Christ *our* Lord and God as 'being holy too,' and as 'having *assisted* His God and Father in fabricating the world,' but omits all reference to the third 'holy.' The Arians observed that in the baptismal formula the Holy Ghost came last. It was on this principle that the formula for consecration in this liturgy was constructed. The subordination of the Son to the Father had been sufficiently maintained in the Preface. Here the subordination of the Holy Ghost to the Son is just as sharply defined. The Holy Ghost is not invoked to *make* Christ present as in other liturgies—Christ being supposed His superior—but to act merely the subjective part assigned Him in all the Arian Creeds and in these Constitutions: namely, that of exhibiting Christ to the receivers; in other words, of acting on the hearts of the receivers, and thus enabling them to discern Him, already made present in another way, as yet undefined.

Thus at last the flimsy disguise thrown over this liturgy so long has been stripped off, and it stands confessed for what it is worth. This, however, has no sooner been done,

---

[1] *Op* i 1-30 ed De la Baune
[2] Gieseler, *E. H* § 84, notes 18 and 22, § 85, note 38

than a host of minor blemishes that have passed muster hitherto reveal themselves. In the first place, the liturgy proper commences with 'the grace,' not of our Lord Jesus Christ, but 'of the Almighty God,' which looks like Scripture deliberately misquoted to derogate from the Son, as not being a true fountain of grace. Next, the celebrant says: 'Lift up,' *not* your *heart*, but 'your intellect': a change which might have proceeded from Arius himself. Next, in describing the acts of our Lord in consecrating, He is said to have 'looked up,' as any man might do, which is *not* in Scripture; but not to have blessed, or given thanks, which *are* both in Scripture. Thus His act of breaking the bread, which is again merely that of a man, stands alone. Further, in regard of the cup, the human act of mixing the water and the wine together is attributed to Him, which is *not* in Scripture: while the giving of thanks, which *is in* Scripture, is omitted. Another act, not attributed to Him in Scripture, but more consistent with Divinity, though applicable to man in a lower sense—that of hallowing what has been mixed—is attributed to Him for the first time now. In what follows, words of S. Paul are given as His words. Previously to this, a more surprising version of His words is given, with which S. Paul has since been credited. For the reading: 'This is My body which is *broken* for you,' which has perplexed so many minds, cannot be traced earlier than this liturgy.[1] Θρυπτόμενον is the word which occurs here; which, S. Basil and S. Chrysostom misliking, changed into κλώμενον, as being the word used for breaking the bread, and thus it has descended to us. Our Revisionists have with good reason ejected it, but they should have restored διδόμενον, which is the word in S. Luke, and which both S. Cyprian and the Vulgate testify to having been the word in S. Paul. The liturgies of S. Mark and of S. James have now both words, showing that *this* was their old word, while

---

[1] The sermon of S Ephrem is a translation from Slavonic, and that from Syriac, not original Greek.

the other was inserted to assimilate them to the liturgies of S. Basil and S. Chrysostom. S. Cyril of Jerusalem, who commences his twenty-second Catechetical Lecture with this very passage, provokingly stops short at this point, as having no need to quote more for his purpose. The last thing to be noticed in this liturgy is that the epithet 'spiritual' is never once applied to the Eucharist in any part of it—indeed, it would have not been in character if it had been—it is applied to the altar when the service was over, but not before. The mere omission of the Lord's Prayer from this liturgy should have suggested mistrust of its contents. It has no claim whatever to be considered a Christian composition. It is a studied insult to the Redeemer and the Sanctifier of mankind throughout.

As an instrument, therefore, put into the hands of the author of evil, and mainly through its insertion in a collection of ordinances supposed to be the work of the Apostles, this liturgy may be called historically the $\dot{\alpha}\rho\chi\dot{\eta}$ $\kappa\alpha\kappa\hat{\omega}\nu$ with perfect truth—the root of all the bloody controversies and false doctrines and interminable divisions that have so long distracted Christendom, in connection with what Christ ordained for a sacrament of love.

Of its composition and date there can be but little doubt. It was composed when Arianism was at its height, when S. Cyril was Bishop of Jerusalem—for thirty years a victim to its malignant spite—and was founded, as long ago pointed out by Sir W. Palmer, on the liturgy called after S. James the Less. The trick of opposing S. James the Great to S. James the Less at once betrays its origin and its purpose. Then, as regards authorship, many circumstances combine to refer it with great probability to Eusebius of Emesa. He was the principal person at the Council of Antioch, A.D. 341, when the see of Alexandria was pressed on his acceptance. He must have known Arius personally when pursuing his studies there some years before. The marked similarity between the letter of Arius, the Creeds of Antioch, and this liturgy, which can be denied by none, prove their literary connection. A further link in the chain is supplied in the fact that Eusebius of Emesa prosecuted his Biblical studies under Eusebius the historian, whose work against Marcellus exactly represents the theological standpoint of this liturgy. Moreover, Eusebius of Emesa was expelled his see soon after taking possession of it, on a charge of magic, to which several extant pieces circulated as his may well be thought to lend colour: for instance, the first and third of the sermons printed as his by Augusti, and notably the magic power attributed in the Latin homily for Easter to the words of our Lord—*never attributed to them before*. But was this an original idea with him, or was it plagiarised from another? We shall be brought again face to face shortly with the striking homily translated by Kohl of S. Ephrem: and then the great probability will be pointed out that this homily supplied the author of the consecration-prayer of the Clementine Liturgy with a model which he seized upon with enthusiasm, and only modified into squaring with Arianism. Eusebius, a graphic writer himself, and a native of Edessa, would naturally be prone to borrow leaves from the discourses of the glowing preacher, who for his avowed preference for it came to be called 'the Edessene.'

That he was a man of mark, and an indefatigable writer of popular works, is attested by contemporaries: and relieved of the cares of his diocese, and living in retirement at Laodicea with his friend George—then its bishop, but who formerly made common cause with Arius at Alexandria—he may well have spent his leisure hours in compiling from all the sources open to him a dramatic work like the Apostolical Constitutions in their present shape, tinged of course throughout with his own opinions.

Further, assuming him to have been their author, yet to have shrunk from ever becoming known as such, it will be easy to understand how they were put into circulation after his death, and how in process of time they came to be palmed upon S. Basil and S. Chrysostom successively with such success. For his death took place previously to the Council of Seleucia, A.D. 359, where Paul his successor signed for Emesa, and George his admirer and biographer took conspicuous part—though S. Cyril of Jerusalem triumphed over his metropolitan Acacius at Seleucia with his aid for once. Now Eusebius, dying before then, may have instructed George to bring out these Constitutions after his death in the way best calculated to secure their incognito. And the name of Clement, as being a Western name, may have suggested itself to one or both of them for that purpose. The great work of S. Epiphanius, where they are first quoted, was not published till sixteen years after—namely, but five years after S. Basil had been ordained bishop, A.D. 376. And five more years had to elapse still before S. Chrysostom was ordained deacon. Thus there was abundance of time for them to get slowly circulated, and as the canon appended to them forbade their being divulged by the bishops to whom they were addressed, they would at first only be studied by bishops, and, divided in opinion as bishops were then, only discussed between friend and friend. Passing from these considerations to their actual contents, let us remember that the palmy days of Arianism had quite passed away by then: fusion was being tried on all sides, and differences extenuated. 'From the date of this council'—the second general, A.D. 381—says Cardinal Newman, 'Arianism was formed into a sect exterior to the Church, taking refuge among the barbarians.' Hence, that this liturgy, coming to them under the venerable name of Clement—Clement of Rome, too—should have been accepted as such by S. Basil and S. Chrysostom, and given the full weight entitled to it on that ground alone, must surely be deemed far less incomprehensible than the high compliments lavished on it by learned and excellent men of our own day, starting with the full knowledge that the name given to it was false— perhaps designedly false—and that it contained Arianism in solution, only requiring careful analysis to be made patent. For S. Basil and S. Chrysostom both lived in an age when the links and gradations between sectarianism were numerous and elastic, and when men frequently passed from one side to another, and then, in some cases, back again. George, Bishop of Laodicea, and Eustathius, Bishop of Sebaste, had each been intimate with Arius in early life, and shared his opinions. But at the Council of Seleucia we find them both warmly supporting the semi-Arians against the pure Arians: so much so, that George was received into communion, though only for a time, by S. Cyril of Jerusalem, as having contributed to his success. From Eustathius,[1] on the other hand, only the year before, S. Basil and his brother Gregory 'received frequent visits, who would sometimes accompany them across the river Iris to Annesi, the residence of their mother, the sainted Macrina, where they would spend whole days and nights in friendly theological discussions.' Then, when the Council was over, S. Basil was to have accompanied his semi-Arian namesake, the Bishop of Ancyra, and Eustathius, on a mission to Constantinople to communicate the semi-Arian resolves to the Emperor.[2] His intimacy with Eustathius lasted upwards of twelve years longer, when he found out how deplorably the man he had gone all lengths to redeem had cajoled him. Now, in what terms was belief in the Holy Ghost expressed in the formula to which the semi-Arians then once more pledged their adherence—namely, the Creed put forth at Antioch A.D. 341, which Eusebius of Emesa probably composed? 'Et in Spiritum Sanctum, qui credentibus donatus est, ad consolationem, et sanctificationem, et consummationem,' *without, however, any profession of His Divinity.* Supposing, therefore, the Laodicean George to have exhibited the Apostolical Constitutions and the liturgy forming part of them, as the work of Clement, to Eustathius of Sebaste: and Eustathius in turn to have exhibited them with enthusiasm to S. Basil, and discussed

[1] Smith's *Christ. Biog. Dict.* ii. 385.   [2] Ib i. 285.

them with him, can we imagine S. Basil finding fault with them on any ground that would not have been, on the one hand, fatal to the Creed upheld at Seleucia by his friend, and, on the other, open to the personal retort that he charged Clement of Rome with being unsound? The Arians to a man would have maintained their genuineness, on account of the teaching they contained: the orthodox, unable to contest their genuineness, would have tried to minimise the countenance lent by them to a teaching of which they could not approve.

Again, S. Basil must have recognised a slight—though possibly, to him, a marked—point of agreement in the formula for consecration of this liturgy with his own. For he calls his prayer for the descent of the Holy Ghost 'the invocation for the declaration of the bread' ($\dot{\epsilon}\pi\grave{\iota}\ \tau\hat{\eta}\ \dot{a}\nu a\delta\epsilon i\xi\epsilon\iota\ \tau o\hat{\upsilon}\ \ddot{a}\rho\tau o\upsilon$).[1] This is just the purpose for which the Holy Ghost is invoked in that of Clement ($\dot{a}\pi o\phi\hat{\eta}\nu a\iota$): 'to declare Christ present.' Some writers, especially S. Chrysostom, insisted most on His objective function, that of making Christ present: others, as S. Irenæus, S. Theophilus, S. Nilus, and S. Proclus, preferred dwelling on His subjective function, that of exhibiting or declaring Christ present to themselves: by enabling them to *discern* Him. S. Basil was of the same mind himself. He was all the more ready therefore to defer to the supposed Clement in the prominence given by him to the artistically constructed, and in most cases *evangelically worded*, recital preceding—and, so far as he could have foreseen then, not in any likelihood of superseding—it. Thus S. Basil, in comparison with S. Chrysostom, may be said to have borrowed freely from the Clementine Liturgy: yet even he will have none of the first part of its Preface, where its character is most pronounced: and in what he borrows from it afterwards he takes care to insert explicit mention of the Son and Holy Ghost, showing their oneness with the Father, and the Divine functions

[1] *De Sp. S* § 66.

attributed to each in Scripture. S. Chrysostom, even with S. Basil before him, either adhered to his old Preface, or composed a thoroughly Christian and orthodox one for himself, of much shorter length : and in invoking the Holy Ghost insists on retaining the word, quoted as existing in his time by S. Cyril, '*make*.'

Now, this word 'make,' let us remember, could not have been understood then to carry with it any such request as '*Change this into*': for otherwise, the later addition 'Changing with Thy Holy Spirit' would have been superfluous, by whomsoever it was introduced. Both S. Basil and S. Chrysostom, it may be remarked in conclusion, rectify the misquotations of Scripture, and omissions of Scripture, which have been signalised in the Clementine: as may easily be seen by comparing them severally with each other, and with it, in the edition of Mr. Hammond. How and where S. Chrysostom shows acquaintance with the Apostolic Constitutions in his own writings has been already pointed out: but it is scarcely possible to doubt his having seen either the original of the Latin homily for Easter, so long attributed in the West to Eusebius of Emesa ; or the sermon of his which gave rise to this homily. For, as regards Eusebius of Emesa, this homily corresponds exactly with the theological views of the party to which he belonged: it has special claims to be considered the earliest exponent of the teaching underlying the consecration-prayer of the Clementine Liturgy : and there are special reasons for assigning it, or a sermon resembling it, to Eusebius of Emesa: the first of which is that he was expelled his see on a charge of magic; which well accords with the power attributed in this homily for the first time to the words of our Lord ; the second is that S. Chrysostom can be proved to have been familiar with his sermons; the third that S. Chrysostom *latterly* propounded the same views himself: and in doing so departed not only from his former views, but from the views of every single Greek or Latin Father who has left a record of his opinions on that subject.

S. CHRYSOSTOM A PUPIL OF DIODORUS.

As regards S. Chrysostom, proofs of this change from his own writings have been already given. Strong evidence for connecting Eusebius of Emesa with this change is supplied by S. Jerome, who tells us that Diodorus of Tarsus, under whom S. Chrysostom studied in early life, left many writings behind him in character resembling Eusebius of Emesa, whose meaning he interpreted, but whose eloquence his own slender acquaintance with secular literature disqualified him from acquiring.[1] If a revered master made the writings of Eusebius his model, is it likely that an enthusiastic pupil would resist, or without resisting escape, their influence? Theodore, Bishop of Mopsuestia, was a fellow-pupil first, and then a warm friend. If the friends ever discussed them together, Theodore would have doubtless upheld the estimate formed of them by his master. The marked resemblance between two sermons on the betrayal of Judas, one by S. Chrysostom, the other attributed with good reason to Eusebius of Emesa, is evidence which may be left to speak for itself.

Assuming the authorship, however, both of this liturgy and of the homily which draws out the teaching, as yet undefined, but latent in it, to have been brought home to Eusebius, we must not on that account be led into crediting him with superhuman foresight in speculating on its remote consequences. But for those consequences, so disastrous and by this time so deeply rooted, one might be apt to make disparaging reflections on the *grotesque* mistake committed by him, and by Tertullian two centuries earlier, in attributing a power of consecration to words used by our Lord, in *administering to communicants* what had been already consecrated by those words of His in blessing and giving of thanks, not a monosyllable of which he permitted either Evangelists or Apostles to record for use by man.[2]

[1] *De Vir Illust* c 119
[2] S Thomas (whose prime authorities are, first, Eusebius of Emesa, and, next, the pseudo-Ambrose) feels, but cannot find any satisfactory solution of, this difficulty. *Sum Th* III, Quæst. 78; comp. Quæst. 75, art 4.

S. CHRYSOSTOM'S PATRONAGE.

How this mistake came to be passed over by S. Basil and S. Chrysostom it is not easy to explain, except on the ground that reverence for the supposed Clement deterred them from remarking on it; but that S. Chrysostom had distinct misgivings on the sacerdotal applications that might be given to those words cannot I think be doubted: after his loud protests, so frequently repeated, against man ever being supposed to act a more than ministerial part in celebrating: and the uncompromising terms in which consecration is in all cases attributed by him to God alone. No other Father is half so stern or outspoken on this point.

At the same time, but *for his patronage*, this liturgy might have remained in the same crystallised state that has so long been its characteristic in the Apostolical Constitutions, without attracting any further notice than what it might receive from scholars. For even S. Basil would never have been followed in his revision, as S. Chrysostom has been in his. Besides, S. Basil has left no sermons to show that, in revising his liturgy by that of Clement, he considered the functions attributed to the Holy Ghost in the old the least affected by what he took from the new. Hence we have fair ground for assuming that S. Basil had *not* seen the homily, which we have strong ground for assuming S. Chrysostom *had* seen, interpreting the new to him. But, again, the sermons of S. Chrysostom, preached on the lines of this homily, failed to enlist adhesion to them in any part of the East, where to this day S. Chrysostom in maintaining them stands alone. So that, perhaps, had this homily never been translated into Latin, the West might never have learnt its teaching from S. Chrysostom. At the same time, too much importance must not be claimed for this homily. Disconnected from the liturgy that it was intended to expound, it would cease to be remembered as soon as read. On the other hand, it would not be remembered to create confusion, had the invocation of the Holy Ghost to *make Christ present* taken *precedence* of the recital of those words, on whose inherent power it dwells: for then it would have been remembered that the Holy Ghost had co-operated in all that Christ either said or did when He walked about on earth. In this way the Arian pitfall would have been bridged over or avoided, into which S. Basil and S. Chrysostom were lured by the supposed Clement: and the East, sooner or later, by their authority. The pitfall consisted, of course, *not* in the devotional recital of the words and acts of our Blessed Lord at the Last Supper, which the Eucharist by commemorating continued—and than which, therefore, nothing could have been more edifying and appropriate— but in doing away with all mention of the Holy Spirit till *after the oblation had taken place*: and then invoking His action only to exhibit or declare Christ present subjectively to all worthy receivers—thus absolutely stripping Him of the higher office with which the whole Church had till then credited Him; as in all the other sacraments committed to her charge—and opening the door wide to speculation and conjecture by what other agency consecration of the oblation had been performed.

Many circumstances prevented this difficulty from being felt practically for a time; the Eastern mind being very tenacious of its old doctrines and customs, and S. Chrysostom himself having taken care to preserve the Invocation of the Holy Ghost in all its primitive fulness and force, and all other Eastern liturgies, except that of S. Basil, remaining unchanged as before. The true character of the change was only realised when the Constantinopolitan liturgy began to be substituted for local liturgies in all dioceses subject to that Church; when Latin and Greek Churches began to compare notes on their diversities, and when the liturgical revision inaugurated by S. Chrysostom found its way into the liturgies of the West. As this branch of the subject will be pursued in a separate chapter presently, no more need be said on it here beyond the fact. But it was just while this movement was being slowly developed that a great theological genius was given to the East in the person of S. John Damascene, who, whether he realised the difficulties of the new position or not, by invoking S. Gregory Nyssen to aid in solving them, introduced carnal conceptions into the subject and paved the way for still more pronounced speculations in that direction, when the authority of Aristotle came to have the high place assigned to it in the exegesis of Scripture that was claimed for it by S. Thomas.

Accordingly, S. John of Damascus, in the thirteenth chapter of his fourth book 'On the Orthodox Faith,' after dwelling on the creation and fall of man, which at length resulted in the Incarnation of the Son of God as its sole remedy, proceeds as follows:—[1]

'But since this Adam is spiritual, it was necessary that His birth should be spiritual, and in like manner His food. But since we are compounds in some sense and double, our birth must equally be double and our food composite. The birth then given to us is of water and of the Spirit—namely, that of holy baptism. The food, He who is the bread of life, our Lord Jesus Christ, who came down from heaven.'[2] For, being about to submit to a voluntary death on our behalf, on the night in which He made surrender of Himself,[3] He executed a new testament for His holy disciples and apostles, and through them for all believers in Him; when, in the upper room of the glorious and holy Sion, having eaten the ancient passover with His disciples and fulfilled the ancient covenant, He washed the feet of His disciples, for a token of holy baptism. Then, having broken bread, He distributed it to them saying, "Take, eat; this is My body, which is being broken on your behalf, for remission of sins." In like manner, having also taken the cup of water and wine, He

---

[1] Drawn from S Greg Nyssen, *Orat Catech* c 37 *ad init*
[2] This is a free quotation from the Liturgy of S James
[3] All this, down to 'beyond reason and conception,' is a continuous quotation from the sermon of S Ephrem extracted from already, p 79, but slightly changed or interpolated here and there.

divided it among them, saying: " Drink ye all of it; this is My blood of the new testament, which is being shed on your behalf, for remission of sins. Do this in My remembrance. For as often as ye may eat of this bread, and drink of this cup, ye show forth the death of the Son of Man and His resurrection till He come."

'If, therefore, the word of God is living and energetic, and if the Lord hath done whatsoever pleased Him : if He said, Let there be light, and there was light; let there be a firmament, and there was one : if by the word of the Lord the heavens were made, and all the hosts of them by the breath of His mouth ; if the heaven and earth, water and fire and air, and all the ornament that attaches to them, were brought into being by the word of the Lord; and, above all, this widely-renowned living creature, man ; if, in fine, God Himself, the Word, of His own accord became man; and of the pure and undefiled substance of the holy ever virgin took flesh to Himself without a father, can He not make the bread His body and the water and wine His blood ? In the beginning He said : " Let the earth bring forth grass," and to this day, after rain has fallen, it brings forth its own productions, co-operating with and empowered by the Divine command. God said : " This is My body and this is My blood ; do this in My remembrance." And by His all-powerful command, till He comes, it is. For thus He said : "till I come." And the rain descends on this new husbandry through the invocation—namely, the overshadowing power of the Holy Ghost. For, as every single thing that God created He created by the action of the Holy Spirit, so now, too, the action of the Holy Spirit accomplishes things which are above nature, which only faith alone can comprehend. " How shall this be to me," said the holy virgin, "seeing I know not a man ? " The angel Gabriel replied, " The Holy Ghost shall come upon thee, and the power of the Highest shall overshadow thee." And now thou askest : " How is it the bread becomes the body, and the water and wine the blood of Christ?" and I say to you, "The Holy Ghost comes down and makes these things, which are beyond reason and conception."'

¹ 'Moreover, bread and wine are used. For God knows the weakness of man, which turns away in perplexity from most things not yet made familiar to it by experience. Hence with His accustomed condescension, by means of things of nature that are familiar to us, He makes those things which are above nature. And as, in the case of baptism, it being a custom with men to wash in water and anoint themselves with oil, He has attached to oil and water the grace of the Spirit, and made this the laver of regeneration; so men, being accustomed to eat bread and drink water and wine, He has coupled His divinity with them, and made them His body and blood; that through things familiar and natural to us we may become conversant with things above nature.

'The body taken from the blessed virgin is body truly joined with divinity; not that the body which has been taken up comes down from heaven, but that the bread itself and wine are transmuted into the body and blood of God. And if thou seekest the manner how it takes place, it is enough for you to hear that it is through the Holy Ghost, as it was also through the Holy Ghost that the Lord took flesh to Himself, and in Himself, of the holy mother of God. And we know no more than that the word of God is true, energetic, and all-powerful; but the manner unsearchable. And it is not worse to say this, that as bread naturally by eating, and water and wine by drinking, are changed into the body and blood of him who eats and drinks, and become no other body but his that existed before, so the bread of the oblation, with the water and wine, through the invocation and descent of the Holy Ghost, are supernaturally trans-

---

¹ The two next paragraphs are due to S Greg Nyssen, *Catech Or*, also, the second more particularly to c 37 *ad fin*, where μεταποιεῖσθαι and μετιστοιχειοῦν both occur, as Le Quien has pointed out in his notes But S. John stops a point short of that theory.

muted into the body and blood of the Christ, and are not two, but one and the same . . .'[1]

[2] 'Further, the bread and the wine is not a type of the body and blood of the Christ—heaven forbid; but the very body of the Lord joined with divinity. For he said Himself: " This is "—not a figure of My body, but—" My body " . . . This bread, the loaves of the shewbread symbolised; this is the pure, to wit, the unbloody sacrifice which, from the rising up of the sun even unto the going down of the same, the Lord declared, through the prophet, should be offered to Him . . .'

[3] 'Although some have called the bread and the wine antitypes of the body and blood of the Lord, as the divine Basil says, "they were not speaking of them after consecration, but before;" calling the oblation by that name.'

This is a disappointing extract when taken to pieces, as it is an attempt to reconcile irreconcilables. S. John Damascene no doubt set the example, which Peter Lombard and the Latin schoolmen followed, of collecting passages from the Fathers and endeavouring to harmonise their views where most dissimilar and strain them into consistency with each other. But he does this here without naming his authors; hence we scarcely know at times when he is quoting from them and when he is introducing ideas of his own. Waterland,[4] commenting on one part of this extract, accord-

---

[1] S Chrysost *Ep ad Cæsarium*

[2] Here he repeats S Peter of Laodicea (Migne, *Pat Gr* lxxxvi 2, *ad fin*) on S Matt xxvi 26, and S Anastasius of Antioch in his *Dux Vitæ* (ib lxxxix p 153), who preceded him by two centuries

[3] This is taken from the last speech of the Deacon Epiphanius in Tom 3 of the sixth Action of the second Nicene Council (Mansi, xiii 266)

[4] Charge, Easter A D. 1739, *Works*, v. 200 'Like as a man's body takes in daily additional matter, and all becomes one and the same body, so our Lord's personal body takes in all new-made bodies of the Eucharist, and thus by a kind of growth or augmentation, all become one and the same personal body of Christ' It is true that Waterland, to make good his charge, refers to a piece declared to be spurious by Le Quien, though printed by him in the same volume with this work (*In Epist ad Zachar et cap quod eam seq Admonitio*, p 652) But this was really the view taken by S Gregory Nyssen in his *Catech Or*, whom S John here condenses

ingly credits him with a view which is not his, nor adopted by him either entirely, drawn from the Catechetical Oration of S. Gregory Nyssen: a view never entertained by any Father but him, and which, therefore, should not have been passed off as Catholic doctrine. Another view put forward in it is clearly drawn from the alleged letter of S. Chrysostom to the monk Cæsarius. But this again is too obscurely stated and too vague to command weight, even if written by him. There was no lack of passages that might have been quoted of the most standard kind from S. Chrysostom. Excepting the 101st Trullan Canon, and this, as some think, spurious letter, he never cites, in this chapter at least, any testimony from Constantinople. Again, S. Basil is only quoted to be corrected by sixth-century writers hardly fit to be mentioned in the same breath with him. The one passage which everybody will remember was long supposed to be the composition of S. John himself till Kohl translated the homily which he found at S. Petersburg in Slavonic, A.D. 1729, purporting to be by S. Ephrem, without the smallest idea that any part of it had been in print before. As Le Quien had published his edition of S. John Damascene seventeen years before, no suspicion of any quotation in this chapter from S. Ephrem ever crossed his mind. Even Peter Benedict, who divined its import at a glance, was long puzzled how to deal with it, till 'casu incidit Johannes Damascenus,' as he naively says, when he settled the question at once by saying that S. John had written it himself. But in the approbation given to this part of his Antirrheticon all that the Prefect of the Vatican can find to say in its praise is that it contains 'nothing at all contrary to good manners or sound doctrine,' which certainly the slipshod way in which he must have read this chapter bears out: for in this chapter the character maintained by S. John throughout is that of a dovetailer of passages either cited or epitomised by him. Then, again, all his passages, except the single reference to the 101st Trullan Canon, are from the fourth century—S. Cyril of Jerusalem, S. Basil, S. Gregory Nyssen, S. Chrysostom—all of them contemporaries and friends of S. Ephrem—with the liturgy of S. James, though in a somewhat later recension. Of these the extract from this sermon of S. Ephrem is behind none in attesting its date. For (1) those words 'Precibus sacerdotis, Sanctique Spiritûs adventu panis fit corpus, vinum sanguis,' echo the teaching of the whole Church in the fourth century; (2) S. Ephrem rehearses here the words and acts of our Lord at the Last Supper to His brethren, as S. Cyril had rehearsed them in his twenty-second catechetical lecture to his catechumens, to bear out his teaching on the Eucharist. Neither he nor S. Cyril throws out the least hint that they were rehearsed in the liturgy then. According to S. Ephrem, too, the words of our Lord once spoken in instituting the Eucharist sufficed, without any further repetition, to produce their effect to the end of time. They were like the words of the Creator: 'Let the earth bring forth grass,' said once for all. Rain descended from heaven to perpetuate the effects of the one: the Holy Ghost came down from heaven to perpetuate the effects of the other. S. Ephrem, in propounding this doctrine, could not have overlooked the teaching of the Clementine liturgy, but must have protested against it had he been aware of its existence. Yet there are no traces of a protest to be found in what he says; it is a natural inference drawn from what had occurred at the creation. Therefore, without intending it, he will be found in direct opposition to the subsequent teaching of the supposed Clement on two points: (1) in stating the purpose for which the descent of the Holy Ghost is invoked, to be to make Christ present; and (2) in not connecting the rehearsal of His words by the priest with consecration of the oblation in any way.

As early compositions—probably the first of their kind in their way—it must be obvious to everybody who will take the trouble to compare them that he who wrote last drew from him who wrote first. And it is just here that the evils of this process of dovetailing are forced on our notice. This extract from S. Ephrem is preceded by a short sentence from the liturgy of S. James that breeds confusion; for this sentence, short as it is, being read first, gives a liturgical colouring to the whole. But this sentence forms no part of the sermon. It was inserted by S. John himself at a time when all Eastern liturgies were being slowly remodelled on that of the supposed Clement, agreeably with the precedents set by S. Basil and S. Chrysostom. And it was natural enough for S. John, living at the convent of S. Sabas, whose metropolis was Jerusalem, to preface this extract with a sentence from the Jerusalem liturgy, by way of avowing his own preference for it. But the effect of his act has been to throw dust into the eyes of his readers in later times by making them suppose that the extract which followed was also part of a liturgy, not of a sermon. Remove this sentence, and the extract which follows is seen to be in the best manner of the earlier half of the fourth century, just of the kind which a popular writer who heard it delivered from the pulpit would be sure to jot down and appropriate to his own purposes at some future time. Let part of this extract be placed in parallel columns with the part answering to it in the Clementine liturgy, and the correspondence between them will be seen at a glance. More than this, it will explain several of the omissions or commissions already charged on this liturgy. Its author, captivated with the dramatic turn of the sermon, put the words down as he heard them, which he wished to remember most, without considering that brevity might well be excused in a sermon addressed to monks; but essential omissions or commissions were decided blots in a liturgy designed for churches frequented by poor as well as rich, illiterate as well as good scholars.

Kohl's Translation of the Sermon.	*Coteler's Translation of the Liturgy.*
'Eâ nocte quâ prodi se voluit, discipulis hoc suis et apostolis testamentum reliquit . . . fractoque pane, discipulis obtulit, dicens: "Accipite et edite. Hoc est corpus meum fractum pro vobis in remissionem peccatorum." Similiter vinum et aquam calici infudit, usque dedit inquiens· " Bibite ex hoc omnes Hic est sanguis meus novi Testamenti, qui pro multis effunditur in remissionem peccatorum Hoc facite in memoriam mei. Quoties enim hunc panem comeditis, et calicem hunc bibitis, mortem Filii hominis annuntiatis "'	'In quâ nocte tradebatur . . . pane accepto, fregit et dedit discipulis dicens· " Hoc est mysterium novi Testamenti· accipite ex eo, et manducate. Hoc est corpus meum, quod pro multis frangitur, in remissionem peccatorum " Similiter calicem miscuit ex vino et aquâ: sanctificavit, et dedit iisdem, dicens : "Hic est sanguis meus, qui pro multis effunditur in remissionem peccatorum Hoc facite in meam commemorationem Quotiescunque enim manducabitis panem hunc et bibetis hunc calicem, mortem meam annuntiabitis donec veniam "'

Neither the liturgy nor the sermon appears to have been altered in any way since they were written. And it is at starting only that they pursue different tracks. The sermon introduces us to the last celebration of the 'old Passover' in the large upper room on 'the famous Mount': for this the liturgy substitutes a more vivid, because more imaginative, picture—that of the Saviour, Who 'having taken bread into His holy and immaculate hands, and looked up to Thee His God and Father'—without further preface, '*brake*.' From this point included to the end they follow the same lines —the same selections from Scripture, the same peculiarities in quoting it, the same misquotations: practically the same Latin equivalents, though rendered in one case from Slavonic, in the other from Greek. The agreement is of course most marked, in attributing no acts of blessing or of thanksgiving to the Saviour—unparalleled in all other liturgies—but thus pointing as with a finger to this sermon as its source. Then, 'in remissionem peccatorum,' put into the mouth of the Saviour without authority by both, as having been uttered by Him in giving His body. This in-

LITURGY COPIED FROM THE SERMON.

accuracy percolated into most liturgies from the Clementine. A worse mistake than this occurs in it at the end, in attributing to the Saviour the words of S. Paul. In this we get a clearer finger-post than before from the liturgy to the sermon. For, though the sermon keeps the words of the Saviour and of His apostles quite distinct in this place, further on it paraphrases 'Hoc facite in memoriam Mei' by 'usque dum Ipse veniat: prout Ipse ait, *Dum venio.*' This is what led the supposed Clement astray. Of the other liturgies, that of S. Mark follows him blindfold: that of S. James corrects him by this very sermon: that of S. Basil assumes him to have been correct: that of S. Chrysostom omits the words altogether, as not being the words of Christ.

It is thus impossible to deny the indebtedness of the consecration-prayer of the Clementine liturgy—putting the question of its authorship altogether on one side—to this sermon of S. Ephrem, though the poles are not more widely separated than is their teaching. And there have been others who have borrowed from this sermon, and yet departed from its teaching, besides the supposed Clement. A nobler and a perfectly truthful exponent of its teaching was long afterwards given to it in a well-known hymn of surpassing beauty: but, again, the poet, imagining it to have been the work of a rival theologian, only served himself of it as a stepping-stone to something else, which for the present we may pass over, thus:

> 'In supremâ nocte coenæ, recumbens cum fratribus,
> Observata lege plene cibis in legalibus,
> Cibum turbæ duodenæ se suis dat manibus!
> Verbum caro, panem verum verbo carnem efficit:
> Fitque sanguis Christi merum, et si sensus deficit,
> Ad firmandum cor sincerum sola fides sufficit. . . .'[1]

Nothing could have represented the system more admirably so far: but just where the action of the Holy Ghost should have been brought in, and given the homage due to

[1] *Thesaurus Hymnol* 1. 251, by Herm. Adal. Daniel (Halis, 1841).

it, another note is sounded, and the sermon is closed. In writing as a theologian elsewhere, the author of this unquestionably beautiful hymn shows that he supposed it was not S. Ephrem, but S. John of Damascus, from whom he had borrowed.

Had S. John of Damascus only therefore named S. Ephrem, and identified himself with his teaching, and not allowed his readers to suppose that he considered any other teaching equally Catholic, S. Thomas would have known, at all events, what he was doing, when he expressed one part of it so faithfully, and *sup*pressed another part of it so unaccountably,[1] both in his hymn and in that portion of his *Summa Theologica* which treats of the sacraments. It is a simple fact, that only two places can be shown in all those countless articles between Quæst. 73 and 83 of the third part, where the operation of the Holy Ghost in the Eucharist is so much as named; and only then as a private speculation of S. John of Damascus himself: yet, even as his private speculation, overawing S. Thomas to that degree, that he shrinks from controverting it.[2] S. John has devoted a section in his 'Sacred Parallels' to 'the Divine Mysteries,'[3] which, though shorter, may well compare with this chapter of his work on the Orthodox Faith, as both bearing the same title, and also pursuing a similar method. That is to say, it consists of quotations—first, from the Gospel of S. John, vi. 51-58; next from 1 Cor. x. 21; next from 1 Cor. x. 23-29; after which follow two long extracts, from 'Sermons of S. Chrysostom'—the last directed against those who, present during the liturgy, leave church without waiting for the hymn of thanksgiving at its close.[4] In the same work is an extract

---

[1] S Thom *Sum Theol* III Quæst lxxix. art. 1, ad 2.
[2] 'Ad primum ergo dicendum, quòd cùm dicitur sola virtute Spiritûs Sancti panem in corpus Christi converti, non excluditur virtus instrumentalis, quæ est in forma hujus sacramenti, sicut cùm dicitur "solus faber facit cultellum," non excluditur virtus *martelli*' S T Part III Quæst lxxviii. art 4; comp. Quæst lxxxii. art 5.
[3] *Lit* ⊖ *Tit* 4
[4] *De Bapt. Christi, ad fin. Op.* vol. ii. 374-5, ed. Montf.

from a sermon on Cain by S. Ephrem, also mentioned by name.[1] In a later chapter of his work[2] on the Orthodox Faith, S. John testifies his respect for the Trullan canons in a way not to be forgotten, by appending to his list of the canonical books of the New Testament 'the canons of the holy Apostles, through—or by—Clement': and then passing over in *emphatic* reticence the Apostolical Constitutions, conformably with the rulings of the second Trullan canon, as we have seen. This, possibly, may account for both the fewness and exclusiveness of his liturgical references: the single liturgy cited by him being that of Jerusalem, or of S. James the Less. One quotation from it has been already noticed. Another, much more marked, because longer and word for word, occurs in a postscript to his letter on the hymn called the Trisagion,[3] where the celebrant, he says, interprets it as it were thus: 'Thou art holy, King of the ages, Lord and Giver of all holiness: holy, too, is Thine only-begotten Son, our Lord Jesus Christ, through—or by— Whom Thou madest all things: holy too, likewise, is Thine Holy Spirit, Who searchest all things, even the deep things of Thee, the God.' Then, further, he testifies to its mixed chalice: to its raising aloft 'of the bread of life' by the celebrant—that is, on exhibiting the contents of the paten to the people, the last thing before communicating them, as S. Anastasius of Antioch had done more than one hundred years earlier[4]; when the celebrant exclaimed 'Sancta sanctis,' and the people responded, as in the days of S. Cyril: 'Unus Sanctus, unus Dominus Jesus Christus in gloriam Dei Patris, cum Sancto Spiritu: Cui gloria in æternum':[5] and then, lastly, with S. Anastasius and S. Cyril

---

[1] *Eclog. lit.* A, tit. 72, ed Le Quien
[2] iv. 17.
[3] *Op* i 496, ed Le Quien, comp. Hammond, *Ancient Lit* p 40
[4] Above, p 145.
[5] S. John D. *Op.* i. 496 and Hammond, *Ancient Lit* p. 49, with S. Cyril, *Catech* xxiii 19 and Toutée's notes Had S. John followed the Clementine, he would have suppressed all mention of the Holy Ghost in both places.

of Jerusalem conjointly, to its prayer for the descent of the Holy Ghost, to *make* Christ *sacramentally* present.

Thus, in spite of the mistakes committed on two different points by each, the resolute stand made by S. John Chrysostom and S. John of Damascus on a third proved the means of arresting the mischief intended by the author of the Clementine liturgy for many centuries in the East, and for this result it is S. John of Damascus who deserves most credit of the two. For S. John of Damascus, in obedience to the Trullan canons, promptly turned his back upon the Apostolical Constitutions and their liturgy, and clung fast to that of S. James the Less, so that his view of its *epiklesis* could not have been described with more truth than it was by S. Thomas when he said: 'Ad quartum sic proceditur. (1) Videtur quod prædictis verbis formarum non sit aliqua vis creata effectiva consecrationis. Dicit enim Damascenus in Lib. IV. Orth. Fid. c. 14 cir. med: " *Solâ virtute Spiritus Sancti* fit conversio panis in corpus Christi."' As I have given his answer in a note two pages back, it need not be repeated. It practically concedes the whole point—his own parallel of the *hammer,* which is inert and inanimate, plainly testifies to the need of a hand—and a Divine hand: 'the finger of God' in this case.[1]

S. Thomas might have quoted isolated passages, favourable to his thesis, from S. Chrysostom: but, again, S. Chrysostom even in those passages invariably pictured Christ Himself the celebrant on each occasion—repeating His own words, unheard and unseen: consecrating the oblation in every case, which had been merely prepared by His appointed ministers.

Further, by continuing to invoke the descent of the Holy Ghost on the oblation to make Christ present in his revised liturgy, S. Chrysostom left it to be inferred that the preliminary rehearsal of the events of the Last Supper

---

[1] 'Tu septiformis munere, *Dextræ* Dei Tu digitus,' *in Die Ientec od Tertiam* Comp S. Matt xii 28, with S. Luke xi. 20

introduced there by him was purely devotional—whatever may have dropped from him respecting them at other times—and not in any way intended to derogate from or interfere with the full effect of that prayer in that place.

A short reference to the charges and counter-charges hurled against each other by the Greeks and Latins, when their final rupture took place, will be found to add force to these remarks in concluding them.

S. Chrysostom has been credited with having introduced other changes into the liturgy bequeathed by him to his see, purely ceremonial in their character. And it was against these that the Roman envoy, Cardinal Humbert, stormed and enlarged most, in his controversial pieces. Not a word was breathed by him against the terms of its invocation of the Holy Ghost, or against the effect attributed to them by the Greeks, or against their making the third hour—9 A.M. —the canonical hour, as long as they abstained from making it the only lawful hour for celebrating the Eucharist, it being the hour at which the Holy Ghost first descended on the Church. It was Alexander I., a martyred Bishop of Rome in the first decade of the second century, who—Cardina Humbert assures them confidently—first ordered the *Passio Domini* to form part of the ceremonial in consecrating the Eucharist: but of its bearing on consecration, if he knew anything himself, he was reticent to a fault in not taking full notice before plunging into matters of minor concern. Unleavened bread—*azymes*—was the principal novelty charged against the Latins by his adversary, the monk Nicetes. In retorting on him, the Cardinal is satisfied to refer in caustic terms to the persistent stand made by the Church of Jerusalem against the unauthorised innovations of the Constantinopolitan ritual. The Latins had received letters from considerable personages at Jerusalem, disclaiming all sympathy with what Rome condemned at Constantinople. At Jerusalem they knew nothing of a spear for dividing the oblation: nothing of a spoon for administering a mixture of the contents of the paten and chalice to communicants: nothing of pouring boiling water into the chalice: nothing of burning or burying what remained of the consecrated elements after communion, instead of reserving them in a coffer specially made for that purpose.

The rupture was scarce consummated that divided the Western and Eastern Churches into two hostile camps, with Rome and Constantinople for their respective leaders, before the same centralising influences were set in motion on either side, with precisely the same results, thus mournfully summarised by the late Dr. Neale, with special reference to the liturgies of the East.[1]

'Of the normal liturgies, those of S. James and of S. Mark were used by the Churches of Antioch and Alexandria respectively, till the time of Theodore Balsamon. This prelate was a complete Oriental Ultramontane. Everything was to be judged by, and squared to, the rule of Constantinople. The Bellarmine or Orsi of the Eastern Church, he was for abolishing every formulary not adopted by the œcumenical patriarch: and endeavoured successfully to intrude the forms of Constantinople on the whole East. Consulted by Mark of Alexandria as to the degree of authority which attached to the liturgies of S. James and S. Mark, he wholly condemns them as not mentioned by Holy Scripture or the Canons: but, chiefly " because," says he, " the Catholic Church of the most holy œcumenical throne of Constantinople does in no wise acknowledge them." The way in which Balsamon treats these offices, more venerable than his own, and that in which Rome has abrogated the Gallican and Mozarabic Missals, are surely marvellously alike. From that time, the Constantinopolitan liturgies of S. Basil and S. Chrysostom have prevailed over the whole orthodox East, except that the office of S. James is used in the Church of Jerusalem, and in some of the islands of the Archipelago, on the festival of that Apostle.'

[1] *Eastern Ch*, Genl Introd. 1. 318.

CHAPTER VI.

THE problem to be grappled with in this chapter, and if possible to be solved from facts, relates wholly to the Roman Canon, and to the following portion of it in particular, on which consecration is, and has been for centuries, in all Churches of the Roman communion, held to depend.

'Who, the day before He suffered, took bread into His holy and venerable hands, and with His eyes lifted up towards heaven, to Thee, God, His Almighty Father, giving thanks to Thee, blest, brake, and gave to His disciples, saying: "Take and eat all of this; for this is My body." In like manner, after He had supped, taking also this excellent chalice into His holy and venerable hands, and also giving thanks to Thee, He blest and gave to His disciples, saying: "Take and drink of this; for this is the chalice of My blood, of the new and eternal Testament: the mystery of faith, which shall be shed for you and for many to the remission of sins. As often as ye do these things, ye shall do them in memory of Me."'[1]

It is a two-sided problem really that is involved in this passage: the first part concerning its insertion, if that can

---

[1] 'Qui pridie quàm pateretur accepit panem in sanctas ac venerabiles manus suas, et elevatis oculis in cœlum ad Te Deum Patrem suum omnipotentem, Tibi gratias agens, benedixit, fregit, deditque discipulis suis, dicens Accipite et manducate ex hoc omnes, hoc est enim corpus meum Simili modo, postquam cœnatum est, accipiens et hunc præclarum calicem in sanctas et venerabiles manus suas, item Tibi gratias agens, benedixit, deditque discipulis suis, dicens Accipite et bibite ex eo omnes hic est enim calix sanguinis mei, novi et æterni testamenti, mysterium fidei, qui pro vobis et pro multis effundetur in remissionem peccatorum. Hæc quotiescunque feceritis, in mei memoriam facietis.'

236 CONFLICTING ACCOUNTS OF ITS AUTHORSHIP.

be shown; the second concerning its application, when and how that commenced.

Having already despatched a similar problem as regards Constantinople, we should encounter fewer difficulties in unravelling this as regards Rome.

And even upon these difficulties we shall get light thrown to some extent at starting by noticing some facts in respect of the Roman Canon acknowledged by all.

1. It is certain that the passage commemorating the Blessed Virgin, the twelve Apostles, and early martyrs of the Roman Church cannot, as it now stands, be dated earlier than Nicene times or the beginning of the fourth century, as the names of S. Chrysogonus, S. Cosmas and S. Damian, all three victims of the persecution under the Emperor Diocletian, occur amongst the martyrs.

2. It is certain that the name 'Canon' was not applied to this part of the Roman liturgy before the seventh century.

3. It is certain that no authentic account of its authorship exists, and that all the accounts which have been circulated on that head are conflicting or legendary. 'It has been ascribed,' says Cardinal Bona,[1] 'by some to Pope Gelasius; by others to Musæus, presbyter of Marseilles; by others to Voconius, Bishop of Castellanum in Mauritania, all of whom, according to Gennadius, composed Sacramentaries. Bishop Aldhelm thinks it was edited by S. Gregory the Great. S. Gregory says himself that it was composed by a scholastic, but omits to add when this was done.'

An element of truth may perhaps be recognised in all these statements. All alike *negative* the notion of its having descended from the Apostles in its present shape, and not one of its reputed authors dates earlier than the last half of the fifth century. Musæus, the earliest of them, bears a Greek name; and Marseilles, the seat of his ministry, was the route by which Greek influences found their way

[1] *Rer Liturg.* ii 11, 2.

into the West, and thence frequently to Rome. Gelasius and Voconius were both of them Africans; and the African and Roman liturgies, if not identic, had much in common. S. Gregory, when he calls his liturgy the work of a scholastic, seems to connect it with one who had pursued his studies—*graduated* may we not say?—at Constantinople, though the scholastic may have merely translated it from the Greek in which it was originally drawn up and for some time used, as has been already suggested. Thus it was his bald and inelegant Latin, probably, that S. Gregory the Great held so cheap. At the same time S. Aldhelm, English Bishop of Sherborne, may not have been far wrong in attributing its revision, in the form used by himself, to S. Gregory. For now we emerge from the world of conjectures into well-authenticated facts and unchallenged history. Now, for the cardinal portion of our inquiry, internal and external evidence go hand in hand.

The first two actual witnesses to any words or sentences now forming part of the Roman Canon are both Englishmen, and Englishmen now, as then, regarded with pride—S. Aldhelm and Venerable Bede. Previously to their time not a word of it is on record. S. Aldhelm, who was slightly senior to Bede, though contemporary with him, is the first extant writer who calls it by that name, and he no doubt brought it from Rome, where it was beginning to be so called when he was last there. He is likewise the first extant writer who reports an addition to it, made, *to his knowledge*, by his *old preceptor and instructor* in early life, S. Gregory. It was he who 'coupled the name of the Sicilian martyr S. Lucia, to ensure their joint celebration, with that of her compatriot and fellow-sufferer S. Agatha,' just as they stand now 'in the daily Canon of the Mass.'[1]

So far, therefore, persons would be warranted in con-

[1] *De Laud Virg* c 42 This surely must mean that he completed his studies *at Rome*, near enough to the times of S Gregory to justify both the statement and his calling S. Gregory 'my pedagogue'

cluding that the prayer beginning ' *Nobis quoque peccatoribus*' was revised, not composed, by S. Gregory. Whether it was given the same place by him in the Canon that it holds now is not decided by this passage.

Venerable Bede, though he never visited Rome, surpasses S. Aldhelm in what he tells us about the Roman Canon and S. Gregory.

Three passages from his works, each relevant in the highest degree to our present inquiry, shall be given here; of these the first and last are well known as far as their words go, though, it may be, they need further interpreting.

1. In the sketch of S. Gregory given by him in Chapter I. Book II. of his ' Ecclesiastical History' we have the following :—

' Likewise, in the actual celebration of Masses, he superadded three words full of exquisite grace: " Diesque nostros in tuâ pace disponas, atque ab æternâ damnatione nos eripi, et in electorum tuorum jubeas grege numerari." '

By ' words' it stands to reason Bede must mean sentences, and the sentences given by him could never have stood alone, nor could they have commenced, though they might have concluded, a paragraph. And by 'the celebration of masses,' as here translated by Mr. Stevenson, he must have meant the liturgy then in use, though in what part of it he omits to state. The question is, therefore, Were they— could they have been given by S. Gregory the exact place which they now occupy with the same prayers following and preceding them ? The word ' Canon ' is conspicuous in this passage by its absence. Facts, it is to be hoped, will throw light on our path as we proceed. Thus much appears clear, that these sentences were inserted in some part of the liturgy then in use by S. Gregory, and, for aught that appears to the contrary, that they were his own composition.

2. To most probably this next passage will be new. In his commentaries on 1 Samuel xxi. 6,[1] pointing out how

---

[1] *Comment* iii 8.

S. GREGORY THE GREAT THE NEXT. 239

indispensable purity was to the Christian priest, he describes him as, ' qui *in sanctas ac venerabiles Christi manus* acceptum panem, in sacramentum corporis Ejus consecratum . . . est sumpturus.' Those italicised words Bede could not be doubted to have borrowed from the existing Canon of the Roman Mass had he lived now ; but who shall decide whether they formed part of the Canon, just as they stand, when Bede wrote, or whether they were, just as they stand, or any part of them, imported into the Canon from this passage ? Who can tell from the context whether Bede is quoting them or putting them together himself for the first time ? Facts again, it is to be hoped, will throw light on our path as we proceed.

One fact, indeed, we have now to start with unrecorded in any previous generation of any previous Pope, but authenticated in this case by two contemporaries of unimpeachable credit—with direct means of obtaining information—that additions were made to the Roman Canon in two definite cases by S. Gregory, the first Pope of that name. Let us now try to gather, from the advice given by him to others on the same subject, the spirit by which he would be likely to be influenced in dealing with it himself.

3. In a never-to-be-forgotten letter of his to our own first Archbishop of Canterbury, preserved by Bede, he thus replies to the second query put to him by the latter :—

' My brother knows the custom of the Roman Church in which he remembers his having been bred. But it is my pleasure you should choose with care whatever you have found either in the Roman, or the Gallican, or any other Church likely to be more acceptable to Almighty God, and transplant into that of the Angles, which is as yet young in the faith, with all requisite circumspection, whatever things you have been able to cull from any number of Churches.'[1]

We could not have desired a better commentary than this on his own practice, which we could not learn either

[1] *E H* i 27

better than from himself. But first let us recall some well-known facts in his life, related partly by others, including Bede,[1] and partly by himself.[2] S. Gregory twice visited Constantinople as diplomatic envoy of Benedict II. and Pelagius II., his predecessors in the see of Rome to the Imperial Court, and on the second occasion he spent three years there. During those three years he commenced, at the instigation of Leander, Bishop of Seville, then also there, and must have made considerable progress in, his celebrated work on morals, otherwise called his 'Exposition of the Book of Job,' besides making great friends with the Constantinopolitan patriarch Eutychius, whose views he corrected on a point to which we shall be soon brought back again. In the ninth year of his pontificate no small light is thrown upon a further subject that must have engrossed his thoughts also during his stay there from the correspondence which it had evidently caused.

But for his visits to Constantinople, we may safely say that letter of his to John, Bishop of Syracuse, to which reference has already several times been made, would never have been penned—would never have been needed. It was plainly the outcome of those visits that he was at length brought to bay by the murmurers who said: 'Quomodo ecclesiam Constantinopolitanam disponit comprimere, qui ejus consuetudinem per omnia sequitur?' This was a wholesale charge which is by no means covered by his reply to it; and we shall be doing him no injustice whatever if we assume that he had in this case fully claimed for himself the liberty which he conceded with so much heartiness to our own metropolitan. In fact, he goes to the length of affirming at last that he is prepared to do the same thing over again for which he was blamed, should he find, either in that Church or any other, anything that he would do well to imitate.

[1] Ib ii 1
[2] *Prol. ad Expos. in Job*, with the Benedictine notes, also *Dict of Christian Biog* ii 779

The details of the charge pressed against him, as he represents them, surely warrant no such warmth on his part in replying to it, yet, in answer to the first and last of them, he supplies two new facts greatly to our purpose.

The first complaint was that ' Alleluia ' was said in Masses by his order at other seasons than that of Pentecost.

His answer is: ' Ut alleluia *hic* diceretur, de Hierosolymorum ecclesiâ, ex beati Hieronymi traditione, tempore beatæ memoriæ Damasi papæ traditur tractum . . .'

Here S. Gregory states it as a fact, and makes S. Jerome vouch for it, that this word 'Alleluia' was introduced into the Roman liturgy from that of Jerusalem only two centuries from his own time—that is, towards the end of the fourth century.

The last complaint was that he had ordered the Lord's Prayer to be recited 'mox post canonem': it having been recited previously ' super oblationem '—that is, before consecration, as we learn from his reply. But with his reasons for the new arrangement we may dispense. Not so the gentle correction with which he prefaces his statement: ' Mox post *canonem*, did you say? No! that is not our word for it. The Lord's Prayer we recite *mox post precem* on this account,' &c.

Passing by the 'Alleluia,' then, as forming no part of the Canon, we have got, between Venerable Bede, S. Aldhelm, and himself, three clear additions made by him to what is called 'the Canon'—the Lord's Prayer—at the end of it, as now; then, as now, too, probably following the prayer, ' Nobis quoque peccatoribus,' with its one word ' Lucia ' due to S. Gregory; and the three sentences, as yet unplaced, which Bede seems to say he composed as well as superadded *somewhere* to the liturgy. What, in addition, is to be said of those four or five words used by Venerable Bede, which have long formed part of the existing Canon, as introductory to the words of institution? But if they stood there previously to the times of S. Gregory, how is it that no Latin writer ever quoted or alluded to them in any genuine work before Bede? After Bede this part of the Canon is quoted freely, but never before. Stories of its pre-existence were subsequently current, but not one that can be traced to any but a spurious source. The author of the tract 'De Divinis Officiis,' now figuring among the spurious pieces ascribed to Alcuin,[1] says of the whole paragraph, ' Hoc quod sequitur Apostoli in usu habuerunt post Ascensionem Domini;' but this statement he probably got from S. Agobard,[2] and S. Agobard from acquaintance, personal or mediate, through S. Gregory, from the writings of the supposed Clement.

The more popular account, attributing it to the martyred Alexander, Bishop of Rome, A.D. 109–19, and the fifth from S. Peter, owes its origin to the False Decretals,[3] and his own biographer of the ninth century.[4]

It attributing it to S. Gregory, we find ourselves on historical ground once more, and doubly so when we contend, in addition, that he borrowed it from Constantinople; and couple with it another prayer of singular interest, and containing still more direct proof of its origin.

But is not the Gelasian Sacramentary proof *against us* at starting? It may simplify matters, as we proceed, not to have left this objection unanswered in our rear. Of the three Sacramentaries printed by Muratori, what is called the Leonine no doubt is the oldest; but not a shadow of proof has yet been offered that it was compiled by S. Leo, and the general opinion now seems to be that the MS. containing it 'was prepared by some ecclesiastic for his own, either private or public, use.'[5] Anyhow, it contains no

---

[1] Migne, *Patrol Lat* c i 1260

[2] 'Unde et ecclesia ex traditione Apostolorum his verbis consecrans mysterium sacri corporis et sanguinis Domini, designanter dicit Dominum dixisse Apostolis, *Accipite et manducate ex hoc omnes* · &c Adv Amalar c 14

[3] 'De sacramentorum oblationibus, quæ inter missarum solemnia Domino offeruntur, passio Domini miscenda est . .' Decret Alex I^{mi}

[4] 'Hic passionem Domini miscuit in precationem sacerdotum, quando missæ celebrantur' *Anast in Vit*

[5] *Dict of Christian Ant* ii 1032; comp Daniel, *Cod. Liturg Eccl Rom* pp 7–8

WHAT STRABO SAYS ON THAT SUBJECT.

Canon. What is called the Gelasian includes a Canon; but a Canon exhibiting all the changes known positively to have been introduced by S. Gregory. Lastly, for what is called the Gregorian as well as the Gelasian there is no direct evidence before the ninth century, and even then only that of Walafrid Strabo for certain; as the passage mentioning a 'Gelasianus codex de missarum solemnibus,' and its revision by S. Gregory, in his life by John the Deacon, is wanting in the earliest MSS. of that work,[1] and as yet no MSS. have been produced of either Sacramentary dating earlier than A.D. 800, as Baluze shows.[2] What Strabo says shall be given at length in his own words:—[3]

'Gelasius, too, fifty-first Pope in succession, is said to have thus arranged prayers composed by others as well as himself. The Churches of France had likewise prayers of their own for use, *which are still used by many*. And because many things inserted by unknown authors seemed to lack definite meaning themselves, blessed Gregory, by drawing all real beauties into close proximity, and weeding out all excrescences and incongruities, compiled a Book of the Sacraments, as it is called, and manifestly declared to be by its title; wherein, *if some things are now found out of character with this intention, they cannot be ascribed to him, but must be considered accretions by less competent hands in a later age*.'

Strabo was earlier by a generation than John the Deacon. Grimaldus, Abbot of S. Gall, who was his contemporary, confirms Strabo rather than him in his preface to the Gregorian Sacramentary, revised by himself for no other reason than because such liberties had been taken with it by later

---

[1] Daniel, ib p 5, note It is printed however still, Lib ii 17.
[2] See his note on Agobard, *De Imag* c 30 The term 'Sacramentarium' probably first occurs in the seventh book of the *Capitularies of the French Kings*, c 202, ed Baluze where it is coupled with 'Ordo Romanus' Amalarius has it, however, *Eccl* iii 40, but seemingly distinguished from the 'Missal'
[3] *De Rer Eccl Exord* c 22, headed 'De Ordine Missæ, et offerendi ratione'

writers as to make most people doubt its having had S. Gregory for its author.[1] Other writers are less positive. Agobard, of Lyons, while denying S. Gregory to have composed an Antiphonary then bearing his name, mentions a 'Liber mysteriorum' with approval as his, and in another place speaks with equal respect of a 'Liber sacramentorum, quem Romana tenet ecclesia,' which Baluze thinks must be the same book under another name.[2] Amalarius mentions a Missal 'qui *vocatur* Gregorialis,'[3] and adds his own belief subsequently that it was by him.[4] But this, again, would appear to have been an Hour-book. The 'Ordo Romanus,' of which he speaks elsewhere, was ceremonial, not liturgical. Hence there were clearly service-books in circulation at that date bearing his name, which had *not been* compiled by him; and even of 'the Book of the Sacraments,' which Strabo says he compiled, we are given to understand by the same writer that some things might be detected in it even then which were not his, and perchance not in harmony with his intentions either. What those things were, Strabo, perhaps discreetly, though provokingly, forbore to name. When he comes to speak of the Canon, he is more reserved still; as he neither tells us with what words it begins or ends, nor, in in fact, quotes any sentence from it. He declares, indeed, in general terms, that it is unknown 'quis primus ordinaverit nobis *ipsam actionem*, qua conficitur sacrosanctum corporis et sanguinis Dominici mysterium,' adding that it was also called 'Canon' by the Romans, and then setting himself to prove that it was 'per partes compositus.' In support of his own arguments to that effect, he cites the parts attributed by the papal biographer to S. Alexander, S. Leo, and S. Gregory, and tries to gather from his words how much each really contributed. There were some then, he tells us, who contended that *all the remainder of the*

---

[1] Migne, *Pat Lat* cxxi 797
[2] *De Correct Antiph.* c. 19, with the note.
[3] *De Eccl Off* iii 40
[4] Ib iv 30, discussed at length in a note further on

Canon following the three sentences introduced by S. Gregory, was composed by S. Gregory. But is not this, he rejoins, opposed to the statements of the papal biographer, that it was S. Alexander who introduced 'the passion' into the Canon, and S. Leo those four words, ' sanctum sacrificium immaculatam hostiam,' further on? Practically, therefore, we should be justified in concluding that *but for the papal biographer*, whose statements he shrank from impugning, Strabo would have acquiesced in this opinion of his contemporaries himself. Still, as it is a question not of composition, but simple compilation, can it be supposed for one moment that S. Gregory would not have retained any words known to have been inserted by S. Leo, though he might place them differently from where they were placed before? Coming back fresh from this survey to S. Gregory, two questions in any further inquiry relating to him must force themselves upon every candid mind : (1) *Had* the statements of the papal biographer respecting S. Alexander and S. Leo been derived *from authentic records*, is it likely that S. Gregory would have been unacquainted with them? Or (2), being acquainted with them, that he would have spoken in an official letter of the Canon, without any reserve whatever, as having been ' composed by *a scholastic* ' ? The high character of S. Gregory, with the doors of the papal archives open to him at all hours, dictates an answer in the negative to both questions. By the word *composed*, indeed, he may quite possibly mean no more than compiled, arranged, or even translated, by this individual.[1] On the other hand, as the term *scholastic* had a special, as well as a general, meaning in his day,[1] it is also possible that he might mean by it one who, like Socrates the historian, or John the collector of canons, afterwards patriarch, was so designated from having pursued his studies, or, as we might say, *graduated* at Constantinople. His statement in that case

---

[1] Hofman, s v with the authorities quoted by him Also Du Fresne, *Gloss Græc.* s v and *Constant. Christian* ii 9, 1.

would be that the Canon received by him from his predecessors had actually been put into shape by a learned Constantinopolitan; and his argument, that he deserved no blame for having revised himself at Constantinople, what one who came from Constantinople put into the shape wherein he had received it as Pope. So much for the contents of his letter: now once more to the events of his life. Being at Constantinople, Bede tells us he proved the means of reclaiming its patriarch, Eutychius, from error on the subject of the resurrection, by dwelling on the character of the glorified body with which Christ rose from the tomb and ascended.[1] While thus engaged, it would only be natural that their conversation should from time to time turn on their respective liturgies; for, though the Roman may have been but little known to the patriarch, Gregory, with his turn of mind, and during those three continuous years passed by him in *New Rome*, cannot have failed to have become familiar with the liturgy called after S. Chrysostom from having been revised by him, and which had been substituted for more than one hundred years at Constantinople by then for the older form. Noticing its peculiarities and its points of difference from his own, he would naturally seek to have them accounted for, and would still more naturally be shown in confidence by the patriarch, whom he had laid under special obligations, the liturgy then supposed to have emanated from the most venerated of all the bishops of old Rome, but who, nevertheless, was not known to have written anything except in Greek. Not being a bishop as yet, Gregory would be shown it under the reserve then equally supposed to have been enjoined by the revered compiler of the Apostolical Constitutions in the last of the Apostolical Canons also put forth in his name.[2] Both the Apostolical Constitutions and the liturgy contained in them were then in the highest repute, though not much talked about, and no suspicion had as yet got abroad of their heterodoxy; for

[1] *E H.* ii. 1.   [2] Above, p. 183.

it wanted more than 150 years to the Trullan Council that forbade their circulation and exposed their blots. Gregory, therefore, with the supposed Clement for his authority and the saintly Chrysostom for his precedent, in making it his model, may well have decided at this time what changes should hereafter be carried out by himself in revising his own liturgy, should this task ever devolve upon him; yet afterwards, when taken to task, in the ninth year of his episcopate, for having made those changes, his answer betrays much of the same embarrassment and dilemma that were pointed out in passages of S. Basil and S. Chrysostom, where they seemed equally put on their defence.[1] He was accused of having borrowed a host of liturgical customs from the Constantinopolitan Church. Of some this was true, but for most he was indebted only to the source from which the Constantinopolitan Church had previously borrowed. Why, then, could he not explain himself and state frankly what had happened? When this letter was written he was a bishop himself, and his correspondent John, Bishop of Syracuse, was a bishop too. But, as the object of his letter was to answer charges brought against him by a third party *who were not bishops*, we can well understand his reply being limited to what he had actually borrowed from the Church of Constantinople— the saying of the Lord's Prayer *mox post precem*, for instance—and his passing over in silence what he had borrowed *at* Constantinople from the Clementine liturgy as being no concern of theirs, and a subject that he was bound not to discuss *except with* bishops, nor, as far as words went, included in their charge.

Thus interpreted, the fair inference from his letter and acts together will be, that he followed S. Chrysostom in revising his own liturgy by that of the supposed Clement, so far at least as relates to that portion of its Canon with which we are now concerned. Further, the mould in which this portion is cast is much too clearly that of the Clementine to be

[1] Above, p. 186.

denied as a fact: and, further still, the precedent of S. Chrysostom is closely followed in correcting the Clementine where it needs correction: and in departing from it where taste might suggest another sentiment or expression. The italics in the Roman denote the corrections.

Roman.	*Clementine.*
' Who, *the day before He suffered*,[1] took bread into His holy and *venerable* hands, and with His eyes uplifted *towards heaven to God, His* Almighty *Father, giving thanks to Thee, did bless*, break, and give to His disciples, saying. "Take and eat ye all *of this*: for *this is My body*."[2] ' In like manner, *after He had supped*, taking also this excellent chalice into His holy and venerable hands, *and giving Thee thanks, He blessed*, and gave to His disciples, saying: "Take and drink ye all of this · for this is the chalice of My blood of the new and eternal testament—the mystery of faith—which shall be shed for you and for many, for the remission of sins. *As often as ye do these things, ye shall do them in remembrance of Me.*' ' Wherefore, mindful,' &c.	' On the night in which He was betrayed, having taken bread into His holy and blameless hands, and having looked up to Thee, His God and Father, and broken, He gave to His disciples, saying: "This is the mystery of the new Testament:[3] take *of it*, and eat; this is My body which is being broken for many, for the remission of sins." ' In like manner also the cup: having mixed it with water and wine, and sanctified, He gave to them also, saying: "Drink ye all of it. This is My blood which is being shed for many, for the remission of sins. Do this in My remembrance. For, as often as ye may eat this bread and drink this cup, ye do show forth My death till I come." ' Wherefore, mindful,' &c.

The decisive points in this comparison are: (1) 'the eyes uplifted towards heaven'; and then the correction 'to God, His Almighty Father,' substituted in the Roman for 'His

---

[1] *Pridie* This word stamps it as the work of a Latin, for it is not exact, the night on which He was betrayed being according to Jewish reckoning the first evening of the *identic* day on which He suffered Our English Office corrects this

[2] By stopping here, with S Matt and S. Mark, the difficulty was got over of deciding between two readings, 'given' or 'broken,' in S Luke and S Paul

[3] This is evidently the foundation of what the Roman says in fuller terms of the chalice; and more consonantly with Scripture, so far as *place* is concerned

EVIDENCES OF HIS USE OF THEM.   249

God and Father' in the Clementine. Next (2), 'My blood of the new and eternal Testament, the mystery of faith': properly placed in the Roman, but expanded manifestly from 'This is the mystery of the New Testament' in the preceding paragraph of the Clementine.

Turning back to the page where the liturgies of S. Basil and S. Chrysostom are similarly compared, we shall find *both passages left out*; so that the Roman must have been copied from the Clementine direct in each case. On the other hand, 'After He had supped' in the Roman was also the correction of S. Chrysostom alone: and therefore must have been borrowed direct from him. 'Shed for you and for many,' borrowed from him also, though shared by S. Basil. Yet there are just three cases where the Roman has taken an independent line of its own: (1) while following S. Basil and S. Chrysostom in supplying all the acts attributed to our Lord in the New Testament, which the supposed Clement omits; and in placing the Lord's Prayer, too, for recital *mox post precem* with them, which in the Clementine finds no place whatever, it rejects that *of sanctifying*, as not attributed to Him in the New Testament which they supply. Then (2), after those words, 'This is My body,' it stops short, agreeably with S. Matthew and S. Mark in point of fact; yet also, possibly, to be saved adjudicating on the reading 'broken,' *originating* with the Clementine, but perpetuated in another equivalent by S. Basil and S. Chrysostom. (3) 'As often as ye do these things' &c. in the Roman is purely original; but the beginning of the next paragraph, 'Wherefore mindful' &c. is common to them all.

I have reserved to the last what appears to me the saddest point of agreement between the Roman and the counterfeit; which alone would prove that one was borrowed from the other, 'Take *of it* and eat,' says the pseudo-Clement—fortified by his reading of $\theta\rho\upsilon\pi\tau\acute{o}\mu\varepsilon\nu o\nu$—as though the Body were broken into pieces for administration, like the bread. 'Take and eat ye *all of this*,' says the Roman, beguiled into misquoting Scripture still more, in deference to a supposed model. I shall show good cause further on for considering this one of those changes in the Canon of which Strabo speaks: introduced, *not by S. Gregory*, but long after his time: and consistent, not with his teaching, but with a teaching that had by then quite superseded his. S. Gregory never would have deserted the Vulgate rendering: 'Accipite et comedite; hoc est corpus meum': which is faithful to the Greek.

Hence, when all the different items brought out in this comparison have been summed up, we seem warranted in concluding, that whoever compiled this portion of the Roman liturgy must have been: (1) a Latin, as the word *pridie* proves, for, not having a Greek equivalent, it would have occurred to no Greek: and besides is not exact, as already shown in a note. Yet (2), whoever compiled it must have worked with the liturgies of S. Chrysostom and the supposed Clement open before him at the same time: and (3), been a person in high authority to venture to depart from them both, or follow one in preference to the other, as he judged right. On the other hand, as he never follows S. Basil or any other, where he departs from these two, it is pretty plain that only these two supplied him with materials. Now all these requirements meet in S. Gregory: and are confirmed by his own personal history, and harmonise with the belief of some who were contemporary with Strabo.

Thus, from internal evidence and authentic history combined, we find this opinion to have been generally correct. Hence, by going yet further into particulars, it is quite possible we may obtain still more light. Our main point in dealing with them, it should be mentioned at starting, will be to ascertain what became of the prayer for the descent of the Holy Ghost, in the hands of S. Gregory? For that he retained it *somewhere* cannot be doubted, after his dogged adherence to the term in use for it in the West; after what has been quoted from the writings of his predecessors, and

his own : [1] from the writings of Bede, and a host of other
Westerns already named, or still to be named in the eighth
and ninth centuries: even if we should not be able to decide
for certain where it stood, owing to the sinister care with
which all traces of it have been obliterated, though some
stray palimpsest may yet disclose this. But, first, the following minor points seem to require notice. The epithet ' venerabiles' applied in what is called the ' Gregorian Canon' to
the hands of our Lord is both singular and unique, being
common to no other liturgy: nor likely to have been chosen
as an equivalent for the word $ἀμώμοις$ in the Clementine by
S. Gregory. As already pointed out, it first occurs in Bede.
And if the anonymous expositor of the Roman Mass, previously noticed, and to be noticed again shortly, wrote before
A.D. 800, he may be merely repeating Bede, when he uses it
himself, not quoting it from the Canon. In all the liturgical
tracts printed among the works of Alcuin, considerable reserve is shown in quoting any part of the Canon, beyond the
first two or three words of a paragraph, as though its precise
form was not yet settled in France: while the quotation
from it at greater length in the Caroline Books [2] seems to
indicate that their author pointedly declined endorsing any
part of this sentence given in Bede: and a corresponding
omission of ' hunc præclarum ' before *calicem* seems to prove
that either this epithet had not as yet found its way there,
or that he refused admission to it as unscriptural. Agobard,
who became Bishop of Lyons two years after the death of
Charlemagne, quotes it as forming part of the Canon in

---

[1] Above, c iv It is strange that Daniel should not have perceived either the historical argument personal to S Gregory or this broad fact Part i c 1 Adnot 12

[2] 'Accepto pane, benedicto ac fracto, hoc salutare discipulis dedit præceptum Accipite, inquit, et manducate ; hoc est corpus meum Similiter et calicem, postquam cœnavit, accipiens, dedit discipulis suis dicens: Accipite et bibite ; hic enim est calix sanguinis mei novi et æterni testamenti, qui pro vobis et pro multis effundetur in remissionem peccatorum Hæc quotiescunque feceritis, in mei memoriam facietis' As this last part is so faithfully given, it certainly looks as though the first part was a correction (ii. 27)

France when he wrote against Amalarius,[1] but this is the earliest explicit mention of it in this connection. If imported into the Canon from Bede, it would account for the well-known epithet since given to him by common consent. A third point, occasioning no small perplexity to Daniel,[2] is that the 'Memento' for the dead is omitted in the Gelasian Canon altogether: and in several MSS. of the Gregorian too. Still, knowing as much of S. Gregory from his own writings as we do, we can hardly think that he would have passed three years at Constantinople, with the liturgies of S. Chrysostom and the supposed Clement to glean from, and left his own liturgy without a prayer of this kind in revising it.

We come next to the wonderful prayer beginning: 'Supplices Te rogamus,' and containing the phrase 'per manus Angeli Tui,' to which the epithet 'sancti' seems to have been soon appended, but which nobody till now has succeeded in explaining, as it stands, satisfactorily. Mr. Maskell says of it: 'Upon the meaning of this passage in this very ancient prayer there is great variety of opinion. Some refer it, but, I think, scarcely with sufficient reason, to our blessed Lord Himself, as "*the angel*, per excellentiam Angelus: sanctus Dei Angelus," &c. Pope Innocent has said well: "Tantæ sunt profunditatis hæc verba ut nulla acies humani ingenii tanta sit ut ea penetrare possit." And, again, according to another Bishop of Rome, quoted also by the Ritualists: " Quis enim fidelium,"[3] &c.' being a passage quoted in a previous page from S. Gregory.[4]

The question is, Was the Roman Canon indebted for this prayer to S. Gregory? There cannot, it may be said confidently, be very much doubt that it was, though it has been altered and differently placed since: and the ground for both statements is of singular interest. First, it is based upon two passages of the supposed Clement: as though designed

---

[1] *Adv Amal* c 14
[2] Ib. Annot 22
[3] *Ancient Lit* 1 100
[4] Above, p 117

to explain one by the other. The long intercessory prayer after consecration ended, the deacon says:—[1]

'Let us, moreover, beseech God through His Christ, on behalf of the gift that has been conveyed to the Lord God let us beseech, that the good God would receive the same through the mediation of His Christ on His altar in heaven for a sweet-smelling odour.'

'Conveyed,' but conveyed by whom? Perhaps the ambiguity was intentional—like many similar expressions respecting Christ in this liturgy. The natural inference from the words as they stand, and from other parts of the context elsewhere, would be that writer makes *Christ bearer* of His own body hither. This is at once toned down, and expressed in the Roman Canon more plainly by the phrase: 'per manus Angeli Tui,' which may well have come from S. Gregory. Who could have suggested this phrase to him? Who but the supposed Clement once more, by designating Christ 'the angel of great counsel' in his Preface? Stated nakedly, this may be called a mere conjecture: but let account be taken of the following fact, and it can hardly fail to command assent. 'Angel of great counsel' are not the words of the Hebrew, nor of the Vulgate, but of the LXX alone.

Now, S. Gregory seldom deserts the Vulgate for the Hebrew or the LXX, probably not above twenty times in all: and Isaiah ix. 6 is twice quoted by him in other parts of his works according to the Vulgate, whose rendering of it is different: but in the first chapter of the twenty-fourth book on Job, the work on which he was engaged *at Constantinople*, he asks *à propos* to Job xxx. 23-4 translated according to the Vulgate, though with a different reading of one word from the received text now: [2] 'Quis est iste angelus, nisi Ille qui per prophetam dicitur *Magni consilii angelus*?' and then dilates on His character as such. As he never again quotes the LXX rendering of this verse, and

[1] Hammond, ib. p 12   [2] *Similibus* for 'millibus.'

as the book on which he was then commenting lay open before him in the Vulgate, and is never once quoted by him according to the LXX, it is at least probable that the version of the LXX was in this case suggested to him *by something that he was then reading in his leisure hours*: and what more likely than this Preface of the supposed Clement, from whom he certainly must have borrowed this prayer and this phrase, for neither S. Basil nor S. Chrysostom can be quoted for them in this connection?[1]

But a still wider question has yet to be asked respecting this prayer. Was it cast in the same mould and given the same place by S. Gregory that it had in the Canon on which Amalarius commented, and has still in the Roman of our own times? There are grave reasons for supposing that, cast in the same mould or not, it had a different place given to it by S. Gregory, and was understood by him in a corresponding sense. First of all, in the exposition of the Roman Mass printed by Martene,[2] and which according to him is contained in a MS. of the eighth century, we have the Canon epitomised in a way that tells another tale.

On the conclusion of what is now called the Preface, the author of this tract says: 'Amid profound silence, the priest with his mind fixed upon God, proceeds to consecrate the host . . . making mention of the Blessed Virgin, Apostles, and martyrs, by whose prayers and good offices he trusts to be assisted . . . and then further prays the Lord to accept of His clemency the offering of His whole family and *command it to be borne by the hands of His holy angel to His altar on high*, and grant that our days may be disposed

---

[1] Hammond, ib p 117; reproduced p 124

[2] 'Hanc enim,' he says of it, writing in A D 1700, 'nongentos annos superare credimus, scriptamque prius quam in Gallis liturgiæ Romanæ ritus inveherentur' *De Ant Rit* i 4, art 11 It was found in the monastery dedicated to S. Albinus at Angers, over which see he presided in the sixth century, being himself of English extraction, as Butler informs us (*Lives of the Saints*, March 1) He explains the title given to this exposition 'Ad distinctionem aliarum liturgiarum, quæ erant tunc in usu, et maxime Gallicanæ'

in His peace: and that we may be rescued from eternal damnation, and included in the number of His elect.'

After this, he comes to speak of, and comment upon, the recital of the acts and words of our Lord, as a thing *next to be described*, and then, in conclusion, offers the following reflections to his readers. (1) That they should consider what a sacrifice this is, which *imitates* continually the passion of the only-begotten Son for their forgiveness. (2) That they need not trouble themselves about the character of the celebrant, as it is the Holy Ghost who mystically vivifies this oblation. (3) That silence pervades the church while the elements are being consecrated: 'quia *Sanctus in iis manens Spiritus eundem sacramentorum latenter operatur effectum*; unde et Græce mysterium dicitur.'

S. Gregory might quite well have written all that has been quoted from this exposition himself: it harmonises with his teaching and that of the Fathers: it attributes consecration of the elements distinctly to the action of the Holy Ghost, it makes the prayer on which we are now engaged a prayer for His action, understanding him to be ' the angel,' or messenger of the Father and the Son *pro hac re*—just the sense which there is every reason to think S. Gregory might have suggested himself—and makes it precede, *not* follow, the recital of the words and acts of our Lord, yet without the slightest allusion to controversies which, had they been in being when this exposition was penned, the writer could not have failed to have noticed.

The weak point in his testimony is that he has withheld his name. Anonymous compositions require to be confirmed by documents that have names to them and can be dated. S. Gregory was not alone when he was at Constantinople, but there was a Western there with whom he became so intimate that he commenced writing his own voluminous commentaries on the Book of Job at his suggestion, and it was a friendship that led to frequent correspondence between them afterwards,[1] and was continued through life. This friend was Leander, who became Metropolitan of Seville, and was succeeded by his brother S. Isidore, with whom, according to Mariana, quoted approvingly by Cardinal Bona,[2] the Mozarabic rite originated, some things in it being due to his brother Leander, who, S. Isidore tells us himself, had made the offices of the Church his special study.[3] Bearing this in mind, if we compare the Mozarabic liturgy with the description, given in a former chapter from S. Isidore, of the liturgy then used in Spain, which he derived from S. Peter—meaning probably the supposed Clement, whose liturgy Leander had employed in revising it—we shall see that what he there calls the 'conformatio sacramenti,' and what answers to it in the Mozarabic rite, is a compound of two distinct things, of which he names only the first as constituting the sacrament; or, in his own words, 'the seventh and last prayers, that the oblation then offered to God, being sanctified by the Holy Ghost, may be conformed to the body and blood of the Redeemer.' How, then, is this expressed in the Mozarabic rite? It deserves to be stated in its own words:— [4]

'Be present, be present in our midst, O good High Priest Jesus, as Thou wast in the midst of Thy disciples. Sanctify this oblation that we may receive the things sanctified in it by the hands of Thy holy angel, O Redeemer, Eternal and Holy Lord.

'Our Lord Jesus Christ the same night in which He was betrayed took bread and, giving thanks, blest, brake, and gave to His disciples, saying, "Take and eat: this is My body which is about to be given for you. Do this, as oft as ye shall eat thereof, in My remembrance." Likewise the cup after supper, saying, "This is the cup of the New Testament in My blood, which is shed for you and for many

---

[1] S Greg. *Ep.* lib. 1. 43, v. 49, ix 121, ed Ben.
[2] *Rer Liturg* 1 11
[3] *De Script Eccl* s v
[4] Daniel, *Cod. Liturg* part 1 87-9

for the remission of sins. Do this, as often as ye shall drink thereof, in My remembrance."'

Let us now restore the prayer 'Supplices Te rogamus' of the Roman liturgy to the place broadly given to it in the Exposition of the Roman Mass said to belong to the eighth century: that is, making it immediately follow the three sentences acknowledged to have been the work of S. Gregory, and be followed immediately by the recital of the acts and words of our Lord, as in the Mozarabic, and then comment on both.

'We most humbly beseech Thee, Almighty God, to command these things to be carried by the hands of Thy holy angel to Thy altar on high, in sight of Thy Divine Majesty, that as many as shall partake of the most sacred body and blood of Thy Son at this altar may be filled with every grace and heavenly blessing, through the same Christ our Lord:

'Who in the same night in which He was betrayed,' &c.

To effect this restoration, a well-known paragraph of the existing Canon, 'Quam oblationem Tu, Deus,' &c., has been omitted. Strong presumptive evidence will be adduced further on, showing that this paragraph was inserted when the above prayer was displaced.

For the present let us restrict ourselves to a close survey of the contrast and resemblance presented between the two revisions of their respective Canons by the two friends. First, let us say of the Mozarabic that it presents numerous other marks of affinity with Eastern liturgies besides this prayer[1]—exactly what S. Gregory tells us himself of the Roman. Secondly, that S. Isidore recognises a distinct epiklesis, or invocation of the Holy Ghost, in it, by which he can only mean the above prayer beginning, 'Be present, be present, &c.' just quoted, in which it is the Son, not the Father, who is addressed, and addressed to sanctify the oblation,

[1] *Dict. of Christian Biog.* ii. 1029.

that His people might receive the things sanctified in it *by the hands of His holy angel.*

This may seem at first sight a strange transformation of the patristic epiklesis ; but, before passing judgment on it, let us recall who Leander was. Leander was a prominent member of the third Council of Toledo, A.D. 589, which added ' Filioque ' to the Constantinopolitan Creed. He has, therefore, remodelled this prayer in the Canon clearly to suit the altered Creed—remodelling it, too, with all the freedom which characterised the proceedings of those Spanish bishops in respect of the Creed, and also making it symbolise their teaching. For they declared, in altering the Creed, that the Holy Ghost in a certain sense proceeds from the Son as well as the Father : that is, in so far as He is said in Scripture to be sent by both. And the author of this portion of the Mozarabic rite similarly goes along with the supposed Clement, in making 'the narrative of the institution' form part of his Canon : but with equal independence maintains the epiklesis in its old place, while giving it a new form based on the new form given to the Creed in the country where that rite prevailed. The Father had hitherto been invoked to send the Holy Ghost from heaven to sanctify the oblation : the Son now being invoked to come and do this Himself, *with* the Holy Ghost for His minister—in the spirit of the Creed—the title by which the Son had been, according to the LXX version of the prophet Isaiah, designated in relation to the Father, might with equal propriety be transferred to the Holy Ghost, in relation to the Son. And there was authority for this in the Latin and Greek Fathers, who had long ago designated the Holy Ghost *vicar* of the Son or of Christ.

S. Gregory, like Leander, went along with the supposed Clement in making 'the narrative of the institution' form part of his Canon ; yet he, too, with equal independence, maintained the epiklesis in its old place, while giving to it a form elaborated by himself, as more consonant with antiquity than that of his friend; so far agreeing with him, indeed, as to designate the Holy Ghost by the same title, but far transcending him in petitioning the Father for the descent of His Holy Messenger—in other words, the Holy Ghost—that the elements might be carried up by His hands to the altar on high where the Son ministered Himself, before the throne of the ineffable Godhead, to be consecrated there, that the union between the faithful on earth and the body which His Son bore for their sake might be consummated in His sight.

Surely there can be no longer any doubt, after this striking comparison, what place S. Gregory gave to this exquisite prayer in his revision, for it is indicated by the place given by his friend to his own version of the same prayer in his. The link between the two prayers stands out in the remarkable phrase, 'by the hands of Thy holy angel,' which is common to both and determines the meaning of both, as well as harmonises their apparent divergence both of petition and address, which is further explained by reference to the standpoint of each author.

All that remains to be shown is that the place given by S. Gregory to this prayer was continued to it for centuries after his death in his own Church, and what was substituted for it when it was removed to the place which it now holds in the Roman liturgy.

Of indirect proof—of facts presupposing and interpreted by this fact—we shall find no lack as we proceed; but there are two remarkable testimonies which for their explicitness and extreme relevancy may be produced at once and be left to speak for themselves almost without comment: (1) in the last letter of the Caroline Codex, which is a letter of Adrian I. to Charlemagne, and has been dated A.D. 791, the Pope tells the King that he had just sent off a copy of the Gregorian Sacramentary to him at his request. This accordingly must have been a genuine copy, coming from the Pontiff himself and from Rome. The Caroline Books, as they were submitted to the Council of Frankfort by the King three years later, must have been commenced very soon after the receipt by him of this Sacramentary. The subject of the Eucharist is brought forward in illustration of their theme several times in these books, and its consecration is described three times by their author in almost identic terms, but he never once refers it to the 'words of institution' as they are called. 'Per manum sacerdotis, et invocatione Divini Nominis,' is his account of it the first time; and there the priest is represented at the altar in his official dress, offering over the elements the very prayer with which we are concerned, after briefly commemorating the passion, resurrection, and ascension of our Saviour, but without any reference to His acts and words at the Last Supper. These follow much in the form given to them in the Roman Canon, but a long way off; and in another paragraph, where they are recited without any bearing on consecration whatever.

It is just possible that in making the commemoration of the passion, resurrection, and ascension of our Lord *a prelude* to this prayer, the writer may have been thinking of the order observed in the Alexandrian liturgy described by S. Cyril in his seventh anathema, to which reference has been already made and will again be made further on. But, be that as it may, this passage furnishes decisive testimony both to the position and the effect ascribed by the writer of it to this prayer, as he read it in the Gregorian Sacramentary just received from the Pope.

(2) The second passage not merely corroborates the first, but makes its entire meaning plain. Paschasius, in his work on the Eucharist that caused so much stir and on which we shall find so much to say in its proper place, recites part of this prayer twice, and the first time he recites it he gives it the place which it then occupied in the Roman Canon. That his words may not lose by being given in English, they shall be set down as they stand:—

'Unde sacerdos, cum hæc incipit immolare, inter cætera,

"Jube," inquit, "hæc perferri per manus angeli sancti Tui in sublime altare Tuum, in conspectu Majestatis Tuæ.'

Cum hæc incipit immolare: 'when he begins to consecrate the elements:' no other meaning can be assigned to these words. He thus bears out all that had been extracted from the anonymous Expositor, from the Mozarabic Canon, and from the Caroline Books, both as to the place then occupied in the Roman Canon by this prayer, and to the effect ascribed to it in each case. For Paschasius himself in the earlier part of his work testifies again and again to the action of the Holy Ghost on the elements, as will be shown abundantly when we come to his work.

And that it was according to the Gregorian Canon that the Eucharist was then consecrated in his monastery may be considered shown incidentally by what passed between Amalarius and Gregory IV. during his second visit to Rome. Amalarius petitioned for copies of the Antiphonary then in use there: the Pope replied that he had none left, as the Abbot of Corbey, where Paschasius was monk when the first edition of his work appeared, had previously carried away with him every copy that could be spared into France. Wala, the then Abbot of Corbey, was a great man, being first cousin to Charlemagne, and if he was so anxious for his monks to be provided with authentic copies of the Roman Antiphonary for saying their office, would he not have been much more anxious that they should possess authentic copies of the Canon, as it was used at Rome, for celebrating Mass? We need not go farther into this matter for the present. We may consider that the true character of the Roman Canon has at length been brought to light, as it left the hands of S. Gregory—that he was certainly not the person who denuded it of all traces of the Catholic epiklesis, but, on the contrary, that, in full accord with his friend Leander, he decided on retaining it in the place which it had always occupied, only recasting it in a new and more transcendent form—petitioning, *not* for the Son to come down, but for the Holy Ghost to be sent as His angel or messenger to raise the oblation of His Church on earth aloft to His altar on high, for union with His glorified body : and raise the souls of the faithful heavenwards, for incorporation with it there too. ' Summis ima sociari, terrena cœlestibus jungi, unumque ex invisibilibus atque visibilibus fieri '[1]—in his own sublime words elsewhere—probably commenting on this very prayer. Had this prayer never been moved out of the place assigned it by him, there would never have been any disputes about the Eucharist in the West.

Moderns are sorely puzzled what to say of this prayer in its present place. As it occurs *after* consecration and not before, people may say, what are we to understand by *hæc*? Certainly that little word supplies one more proof that it was meant to precede consecration, when ' hæc ' would naturally mean the elements, which it frequently designates at an earlier stage. After consecration, it creates an obvious difficulty : ' *not* Christ's body,' says Menard,[2] ' but the memory of His passion'! Durandus, though he invokes S. Gregory to assist in explaining it, prefers understanding by it ' the prayers of the faithful '! Further on, Paschasius is introduced as S. Augustine, saying what even Paschasius has *not* said.[3] Cardinal Bona tries to parry the objection of the Greeks to the words of this prayer after consecration, by taking refuge in the long since disused survivals of the old epiklesis in the West, particularly the Mozarabic rite, whose Canon however he passes over in silence.[4]

We, who have gone through this question historically so far, may still from these fragmentary remains published by Mabillon and others under various names—examined impartially for the light they throw on the past, and without discussing whether the names given to each of them are wholly correct or not—be not only confirmed in the conclusions at which we have arrived already respecting the Roman

---

[1] Above, p 117.
[2] *Ad Lib. Sacram S. Greg.* note 67
[3] *Ration.* iv. 44.
[4] *Rer. Liturg* ii. 13, 4–5.

Canon, but shall also see the steps by which it slowly passed into what it has become now. What, for instance, must consecration have been in the Gothic or Gotho-Gallican Missal for ordinary days, when in the Mass for Easter-eve we read immediately 'post Sanctus'—that is, after the Preface —the following prayer?—[1]

'At Thy command, O Lord, all things in heaven and earth, in the sea and its abyss, were framed. To Thee patriarchs, prophets, apostles, martyrs, confessors, and all saints give thanks. Which we doing ourselves also, beseech Thee favourably to receive these spiritual and devout offerings of bread and wine, praying further, that Thou wouldst bless this sacrifice with Thy benediction, and pour down upon it the dew of Thy Holy Spirit, that it may be to us all a proper Eucharist, such as Thou hast ordained through Christ our Lord: Who in the same night,' &c.

Who can deny this to be the *epiklesis* of all primitive liturgies used at every celebration, and not on great festivals alone, and in this case that of the Churches in the south of France, where the Goths ruled. The 'qui pridie' marks the introduction of another Canon into those parts, which harmonised with the old form for a time well enough as in the Mozarabic liturgy. Then, when the new Canon was revised, the question was, what should be done with this prayer? In no other, accordingly, but this one Mass, is it maintained in its original place. In others it is placed at one time, slightly changed, 'post mysterium,' that is, *after consecration* [2]: like the 'Supplices Te rogamus,' &c. of the Roman. At another, 'post secreta,' viz. after prayers said secretly to himself by the celebrant, now said just before the Preface.[3] In others it disappears altogether, or is superseded by a prayer less decided in tone.[4] In the

---

[1] It may be read in Muratori, *Liturg Rom* ii 594; or Mabill *De Lit. Gallic* iii 251.
[2] Mass for the Chair of S. Peter; in that for the Assumption it appears in another form.
[3] Mass for the Circumcision and for S Leodegar
[4] Masses for the beginning of Lent, for the Tradition of the Creed, and for Sunday.

'Missale Francorum' it has no place given to it, and why? Simply because the Canon printed at the end is later than that of S. Gregory, though not entirely word for word with what Muratori prints as the Gregorian.

In the 'Vetus Missale Gallicanum' this prayer reappears twice 'post secreta,'[1] but in a changed form: possibly copied from Spain, for it runs thus:—

'Almighty God, we pray Thee, cause Thy holy Word to descend on these things which we offer to Thee; cause the inestimable Spirit of Thy glory to descend on them; cause the gift of Thine old largess to descend on them; that our oblation may be made a spiritual sacrifice, sweet-smelling and acceptable; and that Thine invincible right arm may defend us Thy servants through the blood of Christ.'

In the Missa Latina, printed by Flaccus Illyricus, and by Cardinal Bona reprinted as 'Missa Romana variis orationibus interpolata,' a strange composite figures for this prayer in a new place—while the elements are being incensed—yet testifying in its very fragments to its antiquity.[2] Specimens of this kind might be multiplied: but let this one suffice.

The last flickers of a lamp are painfully symbolical of the expiring testimonies to the Catholic epiklesis in the West. S. Gregory I., Venerable Bede, Alcuin, even the Caroline Books, S. Agobard and his friend S. Bernard, Theodulph, all dwell upon it as a matter of course, to the exclusion of any different teaching. After Agobard, those who handed on the torch as they received it are few and far between. In the hands of the rest it waned, wavered, and at last went out.

---

[1] Flaccus Illyricus assumes that it was in general use A D 700 and onwards, till displaced by the Roman, which it may have been interpolated to suit The prayer as given by Bona runs as follows 'Memores sumus, æterne Deus, Pater omnipotens, gloriosissimæ passionis Filii Tui, resurrectionis etiam Ejus, et ascensionem Ejus in cœlum. Petimus ergo Majestatem Tuam, ut ascendant preces humilitatis nostræ unà cum incenso isto in conspectum clementiæ Tuæ, et descendat super hunc panem et calicem plenitudo Divinitatis Descendat etiam, Domine, illa Sancti Spiritûs incomprehensibilis Majestas, sicut quondam in Patrum hostias descendebat ..'

[2] *Rer. Liturg* append. i. 549.

Their aberrations, as they would only cause confusion here, will be best adjourned for separate consideration in a separate chapter. The minority, who clung to the teaching of their predecessors, and whose writings are still extant, consisted of two monks of Corbey in France, a great archbishop in Germany, a monk of S. Albans, and a great archbishop in England—five in all. The writings of all but the last have met with rough handling in modern times for their contents, yet they merely repeat what had been said ages before by the Fathers, to whose very words they adhere. Druthmar, for instance, who seems to have flourished in the fifth decade of the ninth century, says, commenting on S. Matthew xxvi. 26 :—[1]

'He gave the sacrament of His body to His disciples for remission of sins and promotion of love, that, remembering His deed, they might continue to do this *in figure*, never forgetting what He was about to do for them in act. "This is My body:" that is, *in sacramento*. Then "taking the cup, He gave thanks and gave to them, saying" . . . Bread and wine being pre-eminent among all the aliments of life for strengthening and refreshing our weakness, it pleased Him with good reason to employ both as a means of confirming the mystery to us of His sacrament. For wine both exhilarates and increases the blood. Accordingly, the blood of Christ is not improperly symbolised by it: since whatever comes to us from Him makes us overflow with true joy, and increases all our good. As, then, one departing into foreign lands leaves pledges of his love behind him to those by whom he is loved, so God ordained that it should be done by us, Himself making *a spiritual transfer* of bread for body, and of wine for blood: that by these two things we might remember what He had done for us with His body and with His blood, and never fail in gratitude to Him for such unbounded love.'

Druthmar must have been alone with the early Fathers

[1] Ap. Migne, *Pat Lat.* cvi. 1476.

in his cell when he penned these words, in deep unconsciousness of the storm that was beginning to gather in cells not far removed. Ratramn, an inmate of one of them, must have been called upon about the same time by Charles the Bald to let him know, in the tract written at his command, on which side the truth lay. Ratramn, having to speak to the merits of the controversy, could not avoid, of course, making his tract in the main controversial: but into this aspect of it we need not be drawn now: except just so far as to state that the question put to him by the King, to whom he dedicates his work, was: 'Quod in ecclesiâ ore fidelium sumitur . . . in mysterio fiat, an in veritate.'[1] To understand his argument properly, we must know what his thesis was. For, as he rests his conclusions on what he quotes from the Fathers and from Scripture, we can easily gather from his remarks on each quotation what his own views, apart from controversy, must have been.

Here, then, is what he understands S. Ambrose to teach:—[2]

'S. Ambrose saith, that in that mystery of the body and blood of Christ a change is made: and *that* a wondrous *change, because divine*: and ineffable because incomprehensible. Let them who will take nothing here according to any hidden virtue, but will weigh everything as it outwardly appeareth—let them say, in what respect it is here made! For, in respect of the substance of the creatures, *they are after consecration what they were before*. Bread and wine they were before: and after consecration they are seen to remain of the same nature. So that a change hath inwardly been wrought by the *mighty power of the Holy Spirit*: and this is that which faith gazeth upon; this is that which feedeth the soul; this is that which ministereth the substance of eternal life.'

Let it be remembered that in thus interpreting S

---

[1] § 5
[2] § 54, Migne, *Pat. Lat* cxxi 148; comp the *Book of Ratramn*, &c. Oxford, Parker, 1838, p 28.

Ambrose, Ratramn merely reiterates the deliberate teaching of a very great Pope;[1] with whom, and not only S. Ambrose, but S. Isidore and S. Augustine, before quoted by him to the same effect, he is in perfect accord.

If the great Bishop of Mayence, Rabanus Maurus, is not as explicit as Ratramn in expounding his authorities, it is because, living in perilous times, he prefers quoting them in much greater fulness, so as to make their teaching his own. For this he was absurdly traduced in the next generation as an unprincipled plagiarist, who stole from others on purpose to pass for the author of what they had written. We need pursue the subject no further at present. In his principal work, 'On the Universe,' he repeats word for word with approval all that was quoted from S. Isidore some chapters back.[2] In his commentaries on Exodus he repeats S. Gregory first, and after him S. Gaudentius, quoted above likewise. In his work 'De Institutione Clericorum,' we have S. Isidore largely quoted again in B. i. c. 31; and in the 'Ordo Missæ' which forms the next chapter, consecration is mentioned with marked brevity and absence of details: the words of institution having been quoted in the preceding chapter as they 'are read,' not in the Canon, but 'in the Gospel.' Further, in describing what parts of the Canon were due to what Popes, he says nothing about S. Alexander I. or 'the passion.' Yet this order, he says—agreeably with S. Isidore—was handed down by apostolic men to the Roman Church, almost all Churches in the West preserving the same tradition. The 'Additio de Missâ,' with which this book closes, may well be thought due to a later hand, as it commences with a sentence taken word for word from Amalarius. And, more so still, the 'Ordo Missæ' which comes last in a further tract addressed to Thiotmar, and entitled 'De Sacris Ordinibus,' which consists, with two exceptions, of extracts from this work, and actually repeats its 'Ordo Missæ' till the offertory is reached. From this point it departs to comment

[1] Above, p. 119.　　　　　　　　　[2] C. iv

with a minuteness and in a style foreign to Rabanus, on clause after clause of what is now printed as the Gregorian Canon, only going a step further, and commenting on 'Ite, missa est,' and the response 'Deo gratias,' as its conclusion.

A letter or tract of his addressed to Eigilus, Abbot of Prum, on the controversy which had just arisen is no longer extant, though Mabillon thought he had identified it with an anonymous tract of inferior stamp printed by him from a Gemblours MS.[1]

We pass from foreigners to two household names, separated, indeed, in point of time by more than a century, and by race and probably by station too, but in perfect agreement on the point which concerns us here, though controversy was then at its height. Ælfric the Anglo-Saxon, 'monk and mass-priest' as he calls himself, and S. Anselm, a native of Savoy, who studied under Lanfranc, an Italian, and succeeded him first as Abbot of Bec in Normandy and later as Archbishop of Canterbury. Ælfric completed his education at Winchester in the celebrated school of its then Bishop Ethelwold. By his successor Elphege he was transferred to the Abbey of Cerne in Dorsetshire, that had just been endowed there, A.D. 987, and was in want of a head. He composed, or rather compiled, while there two sets of homilies to be recited in church during the year—each set containing forty[2]—dedicating them to Sigeric or Siricius, Archbishop of Canterbury, by whom they were approved and authorised for use. It is with these, not with his subsequent history,[3] that our business lies. They were translated by the late Mr. Thorpe and fill two volumes.

---

[1] Gieseler, *E H*, Per. III div. 1 § 14, whose notes there, and on Dio. II § 29, cover the whole ground. A fragment of a ninth or tenth century MS at Avranches, printed in the *Report of M Ravisson* (Paris, 1841, app XII), may well be thought to be part of this missing letter, not only from its contents, but also from the furious way in which its last page has been so scratched through as to be no longer legible

[2] Preface to the second set Thorpe, II 3.

[3] For which see Soames' *Anglo-Saxon Ch*, p 184 *et seq* ; Lingard's *Anglo-Saxon Ch*, II 310-20, and then pp. 452-77

Before proceeding to quote from them, however, several facts, ancient and modern, should be recalled: (1) that Ælfric was junior by 250 years at least to Bede; (2) that, as Mr. Warren truly remarks in his excellent Introduction to the Bodleian gem of this species—Leofric's Missal [1]— 'considerable alterations had taken place in the Roman Office-books since the time of Charlemagne'; (3) that 'immense numbers of codices'—of the said Office-books— 'written by his order had been dispersed about everywhere'; (4) that of what is now called the Gregorian Canon 'no MS. has yet been shown earlier than his time'; (5) that 'all the important codices printed or collated of it were written north of the Alps and mostly within what was then France.' It must, therefore, be taken for granted (6) that it was used exclusively throughout England very soon after his time, so that all traditionary reminiscences of any prayer for the descent of the Holy Ghost on the elements must have been extinguished in the minds of those who recited it a full century before Ælfric was born. It follows, accordingly, that we must not look for any distinct reference to it in his homilies, which were drawn mainly from his own experiences, or from the writings of late ninth-century divines. Nevertheless, if his homilies are carefully searched for that purpose, it will be found presupposed in them all through; (7) his modern commentators, one and all, blind to this fact, have frequently misconstrued his meaning.

In his sermon on the Nativity, which is the second of the first set, he says:—[2]

'Bethlehem is interpreted *Bread-house,* and in it was Christ, the true bread, brought forth. . . . This holy bread we taste when we with faith go to housel, because the holy housel is *spiritually* Christ's body, and through that we are redeemed from eternal death.'

---

[1] Of this the part he marks A is a Gregorian Sacramentary, written, according to him, in Lotharingia early in the tenth century. Leofric accompanied Edward the Confessor into England A D 1042, and between that and 1050 was installed Bishop of Exeter (*Introd.* pp. xx xxvi. and xxvii)

[2] Thorpe, 1 25

In the next sermon, which is on S. Stephen's Day, we are told:—[1]

'Our spiritual gifts are our prayers and hymns and housel-hallowing and every other gift that we offer to God, which we should give to God with peaceful heart and brotherly love.'

Again on the Lord's Prayer:—[2]

'The ghostly bread is the commandment of God, on which we should daily meditate and with works fulfil. . . . The ghostly bread is also the holy housel with which we confirm our belief, and through partaking of the holy housel our sins will be forgiven us, and we shall be strengthened against the temptations of the devil.'

One clue to this teaching is supplied on the seventeenth Sunday after Pentecost:—[3]

'There is no forgiveness of sins, but through the Holy Ghost. . . . Verily the work of the Holy Trinity is ever indivisible, yet all forgiveness belongs to the Holy Ghost, as birth belongs to Christ alone.'

Or, as on the Epiphany:—[4]

'Baptism washes us from all sins: housel hallows us: true penance heals our misdeeds.'

Passing from these to the often-quoted sermon for 'the Easterday sacrifice,' we get a still plainer clue to their meaning in a passage that should have been detached from its place near the end and made to serve for a general introduction to the whole:—

'We would have long since treated of the lamb which the old Israel offered at their Eastertide, but we would first relate to you concerning this mystery and afterwards how it is to be eaten. . . . The people of Israel were not accustomed to raw flesh, though God commanded them not to eat it raw nor sodden with water, but roasted at the fire. He will partake of God's body raw who without reason

---

[1] Thorpe, 1. 55.   [2] Ib. 266-7.   [3] Ib. 500-1.   [4] Ib. 11. 49

weens that He was a simple man like unto us and not God. And he who, according to human wisdom, will inquire into the mystery of Christ's Incarnation does as though he seethed the flesh of the lamb in water, for water in this place betokens human knowledge. But we are to know that *all the mysteries of Christ's humanity* were ordained through the might of the Holy Ghost. Hence [1] eat we His body roasted at the fire, because the Holy Ghost came in form of fire to the Apostles in various tongues.'

This comes to us direct from the Fathers, particularly S. Gaudentius and S. Gregory, and explains exactly what he means in various passages occurring earlier in his address, e.g. :—

'The people of Israel ate the flesh of the lamb at their Eastertide when they were delivered, and we now partake *spiritually* of Christ's body and drink His blood when with true belief we partake of the holy housel. . . .

'Certain men have often inquired, and yet frequently inquire, how the bread which is prepared from corn and baked by the heat of the fire can be changed to Christ's body, or the wine which is wrung from many berries can by any blessing be changed to the Lord's blood. . . .

'Without they appear bread and wine, both in aspect and in taste, but they *are truly*, after the hallowing, Christ's body and His blood *through a ghostly mystery*. A heathen child is baptised, but it varies not its aspect without, though it be changed within. . . .

'Great is the difference between the invisible might of the holy housel and the visible appearance of its own nature By nature it is corruptible bread and corruptible wine, and is by the power of the Divine Word truly Christ's body and His blood—not, however, bodily, but spiritually. . . .

'This mystery is a pledge and a symbol . . . . but it is, as we before said, Christ's body and His blood—not bodily,

---

[1] Thorpe, 'then,' ib 281.

but *spiritually*. Ye are not to inquire how it is done, but to hold it in your belief that it is so done.'[1]

This is his honest refrain all through. Now and then he cannot avoid arguing as a controversialist, but in general his expressions are strictly drawn from the Fathers, and where we might expect he would quote the Canon he quotes Scripture. The bread and wine by being hallowed become what Christ declared them to be, the Holy Ghost at every celebration giving effect to His words. For 'all the mysteries of Christ's humanity were ordained through the might of the Holy Ghost.' The sacrament of the altar, no less than that of the font, has an outward as well as an inward part, so that we may speak of it in two different senses with perfect truth and call it by names applicable to what is seen or to what is unseen. In all this Ælfric is in marked contrast to Amalarius (as will be shown in the next chapter), whom he nevertheless calls 'a wise doctor' in his homily for Septuagesima Sunday,[2] and speaks with approval of his 'book on ecclesiastical customs and services of yearly recurrence.' But, on the other hand, he is in distinct accord with his native traditions; for among the extracts given by Martene from the two oldest Anglo-Saxon Pontificals that have come down to us we read, in a MS. dated A.D. 800 by him, of that of Egbert, Archbishop of York, a prayer for consecrating the altar after dressing it, to this effect:—

'Let Thy Holy Spirit, O Lord our God, we beseech Thee, descend on this altar, that He may sanctify the oblations of Thy people, and worthily cleanse the hearts of those who are partakers of them.'

In a longer prayer for commencing its consecration we read:—

'May the libations (of the chalice) on these *tables* be acceptable to Thee, may they be well-pleasing, and always replete with the dew of Thy Holy Spirit . . .'

---

[1] Ib pp. 267-77 The Catechism of the Council of Trent, quoted in a note further on, repeats the last sentence word for word here quoted from him.

[2] Ib. ii. 85.

ANGLO-SAXON LITURGIES. 273

In another prayer preceding its consecration:—

'O Holy Lord, Almighty Father, Eternal God, mercifully and favourably deign to hear our humble prayers, and look down on the holocaust of these altars: that, not being consummated by visible fire, but by the pouring out of Thy Holy Spirit, it may ascend a sweet-smelling odour, and become a Eucharist of healing to all worthy partakers of the same, to their eternal salvation.'

For consecrating the corporal, the consecrator says:—

'Look down, O God, who desirest that we should imitate the devotion of those who serve Thee worthily: and bless this corporal and these linen cloths set apart to the uses of Thy service: sanctify, purify, consecrate them, with the power of Thy heavenly benediction: and may Thy Holy Spirit descend on them that He may bless the oblations of Thy people: and graciously perfect the hearts and bodies of the receivers of them.'[1]

As Mr. Maskell points out, this Pontifical has only been edited in part by Martene, so that we cannot be certain what Canon it contained. If its Canon was the so-called Gregorian, these extracts plainly testify to a disused Canon of older date, where the epiklesis, or invocation, of the Holy Ghost, occupied the place and fulfilled the purpose assigned to it in the primitive Church.

The other Pontifical, also dated A.D. 800 by Martene— that is, 900 years old in 1700, when his work was published, which Mr. Soames, whose translation of a part of it will be used presently, mistakes for A.D. 900—certainly contains interpolations, the chief of which is printed in capitals by Martene.[2] But, on the other hand, it makes up amply for them by retaining the old form intact for consecrating both the paten and chalice; which we are left to guess in the

---

[1] Martene, *De Ant. Rit.* ii 13, Ord. ii Most of them are likewise given by Mr Maskell, *Monum Rit. Eccl Angl* i. 150-1 or 162 *et seq.*

[2] Ib p 263 It occurs at the end of the fourth form of the '*benedictio tabulæ,*' 4to ed

T

MS. of the other Pontifical, unless it is Martene to whom we owe the '&c.'[1] This MS. was in the hands of the monks of Jumièges in Normandy when Martene discovered it, possibly where it was written. 'In this venerable formulary,' says Mr. Soames, 'the bishop says in consecrating the paten:—
'"God who, after the typical passover, and the lamb's flesh eaten, deignedst to take bread out of a dish, *as a representation of Thine own body*,[2] and distribute to the disciples, we pray Thee, with earnest devotion, that whoever may partake with his mouth out of this paten *of consecrated bread*[3] may with his heart desire, and take Thee, the living and true bread . . ." Over the chalice the bishop says: "May whoever shall taste out of this chalice with pure heart *the mystical commemoration of Thy blood*[4] obtain from Thee the most merciful pardon of all his sins, and eternal joys."'[5]

By these authoritative documents of his Church, every word quoted from Ælfric on this subject is covered; and these documents themselves are covered by corresponding expressions in the Fathers, and in the liturgies of the primitive Church, which they merely reproduce. Putting aside the legendary matter contained in them, but mainly due to his age, the homilies of Ælfric may still edify the English reader by their simple language, straightforward character, and devout tone; rendering them almost fit for present use in a village church, and placing them in marked contrast to the vapid sentiment and turgid style of the pseudonymous literature that, affecting to be the newly-discovered remains of the most standard of the Fathers, was stealthily superseding their teaching, and sowing the seeds of error in doctrine and discipline broadcast in the West. Works of this description were soon after his time brought over in

---

[1] Ib 258
[2] 'In proprii comparatione corporis'
[3] 'Panem sacratum.' Hilduin, Abbot of S Denys in the ninth century, to the same effect ' Hora, qua *frangebatur panis sanctus quo ipse et populus communicare debebant*, &c'—*Vit S Dionysii*, c 29
[4] 'Mysticam sanguinis Tui memoriam.'
[5] *Anglo-Saxon Ch*, p. 219; comp Martene, ib Ord iii p. 265-6.

abundance by foreigners, introduced in the next generation into English sees, and determined, in common with the Lotharingian Leofric and his compatriots, on assimilating the Anglo-Saxon Church to that of the Churches across the Channel.[1] The homilies of Ælfric in this way were speedily forgotten, when the Italian Lanfranc became head of the English episcopate, famous as Prior of Bec, years before, for his writings against Berengarius; which S. Anselm, had he been heard, would fain have reconciled with the Fathers and with common sense. But it was by that time too late to ask men to be reasonable. The mischief had been slowly but surely done, and was past recal. Spurious and genuine works lay heaped together in one confused mass, each exercising co-ordinate sway; or, where it was possible, the genuine made, by means of interpolations or additions, to accord with the spurious. By dint of the changes introduced into Latin Missals and Pontificals everywhere, from the ninth century downwards, to suit the latest revision of the Roman Canon, which was sooner or later substituted in all Western Churches for their own, all vestiges of the primitive epiklesis were gradually swept away, till at length it became clean forgotten. Nor was any tradition of it preserved from henceforth, but in scattered fragments of a few public Office-books, too decayed to serve for palimpsests; or among the private devotions drawn up for celebrants by some learned divine conversant with the genuine works of the Fathers, and attached to their teaching.

Thus, among the prayers compiled for use before celebrating by S. Anselm, the twenty-ninth begins in these words :—

'Most high priest and true Pontiff, who didst offer Thyself on the altar of the cross to God the Father, a pure and immaculate victim for us miserable sinners, and who didst give to us Thy flesh to eat and Thy blood to drink : and *hast vested that mystery in the power of Thy Spirit,* saying,

[1] Warren, *Introd.* p xxiv.–xxv

"This do ye, as often as ye shall do it, in My remembrance . . ."'

Towards the end of the same prayer he adds:—

'I beseech Thee, grant of Thy clemency, O God, that the fulness of Thy benediction and the sanctification of Thy divinity may descend thereon: O Lord, may that invisible and incomprehensible majesty of Thy Holy Spirit likewise descend thereon, as He descended on the sacrifices of our forefathers in olden time: may He both make our oblations Thy body and blood, and enable me, unworthy priest that I am, to celebrate so great a mystery with all becoming devotion and purity of heart.' . . .[1]

This last part is borrowed from a prayer attributed to S. Ambrose, and culled by him, in all probability, from the liturgy bearing his name, though it was really that of his Church. It is in strict keeping with the teaching of this prayer that S. Anselm tells Waleran, Bishop of Newburgh, who consulted him on the merits of leavened or unleavened bread: that when 'we'—the Latins—'celebrate with unleavened bread, it is not that we consider *unleavened* bread in any way typical of Christ: but that we use bread in celebrating, as He did Himself, that it may be made, by the power of God working on it, His body.'[2]

Stronger language than this is never employed by him in any prayer, however fervent, or in any dogmatic piece known to be his, on this subject. In his twenty-seventh prayer:—

'Up, my soul,' he says: 'prepare the guest-chamber of thy heart to receive the body and blood of thy Creator. . . . Inspect all the senses of thy body with diligence: with diligence pass them gathered together in review before thee: and cast out everything thou findest in them tainted or impure. . . . Then, all things appertaining *to the consecration itself of this august mystery performed* . . . whilst thou holdest in thy hands the body and blood of Thy Redeemer,

[1] *Op* p 267-8, ed. Ben, 2nd ed 1721.   [2] Ib p 135

entreat Him of His infinite mercy to forgive thy sins, and prevent thy returning to them ever again . . . believing of the body which thou thus holdest, that it is truly that body which was born of a virgin, was crucified, was laid in the grave, rose the third day from the grave, ascended into heaven, and now sits at the right hand of the Father.'

In prayer twenty-eight his words are: 'This *mystery* of Thy body and blood.' In prayer thirty-two: 'This *sacrament* of Thy precious blood and holy flesh.'

We may pass from these devout utterances to the two pieces dealing with this subject, brought to light and placed at the end of his Epistles by their latest Benedictine editor.

The first of them is a letter, like the rest, in his unmistakable style. But it exhibits initials only, not names, in the heading prefixed to it.

'Domino G. Abbati, olim carissimo filio: nunc, Deo propitio, venerabili Patri: frater A.'[1]

Yet the explanation which can be given of this reserve seems unexceptionable. There was a monk named Gislebert who had studied at Bec under S. Anselm, as prior; and became Abbot of Westminster either just before S. Anselm ceased to be prior, or just after he likewise took the title of abbot. S. Anselm had sent him over into England on some business with Lanfranc, then Archbishop of Canterbury: and Lanfranc detained him for Westminster Abbey, then in want of an abbot. It so happens that a letter from S. Anselm to him has been preserved, congratulating him on his elevation, where both names appear in the heading, which in other respects is identic in style with that of the letter exhibiting the initials only, not the names.[2] The headings alone might be taken to prove the correspondents were the same; but for the initials in one case, and the

---

[1] *Ep* lib iv 106
[2] *Ep* lib ii 16 · 'Suo dilectissimo, olim, Divina dispositione, filio · nunc, Dei gratia, coabbati Gisleberto, frater Anselmus'

names in the other, a further reason may well be sought. One, then, is a letter of congratulations, which S. Anselm would be desirous that his old master the Archbishop should see, to prove that he was pleased at the appointment, though he regretted the loss of his envoy. The other letter referred to a subject on which he could not agree fully with his former master; and therefore, for fear it should ever find its way to Canterbury, it is addressed in a way that would fail to identify the actual correspondents. This is the clue to the initials. Had the learned authors of the *Histoire Littéraire de la France* read a little more between its lines, they could never have transferred a letter so remarkable, and, construed side by side with his twenty-seventh prayer, so like Anselm, to one whose main claim to it lay in this: that his own name began with an A, and that of his biographer with a G.[1]

There are passages in it, certainly, whose meaning is obscure: reading as though they had been tampered with or ill transcribed; and the string of authorities appended to it may be dismissed at once, as the clumsy work of a later pen. But its teaching is decidedly that of S. Anselm from first to last. The title prefixed to it is 'De Sacramento Altaris.' Among the salient points in it are the following:—

(1) 'I believe that the Lord's most holy body, which is daily consecrated on the altar *by the ministry* of the priest, is beyond any doubt His true flesh which suffered on the cross, and the true blood which flowed from His side; as He who is the true testified when He said, "My flesh is meat indeed," &c., and again, in giving the bread to His disciples, "This is My body." I know of no other body that was given for our salvation but this. . . . They who think that after consecration it is materially bread, and but figuratively, and not truly, the Lord's body, being both carnal and carnally-minded, act inconsistently with faith in no small degree; trusting to the eyes of their body rather than to His express

[1] Vols. viii 165, and ix. 439, adopted by Migne, *Pat. Lat.* clix. 254-5.

words.' (2) But that the sacrament is called bread after consecration, as well as flesh, I concede without rebuke: and agreeably with the dictates of reason and faith, as a Catholic admit and approve. For that it is called bread by the orthodox, nobody doubts who is honest and wise; seeing that He who is the truth also says, 'I am the bread which came down from heaven,' &c. And a sacrament, too; for under those visible tokens which the eye beholds, a hidden consecration of the flesh takes place by the power of God: so that what it is inwardly by power, it is believed to be truly by faith. And a figure no less, that which is apprehended mentally being one thing, and that which is outwardly seen and tasted another. Hence, after consecration of so great a mystery, I so consider it a real eucharist of the Lord's body, which I receive, that I nevertheless in no sense deny that it is in a sacrament or figure. For if I thought it was *not* in a sacrament that I devoured with my teeth the Lamb of God, I should, in the words of S. Augustine, be chargeable with a great crime. The more fully, therefore, the sacrament or figure, with the light shed upon it by the Holy Ghost, is contemplated by me, the greater edification I derive from the reality.

'These statements of mine, let me request you dutifully to bear in mind, I could confirm by innumerable testimonies of the holy Fathers, but for the dread I have, to say the truth, of the length to which it would extend my letter.'

With these words S. Anselm would naturally lay his pen down. Either an officious scribe, to show his learning, or a disciple wishing to place the orthodoxy of his master beyond question, afterwards did for his letter the very thing he deprecated doing himself.

But his own writings supply the best comment on what he has said here. First, he lays down in express terms everywhere that Christ is truly present in His sacrament after consecration with the same body that was crucified for man. But, secondly, no passage can be quoted of his in which consecration is ascribed to the act of the celebrant or to any words pronounced by him. The power of God—that is, more specifically, the operation of the Holy Ghost—makes the sacrament, according to S. Anselm, invariably what Christ meant it to be. Thirdly, S. Anselm never shrinks from calling the Eucharist after consecration a sacrament or a figure. Fourthly, never is the word transubstantiation, or its compounds, or its equivalents, employed in his writings. The only places where the word 'substance' occurs in connection with this subject is where bread, leavened or unleavened, is pronounced substantially the same.[1] He distinctly lays down in one place that bread remaining *materially* bread is no proof that after consecration Christ is not truly present in His sacrament.[2]

In all this S. Anselm, in full and loyal accord with the Fathers, notwithstanding that all traces of their epiklesis had been expunged from the Canon then used in England, as in every Western Church. And on the first point he will also be found in full agreement with his predecessor in the see of Canterbury, when we are brought face to face with the writings of Lanfranc in the ensuing chapter.

Meanwhile the remaining piece claimed for S. Anselm by his latest Benedictine editor, and accepted as his by the authors of the *Histoire Littéraire*, and printed as Ep. cvii. in the fourth book of his Epistles, requires some notice.

First, whatever its original shape may have been, what is now given us is a mere fragment with this title: 'Sanctus Anselmus Cantuariensis archiepiscopus, de Corpore et Sanguine Domini.' If it ever, therefore, was a letter, the address and commencement of it are not here given, and it ends without salutation and abruptly so far as the general argument is concerned. Further, there is a rent in the context of the sentence beginning with the words 'Quare autem corpus Christi,' &c., showing that a tampering with the text commenced at that point and was continued, almost

[1] *De Az. et Ferment* c 1   [2] Above, p 276.

uninterruptedly, to within a few lines of the end. Just this one sentence—' Non est quærendum quid fiat de corpore : Deus enim conficit sicut scit '—may be set down as it stands to S. Anselm. All the rest is interpolation, and interpolation savouring of the Lanfrancian school, just as the appendix to the foregoing piece may have been the addition of a disciple. Both pieces, as they stand, cannot well have been penned by the same person ; yet there is nothing in the first part or concluding lines of the second that is not in full accord with the first piece. Witness the concluding lines of the second :—

' Because we sin daily . . . . therefore Christ is immolated in *a mystical sense* daily for us. Within the Catholic Church, in the sacrament (*mysterio*) of His body, neither less is received from a bad nor more from a good celebrant ; for consecration is in no way dependent on the merits of the consecrator, but is effected by the word of the Creator and the power of the Holy Ghost ; for if it depended on the merit of the celebrant, it would not appertain to Christ. But now, as it is He who baptises, so it is He who, through the Holy Ghost, causes this bread to be tranfused into His flesh and this wine into His blood.'

He merely repeats here language which had once been universal, but that portion of it relating to the Holy Ghost found expression no longer in any Western Church nor in the teaching of the West either, after S. Anselm. Peter Lombard quotes this passage word for word, except just at the end, as from a work bearing the same title by S. Augustine; but it is in quitting the subject and in reference to consecration by heretics and evil-livers, not as having any direct bearing on the Real Presence, which had already been discussed by him on another hypothesis and confirmed by spurious authorities at great length.[1]

Mr. Maskell, in an additional note to the Uses of Sarum and Bangor, York and Hereford, says :—[2]

[1] *Sentent IV*, dist. xiii   [2] § ix p 201

'The following prayers are taken from a MS. Missal in my possession of the thirteenth century. It formerly belonged to some English Benedictine monastery. The prayers are very remarkable, and I do not remember to have seen them in any other Missal. They are placed immediately before the Prefaces, after the ordinary.'

In the last of them we have probably the latest extant relic of primitive tradition on this point :—

'*Over the host placed on the chalice.*[1] Accept, Holy Lord, Almighty Father, Eternal God, this sacrificial oblation which I, unworthy sinner, offer humbly to Thee, the living and true God, and deign to send Thy Holy Spirit from heaven, who, by His commixture with it, may sanctify this offering of our hands to Thee.'

Mr. Maskell includes this prayer among those which he says he cannot remember having seen '*in any other Missal.*' Had he, then, so soon forgotten some that he had placed with his own hand in parallel columns with the Roman not very many pages back, but *having nothing opposite to them in the Roman*, where the celebrant prays for the gift of the Holy Ghost that he may be able to celebrate worthily [2] and that he may enter on his task with clean hands,[3] where the assistants pray that the Holy Ghost may illumine both his heart and lips,[4] and where he prays finally that he may so communicate as to receive remission of his sins and be filled with the Holy Ghost?[5]—all relics of the primitive Canon, where the descent of the Holy Ghost on the elements was invoked, *as well as* His action in the hearts of the celebrant and communicants, and, *therefore*, finding no counterparts in the Roman because foreign to the Roman Canon then in

---

[1] Martene, *De Ant Eccl Rit* 1 c 4, art. 6, § 16 · 'Unum est quod hic observare debemus calicem scilicet unà cum pane simul unica oratione oblatum ; id quod non solùm in citatis Missalibus, sed insuper in Antissiodorensi, Catalaunensi, Lugdunensi, aliisque quàm plurimis advertimus '—v pp. 391, 458, 571, 575, 596, 601, 609, 616, 620, 625

[2] Ib p 8

[3] Pp 64–5

[4] P. 68.

[5] Pp. 114 and 118.

use, as Mr. Maskell had excellently said himself still further back :—

'The direct prayers in the primitive forms had the sure and good effect of keeping up in the minds both of priest and people a remembrance of the solemn truths which were expressed in them. Plainly to pray for the descent of the Holy Spirit upon the bread and wine and in plain words to offer up the sacrifice could not but be followed by a corresponding faith. Practice and belief would go hand in hand.'[1]

Accordingly, before closing this chapter, I desire to particularise two facts in advance for special notice, which anybody who will may verify for himself in the chapter which follows, the more easily from having had his attention bespoke for them now.

The first of them is that the gradual disuse by the Latin Churches of the primitive epiklesis, or prayer for the descent of the Holy Ghost, in their communion offices or liturgies, caused by their gradual adoption of the *so-called* Gregorian Canon, from which all traces of it had been expunged, exactly synchronises with the rise and progress of carnal ideas and expressions in their teaching on the Eucharist, derived in the first instance from spurious documents, but emphatically disclaimed in all the genuine writings of the Latin and Greek Fathers and in all the primitive liturgies commented on or used by them.

The second fact is that the word 'spiritual,' bereft of the natural interpretation put upon it by this prayer, which was its correlative, came to be expunged too; then, from having been expunged, to be considered of ambiguous meaning in the West; at last to be discredited, as though equivalent to what was *un*real, or only typical or figurative. Hence they who talked of our Lord being spiritually present in the Eucharist after consecration of the elements began to be suspected of heterodoxy, being supposed to deny that

[1] Pref. p. cxvii.

He was really present, unless they would add corporally, bodily, substantially, materially, locally, present with His flesh and blood on the altar—just as when He walked about on earth—expressions unknown to the Fathers, disallowed by Ælfric, and avoided by S. Anselm as such. Fortunately, no such expressions ever found their way into the liturgies of any country, nor the doctrine of 'a *carnal presence*' into the formal teaching of any Church.[1] Still in no part of the so-called Gregorian Mass is the epithet *spiritual* to be found in any connection, *nor in the modern Roman either*, both presenting in this respect a marked resemblance to the Clementine liturgy—too marked from one point of view to have been fortuitous, and from another for S. Gregory to have been a party to it in any way. The special *Post-Communions* and *Secreta* for holidays, in which alone this epithet may still be seen in the so-called Gregorian, and is still applied in the modern Roman—as *hostia spiritalis, cibus* (or *alimonia*) *spiritalis, sacrificia spiritalia, sanctificatio spiritalis*—are simply relics of the old rite preserved in the fragmentary survivals of the Gelasian and the Leonine. Except on such occasions, the only places where the Holy Ghost is so much as named in the so-called Gregorian are the doxologies and the Creed. The modern Roman has improved on this so far that, instead of commencing at once with the Introit, the celebrant professes that he enters upon his appointed task ' In the name of the Father and Son and Holy Ghost,' and pledges himself personally to it in the word ' Amen.' Would it might prove the first step of a palinode!

[1] Even the Council of Trent teaches that 'in the Divine sacrifice which is celebrated in the Mass, Christ is contained and immolated in *an unbloody manner*, who once offered Himself in a bloody manner on the altar of the cross', and calls it 'a sacrifice, such as the nature of man requires, whereby that bloody sacrifice might be *represented*, and the memory thereof remain even unto the end of the world'—*Sess* xxii c 2 and 1 And its Catechism ' Illud sæpissime in sanctis Patribus repetitum fideles admonendi sunt, ne curiosius inquirant quo pacto ea mutatio fieri possit Nec enim percipi a nobis potest nec in naturalibus mutationibus, aut in ipsâ rerum creatione ejus rei exemplum aliquod habemus. Verùm, quid hoc sit, fide cognoscendum est, quomodo fit, curiosius non inquirendum '— Part II iv. § 41.

CHAPTER VII.

THOUGH it may seem a mere trifle that we shall have to grapple with henceforth—the actual place given by S. Gregory to a single prayer, preserved as recast by him in the Canon now used—it is in reality the key of the position. Moreover, being the coping-stone, the colophon, of a colossal work in the history of the world variously carried out during the ninth century, pregnant with consequences on the whole for good—yet good, in no small number of cases, brought out of evil—the work of welding all the heterogeneous, but hopelessly scattered or intermixed immigrants in the west of Europe, most of them already Christianised, into formal corporate, social and political union under one head: it can no more be dissociated from that work than a part from the whole. Hence, too, not only must the process by which that work was accomplished be scrutinised in detail, but its final outcome must be studied by the light of each of its component parts belonging to the same category, and given a name that will suit them all. So far, then, as ecclesiastical matters were comprised in this work, its outcome, whether intended or not, was plainly the Gallicanising of the whole Western Church.

It was well doubted by one cut off too prematurely to make good his words, whether the eighth or tenth centuries filled as important a position as the ninth alone. For 'the system which Charlemagne established in the Church as well as in the empire, had no fair room for displaying its real nature, and for the development of its legitimate results, while the strong arm and masterly genius of its founder were at hand to check or direct its progress.'[1] Of all the great personages in history, Charlemagne probably was second to none in promoting learning and good government according to the means at his disposal, and he did a vast deal for religion too, though it was for the religion of his own times: taught and administered as he thought fit to direct. In both doctrine and discipline he claimed to be the final appeal; he would hear arguments, and consult authorities, but in pronouncing his decision he would brook no control. That he laid the foundations of modern Europe both ecclesiastically and politically, when he caused himself to be solemnly crowned on Christmas Eve, A.D. 800, at Rome by Pope Leo III., is a plain historical fact. But he left many details unfinished or unattempted in his own lifetime to be filled in at intervals by his successors. He never lived to see the interpolated Creed of Spain, patronised by himself, adopted by Rome; though, to secure the adhesion of Rome to it, he professed his willingness to introduce first the Roman Chant, and then the Roman Mass, or at least Canon, throughout his dominions. As he was always blowing hot and cold on this point, ritual got into such tangles that scarcely two dioceses at last had the same, and many were the versions of the so-called Gregorian at one time north of the Alps. When and under what circumstances its final revision was effected, we may be able to discover. Yet the same mystery may be said to brood over its authorship of that revision, as over that of the False Decretals, and over its adoption by Rome, as over the acceptance of the Creed of Reccared and Charlemagne by the Popes.

Glimpses of the struggle—for a struggle there was in each case—present themselves in sufficient clearness here and there, to warrant conclusions based upon authentic history. Those glimpses have been kept out of sight, or at least in the background, hitherto.

The second Nicene Council was held, as everybody knows,

[1] *Life and Times of Hincmar*, by Rev James Prichard Oxford, 1849

A.D. 789, and foremost in formulating its decrees, and first in subscribing to them, were two legates from Rome; and foremost in accepting them was the reigning Pope, Adrian I., by whom they were subsequently defended in a long letter on being attacked by Charlemagne. When 'the Capitulary directed against this synod,' as the Pope calls it,[1] was received by him, we are not told, but it was exhibited seven years afterwards in four books, since called the Caroline Books, to the Council of Frankfort, where the rejection of the second Nicene Council was formally decreed; and *that*, not more for the resolute stand made by it against the Iconoclasts, than for its persistent adhesion to the Nicene-Constantinopolitan Creed without any change.

During the seven years which intervened between the two synods, concurrent efforts were made by Charlemagne to conciliate the Pope by affecting to press the adoption of Roman usages on all Churches within his dominions on one hand; on the other, to get the interpolated Creed adopted throughout the West by pressing its adoption in good earnest upon the Pope. The long and laboured apology made for it at the Synod of Friuli, A.D. 791, summoned at his instance by the venerable Bishop of Aquileia, Paulinus, and of all his theologians the most distinguished, was intended to prove that its interpolated clause—*Filioque*—was not only consistent with orthodoxy, but with the precedent set by the Constantinopolitan Fathers themselves in what they added to the Nicene formula, though Paulinus was unable to show equal authority for the clause patronised by his master: and this was just the point which the oath then taken by the Popes, preliminary to their consecration, bound them to regard most. Charlemagne, to whom the oath taken by them could have been no secret, was meanwhile busy with his acknowledgments of the pre-eminent claims of the Roman See, and the measures to be carried out by him for his exaltation. It was better, he thought, to have two strings to his bow than one. Cardinal Bona was able, therefore, to refer his readers to a glowing chapter on the privileges inherited by the Church of Rome from her founder S. Peter, in the books written against the second Nicene Council,[1] and hence, by implication, against the living head of the Roman Church who confirmed it, where conclusive proof—according to the Cardinal, overlooking this inconvenient fact—will be found that 'ancient rites were abolished in the Churches of France by command of the most pious kings, Pepin and Charles, and Roman introduced in their stead about 900 years from his own time.'[2]

But when we come to peruse this chapter, we are reminded, in spite of our utmost desire to be serious, of the mountain and the mouse. Nothing can be more overflowing than its commencement: but the actual statement which is reached at last amounts to this—that the Churches in the dominions of the writer which had hitherto declined accepting the Roman tradition in chanting the psalms, had in most cases given way, and were then striving to perfect themselves in it with praiseworthy zeal.

It is true that Pertz has placed among the Capitularies of Aix, A.D. 802, the following questions to be asked of presbyters before their ordination: '4. Are you well acquainted with, and understand your Mass, according to the Roman order?'

And '7. Are you well able to chant the Divine Office according to the Roman rite on the appointed festivals?'

And again, amongst the things which all ecclesiastics have to learn:—

'4. The Book of the Sacraments perfectly; both as regards the Canon and the special Masses where changes have to be made.'[3]

But these regulations are not quoted by the Cardinal; nor are they found in the older collections. It may be said of them all that, if dated rightly, they were not issued till after the coronation; of the first two likewise that the terms

[1] *Lib Carol* 1 6   [2] *Rer Liturg* 1 12, 1   [3] *Legum*, i. 107

'Missa' and 'Officium Divinum' may there be synonymous, and only refer, therefore, to the chanting of the psalms and antiphons in the daily office, while there is nothing to show that it was either the Roman Canon or Sacramentary with which the third deals. The only Sacramentary mentioned by Amalarius was that of his own Church of Metz. The 371st Capitulary, to which Bona must refer (*not* the 219th), of the fifth book stands on no higher authority than that of Benedict the Levite, from whose collection it is taken; and this provides merely that presbyters shall use sandals when they celebrate Mass, as the Roman Ordo prescribes. The genuine Constitutions of A.D. 788 [1] and of the year following have reference to the Roman Chant alone, which Pepin made great efforts to introduce, and substitute for the Gallican.[2] What actually passed between Pepin and the Popes of his day is best learnt from their own letters preserved in the Caroline code. From one [3] we learn that he was sent an Antiphonal or Responsal by Paul I. From another,[4] that he requested the monks of his brother, then Archbishop of Rouen, might be taught singing at Rome by a Roman named Simeon, who was formerly choir-master at Rouen. Not a word is, however, breathed on this subject in the forty-nine extant epistles that passed between Adrian I. and Charlemagne, strange to say; although the exaltation of the Roman Church is a fruitful topic in them all, especially the donation to it of temporalities said to have been made by Constantine, Pepin, and his successor, the reigning king. In the last epistle, dated A.D. 791, the same year in which the Synod of Friuli met, and therefore perhaps wanted for some purpose connected with it, Adrian tells Charlemagne that, agreeably with his request, he sends him a Gregorian Sacramentary. Now it so happens that in the twenty-seventh chapter of the second of the Caroline Books, it would appear that its author

---

[1] 'De emendatione librorum et officiorum ecclesiasticorum,' Baluze, *Capitul.* i 203
[2] Ib 239 'Decertavit ut fieret, quandò Gallicanum cantum tulit'
[3] *Ep* xvi ed Migne
[4] *Ep* xxxvi ib.

either repudiated certain expressions of the so-called Gregorian Canon as it has come down to us, or else that the Sacramentary sent him by the Pope was *not* the so-called Gregorian. Anyhow, this is the sole mention of any liturgical work in their whole correspondence; nor are we told why Charlemagne wanted it, nor to what purpose it was turned by him. In those illiterate days, indeed, the adoption of the Roman Chant might indirectly lead to the adoption of antiphons and responses set to it in what we may call by anticipation the Roman Breviary. But, again, the offices of the Breviary formed no part of the Sacramentary. Mabillon,[1] to be sure, contends that the book then called Antiphonary contained 'introits' of the Missal as well. But in the work of Amalarius on the Antiphonary we find no mention at all of the Mass; nor even in the 'Eclogæ de Ordine Romano . . . in Missâ,' given to him also, do we find any directions for chanting. Choirs and choristers are naturally dwelt upon in his larger work 'De Officiis' dedicated to the Emperor Lewis. And, commenting on the 'Offertory,'[2] we find him saying: 'While the celebrant passes to receive the oblations, the choristers chant, according to ancient custom.' For Metz had been a school of music over thirty years when he wrote this. But sing what? Hymns, probably; *not* sentences from the liturgy, or he would have named them. Antiphons, indeed, taken from the Psalms, were just about that time beginning to find their way, and thus import singing, into the Mass; for 'the Mass formerly began with lections,' as he says himself.[3] Further on,[4] forgetful of his own remark, he gives a long extract from the well-known letter of S. Gregory the Great to show, as he says, when 'Alleluia' was first *sung* at Mass in Rome. But, as though to furnish us with a specimen of his own inaccuracy, the word employed in the very passage which he quotes is uniformly throughout, *not* sung, but

[1] *Liturg Gall* i 5
[2] III 19
[3] Ib iii 5
[4] Ib iv 26

'*said*'—in respect of 'Kyrie eleison,' as well as 'Alleluia.' Then another pertinent observation of his own respecting 'Kyrie eleison' is, that it preceded the Lord's Prayer always at the *conclusion of matins and vespers* in the Gallican Church, adding, 'Nam quod *nos Galli*, finitis psalmis nocturnalibus, *solemus cantare orationem Dominicam*, Romana prætermittit ecclesia.' Nor was this the only point on which the Roman Chant of those days fell short of the requirements of the Gallican. For, according to the dialogue that passed between the legates of Charlemagne and the next Pope, Leo III., A.D. 809, the Creed, which was then said, but *not* sung—in church, but *not* at Mass in Rome—was, by licence specially procured from Rome, sung in the chapel annexed to his palace. But the Pontiff, on learning it was the interpolated Creed which *was sung there*, withdrew his licence, lest the custom of chanting it in that form should be copied. Lastly, neither in Rome nor in France was the *Canon* of the Mass ever chanted, so that the mere introduction of the Roman Chant into France would not of itself be the least likely to suggest, much less dictate, changes in the Canon.

But, after all, if we want to know what consideration was actually sought or obtained for the Roman Chant in the reign of Charlemagne, we may get fuller and surer information than the annalists of his own day would have dared to give, copied from the archives of his dominions by one sufficiently removed from his times to be able to publish his extracts without fear. 'Ademar,' says Pertz[1] of a monk of Angoulême, whose three books of histories end with A.D. 1023—marking his age—'may be trusted for almost anything connected with the province of Aquitaine'; to the men of which, therefore, the following incident reported by him alone may well be referred. Charlemagne spent the Easter of A.D. 787 at Rome. This we learn from the Annals of Eginhard and of Laurisham as well as from him. 'During the

[1] *Monum. Germ Scriptores*, IV. 108

days of the festival,' he continues, 'a violent altercation arose between the Gallican and Roman choristers. The Gal'icans affirmed they sang better and with more taste than the Romans. The Romans said their chants were the purest and most strictly Gregorian, and that the Gallicans had corrupted them. The dispute waxed warm on both sides. At length Charlemagne, reminding his own subjects that the fountain must be purer than the stream, bade them go back to the fountain.' Being at Rome then, he could not have well said less. To compliment his host still more—and, let us by no means forget, the second Nicene Council was then assembling—Adrian was requested by him shortly afterwards to let him have two choristers from Rome to correct the defects of the French. Two were selected accordingly for that purpose; and one being settled at Metz and the other at Soissons, all the choir-masters of other dioceses were commanded to repair thither respectively, to learn the true Gregorian Chant, and to sing antiphonally like the Romans. The same Roman choristers taught the French how to play on the organ. And grammarians and arithmeticians, Ademar tells us further, were taken at the same time back by Charlemagne from Rome to instruct his people. In a word: 'ubique literarum studium expandere jussit.' Choristers and musicians, grammarians and mathematicians, all went from Rome, where they abounded most, to France, where they were well-nigh extinct, in *the interests of learning generally*, so far as he was concerned; yet, in a way, all would alike further his political ends. Further, let us not fail to observe the geographical position of Soissons and Metz, easily reached from each other, as well as from Aix-la-Chapelle, where he resided himself. The province of Aquitaine was the furthest removed in his dominions from all three.

Barely fifty years elapsed between this transaction and the publication of the Life of S. Dionysius, the supposed Areopagite, by Hilduin, Abbot of S. Denys, undertaken by command of the Emperor Lewis A.D. 835. Yet events in those days moved rapidly, and churches and seats of learning were comparatively few. A passage from the dedicatory letter prefixed to this Life,[1] quoted in the first instance by Le Cointe,[2] from having been afterwards repeated by Bona,[3] has become well known; in which Hilduin appeals for confirmation of what he is then stating to ' decayed Missals of most ancient date, containing the order of Mass, according to the Gallican rite, which had, from the time when France was first converted to the faith, prevailed there, till it received the Roman order which it now uses.'

Hilduin, we must remember, had a heavy fall in his career. From being in high favour at Court, he was suddenly disgraced and exiled; A.D. 830, or thereabouts, he followed Agobard and others in taking part with the sons of Lewis against their father. At the end of two years he was restored to his post; and it is easy to see from his measured words after this how conscious he was of treading on delicate ground, and resolved that he would never offend again. Yet he testifies, even in recording what he thought his master would be pleased to know, how clean the sweep had been of the old Office-books, which had been displaced by the new use, though for how long, or under what circumstances, he forbears to state.

Let us carefully note this expression—*not*, ' which it has long used,' but, '*which it now uses.*' He testifies to the high antiquity of the oldest books containing the Gallican rite, but omits to tell us a word about what he calls the Roman, beyond its being in present use. He leaves us to find out if we can, when that change had been made; yet, strange to say, he puts us on the road to its discovery, without knowing it, in the same breath. For he proves, in the same chapter, that it was the Roman Clement who directed the Areopagite Dionysius into France, from ancient documents recording his martyrdom. And in proof of their

[1] § 5, Migne, *Patrol Lat* cvi 17
[2] *Annal. Eccl. Franc.* A.D. 601, n. 18.   [3] *Rer Liturg* i 12, 5.

antiquity he refers more particularly to 'two Masses contained in these volumes,' of which he says 'that Masses of this kind, in which the Acts of martyrs were recited at great length and in touching strains, had long been discontinued in France, the letters extant among us of Innocent, Gelasius, and still more recently Pope Gregory, to the bishops of France, and from the bishops of France to them, on imitating the Roman custom in all Offices put forth by authority for public use, may be taken to prove.' On the other hand, he forbids our 'inferring from the Mass introduced into France by S. Dionysius and his companions that they had departed in any way from what had been instituted by the Apostles; as there was *abundant proof extant* of what the true meaning,[1] both of the Apostles themselves and their successors, and of the Church of Rome too, was.'

That these last words contain a clear reference to the Clementine liturgy will be shown later; let us here limit ourselves to the letters of Innocent, Gelasius, and Gregory, to the bishops of France, and from the bishops of France to them, said to be then extant, and to have caused the custom of reciting the Acts of martyrs at Mass to be discontinued in France.

Here let it be remembered, in the first place, that this custom was not peculiar to France. 'The third Council of Carthage,' says Bingham, 'which forbids all other books to be read in church besides the Canonical Scriptures, excepts the passions of the martyrs, as books that might be read on their anniversary-days of commemoration. S. Austin, and Popes Leo and Gelasius, often mention the reading of such histories in the African and Roman Churches. Cæsarius of Arles, Alcimus Avitus, and Ferreolus speak of the same in

---

[1] 'Sensus proprii abundantiam notam esse' (Surius, *De Prob Sanc Hist* tom v 638, Oct 9) a harsh expression, no doubt, but rendered unintelligible in Migne by a misprint, the leaving out of 'abundantiam' Surius absurdly deduces in the margin from these letters, 'Gallia in missa morem Romanum sequi quando cœperit.'

the French Churches.'[1] The book containing such histories, when they became so numerous and voluminous as to demand one, was called 'Passionarium' or 'Passionale'; and according to Merati,[2] the place for reciting them at Mass was just before the Epistle and Gospel: 'et hinc est, quod eadem acta quibusdam missalibus et sacramentariis inserta fuerunt,' as he remarks himself; adding that this custom was preserved in France till the ninth, and in Spain till the tenth century, as the Gallican liturgy proves.' Yet, almost in the same breath, he maintains that the Roman Church never allowed such histories to be inserted in her Missal; because, forsooth, no such histories are found in the extant MSS. of the Gelasian and Gregorian Missals or Sacramentaries, none of which can be proved to have been written earlier than A.D. 800; and most, if not all, exhibit proofs of having been written in France. Even of these, too, truth compels him to admit that 'the prefaces contain short notices of the martyrs and of the sufferings endured by them; culled, indeed, with such caution, that they cannot be charged with containing anything that is false.' Yet, after making this admission, strange to say, he tells his readers that they will be warranted in inferring 'that when the reading of such Acts is prescribed in a Roman "Ordo," we must understand it of the lections appointed to be read *in officio*—viz. in the Breviary—or conclude the "Ordo" really belongs to other Churches, not to the Roman.' This is one way of getting out of a difficulty, making it apparent, however, that no other escape from it could be found.

Next, let it be asked what is the worth of those letters to which Abbot Hilduin refers? Letters are still extant of Innocent, Gelasius, and Gregory to bishops of France, though not exclusively to them by any means, in which the Roman Church is held up in general terms as a model for all other

[1] *Ant* xx 7, 5; comp Mabillon, *De Curs Gall* §§ 30 and 35
[2] *Ad Gavanti Comment. Thesaur.*
tom. ii 144, 'De Lect' § 9; comp Martene, *De Ant. Eccl. Rit* i. 4, 4.

Churches to follow; but not one which asserts that the Roman Church ever forbade the recital at Mass of the authentic Acts of any martyr, either in her own case or in other Churches. That the decree 'De apocryphis Scripturis' attributed to Pope Gelasius is itself apocryphal will be shown further on: but, admitting its genuineness, we shall find it would prove too much or too little for the contention of the good abbot. For it first states indiscriminately that, in accordance with ancient custom, the Acts of martyrs were not read in the Roman Church; but afterwards gives instances of the worthless character of the Acts affected by this rule. Then, further, we meet with no distinction in the Church services to which it should apply; as though it applied to all alike.

Thus far only, therefore, can the statement of Hilduin be said to hold good: (1) that the Gallican rite had been displaced by the Roman at S. Denys and in the north-east of France sufficiently for all traces of it to have been effaced in every Missal to be found there, except the oldest—and those too decayed to be remodelled for further use—when Hilduin dedicated his work on the supposed Areopagite to the Emperor Lewis, A.D. 840 or thereabouts; and (2) that this change was in keeping with the general maxims laid down by the three Popes he names, although it is certainly nowhere dictated in their letters.

Abbot Hilduin, therefore, construed by his surroundings, affords no more countenance for the conclusions of Cardinal Bona than the Caroline Books. Nobody wants to be told that numberless things would never have happened in Europe *but for Charlemagne*. What has to be made plain is: how much was actually planned and executed during his reign, and what was filled in afterwards by his successors; and when, where, by themselves, or by whom (as M. Rohrbacher says of him with entire truth [1]); Charlemagne set everybody that exhibited any talent working in the in-

[1] *Histoire Eccl.* xi 274

terests of learning and literature throughout his dominions; and it was to the East that he turned mainly for direction and information. It was with this object that he sent to Rome for choristers, arithmeticians and grammarians, as we have seen. It was for the same purpose that messengers were constantly passing and repassing between Aix and Constantinople; and monks from his palace to their Latin brethren on Mount Olives. It was there that the experiment of chanting the Creed with the Latin interpolation appended to it was first tried in the East; it was there that reference was first made to 'the Faith of S. Athanasius' in support of its teaching. At home, the homilies of S. Chrysostom on the Epistle to the Hebrews, either in the translation of them made for Cassiodorus,[1] or in one made for himself—anyhow reproduced largely by Alcuin[2]—contributed in no small degree to the spread of those views which were destined to take possession of the Latin mind on the subject of the Eucharist, and bring about changes in its ritual and its doctrine before very long.

Pinius the Jesuit,[3] in his learned comments on the Mozarabic liturgy, says of the ninth century when he reaches it, that, for anything to be gathered from it on liturgies, 'it is as barren as a tamarisk tree; producing no fruit on which any student can thrive.' Sismondi makes a striking observation on the reign of Charlemagne, which is to the same effect.[4] His words are: ' L'on ne peut même affirmer s'il fut avantageux ou pernicieux pour l'humanité.' Previously to this he had compared it to a meteor; but a meteor dies brilliant, and is only remembered for the light that it shed whilst it lived. Charlemagne made many good laws, but he left his dominions a chaotic aggregate without cohesion: he upheld religion, but he bequeathed the palace

---

[1] *De Inst Div Lit* c 8
[2] In his own exposition In Migne's ed the passages are marked all through as quotations *Pat Lat* c 1031 *et seq*
[3] *Tract. Hist Chron* c v 1
[4] *Hist des Français,* tom ii 421 and see the picture drawn from facts in Sismondi, tom ii 429-31.

which he inhabited a foul Augean stable to his son: he promoted learning, but to the spurious literature commenced in his reign, and multiplied a hundredfold amid the troubles in which his son was involved, we are still bound hand and foot in all the disastrous consequences to Church order, and Church ritual, and Church doctrine which it has entailed in one form or another ever since.

For during the confusion of interests and the shiftings of parties and the general insecurity to life and property caused by the savage wars between the Emperor Lewis and his sons, and his own endless partitions and repartitions of territory for the benefit of the child of his second wife, Charles the Bald, with whom we shall have soon to do, the forger who had learnt his craft under the first Emperor, but was restrained by fear of detection from adventuring in it too far then, could work at it without stint in any secluded corner, while the sons of the second Emperor were fighting with doubtful success amongst themselves, and be sure that no eye would care to disturb his privacy while his work was in progress, nor any critic find leisure to impeach its authenticity when finished and circulated noiselessly from convent to convent.

It must not, however, be forgotten for one moment in whose reign the forger had served his apprenticeship, nor to what achievements of the establishments in which it had been passed he must have been privy.

Charlemagne liked having his friends about him and well knew the advantages of centralisation. It was at Metz and Soissons, then, as we have seen, that the two choristers from Rome, who were to teach all the other choirs in his dominions the Roman Chant, were to be installed. It was at Aix-la-Chapelle that he resided himself, surrounded by all the members of his Court and learned divines of all ranks in his Church. Mayence, then the most renowned archbishopric in his dominions, was about the same distance from Aix and from Metz that Aix was from Metz and from Soissons. We have thus a geographical quadrilateral, formed by the junction of two equilateral triangles; and it is a well-authenticated historical fact that either within this quadrilateral, or, at any rate, between it and Rome, all the great Western forgeries of the ninth century were concocted, be the authors of them who they may and the exact time or manner of their issue ever so open to question.

The appendices to the Benedictine editions of the Fathers alone show the extent to which the writings of the Fathers were interlarded with false pieces attributed to them, and there were numbers judged too unworthy by the editors even to be given a place there. This was, for the most part, the work of the ninth and tenth centuries.

But it is for a still worse species only that we could here find space; nor can we do more than notice the principal with which we are most concerned.

1. Adrian became Pope A.D. 772. Two years afterwards, at his request, Charlemagne turned his arms against the Lombards, and having all but completed their subjugation, repaired to Rome to keep Easter and receive the thanks of the Pope for it. What actually passed between them will, perhaps, never be known, but, from the documents which have come down to us, it is easy to see that a deep game was played on both sides. Three days were spent in showing the Conqueror over the principal churches and buildings, and in celebrating fêtes for his victories. On the fourth day, being, according to the papal biographer, pressed to fulfil the promises made by his father and by himself at various times—' pro concedendis diversis civitatibus ac territoriis istius Italiæ provinciæ, et contradendis beato Petro ejusque omnibus vicariis in perpetuum possidendis '—he executed what has since been called the 'Caroline Donation' in very solemn form, full details of which and of its extent are then given. This, if it ever took place, was of course a masterstroke. Yet Adrian is found in later epistles petitioning for additions of territory, stated to have been granted to him

by this document, as still not in his possession, and only promised.

Neither Le Cointe¹ nor Cennius² can shut their eyes to this contradiction, and lose themselves in explaining it.

2. As a set-off to this donation, we have the Acts of a synod held at the Lateran, while Charlemagne was still in Rome, where we are told Adrian, with the full consent of 153 bishops and abbots attending it, bestowed on Charlemagne the right of choosing the Pope, and of inducting him both into his temporalities and his see. Bishops and abbots were bound by the same ordinance to resort to him for investiture, previously to their consecration. This, had it actually taken place, would have supplied Urban II. with an unassailable precedent for the Sicilian monarchy granted by him, A.D. 1098, to Count Roger of Sicily, which Cardinal Baronius incurred the wrath of Spain for calling in question.

Mansi calls this council 'partim fictitia, partim dubia,' without deciding which it is most.³ Sigebert of Gemblours is the main authority for it, but it is omitted in some MSS. of his work. Those who reject it, accordingly, maintain it was the addition of a partisan in those MSS. which contain it, forgetting that partisans have been known to omit, as well as to add. Gratian not only records it as official, but caps with it a similar concession made to the first Otho by Leo VIII., who quotes the act of Adrian in justification of his own.⁴ Fictitious or not, it points to the fact that there were three parties interested in the work assigned to it: an imperial, a papal, and a liturgical, each bent on advancing schemes of its own.

Several other transactions of minor importance, said to have taken place that year, point the same way. Thomas, Archbishop of Milan, is generally reported to have crowned

¹ A D 774, n 6
² *Monit ad Adrian Ep* c 29 et seq
³ *Conc* xii 883-88.
⁴ *Dist* xliii c 22-3; comp *L'art de Vérif les Dates*, 1 271, s v, 'Léon VIII'

Charlemagne, king of Lombardy, with the celebrated iron crown at Monza, some saying the ceremonial used was that of the 'Roman Ordo,' others, that of the Ambrosian Missal.[1] Another story represents the Roman rite substituted for the Ambrosian by peremptory command of Charlemagne, and only saved through the prayers and exertions of a Gallican prelate named Eusebius, perhaps hoping in this way to prevent the suppression of his own.[2]

3. Another document of prime importance dwelt upon at some length by Le Cointe, in connection with this visit of Charlemagne to Rome, is an epitome of canons discovered in a monastery by Canisius, and published by him at Ingoldstadt A.D. 1608, with an inscription on it declaring that they were presented in one volume by Adrian to Charles, king of the Franks and Lombards, and patrician of the Romans, at Rome, and an acrostic dedication by the giver of it referring to the victories just won. This had no sooner appeared than its true character was divined by Sirmondus the Jesuit, whose learned comments on Gallican councils and constitutions added great weight to his contention, that it was not this epitome, but the collection of canons epitomised in it, which Adrian presented, and Charlemagne received, on his first visit to Rome. Search was accordingly set on foot in all the libraries and monasteries of Europe for MSS. of the collection thus characterised by him, which the latest editors of S. Leo, the Ballerini, tell us had only to be looked for to be found in great abundance, though they omit to add where they found it called 'Hadriana collectio,' before calling it by that name themselves, and treating it all through the learned discussion which they have given to it as distinct from the Dionysian. Others, indeed, as Wendelstine, A D. 1525, and after him Pithæus, had published a collection entitled by them 'Codex canonum vetus ecclesiæ Romanæ.'

---

[1] Le Cointe, A D 774, n 30
[2] Muratori, *Rer It Script* iv 73 et seq Landulph, however, belonged to the eleventh century Ughelli, *Ital Sac* vi 31, tells it more plausibly

Quesnel, A.D. 1675, in an appendix to his edition of the works of S. Leo, brought out another—his principal authority for it being a MS. in the archives of Oriel College—which he considered had higher claims to that title. But these, not having been connected by their editors in any way with this epitome, nor with the gift of Hadrian, need not concern us here, being all but forgotten now. On the other hand, Professor Maassen, following in the track of the Ballerini with far greater means at his command, has succeeded in tabulating a list of seventy-one MSS. named according to the different archives that possessed them, of what he calls the 'Dionysio-Hadriana collectio':[1] and headed by two, which he says exhibit the acrostic dedication of the Canisian epitome.[2]

We must not be deterred by this array of MSS. from questioning the correctness of the hypothesis to which it is due—namely, the *dictum* of a single, though a learned man. The Ballerini themselves shrink instinctively from grappling in any way with the Canisian epitome: they barely mention it; they do all they can to divert attention from it, designating it a 'so-called piece,' which after the remark upon it by Sirmondus, they are dispensed from naming except in scorn.[3] Maassen is more liberal, but he fails to comprehend its point.[4] Mansi places himself in marked contrast to the Ballerini, by making no mention of their conclusions, while giving it entire.[5] Le Cointe draws attention to its singular characteristics, and thereby supplies us with the key to its origin, which shall be put into the lock forthwith, some rust clinging to it having to be got off first.

There is one section in the learned dissertations of the Ballerini that does honour to them even as controversialists: it is the section treating of the Dionysian collection, in other

---

[1] *Quel und Lit can Rechts*, § 586
[2] Viz *Cod Paris Suppl Lat* 331, and *Cod Lat Sangerm* 367
[3] 'Uti appellant, p 187 and then p 188, at the end of c 2, part III
[4] § 604
[5] XII 859.

words, the collection made by the Scythian monk, Dionysius Exiguus. They could not have considered him their best friend by any means, yet they print at full length the high praise bestowed on him by his friend and patron, Cassiodorus, not only for learning, but honesty, making him a glorious model for his pupils to follow: and to his collection they do full justice, by scrupulously recapitulating all the details given of it by himself. It consists of two parts, which are perfectly distinct, and must not be confounded, as one was published some years [1] before the other was even taken in hand: and therefore must have constituted a separate volume for some time and may have continued to be circulated separately longer still. For each part has a title peculiar to itself, incapable of comprehending the other, the title to the first part being—as now printed—'Codex canonum ecclesiasticorum Dionysii Exigui': the title to the second, 'Collectio decretorum'—Dionysius himself calls them *constitutorum*—'pontificum Romanorum, auctore Dionysio Exiguo.' It is a perfectly gratuitous assumption, therefore, which Sirmondus makes when he lays down that a document headed, 'Epitome canonum . . . *in uno volumine*, &c.' should have included all the papal Constitutions of the second part.[2] At that date no doubt each part formed a separate volume, though they might in some cases have been tacked together. Both parts are clearly distinguished by Pope Zachariah in his letter to Pepin and the French bishops, the second part being called by him 'Liber Decretorum' in citing the letters of the Popes contained in it to which he refers.[3] And the Ballerini tell us of their own accord that the title given in no less than ten MSS. to the rival collection published by Quesnel is 'Codex canonum ecclesiasticorum, *et* constitutionum sanctæ sedis apostolicæ.'[4]

That the 'Dionysian collection of Canons' was adopted

---

[1] See his own letter to Julian prefixed to the Decretals
[2] *Conc Gall* ii 117
[3] Mansi, xii 326-34
[4] *Append ad S. Leon Op.* 14, note

almost immediately for general use by the Roman Church is stated in express terms by Cassiodorus, and free reference to it occurs in the letter of Pope Zachariah, where citations from the second part occur also. Further, that it came to be called 'codex canonum' in the West generally may be shown from facts: and that, in process of time, numerous varieties of it appeared with additions not always authentic. But the title given to it of 'Code of the Roman Church,' and the distinction drawn between it and the 'collection of Adrian,' were neither of them known till comparatively modern times.

The Ballerini contend that it was 'the Dionysian *collection* with certain *additions*' which was presented by Adrian to Charlemagne.[1] The truth is, it was the Dionysian collection *of canons* with certain *subtractions* which formed the gift. The despised epitome makes everything as clear as day. It deals only with the first part of the Dionysian collection—only with canons, that is—because but '*one volume*' containing canons was sent. And it epitomised faithfully, beyond any doubt, all the canons which that one volume contained. The divergences between it and the collection are pointed out in detail by Le Cointe, who shows no desire to minimise them; but except in the African canons, which come last,[2] and which need not detain us here, they are purely nominal. When Le Cointe notices that the epitome stops with the African canons, he should have remembered that Dionysius himself stops there too, so far as canons are concerned. But in the Dionysian collection, as stated by Dionysius himself in his dedicatory letter to Bishop Stephen, after the canons of the Apostles immediately follow the Nicene canons, and after the canons of Ancyra, Neo-Cæsarea, Gangra, Antioch, Laodicea, which he places next, come the canons of Constantinople and Chalcedon, with which he tells us the Greek canons end. In *this*

---

[1] Pt iii c 2, p 184
[2] And where the MS is defective as Mansi points out, xii 879.

CANONS OF GENERAL COUNCILS OMITTED.

epitome, the Canons of Nicæa, Constantinople, and Chalcedon —the only General Councils whose canons are given by him— are *passed over entirely*, not one is epitomised. Le Cointe, though he notices it, shrinks from attempting to account for this omission. And well he might! For is it likely for one moment that, had these canons formed part of the volume presented by Adrian to his guest, they would not have been epitomised with the rest? For they stand neither first nor last, but in the very centre of the collection of Dionysius. And the epitomiser tells us himself that what his work professes to be is 'a compendium of the canons, Eastern and African, which Pope Adrian of happy memory presented in one volume to Charles, king of the Franks and Lombards.' Nor can he be blamed for not epitomising any canons not found in this volume. He was bent on giving us a compendium of it as it stood. It turns out, therefore, to have been *the Dionysian collection of canons*, with *important subtractions*, one result of which is obvious enough—namely, that next after the provincial canons of Ancyra, Neo-Cæsarea, Gangra, Antioch, and Laodicea, come the Sardican canons sanctioning appeals to Rome, all the canons of Nicæa, Constantinople, and Chalcedon recognising or enlarging the jurisdiction of other sees independent of Rome being suppressed. Hence the very first mention of Rome that meets us in this epitome runs thus:—[1]

'That bishops of the same province should hear causes between bishops who disagree. But should the bishop who has been condemned by them appeal to the Roman Pontiff, whatever he may determine must be observed.'

A little further on we read:—

'That a provincial synod may be revised by vicars of the Roman Pontiff, should he so decree.'[2]

Each of these statements is tersely, though not unfairly,

[1] 'Ut inter discordes episcopos comprovinciales episcopi audiant Quòd si damnatus appellaverit Romanum pontificem, id observandum est, quod ipse censuerit'

[2] 'Quòd provincialis synodus per vicarios Romani pontificis retractari possit, si ipse ita decreverit'

x

put: yet the canons represented by them are stronger still: and it is a canon omitted in this epitome which imparts additional force to them all, by making them take the form of a proposal from Osius—who not only presided at Sardica, but at Nicæa too—'to do honour to the memory of the Apostle Saint Peter,' in passing them.[1]

And then, lastly, the suppression of all the preceding canons of three General Councils, distinctly limiting their operation, must of itself have ministered to the idea that they were to be regarded as ordinances for the whole world.

Thus the survival of this epitome discloses to us in the plainest terms to what extent the volume presented by Adrian to his guest represented the Dionysian canons, and to what extent it fell short of representing them. The only point that can remain doubtful is, with what object the omitted portion was suppressed. First, then, it is simple nonsense to pretend that the collection of canons made by Dionysius was ever called, or considered, in ancient times 'the code of the Roman Church,' though its intrinsic recommendations made the Popes refer to it constantly, and quote from it too, when it suited their purpose. Previously to its appearance, the Popes steadily refused to consider themselves bound by any canons but the Nicene, which *they interpolated*, and the Sardican, which *they tacked on to them*, as possessing equal authority, but whose spuriousness has at length been acknowledged in a recent work printed at the Vatican. These Sardican canons were quoted as Nicene by Popes Zosimus, Innocent, and the first Leo. And at the Council of Chalcedon the legates of the first Leo formally quoted the sixth Nicene canon with this interpolation prefixed to it: 'Quòd ecclesia Romana semper habuit primatum,'[2] which was exposed on the spot. Nevertheless, strange to say, it was reproduced in an enlarged form by the author of the 'Prisca Versio,' published by Justellus. To the canons of Chalcedon and Constantinople the Popes, down to Adrian at

[1] Can 3 in Dion Ex   [2] Mansi, vii 443

least, could never be made to assent. Dionysius himself would not include the twenty-eighth Chalcedonian canon in his collection; though the ninth Chalcedonian and the second Constantinopolitan between them embody the whole sting of the canon which he omits.

Adrian, therefore, merely followed in the footsteps of his predecessors in ignoring these canons; while, to have quoted the Nicene, he must have either broken with the Dionysian version in adopting the interpolation of the legates of the first Leo, or pronounced against their interpolation in adopting the Dionysian version. If he omitted them entire, they would tell no tale. The prefaces to the Ancyran and Gangran canons in the epitome, where mention of the Nicene canons occurs, form no part of the Dionysian collection proper, but are repeated from the 'Prisca Versio.' Adrian had never informed Charlemagne that the volume which he sent him was the Dionysian collection of canons, and as he was not therefore palming it upon him as such, he could omit what he would. By omitting all mention of the Nicene, the Sardican canons would stand out, he may have judged—and judged correctly—when they came to be perused, in high relief.

Astute policy, then, is the heaviest indictment that can be sustained against Adrian on the showing of this epitome. But his own writings prove that he could go several steps further when policy required, and his subject-matter enabled him to be more bold. For who could know half as well as himself what his own archives contained: and who kept the key of that lock but himself? Accordingly, within three years of the presentation of these canons, Adrian, to enhance the righteousness of his oft-reiterated, but as oft-evaded, plea for the exaltation of 'the holy Catholic and Apostolic Church of Rome,' or rather 'of S. Peter the Apostle,' and for the enlargement of its temporalities, addressed a glowing letter to his powerful patron, in which are set forth what splendid donations the first Christian Emperor Constantine, and other emperors and patricians, treading in his steps, had at different times made to the Church of that Apostle—donations which were still producible for the most part from his writing-desk at the Lateran, though the wicked Lombards had long usurped the property therein conveyed. 'Hence, what,' he asks, 'could the new Constantine, whom God had raised up, and constituted a universal benefactor of that same Church, do but restore them in all their integrity to it without delay?'[1]

4. The apology which Cennius makes for this statement is a mere substitution of one forgery for another,[2] having for its result the discrediting two Popes instead of one. Over and above this, one link in the connection of Adrian with the Acts of Pope Silvester is acknowledged. Another link,[3] as it occurs in a letter addressed by Adrian himself to Egilas, a bishop of Spain, speaks for itself. A third link requires careful treatment to be made plain.

5. Five more years had elapsed; and we gather from the letters of Adrian, still full of the same plea, that his appeal to the precedent of Constantine, and the authority produced for it, had as yet elicited no response. But, at the end of that time, a bishop designate, named Peter, sent by Charlemagne to receive consecration from the Pope, brings with him and presents the Pope with an epitome (*breviarium*) of the Acts of the Council of Chalcedon, which the Pope characterises after examination a 'pseudopittacium,' and expresses no small indignation and surprise that it should have been sent to him; protesting that he embraced the *genuine* documents of that Council in their entirety with all his

---

[1] *Cod Carol Ep* lx ed Migne, *Pat Lat* xcviii 306

[2] 'Desipiunt Muratorius aliique Adriano objicientes donationem Constantinianam haud dum natam Ex actis enim Silvestri, quæ, licet supposita, tamen in libros apocryphos rejecta non erant, mutuatus est Adrianus, quæ hic habentur'

(*Ad l*) Yet the long letter of Leo IX, who avails himself of 'the Constantinian donation' to the full, commences with a distinct reference (§ 10) to the Acts of Pope Silvester, proving their connection —Mansi, xix 641-5

[3] *Ep* lxx *ad fin*

heart. Was this epitome, which he confesses to have been 'a vestrâ excellentiâ nobis directum,'[1] *directed to him in mock irony by the sender*, in return for having had the Acts of Pope Silvester quoted to him as authentic, which his divines knew to be false? We may well imagine the grim smile with which this pseudonymous piece was handed to Peter to present *after consecration*, and the sharpness of the sting inflicted by it after perusal. The document itself might hardly be worth protesting against; but could the Acts of Pope Silvester be permitted to be dragged down to its level? Either they must be given a *locus standi* without delay, or the less said about them in future the better. Adrian may or may not have been privy to the fabrication of this version of them, but these facts anyhow are beyond dispute. A different version is given of them one hundred years earlier by S. Aldhelm, who must have got it from Rome. This version attributes the cure of Constantine from leprosy to the sacrament of baptism, but without stating by whom administered, or when or where received. It relates the confutation of the Jews by Pope Silvester, but leaves us to infer it happened at the Nicene Council. It makes Constantine dream his dream *at Constantinople*, and Silvester appear in a vision there to interpret it for him. And what the dream symbolises is the splendid future, and uprising of magnificent churches for *the new capital*, without adding a word about the old.[2]

6. The version given of them by Adrian is first quoted by himself; and the document which shields them from criticism was quoted for the first time some seven or eight years later

[1] *Ep* lxxiii *ad fin*
[2] *De Laud Virg* c 25. According to the poem on the same subject, indeed, baptism was administered to him by Silvester; but only the destruction of pagan temples in Rome followed there Migne, *Pat. Lat* lxxxix. 122 and 218 Another version of these acts may be read in Surius, *De Prob.*

Sanct Hist vi. 1052, and a third in Greek, nearly the same, was published by Combefis at Paris, 8vo A D 1659 The Constitution of Silvester may be read in Mansi, ii 618 *et seq* and the Donation, ib 603–11, but Adrian is the first who connects any donation with his version of the Acts.

in his pontificate. This document is the well-known decree said to have been formulated at a Council of seventy bishops under Pope Gelasius, A.D. 494. Its spuriousness has been elsewhere maintained.[1] It may have been built upon old foundations, but it betrays, as now seen, a style of architecture much too redolent of the manner and aims of the ninth century to bear antedating. It ministers confessedly to what was wanting then. The genuine pieces of the Popes collected by Dionysius Exiguus are called by himself 'constitutions'; Pope Zachariah calls that collection of them 'liber decretorum.' This decree preconises another set not yet given to the world, when it enumerates, among books to be received, 'Item *decretales epistolas,* quas beatissimi papæ diversis temporibus ab urbe Româ dederunt'; and adds, further on, under the same heading: 'Also the Acts of blessed Silvester, prelate of the Apostolic See, though the name of the writer of them is unknown; as being read by many Catholics in the city of Rome, and many Churches long accustomed to follow their example.'[2] Yet, almost in the same breath, it had been declared that the Acts of martyrs were not read in the Roman Church as '*being anonymous compositions.*' There was a present purpose to serve, both in getting clear of the one and upholding the other.

Accordingly, with this decree to back him, Adrian ventured on a bold stroke of policy after waiting two more years in suspense. The plea founded on the Acts of Pope Silvester had been sufficiently disregarded by Charlemagne; it might be received with more favour in the East, whither the Pope was now asked to send help, such as could only be sent by him.[2] Legates were therefore despatched by him to Constantinople to be present at a Council about to meet, to reverse the nefarious acts of the iconoclasts who had defied his predecessors. His legates took with them a

[1] *Dict of Christian Ant* 'Roman Councils,' ii 1815
[2] Mansi, viii 162-3. In the note to p 146, the earliest reference to it in this shape is suppressed
[3] The letter of the Empress Irene and her son inviting him is dated Aug. 29, A.D. 784—Mansi, xii. 984.

letter addressed to the Empress Irene and her son, and read at the opening of the Council, assuring them of his hearty good will, but reiterating the plea next his heart, that they would procure for him, by all the means in their power, the restoration of all the territory bestowed on Pope Silvester by the founder of their capital, but since then wrested from his representatives by a succession of usurpers. When his legates returned, and reported the Council a great success, Charlemagne must have felt that he had been outwitted for once, and had no time to lose. Without loss of time, therefore, a work was concocted between his divines and himself, attacking the decrees of the second Nicene Council respecting images, and opposing the Creed of his adoption to theirs. This work, already noticed, has been called the Caroline Books. At the end of the thirteenth chapter of the second of its four books occurs the earliest extant mention of the Gelasian decree, which is there deliberately made to concur in the following sharp attack upon the Acts of Pope Silvester, which that decree was meant to uphold. 'Hence the book of the Acts of Silvester of happy memory, when it speaks of the images presented to the Emperor Constantine, may be contradicted; because, though it may be read by many Catholics, it has plainly no business to be quoted for settling points in dispute, as is more fully demonstrated in the book of Gelasius of happy memory, Bishop of Rome, which is entitled *Decretalis de recipiendis sive de non recipiendis codicibus.*'[1] Adrian, in his long-drawn reply to this work, drops all mention of the Acts of Silvester,[2] and refers to what passed at the Nicene Council for proof of the honour in which images were then held; of which proof, it is needless to say, no record exists. But in concluding his subject he naively lets out that, though his Eastern potentates had abandoned their errors about images, they had not yet given back what belonged to his see. And this leads to the further remark, intended for still wider application, that if restitu-

---

[1] Migne, *Patrol. Lat.* xcviii. 1078.   [2] Ib. 1285.

tion were refused, he should be constrained to proclaim him a heretic who persisted in an error of this sort.'[1]

This work and the answer to it sufficiently reveal the real issues between them, and the arms that they used. Another conspicuous illustration of both shall be given from the same source.

7–8. Charlemagne was just as eager to get his interpolated Creed adopted by Adrian as Adrian to get the territory which he claimed confirmed to him by Charlemagne. One wanted to lay the foundations of a new empire in a Creed that should be distinguishable from the traditional Creed of the old; the other wanted to add temporal to the spiritual dominion that had been already gained for his see. Adrian quoted the Acts of Pope Silvester to support his claim to the territory which he said was his; Charlemagne produced two Creeds, both of them counterfeits, to bear out his Creed.[2] About the first of these there can be no dispute, for it literally stands confessed. It appears at full length in the first chapter of the third of the books bearing his name; and at the end of it, either he says or his divines say for him: 'Such is the tradition of the Catholic faith in its integrity, which we profess and believe from our heart, and have set down in the words of S. Jerome.' That S. Jerome was not the author of it, his theologians were too well versed in the writings of S. Augustine not to have known: that it must have been interpolated in order to serve the purposes of this work is only too plain; for otherwise it must have testified *against* the interpolated Creed of Charlemagne.[3] Pelagius, a

---

[1] Migne, *Patrol Lat* xcviii 1292

[2] 'The Franks,' said Baluze, in 1666, the highest authority then on these points, 'repudiated the decisions of the second Nicene Council about images all the more vehemently from fear that, if they accepted them, they might again become part and parcel of the Greek Empire' Quoted with approbation by Gallandius, *Bibl Vet Pat* xiii 457, note Comp. *Proleg.* p. xiii.

The same may be said of their adherence to the 'Filioque' clause, in support of which *alone*, let us never forget, the Athanasian Creed was first cited

[3] Hence Migne, 'Addidi *Ex Patre et Filio procedentem*, volente et jubente Carolo infra c 3, et c 8' Rabanus Maurus, *De Sac Ord.* c 9, has 'Filioque,' no doubt on the strength of this passage.

very different person from S. Jerome, composed it; and this fact could have been no secret to any readers of S. Augustine, who twice quotes it,[1] as being the 'libellus fidei' despatched by his opponent to Rome, where Baronius found it in safe keeping among the letters of Pope Zosimus, by whom it was favourably received. But in the original, which is loyally reproduced by Baronius, the Holy Ghost is described to be 'Verum Deum ex Patre procedentem.'[2] The '*Filioque*' being indispensable to the argument, it was put in here. Rabanus Maurus, in quoting this Creed, quotes it with this additional clause, which had become law in the whole West by then; but he had too much respect for S. Jerome, and was too familiar with his translation of the work of Didymus 'On the Holy Ghost,' to think of ascribing that Creed to him, especially with that addition.

As to the second Creed, if Lambecius is to be trusted, it cannot have been long after the completion of this work that Charlemagne despatched the celebrated psalter preserved at Vienna, written throughout in letters of gold, to Rome: commencing with an inscription in verse, describing it as a gift to Pope Adrian from King Charles: and finishing with an appendix in which the Athanasian Creed, never before produced entire, still less ever before designated by that title, comes last.[3]

Lambecius is careful to tell us that Pope Adrian died in December, A.D. 795; so that, if his view of this psalter is correct, the Athanasian Creed must have been in existence by then; yet as it is nowhere quoted or named in the Caroline Books, their reticence goes far to establish its non-existence when they were composed.

On this Creed I discoursed in a book more than twelve years old, at sufficient length to dispense me from any further remarks on it now save this: that the view there

---

[1] *De Gratiâ Christi*, c 31-33, and *De Pecc Orig* c 17 and 23
[2] A.D. 417, n 32
[3] *De Bibl Cæs* vol 11 261 *et seq*.

taken of its composition is the only view to which authentic history lends any support: and that it receives additional illustration from the facts brought out in connection with the Creed from which we have just parted. Nobody can deny *that* Creed to have been published under a false name by Charlemagne: nor, till an earlier work of undoubted authenticity can be produced where the 'Quicunque vult' is designated 'the Faith' or 'Creed of S. Athanasius,' can anybody deny Charlemagne to have been the first in whose writings, or the writing of persons acting under him, it is ascribed—and ascribed falsely—to S. Athanasius, and paraded as a Creed possessing all the authority that would attach justly to his name. Thus, if this psalter was really presented to Pope Adrian I. by King Charles the Great, it is himself who first gives the Athanasian Creed the title which it has ever since borne. If this psalter was not his gift— which just may be [1]—then the 'Quicunque vult' got its title first given to it either by his monks, who sang the interpolated Creed on Mount Olives, and forthwith justified their act to the successor of Adrian, Leo III., by declaring that it was so said in the 'Faith of S. Athanasius'; [2] or else by Theodulph and Alcuin [3] in tracts published by his command against the Greeks: and, as Alcuin died on Whitsunday A.D. 804, written a year or more before then. In these tracts extracts are made from it at sufficient length to leave no room for doubt that by 'fides Athanasii' the title given to it at that date was meant—and it was a very common meaning

---

[1] For there is nothing in the dedicatory verses to prevent 'King Charles' from being Charles the Bald, and 'Pope Adrian' from being Pope Adrian II See this point argued *Athanasian Creed*, pp 303-7

[2] Neale's *Eastern Ch* Genl Introd ii 1155-8, as transcribed by Le Quien from *Miscell* vii p 14 of Baluze, *Oriens Christian* iii 347 But it is without date, the only clue to which is that Charles is styled Emperor.

[3] Migne, *Patrol. Lat* cv 247, and ci 73 and 82 respectively Alcuin quotes it twice, and in the second passage gives its concluding words on the Trinity Immediately preceding his first quotation the decree of Pope Gelasius is evidently cited in its justification That Alcuin wrote this tract is shown in the *Præv Monit* to it by Migne.

for 'fi es' = πίστις then—what has since been called the Athanasian Creed in its present shape. Two Creeds accordingly were put forth at intervals by Charlemagne: and on each occasion it was in controversy with the Greeks. The first he paraded as the Faith of S. Jerome, a doctor of the Latin, and the second he called the Faith of S. Athanasius, a doctor of the Greek Church: and the latter, in his Capitularies of Aix, A.D. 802, he ordered all his clergy to learn by heart, giving precedence to it over the Creed of the Apostles.[1] How he came by it is another question. But whether concocted in his reign or not, it was published by him under a false name. His first Creed—of whose character, authorship, and date we could not well have clearer evidence—he not only published under a false name, but interpolated. The counterfeit charter employed by the Pope stated as facts things which were not facts; the counterfeit Creeds employed by the King claimed to be both authentic and authoritative without being either. Europe has for centuries groaned, and in many ways is still groaning, under the effects of all three. Let me not be supposed, however, to imply that fictitious documents were peculiar by any means to the West at this period. Half the documents quoted and received with approval at the second Nicene Council were just as disastrous, because just as false. But it is to the manufacture now going on of such documents within the quadrilateral of Charlemagne previously described, and to the reciprocity between it and Rome, that I want to direct full attention, by way of clearing the ground for my own special branch of the subject when it is reached.

9. The ninth document of this kind is one which has puzzled commentators, and divided them, almost as much as the Athanasian Creed: and well it may, for it has come down to us with two distinct titles, perhaps indicating a joint responsibility. The title given to it in Mansi,[2] which Hinschius tells us no less than thirty-one MSS. support, runs

[1] Pertz, *Mon. Germ. Legum*, 1. 107.   [2] XII 903 *et seq*

thus: 'These Capitularies were *collected scatteredly* from Greek and Latin canons, and Roman synods, and decrees of Roman prelates and princes, and given to Ingilramn, bishop of the city of Metz, at Rome, by Pope Adrian of happy memory, on September 19 of the ninth indiction—*quando pro sui negotii causa agebatur*'—which each reader may translate for himself. It never varies in any form of either title that I can discover. *Sparsim collecta*: 'scatteredly collected' is another phrase that never varies under either title; indeed, it might be called the *trade-mark* of this species of pseudonymous issue from the quadrilateral. Another point that never varies under either title, is that their presentation took place at Rome. The indiction assigned for it is variously numbered under both titles: but the ninth, which is the prevailing one, corresponds with A.D. 785. And the pith of the other title consists in this: that it affirms them to have been presented by Ingilramn or Angilramn, according as his name is spelt, to Pope Adrian. Le Cointe,[1] recalling the Book of Canons presented to Charlemagne by Adrian eleven years before, much prefers this title: but, interpreted by its epitome, the ring of this book and of these Capitularies is only fainter in one than in the other. By those who support the first title they are called 'the Capitularies of Adrian': by those who support the second they are called 'the Capitularies of Angilramn.' Meanwhile the fact of a twofold title suggests a joint composition, and the fact of their having been presented at Rome, and accepted without protest, a joint adhesion to their contents. Policy, we may well believe, prompted or tolerated the very scant reference contained in Chapter VI. to the privileges conferred on the see of Constantinople by the ninth canon of Chalcedon: as the letter of the Empress and her son, inviting the Pope to send legates to the Council which they were preparing to assemble, must have been in

---

[1] *Annal* A D 785, n. 16 *et seq*

his hands at the time.[1] Besides, Chapter VI. is overshadowed in advance by Chapter III., than which no fuller assertion, in a few words, of the claims of the see of Rome could be found.

There have been some who maintained that these Capitularies were drawn from genuine sources in every case; it is acknowledged by all now that the documents characteristic of them are for the most part spurious. The contention of Hinschius, whose exhaustive work on the Decretals of the pseudo-Isidore[2] leaves nothing to be desired that the argument *from internal evidence* could supply, comes to this: that the pseudo-Isidore borrowed from these Capitularies, and from the Capitularies of Benedict the Levite, and that the Capitularies of Benedict the Levite furnished a good number of these Capitularies also. Thus, according to him, it would follow that these Capitularies were compiled *after* Benedict had compiled his, and perhaps, he adds, simultaneously with the compilation of the pseudo-Isidore, so that the pseudo-Isidore might have been quite possibly the compiler of both sets. What, then, is to be said of the twofold title given, amid endless varieties, with so much unanimity to these Capitularies in so many MSS.? Hinschius assumes that both titles are false: and justifies his conclusion on the further assumption that no proof in writing exists that Angilramn was ever at Rome.[3] All his fine-drawn conclusions, therefore, from internal evidence were rudely shaken when Wattenbach, by a fine touch of criticism, got Alcuin to depose to the fact that Angilramn had once been bearer of his respects to a monk at that time, but afterwards abbot, of S. Saviour, on Mount Amiato, near Radicofani, named Usuard, leaving us to infer naturally that he was then *en route* for Rome. 'At Rome, therefore,' continues Wattenbach, 'I make no doubt he was, on September 19, A.D. 785, agreeably with the title prefixed to

---

[1] Note to p 310 [2] Leipsic, 1863, 8vo.
[3] Ib *Proleg* clxix

these Capitularies.'[1] What took Angilramn to Rome the Capitularies of Frankfort, A.D. 794, explain in a way that would have satisfied everybody but for those six colourless words—perhaps from design—as they stand now: '*quando pro sui negotii causa agebatur*.' One thing is certain, that if we touch them at all, we must put no meaning on them that history will not bear out. Accordingly, when Charlemagne says in his fifty-third Capitulary[2] that 'licence had in time past been obtained by him from the Apostolic See— that is, from Pope Adrian—to keep Angilramn continually by him at his palace, *propter utilitates ecclesiasticas*,' we should consider he as good as tells us that the business Angilramn went to transact in person at Rome was to procure this licence from the Pope. To represent him going thither as an accused person[3] to defend himself, is simply to contradict all we know of him, and quite irreconcilable with the high terms of respect addressed to him by Paul Winfrid the deacon, in concluding his monograph on the previous bishops of Metz.[4]

We are thus thrown back upon the old school headed by Baronius, who, nothing doubting, makes Adrian author of these Capitularies: and on Pagi,[5] who bids us notice that they were ascribed to him by Hincmar—consecrated archbishop of Rheims little more than half a century from his death—nothing doubting either, in controversy with his nephew:[6] and also that Riculfus came back in A.D. 785

---

[1] *Bibl Rer Germ* tom vi, *Monum Alcuin* p 514-15, with the notes Usuard became abbot A D 794, which is the date given to this letter Angilramn died A D 791

[2] Baluze, *Capitul Reg Franc* i 270

[3] 'Ut causam suam adversus falsos accusatores defenderet,' says Baronius, who then adds, 'quem absolutum hisce canonibus et communitum [pontifex] remisit ad suos' According to this, Adrian not merely compiled these Capitularies, but acted on them as soon as compiled, A D 786, n 6, but rightly corrected by Pagi to 785

[4] Migne, *Patrol Lat* xcv 710

[5] As above and also n 9

[6] This was in 869, *Opusc et Ep in Causa Hinc Laudun* c 24 The two statements are within two pages of each other Migne, ib cxxv 377-9, in his tract *De Presb Crim* calls the author of the False Decretals, *Isidorus episcopus Hispalensis* (c 21), not distinguishing between him and his namesake

NOTICES OF RICULFUS. 319

from Spain, bringing with him, as Pagi rightly makes Hincmar say, 'the Book of Isidore Mercator,' for the description given of its commencement by him identifies it with the collection so long known under that name, which, 'as *taking particular interest in works of this kind*, and in the royal Capitularies,' on becoming archbishop of Mayence the year following, he caused to be circulated up and down throughout those parts. But Hinschius, on the other hand, by exhibiting a long list of MSS. of it, classified according to countries, in which Spain is credited with next to none, and Portugal with none whatever, proves unconsciously that by Spain Hincmar must have meant what used in days gone by to form part of the Gothic kingdom in Spain, yet was north of the Pyrenees, and was still inhabited, as we learn from the Capitularies of A.D. 812, by a Spanish population [1]— in modern parlance, the Basque provinces.

10. The learned authors of 'Gallia Christiana'[2] protest against the unfairness of crediting Riculfus with the authorship of the False Decretals; but one thing has just been established—namely, that they were manufactured north, *not south*, of the Pyrenees. Another fact is that the remark of Hincmar in characterising Riculfus as '*hujusmodi studiosus*' finds illustration in two Capitularies: the first of A.D. 803, 'De Purgatione Sacerdotum,' where we find he produced a letter of 'Pope Gregory of happy memory' bearing on this subject, which was accepted as decisive by Charlemagne; but it was a letter of the second Gregory, not of the first. Three years later [3] we have part of the 'Consti-

---

[1] 'Pro Hispanis qui in regnum Karoli confugerant' But numbers had never left those parts Repeated A D 815 by Lewis, being his very first precept Baluze, 1 pp 499 and 549

[2] v 444–5

[3] Baluze for the Caps 1 386 and 458 Hinschius for the pseudo-Is p 449 It is not a little curious that one of the very few letters of S Gregory the Great which the pseudo-Isidore has ventured to insert in his collection should have been grossly interpolated in that part of it which relates to this subject *Ep* lib ix 52 with the Benedictine note 'Hæc epistola facilius expungeretur quàm sanaretur In Isidorum Mercatorem multi rejiciunt'

tutum' of Pope Silvester quoted with approval on the same subject: and it happens to be this time the part selected for insertion in his collection by the pseudo-Isidore, though it forms also the seventy-second of the Capitularies of Adrian or Angilramn. From whom did Charlemagne get it? from Adrian or Angilramn, who were long since dead, or from the book brought into France by Riculfus, who was in high force just now? There are some facts connected with him that have never been sufficiently brought out, from having come down to us in disguise. The special favourites at the Court of Charlemagne had all a name given to them by him, symbolising roughly the estimation in which they were held there. Angilbert was called Homer, as having a lofty turn of mind; Riculfus was only Damœtas, as having a bucolic turn. Alcuin called him his 'son' when their acquaintance first commenced; and is eloquent both in prose and verse over the formidable two-headed monster carved on an ivory comb received from him. 'Fisherman' is his next term for him in congratulating him on becoming archbishop. 'Venerable father' in A.D. 800: 'tried friend' two years later, when Alcuin was in trouble and needed his support. In most of these letters there is a caution against worldly-mindedness. 'O fili, *inter occupationes seculi* non obliviscaris tui,' addressed to him in his youth is reiterated more strongly than ever in his last epistle to his 'tried friend.' But it is the letter addressed to him in A.D. 800 that requires most comment.[1] It discloses the fact that Riculfus was absent in Rome, taking part in the farce that was being played there then of a mock trial for frightening Leo III., the victim of a murderous assault but a year earlier, into crowning Charles emperor, and thus breaking definitively with the East.[2] Two points in these transactions, and in this letter of Alcuin,

---

[1] *Ep* 123 in Migne, *Patrol Lat* c 357; with the note The others are, 44-6 and 122 But the last is 211 in *Monum Alcuin*

[2] On this see the art 'Leo III' in *Dict of Christian Biog* iii 674-77

which of all contemporary documents throws most light upon them, should never be forgotten by us in this inquiry. The letter of Alcuin has been accurately dated by Wattenbach 'end of 800 or beginning of 801';[1] for tidings must have reached Alcuin of all that had been consummated at Rome by them, when he told his spiritual father how all his anxieties had been dispelled, and how his heart had bounded with joy, on learning how prosperously things had gone—*et quomodo stetisti cum domno Apostolico*—on peace being restored to the Church there, mainly through his exertions.[2]

How had Riculfus been the prime mover in restoring peace that he is here represented to have been? Let events speak for themselves—events spread over three days. On the first day a number of archbishops, bishops, and abbots, met by order of Charles in the church of S. Peter to hear charges preferred against the Pope. What those charges were we learn from another letter of Alcuin, written some little time before to Arno, metropolitan of Salzburg, also then at Rome, which the writer had possibly learnt from Riculfus. 'I understand,' he says, 'there are many, who from motives of jealousy, are trying by crafty suggestions to compass the deposition of the said Pope; endeavouring to fasten upon him charges of perjury and adultery, and then to draw him into purging himself by solemn oath from those crimes; hoping in secret, by advising this course, to get him to lay down his pontificate without swearing, and pass the remainder of his days in any monastery that he pleased in peace.'[3] The party led by Riculfus prevailed. 'They exclaimed—archbishops, bishops, and abbots, all of them'— says the Papal biographer, 'with one mouth, "We dare not

---

[1] *Monum Alc* p 586
[2] 'Quidam, meliori consilio vetera reformare, et in antiquum reponere ordinem; cum quibus vestram sanctissimam sollicitudinem laborare audivimus. Et placuit mihi multùm, piæ pacis atque ecclesiasticæ concordiæ vos secundum Deum seminatores esse; in quâ vestiam benevolentiam semper sudare exopto'—Ib p. 588
[3] Ib p 489

judge the Apostolic See, which is head of all the Churches of God; for by it and by its vicar, all of us are judged ourselves, whereas it is judged by none, *conformably with ancient custom.*"' The Pope then came forward, and offered, 'following in the steps of his predecessors, to clear himself by oath from the crimes laid to his charge.' On the second day he did this in their presence. On the third day in their presence, and that of a much larger concourse, by prearrangement he crowned Charles.[1]

Now, if the exclamations attributed to the bishops and archbishops on this occasion by the Papal biographer have been correctly reported, it is from the book of Riculfus alone that they can be explained. The fabled Synod of Sinuessa might have supplied a precedent and a principle combined of the clearest and closest relevancy to the matter in hand, ' Prima sedes non judicabitur a quoquam,' as it was believed to have ruled.[2] But had it not been confirmed by the Book of Riculfus, how could the bishops and archbishops have ventured to say of its ruling, '*quemadmodum et antiquitus mos fuit*'? Every word that fell from them is founded on some maxim oft repeated in the False Decretals, and could not have been gainsaid by those who believed them true. Their utterances about the see of Rome were culled nearly word for word from the third decretal of Anacletus,[3] who comes next but one to S. Peter in that collection, and is there described as having been ordained presbyter by him, but *placed in the Apostolic See by the Lord*, 'which Apostolic See,' says Anacletus, ' was made both head and hinge, so to speak, by the Lord, and owes its appointment to no other; thus, as a door is governed by its hinge, so all the Churches are, by disposal of the Lord, governed by the authority of this Holy See.' Alexander I., Sixtus I., Pius I., and others down to Melchiades, the last of his ante-Nicene

---

[1] Mansi, xiii 1044
[2] Baron. A D 303, n. 98; comp Pagi *ad Baron* n. 18, A D 302
[3] Hinschius, p 84

successors, claim the same privileges for themselves by divine right in as lofty terms.[1] Other maxims, only general in their import till then, had, from their point of view, a primary meaning too for themselves; such as, 'The greater cannot be judged by the less . . . the disciple neither ought to be nor can be above his master.'[2] 'He cannot be condemned by human trial whom God has reserved to His own tribunal . . .'[3] Or more plainly put, 'Who is he who judges another whom the Lord has reserved to Himself and to this holy see to be judged?'[4] It was one thing for language respecting the privileges claimed for the Roman See to have grown inflated in proportion to their actual extension as time went on; it was another thing for its *earliest* bishops to be credited with having all along far exceeded that language in claiming them as due from all and as inherent in their see by divine right. Accordingly, those who were shown the book of Riculfus in confidence beforehand, and believed it authentic, could have made the declaration attributed to them by the Papal biographer in perfect good faith, and have wound it up without fear of contradiction by asserting that it was in strict accordance with ancient custom. It was allowed to pass unchallenged by Charlemagne, as it led by natural sequence to the next act, already determined upon with his full consent. For in the act of Leo, whose oath has been preserved [5]—and it is certainly the first, if not also the last, of its kind on record—the hand of Riculfus is as conspicuous by its presence as his book is by its absence. Canonical purgation, as it is called, purgation by oath, is nowhere prescribed, or even hinted at, in the False Decretals. Authentic instances of it occur in the Epistles of S. Gregory the Great, the first Pope by whom it was employed;[6] though his namesake, Gregory II., was the first Pope who

---

[1] Hinschius pp 95, 108, 116-7, 243
[2] Ib pp 45,
[3] Ib pp. 99, 126, 163, 193.
[4] Ib p 129.
[5] Mansi, xiii 1046.

[6] *Ep* lib ii 33, for the case of a bishop, and *Ep* lib vii 18, for the case of a deacon and abbot, where the Benedictine note is fullest

prescribed its use. The Capitulary 'De Purgatione Sacerdotum,' said to have been published at Aix, A.D. 803, has been already noticed, as furnishing evidence of the most conclusive kind that it was Riculfus to whom Charlemagne was indebted for this information. What has not yet been pointed out—though it was guaranteed by Hincmar within fifty years of its occurrence—is, that the subject was under consideration by Charlemagne four years earlier, A.D. 799, when what forced it on his attention must have been the Pope's own case. His short letter, proposing it for general inquiry, must be read between the lines to be understood, as it is there made to concern only presbyters charged with crimes which they denied, and their accusers could not prove. And he concludes with mock gravity, that he had sent to consult the Pope what course was to be pursued in their case—which was just his own also—and was waiting for his reply.[1] Then, in a subsequent Capitulary, dated by its contents, he makes known to all whom it may concern how this perplexing question was at last settled at a large gathering,[2] where the Pope was present, including bishops of the Roman and of the Greek Church and of his own dominions; priests and Levites,[3] magistrates and other laymen, *conformably with the precedent set by the Pope himself*, who had twelve presbyters. Hincmar says, bishops joined with him in making oath of his innocence, though the number of witnesses might be varied in each case. From another Capitulary, published about the same time,[4] we get the further information which has been anticipated— namely, that he was in ignorance of the previous ruling of this point by Pope Gregory, till shown a letter of his by

[1] Baluze, *Capit* 1 327, and Hincmar, *De Presbyteris criminosis*, c 1
[2] Ib p 384 It is given in full by Gratian in his second part, ii 9, 5, c 19
[3] Knust italicises and raves at this word 'Quidnam sancti patres atque *levitæ* statuerunt ' ! quite forgetting, or else not knowing, that *abbots* were rarely then in more than deacon's orders and that abbots always formed part of these assemblies—Alcuin, for instance Hinschius corrects Knust on many points, pp cliv –lx.
[4] Baluze, 1 386

Riculfus, Archbishop of Mayence, where the following words occurred: 'Concerning a presbyter, or *any priest whomsoever*, accused by the people: in the event of there being no witnesses capable of proving the crime laid to his charge, an oath shall be lawful, and he may call upon Him to whom all things are naked and opened, to attest his innocence, and so remain undisturbed in his office.' Gratian repeats all these Capitularies in the second part of his Decretum consecutively to the oath taken by Leo; testifying to his belief of their connection,[1] Knust recklessly pronounces them spurious,[2] just because he fails to see their application, and the light thrown on the doings of Riculfus at Rome by the letter of Alcuin intended for his eyes alone, based on tidings furnished by himself. Is not the light thrown on the events in question by this letter of Alcuin reflected back on his letter by these Capitularies, thus establishing their own genuineness? Meanwhile, there are more letters of Alcuin to be consulted before we have done with him, or Riculfus, or Charlemagne.

Taking Charlemagne first, let us take care not to forget that what is placed last in his Capitularies of A.D. 806[3] has been extracted from a Constitution of Pope Silvester: whose Acts he had quoted with disapproval in writing against the second Nicene Council, when Adrian was Pope. But as the passage now quoted and endorsed by him happens to appear nearly word for word in the book of Riculfus also, perhaps it was through Riculfus—as being '*hujusmodi studiosus*' —that it was inserted here, or as being confirmed by his book. For it is likewise found in the Capitularies which Angilramn either took with him to Rome or brought back from Rome.[4] Next, in the sixth chapter of the first of the Caroline Books, we find the digression on the privileges of the Roman Church introduced by a well-known extract from the preface

---

[1] Cause II quæst v c 18, 19.
[2] Pertz, *Monum. Germ. Legum*, ii. append p. 32
[3] Baluze, 1 458, also Pertz, *Legu* i. 148.
[4] C. 72.

to the Nicene Council in the book of Riculfus—the pseudo-Isidore; to the effect that the Roman Church owes its primacy to no synodical decrees of Councils, but to those words of Christ: 'I say unto thee, that thou art Peter,' &c. But this, again, is introduced almost in the same terms into the Gelasian decree. Further, in the objurgatory letter addressed by Charlemagne to Alcuin only two years before his death, we find a third double reference: [1] the actual words quoted— 'Nulli criminoso alterum accusandi dari licentiam'—being all but identical in words with the forty-third of the Capitularies of Angilramn, but identical in substance too with the first pseudo-decretal of Anacletus, and the second of Eutician,[2] where they treat of the same point. Alcuin himself, too, refers in the letter which had drawn down this reproof on him to the canons and Acts of Pope Silvester: though he there mistakes the twenty-second canon of the fifth Council of Orleans for a canon of his.[3] And in his letter to Arno, then at Rome, two years before,[4] besides quoting the Constitution of Pope Silvester, imported afterwards into the Capitularies of A.D. 806, he says he remembers having read *other canons*, in which it was laid down 'that the Apostolic See was judiciary, but could not be judged.' Those canons he had probably read in the book which he knew his friend Damœtas to be then using at Rome; so that his reference to them may have been dictated by the wish of securing their acceptance by Arno.

Finally, there was another bishop with whom Alcuin was in constant correspondence just now—Remedius, bishop of Coire, a suffragan of Mayence—whom Frobenius, commenting on a letter from Alcuin to him (and, as Alcuin died A.D. 805, necessarily written before then), styles author of a collection of canons ordered by Charlemagne; but all of them, it turns out, drawn from the book of Riculfus, or the

---

[1] *Ep* 158, ed Migne, with the notes of Baluze
[2] Hinschius, pp. 68 and 211
[3] *Ep* 157.   [4] *Ep*. 108.

False Decretals, so far as they are still extant. Goldastus, who first printed them, says they were put in hand A.D. 813, or the year before Charlemagne died.[1] Hartzheim reprints them,[2] but misdates their author, from not knowing that he corresponded with Alcuin, and therefore fails to realise the proof supplied by his letters, that the False Decretals *were* known to Charlemagne, notwithstanding all the special pleading of the Ballerini to prove the contrary.[3] Wattenbach[4] evidently shrinks from dealing with this fact. Heedlessness of this fact—though as well authenticated as any fact of this kind in the annals of the past ever was—and undue deference to the conclusions of the Ballerini brothers has been the characteristic of most who have written on the False Decretals since their time, notwithstanding the high praise bestowed upon Blascus by the censor of his eminently more historic work, reprinted by Gallandius.[5] The Ballerini contended, first, that the False Decretals could not have compiled before the Synod of Paris, A.D. 829, because there are passages in a False Decretal of Urban I., and in another of John III., which appear to have been taken bodily from canons passed at this council. Instead of which it is the reverse that is true. The Caroline divines, being acquainted with the False Decretals, used them to that extent in framing these canons. The quotations are not long in either case: indeed, it is stretching a point to say that the ante-Nicene Decretal is quoted at all. And Blascus considers the pseudo-Decretal of John III. a later addition. The Ballerini contended, secondly, from the words of Benedict the Levite, that the False Decretals were not put into circula-

---

[1] *Antiq Alem* tom ii pt 2, p 154
[2] *Concil. Germ* ii 414–26 and 428
[3] *De Ant Coll* pt iii 1, 6, § 13
[4] Without alluding to what Frobenius had said of Remedius, all he finds to say of him himself is 'De cujus ætate nihil certi constat, Anno 820 obiisse dicitur,' *Monum Alc* p 709, note The edition of Frobenius appeared A D 1777, just twenty years after the Dissertations of the Ballerini, which therefore he must be understood to have dissented from on this point
[5] *Sylloge Diss de Vet Can Collect*, Venet. 1778, iol Præf. p. xiii.

tion until after he had used them for his Capitularies. They have mistaken his words, and in consequence miscorrected Hincmar. Hincmar speaks in definite terms of 'the book of Isidore with the collected epistles,' as being the book which Riculfus, while yet a presbyter, brought back with him from Spain; Benedict never once names it, but states that, in collecting materials for his own work, he was indebted more largely to 'schedules' (*sicut in diversis synodis ac placitis generalibus edita sunt*) discovered by him in the cabinet of Riculfus—which Autcar, the next successor but one to Riculfus in the see of Mayence, when dying, enjoined him to publish—than to any other source.[1] As Riculfus was a collector of documents of this kind, according to Hincmar, we are quite justified in concluding that— in addition to the book which he brought back with him from Spain while yet a presbyter, if still in his cabinet at his death— would be found amongst his stores a large collection of *home-papers* amassed by him during the twenty-eight years of his episcopate. Not a few of these domestic papers we may, with equal reason, set down to his personal intimates, intimates like Paulinus and Alcuin, neither of whom, judging from the confidential letters that passed between them and him, could have been unacquainted with the contents of the book imported by him from Spain—a book of high interest to them all. One such letter addressed to Alcuin by Arno when at Rome, 'De Moribus Apostolici,' *on the morals of the Pope*, Alcuin tells us he burnt himself, lest it should be stolen and its secrets divulged.[2] Accordingly, what can be more probable than that Benedict is stating what is strictly true when he describes his third book, numbered seventh in Baluze, from being reckoned continuously with an earlier collection of Capitularies in four

[1] *Capit* v Præf Baluze. i 803; Hartzheim describes the state in which the papers of Riculfus were found by Benedict with great candour, and makes no mention of the False Decretals as being among them *Conc Germ* i Præf 8

[2] Frob *ad Ep* xcii note *k* (in Migne, cviii)

books by Abbot Angesisus, as consisting in part of extracts from ' canons scatteredly collected by Bishop Paulinus, Master Albinus, and other masters at the behest of the high and mighty Prince Charles'? Why should not Paulinus and Alcuin have deposited with their archæological friend Riculfus rough drafts of collections made by themselves, but ordered, like that of Remedius, by Charlemagne, to be drawn from, as his needs required, in making fresh laws? One such abstract relating to country bishops may be named as a specimen.[1] It embodies the result of negotiations on that head which Arno was instructed to bring on the *tapis* during his stay at Rome, terminating with the coronation. As we know, he could not have spent less than a year there then, he must have engaged in many such discussions, if only to find occupation for himself.

With the work of Benedict the Levite we are not now directly concerned: still, as we have named him, authentic history may be served by stating that it has not proved him a forger in proving that the sources from which he drew are to a very great extent spurious.[2] The Capitularies of Angilramn and the book of Riculfus were both in existence, and familiar to many, and used for many purposes, before he could have put pen to paper. Both saw daylight in the quadrilateral, whoever composed them: and both were produced among the documents from time to time consulted in negotiations between Aix and Rome. By furnishing, between them, a standpoint for those bishops who declined sitting in judgment on Leo III., they made the coronation of Charles by him possible, with the restoration of empire to the West for its result. Why they should have lain comparatively dormant for so many years after this, until Benedict, by

---

[1] III 260, marked by Knust, but only because containing reference to the False Decretals 'Benedicti figmentum.' Mansi receives it as historical, but dates it A.D 803, xiv. 5.

[2] Blascus, *De Coll Can. Is M.* c 6, reiterates the opinion expressed by Baluze, Præf 45, that Benedict was not even a receiver of stolen goods knowing them to have been stolen.

bringing out his three books of Capitularies at Mayence, caused inquiry to be made for them, and copies of them to be multiplied and accepted everywhere with enthusiasm, may be explained on grounds perfectly consistent with facts. First and foremost of the causes why they lay dormant was the pertinacity with which Leo, deaf to threats and promises alike, refused to abandon the uninterpolated Creed, breaking off at intervals all communication between him and Charlemagne, till at last it entirely ceased. Charlemagne would seem to have signalised the year following his coronation by a remarkable Capitulary, 'De honoranda Sede Apostolica':[1] which, though guarded in tone, may be construed to mean he was willing to go much further in that direction, if the Pope would only meet him half-way. But this overture failing to elicit any response from Leo, there was a complete cessation of correspondence between them for three years. A trivial pretext was invented, A.D. 804, to induce Leo to cross the Alps, and once there, he was prevailed upon to spend his Christmas in France. But only compliments were exchanged on both sides while they were together. Soon after separating, indeed, letters passed between them on business once more [2]—seven between A.D. 806-9 from Leo: the only record of acknowledgment extant from Charles being the engrafting of a portion of the Constitution of Pope Silvester on to the Capitularies of A.D. 806, already mentioned. Then another break of three years. What occasioned this break? Cennius is reticent on everything relating to it. A.D. 809 was the year in which Abbot Smaragdus sped with a deputation from Aix to Rome, bearers of a characteristic letter from Charlemagne to the Pope, with a view of obtaining from him a formal recognition of the interpolated Creed.[3]

---

[1] Baluze, i 357, with the note, ii 1055 Pertz omits it, but Hartzheim reprints it without hesitation, i. 356.

[2] Cennius, *Monum Dom. Pont* ii. 47-71

[3] Hartzheim, to his credit, reprints all the documents except the profession of Leo, i 390-7

How Cennius could have persuaded himself that his
'Codex Carolinus' could be considered in honesty complete
without this letter, or the letters of Leo printed by him
without the letter of Leo which produced this letter of
Charlemagne to him, or how Hartzheim could omit the
dogmatic profession of Leo forwarded in his letter to Charlemagne, or Jaffé follow [1] Mansi in dating this profession of
Leo vaguely A.D. 795–816, when—if really due to his pen—
it is distinctly recorded to have been elicited from him on
this occasion, I should much like to hear explained by
anybody who can without attributing a *suppressio veri* to
any. Neither Baronius nor Pagi could be charged with it,[2]
these documents having come to light since their time. To
sum up therefore, briefly, what passed on this occasion.
There were three acts to this drama, just as there had been
to the coronation nine years before. The performance
commenced with the Latin monks on Mount Olives singing
the interpolated Creed at their services, in a way calculated
to excite public attention and to challenge remark. On
being attacked for it, they defended themselves by trans-
mitting to the Pope an account of what had passed, which
he forwarded in turn to the Emperor with a letter from
himself, enclosing a profession of faith that he had already
sent to them. This formed the second act: the deputation
from Aix to Rome forming the third. On what passed
between the deputies and the Pope we need not here dwell.
It may be read at length in the great work of Dr. Neale.[3]
Two facts connected with it, unnoticed by him, deserve
pointing out. (1) That the letter brought by the deputies
from Charlemagne passes over—as though it had never been
written—the profession of faith which Leo forwarded in the
letter that led to their coming, but affects, on the contrary,
to teach the Pope what the true faith was. Leo, with equal

---

[1] *Regest Pont Rom* p 220
[2] Baron A D 809, n 52, and Pagi *ad l.*
[3] *Eastern Ch* Introd II 1163–7, translated from the Latin, which may be seen in Hartzheim, 1 394–7.

reticence, barely mentions the receipt of the letter, but returns warm thanks for the *splendid present* that accompanied it, *in a letter addressed to Riculfus*, who, just as at the coronation, would seem to have been a prime mover in this matter too.[1] But the finale was very different from what had been planned. The recital of the interpolated Creed in the Imperial chapel, if not interdicted, was energetically dissuaded. Earnest appeals for a renewal of intercourse between Rome and Constantinople from Theodore Studites, and a synodical letter from the orthodox patriarch, Nicephorus, that should have arrived sooner, with a profession of faith in accordance with the interpolated Creed, brought old and new Rome into *rapport* once more.[2] To crown all, the uninterpolated Creed, engraved in large characters on silver plates, was hung up over the confession of S. Peter, to be seen by all. After this, Leo might petition for help as much as he would, but help would not come. His three letters written A.D. 812–13 elicited no reply. Nevertheless, he outlived Charlemagne; but, on the other hand, the work of Charlemagne, forced in process of time upon his unstable successors, long outlived his.

For the moment, indeed, the triumph of the work of Charlemagne was retarded by his death, which took place five years later, A.D. 814, almost as much as the circulation of the book of Riculfus was by his death, which took place the same year by a singular coincidence. Their successors were both of them unambitious, unworldly men, whose ways were not the ways of their predecessors. The Emperor Lewis had no taste for political schemes or intrigues, nor Archbishop Haistulf for out-of-the-way Church or State papers. Again the old school of divines and diplomatists was fast dying off. Angilbert died the same year as Riculfus and Charlemagne. Metz had been without a bishop ever

---

[1] Mansi, xiii 977, gives the letter without comment Le Quien, *Or Christian* iii 353, hardly perceives its full relevancy
[2] Baron A D 809, n 18–24, and 811, n 20–43

since the death of Angilramn, A.D. 791. Paulinus and Alcuin had both been dead ten years. Theodulph and Arno lived on; but their sees were far apart, and neither of them near Aix; besides, of their occupants, one was most famed for his missionary zeal, the other for his diocesan visitations and rules. Autcar, or Otgar, succeeded Haistulf, A.D. 826, as Archbishop of Mayence, which he continued to be for twenty years or more. From Benedict the Levite we learn that he was related to Riculfus, but so far as any record exists of his acts he would never seem to have been employed similarly. We never find him sent on any political mission to Rome by the Emperor Lewis or by his sons. He held councils, baptised a Danish king and queen with a number of their subjects, interested himself in the affairs of monasteries.[1] But, being related to Riculfus, he would naturally care for his papers. Still, as long as the son of Charlemagne lived, he seems to have considered it useless or impolitic to draw public attention to them by having them put in order or copied. But when Lewis was dead, and he perceived his own end approaching, he gave the word to his deacon Benedict that recalled public attention to them in a way that could never have been forecasted by him, and in process of time led to a great part of them becoming law. The very year in which this injunction was laid upon Benedict saw Hincmar consecrated Archbishop of Rheims, and from that time forth his nephew and namesake, whom he consecrated Bishop of Leon, A.D. 858, was his constant attendant. Writing against Gotteschalcus the year after consecrating his nephew, the Archbishop himself quotes the False Decretal of Anacletus; and nine years later writing to Charles the Bald to excuse his nephew, he quotes the False Decretals of Urban Lucius and Stephen. The whole dispute that ensued between him and his nephew subsequently turned upon the False Decretals that his nephew had meanwhile long studied and copied in part, till at length he made them his stand-

[1] *Gall. Christia* v. 445-6.

point, and exhibited a full collection of them in self-defence. Such collections, his uncle thereupon tells him, were by no means rare; as these Decretals had been known to many long before either of them was born.[1] Their acceptance, where they were found at variance with the canons of Councils universally received, was another thing. Rabanus Maurus would have nothing to say to them, because they were not in his line. Hincmar opposed them at first, but after they had been accepted by Pope Nicholas, he bowed to the inevitable. By Gratian they were placed side by side with the Fathers and General Councils that had commanded the assent of Christendom from the earliest time downwards. And from him they passed into the canon law of the West. The Catechism of the Council of Trent quotes them as authorities of the first order on every doctrinal and disciplinary point to which they can apply. The Vatican Council, had it lived long enough, would have probably done the same. Who the forger of them was has been much disputed in modern times. But Hincmar quotes from the first book of the Capitularies collected by Benedict the Levite, without dropping a hint that it contained any forged by its collector. He is also far from charging Riculfus with having forged any part of the book brought by him from Spain. From what Alcuin says of Riculfus we may infer him to have been a worldly pretender, fond of display, and given to diplomacy, but nothing worse. From what Hincmar says of him we may infer him to have been a virtuoso collector of works of art and MSS., valuable for their contents or early date. If he supposed the MS. purchased by him in the Basque province to have belonged to S. Isidore, or been compiled by him, and if, in addition, the earlier parts of it were written in Gothic characters, he would naturally be fond of exhibiting it to his friends, and dilating on its unique worth. And if what Benedict tells us of Otgar is correct, his relationship to Riculfus alone will suffice to

[1] C. 15.

THE FALSE DECRETALS REFLECT THEIR AGE.

account for his taking steps to prevent the papers inherited by him of his relative from being scattered to the winds at his death.

The truth is, these False Decretals were the natural production of the age during which they appeared, and were no bad reflection either of its style. It was by the process of dovetailing that its most esteemed works were put together: and in this process the new and the old were so blended together—and the old so frequently recast by subtraction, addition, or textual alteration—that not only was the original meaning of the old lost, but it became difficult to say where the old ended and the new commenced. Again, the mistakes committed through ignorance or inadvertence were surprisingly common even in those writers who were then accounted oracles. Pages might be filled with errors of this kind in Alcuin alone. Specimens are given in pp. 73-74 of the Appendix to my own book on the Athanasian Creed. Further, the publishing works under time-honoured names was not considered any sin at all, though it has proved of incalculable mischief and confusion to succeeding ages. If this device was not invented by Charlemagne, it was at any rate practised, and to that extent encouraged, by him.

It is a simple fact that he published the profession of Pelagius as the profession of S. Jerome in the third book of his work against the second Nicene Council: and the 'Quicunque vult' in his Capitularies of A.D. 802 as the Faith of S. Athanasius. He wanted the sanction of antiquity likewise for the ecclesiastical system which he thought best suited and most likely to cement and consolidate the Latin-speaking empire that he was bent on founding in the West, and on so constructing, too, that the East might be brought into corporate union with it at any moment, and form one cosmopolitan whole.

Now it cannot be denied, as a matter of fact—putting their authorship on one side—that this was done to his hand in the False Decretals: which, had he lived long enough, he would have no doubt reproduced in his Capitularies to that extent, after divesting it of everything incompatible with his own sovereign jurisdiction. This is indicated in the jealous reserve shown by him in accepting the Constitution of Pope Silvester, from whose central clause the word '*laicus*' has been eliminated, making it only concern ecclesiastics. Still, on the whole, they fitted in with his policy well enough; and they have literally become the ecclesiastical Code Napoléon of mediæval and modern Europe to this day, from their adoption by Pope Nicholas onwards, though to the benefit of the Pope by a good deal more than of the secular power, owing to the turn of events, till quite recent times. For they attributed to the see of Rome a sovereign supremacy by divine right over all Churches and persons throughout the world: they declared not only bishops, but metropolitans and primates, apostolic institutions: and they declared laymen incompetent to try cases in which the clergy were concerned.

Nor were the Caroline divines and canonists stepping an inch beyond their legitimate right in asserting these principles, if they honestly believed them: and making them the basis of their legislation in view of their actual or impending circumstances. They were plainly far better judges of their absolute requirements than we can be; and in an age when power was centred in brute force, and education was entirely confined to the clergy, to protest against being judged by laymen was only to protect themselves from being judged by those who could neither read nor write.

But they had plainly no business to assume legislating for the whole Church of their day, or invent to the confusion of ages unborn a gross imposture, like that of antedating their system by veiling its origin under false names: and of claiming antiquity for either their laws, their dogmas, or their practices, when it was, in point of fact, *from antiquity* that in each of these particulars they broke loose. If it was the action of the secular power of their own times that they sought by these means to stem, they had no business, as Christians, to seek to oppose force by fraud. It was not by fraud that primitive Christianity made a conquest of pagan Rome.

Besides, it was really *with the secular power* that these Caroline divines and canonists were leagued at first, and with the secular power that they worked doggedly for a time both against the East and against Rome—so much so, that it was only by *accepting their terms* one by one that Rome was enabled, as time went on, to become their sovereign power both in Church and State.

This is a point that cannot be too often or too plainly reiterated, too narrowly scanned or too closely pressed in all its bearings, as without it history cannot be read aright.

For the interpolated Creed imported into France from Spain, Rome not only discarded, but eventually discredited, the genuine Creed of œcumenical Councils which every Pope before consecration, down to the middle of the ninth century, made solemn oath *usque ad unum apicem* to maintain inviolate.[1]

For the principles of the False Decretals—also said to have been imported from Spain, but actually so well suited to the requirements of the Latin Empire founded by Charlemagne that it is impossible to doubt their having been compiled in its interest, and within its limits—Rome was the more content to trample under foot the decrees of Councils that her bishops had also sworn to observe: for in the textbooks of the new system she saw herself recognised mistress of the whole Church by divine right.[2]

---

[1] Two forms are given but in both he swears as elect, and not yet consecrated, and the only difference between them is that one is of later date than the other. What is called 'secunda professio fidei' is constructed quite differently from either. See the *Liber Diurnus Pont Rom* in Migne, *Pat Lat* cv 44, first printed by Garner

[2] 'Ancient canon law,' says Baluze, 'was contained in a single

At the Council of Troyes, A.D. 878, in the presence of Pope John VIII., who was passive, and never uttered for or against the transaction, the knell of the old system was struck: when its venerable champion, the elder Hincmar, was delated to him for not receiving the *decretal epistles* of the Popes; and the younger Hincmar, who had been deposed for numerous acts of canonical disobedience to his metropolitan, and punished with the loss of his eyes for numerous acts of contumacy to his lawful sovereign, was condoned and set free.[1]

For the moment, indeed, the ground was slippery, and by no means assured. And this, though the last, is certainly not the least important point to which our attention should be given, in dealing with the tangled complications of the ninth century.

Charlemagne willed a complete separation between the temporal and ecclesiastical orders of his realm, and ordained a graduated scale for both, culminating always in himself. His inferior clergy were to be ruled by their bishops, his

code, which comprehended the canons of ancient Councils and the decrees of a limited number of Roman pontiffs in addition Such was the code received and used by the Church up to the times of Charlemagne Then, as it were by some fatality, because kingdoms were changed, canon law must needs be changed too That is to say, the old code which had been in force for upwards of 700 years was superseded by a new code, drawn from the spurious epistles of the martyred Bishops of the Roman See, published by that impudent impostor the pseudo-Isidore, and from the novel Constitutions of those who subsequently to the times of Charles filled the Apostolic See. Thus it was introduced in the age of the great Charles—an age more favourable to it than any other, on account of the vast confusion produced in the ecclesiastical world by the wretched and amazing ignorance of the bishops and other clergy, and their unacquaintance with the ancient canons It was in this terrible disorder of things that those famous and renowned letters attributed to the primitive bishops of Rome saw daylight; sending a thrill through the minds of all by their apparent antiquity And because they bore the names. of such holy bishops on their titlepage, soon it became a settled maxim with all, that it was not lawful to question any principles contained in those sacred monuments of antiquity' *Præf ad Ant August Dial* p 1, quoted by Cave, *Hist Lit* ii 21-2, with cordial approval

[1] See the *Life and Times of Hincmar*, p 486-9, by Rev James C Prichard, late Fellow of Oriel (Littlemore and Oxford, 1849); a work much in advance of its date

bishops by their metropolitans, his metropolitans by their primates, his primates by the Pope. To the Pope he accorded, as of divine right, unlimited power over ecclesiastics of every grade, and over laymen in spiritual things, controlled only by himself.

But systems in this world have necessarily to be carried out by men, and men have never yet failed to discover practical anomalies in every system. However positive the lines of demarcation drawn by Charlemagne, mixed questions would arise constantly between his subjects and the Pope, and between the Pope and himself. At one time he would invoke the intervention of the Pope between himself and his subjects; at another time they would fly to the Pope for protection against him; at another time they would combine with him heart and soul against the Pope. Freedom and immunity would be sure to be desired by all in turn. Any philandering with alien powers would be sure to provoke reaction. The Popes themselves prevented the supremacy which Charlemagne willed them in theory from being accepted in his dominions, as long as he lived, by refusing to break with Constantinople. His clergy rallied round him from mixed motives; in part because they were proud of, as well as in dread of, their sovereign; in part because he upheld their Creed; in part because they disliked the notion of exchanging their traditional freedom for complete subjection to the Pope. The tension superinduced at times by the resumption of amenities between old and new Rome more than once pointed to the setting up of a national Church in France bounded on the south-east by the Alps. Two prime specimens of this tension, never having been as carefully scrutinised hitherto, perhaps, as they deserve to be, will, by being brought out at last in high relief, tell their own tale and leave a lasting impression behind them on our minds as we return from our somewhat lengthy digressions to our immediate subject. One of them has been in part anticipated, for it occurred near the beginning of the period on which we are now engaged; the other nearer the end of it. One was the work of Charlemagne, the other the work of his son Lewis—the Synod of Frankfort, A.D. 794, and the Synod of Paris, thirty years later, A.D. 824.

1. In A.D. 778 Charlemagne crossed the Pyrenees and wrested Arragon, Navarre, and Catalonia from the Saracens, and added those provinces nominally to his empire. He lost no time in making acquaintance with the remnants of the Christian Church which he found there, and either from preference or from policy before long adopted the Creed interpolated by the Gothic king Reccared two hundred years before with the *Filioque* clause. But it was otherwise with the liturgy then used in Spain. Felix, bishop of Urgel, in Catalonia, must have been developing Adoptionism in concert with Elipandus, archbishop of Toledo, just at the time when his see passed into the hands of Charlemagne. Not many years elapsed before they were both called to account for their opinions, and the bishops of Spain were formally warned against them by Pope Adrian in a letter now forming part of the Caroline code, though its date cannot be fixed.[1] A letter from Elipandus in justification of them was commented upon at the Council of Frankfort in four different refutations of them read there, which it elicited. Of these the first letter professes to come from the Pope, but it is headed quite differently from any of his acknowledged letters, and makes no mention of having been despatched by his legates to any Council, and is, like the other, without a date. The second purports to be from the bishops of Italy; but it was composed, as it states, by Paulinus, bishop of Aquileia, and, after the manner of his synodical letter addressed from Friuli to King Charles, upholds the twofold procession of the Holy Ghost. The third purports to be from the bishops of France and Germany, but *on that point* they are just as silent as the Pope. Its chief interest consists in this—that it notices the defence set up by Felix and

[1] *Ep* 97

Elipandus for their opinions from expressions occurring in *their national liturgy*, which the bishops of France and Germany say only shows what parents they had in Eugenius, Ildefonsus, and Julian, archbishops of Toledo, whom they profess to follow.[1] The fourth refutation is that of the King himself, strong in the perfect agreement existing between him, the bishops of his dominions, and the Pope; and concluding with a formal dogmatic profession of his own, in which the twofold procession of the Holy Ghost is asserted in two consecutive sentences with marked emphasis,[2] as though to proclaim his full acceptance, to those whom it concerned most, of the Creed accepted in Spain.

Thus it was by a Creed imported from Spain that a heresy developed in Spain was sought to be crushed. Yet from A.D. 778 when it first showed itself, to the end of the century when it died out, Adoptionism continued to supply ground for frequent communications between Spain and France; so that Riculfus may well have been returning from some mission in connection with it when he purchased the book containing the False Decretals of the Popes; and which he was therefore credited with having brought back from Spain.

But for its first canon we should hardly be able to identify the four refutations of Adoptionism already noticed with the Council of Frankfort, as Frankfort is nowhere mentioned in them by name. But for its second canon we could not have guessed that any further doctrinal question had been decided there; for in this case the documents submitted to the Council form no part of its acts. But for the statement of Eginhard, the Imperial secretary, then a very young man, and those who borrowed from him, we could not have guessed that legates from Rome were present at any part of its proceedings. Charlemagne speaks of the Council in his letter as having been summoned by him from all parts of his kingdom, to deliberate what answer should be returned

[1] Mansi, xiii. 886.   [2] Ib p 905.

to the communication just received from Spain: of the messengers that had sped from him three or four times to the Pope to inquire what he thought of it; and of the letter he was then sending to Spain along with his own, in which the opinions of the Pope, his Church, his bishops, and his learned men would be found, but of legates from Rome not a word. The first canon speaks of the Council as having met by favour of God, apostolic authority, and command of King Charles—who was present, it adds, in person—and as being composed of the bishops and priests of his kingdom. Eginhard is in agreement with both so far. What follows is his own :—' Adfuerunt in eadem synodo et legati sanctæ Romanæ ecclesiæ, Theophylactus ac Stephanus episcopi, vicem tenentes ejus a quo missi sunt, Adriani papæ.' [1]

This statement has to be reconciled with the undoubted fact, that the second canon of this Council embodies a direct condemnation of the second Nicene Council, at which the same Pope Adrian was certainly represented, of which he approved formally when it was over, and which he defended after the condemnation passed upon it in this canon to the day of his death. And, further, that its condemnation was due to a volume directed against it, and afterwards sent to Rome, which Hincmar tells us he read at the palace when a boy.[2] Could any legates from Adrian have been present when this volume was read; could they have gone back, without protest, in company with it—to wit, the Caroline Books—to Rome?

Meanwhile there is not a shred of evidence to show that the Pope was consulted beforehand on the subject of those books, or had been given to understand that they would be produced and read at Frankfort, or that the Council confirmed by him would be condemned on their showing. Not a letter of any description has been preserved either from Charlemagne to Adrian, or from Adrian to Charlemagne, between A.D. 791-4; and the letter of Adrian acknowledging

[1] *Annal* A D 794, ed. Pertz.   [2] *In Causâ Hinc Laud.* c 20

the receipt of the Caroline Books, and defending the Nicene decrees notwithstanding their attack upon them, continues to be printed in a corner by itself, instead of appearing among his other letters.[1] In a recent edition of the 'Monumenta Carolina,' professing absolute completeness, it is not given at all.[2] The abstract of it in the 'Regesta Pontificum Romanorum,' brought out sixteen years earlier by the same author, only serves to mask its importance.[3]

Thus, if Adrian was consulted before the condemnation of the second Nicene Council was resolved upon at Frankfort, its condemnation cannot possibly be supposed to have been resolved upon with his consent. If he was not consulted before that matter was taken in hand, we see with what assurance these Caroline divines could legislate for themselves in matters affecting the whole Church, doctrinal and disciplinary, without consulting any Church but their own, and in crass ignorance or even wilful contempt of the decrees of any number of œcumenical Councils, so that they had their king with them or were carrying out his behests.

2. Thirty years later—A.D. 824—as has been said, found their successors guilty of the same conduct again in an aggravated form. In that year—the year in which Eugenius II. became Pope—messengers arrived from Constantinople bringing with them a letter addressed to 'Lewis, King of the Franks and Lombards, but called their emperor,' from Michael the Stammerer and his son Theophilus, then joint emperor with him, expressing their strong desire to have the decrees of the second Nicene Council submitted for reconsideration to the whole Church, on account of the numerous irregularities which they were supposed to sanction, and praying that their messengers might be conducted in safety to the Pope with a letter addressed to him by themselves on the subject. The heading of their letter to the Emperor—'De non adorandis imaginibus'—sufficiently

---

[1] In Mansi, for instance, xiii. 759-810
[2] By Jaffé (Berolini, 1867).
[3] P. 214.

resumes its contents for our purpose, though it treats of other subjects besides.

Their messengers were duly sent on from France to Rome, and we learn from Lewis himself that Freculphus, bishop of Lisieux, also went thither from him to obtain leave for a collection of authorities on the subject to be made by the French bishops. Permission having been accorded or assumed, a Council met in Paris on November 1, A.D. 825, for that purpose. Its labours resulted in the collection which occupies forty pages in Mansi, yet its fifteenth chapter breaks off unfinished, leaving us in doubt whether it ended with that chapter or not. It was received by the Emperor on December 6, so that it cannot have taken more than a month to make. With its contents we need not concern ourselves further than the following extract from them by M. Rohrbacher will cover:—[1]

'Voici en quels termes les évêques parlent à l'empereur de ce qu'ils ont fait : "Nous étant assemblés par vos ordres à Paris le 1er de Novembre, au sujet des images, nous nous sommes fait lire d'abord la lettre que le Pape Adrien écrivit autrefois à Constantin et à Irène pour le rétablissement des images ; et autant qu'il nous a paru, comme il a condamné avec justice ceux qui osent briser les images, *il a mal fait de commander qu'on les adorât superstitieusement.*" Ils rejettent de la même manière le second concile de Nicée ; sur quoi ils parlent à l'empereur en ces termes : "Votre père, de sainte mémoire, s'étant fait lire ce concile, *et l'ayant désapprouvé en bien des choses,* marqua ces endroits, et les envoya au Pape par Angilbert, afin qu'il les fît corriger. Mais Adrien, prenant la défense de ceux qui, *à son instigation,* avaient ordonné ces superstitions, *a répondu à ces articles ce qu'il a voulu, et non ce qui convenait.* . . . Cependant, à la fin de son apologie, il déclare qu'il n'a pas d'autres sentiments sur la question présente, que ceux de saint Grégoire. Ce qui fait voir, qu'il *a plutôt péché par ignorance.* Car s'il n'avait

[1] *Hist. Univ. de l'Eg* xi. 467–8.

pas été retenu par les liens de la vérité et par l'autorité de saint Grégoire, il eût pu tomber dans le précipice de la superstition." '

Charlemagne and his bishops, whatever they may have said of the second Nicene Council, never, certainly, ventured on such criticism of the official utterances of the Pope who confirmed it as is expressed in the italicised portions of this extract. But these French bishops, far from entertaining any misgivings that they had gone too far, had also the face to supplement their collection with two letters composed by themselves, one which they considered the Emperor should send in his own name to the Pope, the other which they considered the Pope should send in his own name to the East, in answer to the letter which the messengers of the Greek Emperors had brought to him. The first of these letters Mansi prints entire; the second ends with a 'cetera desunt,' but whether from erasion or decay we are not told.[1]

Jeremiah, archbishop of Sens, and Jonah, bishop of Orleans, were sent with this collection to Rome by Lewis, after reading and approving of its contents, as he tells us in his 'Commonitorium' to the two bishops; but they were to extract such portions of it as they thought most telling and least likely to imperil its rejection, for perusal by the Pope, whom they were to take special pains to win over by seeming deference to the *media via* desired by them, and not by overt resistance to confirm in obstinacy. Further, they were to propose that, in the event of any delegates being sent by himself to the Greek capital, delegates from the Emperor should accompany them.

As nothing is said in this document of the two letters appended to the collection, we must suppose them cancelled by the Emperor. His messengers took a letter with them from him to the Pope, representing what had been done as

---

[1] Ib xiv. 461–74 Mr. Rohrbacher amusingly characterises them as 'deux pièces *d'une nouvelle invention.*'

having been done with his sanction ; and the despatch of its results now submitted to him, 'non ut hìc aliquo velut magisterio officio fungerentur, aut hùc docendi gratiâ directi putarentur'; but in the hope that he might find it of service to him in the matter to which it referred—a matter which he well knew was causing endless dissension and discord in the Greek empire just then. Accordingly, departing from the submissive tone which he had employed hitherto, Lewis here tells the Pope that it is *his duty* to send delegates to the East with such a reply from him as nobody, whether Greek or Roman, will be able to blame, *such as, in truth, should in all cases proceed from his see.* Lastly, when it is asked that delegates from France should be sent with his delegates into the East, it is not meant to imply that his delegates were not competent to act alone, but only that the Emperor and his subjects are willing to lend their aid in every case where the necessities of the Pope or his inclination may prompt him to ask for it.

Practically this letter omits nothing that the French bishops had urged in theirs; it has only the merit of being shorter and less discursive.

Le Comte tells us that this collection and its accompaniments 'lay hid in a corner'—as is not surprising—'till 1596, when it was printed at Frankfort-on-the-Main for the first time with this heading : ' Synodus Parisiensis de Imaginibus, A.D. 824, ex vetustissimo codice descripta, et nunc primum edita.' It was attacked by Bellarmine forthwith, and no wonder either—in an appendix to his work 'De Cultu Imaginum'; then by Baronius, A.D. 794 and 824-5 ; and next, on that account, refused insertion by Binius in his Collection of Councils. Sirmondus could only bring himself to print the letter of Lewis to the Pope, and his 'Commonitorium' to Bishops Jeremiah and Jonah; but Delalande, who continued the collection of Sirmondus, printed all the remaining pieces as one document.[1] Mansi, whose collection appeared

[1] Pp. 106-138, ed Paris, 1666. Fol.

a whole century later, takes credit to himself for having been the first to do what Delalande had already done.[1] Yet, like Delalande, he omits the two pieces printed by Sirmondus, referring us, however, for them, not to Sirmondus, but Baluze, who says as little about them as he can help.[2] Eugenius remained Pope till August, A.D. 827, quite long enough to have deliberated on the whole matter, therefore, and to have formed his decision. Yet, either he was too prudent to send any written reply to the Emperor Lewis, or to the synodical act of his bishops, or his own successors have been too prudent to keep, or at any rate to let his reply be seen. Theophylact, his *nomenclator*, and Leo, bishop of Cività Vecchia, were sent by him in the month of June, A.D. 826, to Inglesheim, where Lewis and his magnates were then assembled in council. 'Quæ autem isti attulerint,' says Baronius, 'altum ubique silentium.'[3] We scarcely need utterances, however, where facts converge. Eugenius had not been dead a month when ambassadors arrived from Constantinople to Lewis, then at Compiègne, not to make fresh overtures, but to *confirm* a treaty—a treaty, therefore, whose basis had been discussed and settled on either side before then. And Lewis, we are told, gave them an honourable reception, and concluded their matter.[4]

The last act of Eugenius, we may be quite sure, was of a piece with his first act. His own election to the pontificate had been disputed, and the Emperor had intervened and had pronounced for him. Eugenius, to ward off any further cabals in his own case and to prevent their recurrence for his successors, thereupon exacted a solemn oath of fealty to the reigning Emperor and his son Lothaire from the Roman clergy and people, with a salvo to the fealty before promised to himself, and made them further swear that they would never in future be parties to the consecration of any Pope

[1] XIV 415-16
[2] *Capit Reg Franc.* i 643-6, and ii. 1110.
[3] A D 826, n. 8.
[4] Le Cointe, A.D 827, n. 70-1.

who might be chosen till he had in their presence, and in the presence of the Imperial envoys, taken a similar oath to what had now been sworn by them all. All accounts agree that this ordinance was faithfully carried out at the consecration of the next Pope, Gregory IV., and Pagi says it continued in full force with occasional interruptions till the eleventh century.[1]

But for Pagi, whose learned criticisms on Baronius during this period were not published until six years after his death by his nephew, A.D. 1705, this oath, exhumed by M. Freher, the oldest collector of the 'Conditores Franc. Hist.,' A.D. 1613,[2] might have 'lain in a corner' unknown until now. Baluze reproduced it, indeed, A.D. 1677, but without comment of any kind, or even heading to show by whom it had been imposed.[3] A year later Le Cointe passed it over altogether. Muratori reprinted the fragment containing it without comment in A.D. 1725 and on second thoughts only.[4] Bouquet in A.D. 1749 reproduced Baluze first in a note,[5] but afterwards the oath itself, as it stands in the fragment, illustrated in a note from Pagi.[6] Rohrbacher, to his credit, gives us the oath in his text, translated into French; but by printing the salvo to the imposer in capital letters and omitting the 'et' following it in the Latin, he seems to insinuate that a similar salvo was to be continued in the oath when taken by the Popes themselves previously to their consecration, as though fealty to the dead could be binding after their decease.[7] Neither Mansi nor Migne so much as allude to it in connection with the decrees or acts of Eugenius II.

These several facts must have been comprehended in their full import and estimated at their full gravity by the learned men who thus shrank—and, entertaining their principles, shrank naturally—from scrutinising them further

[1] *Ad Baron* A D 825, n. 29–31.
[2] Part I p 181.
[3] *Caput* 1 647
[4] See his *Monit* vol i part 2;
Rer. It. Script p. 182
[5] *Recueil des Hist. Fr* vi. 106.
[6] Ib p. 173.
[7] *Hist de l'Egl* xi 460

themselves, and endeavoured to throw a veil over them for others. This only makes it all the more incumbent on us to consider them in their full import now. The history, then, of these two Councils, following on each other in two successive reigns, has only to be fairly stated to illustrate the spirit which animated the founder of the Latin Church on its becoming the Church of his dominions, and to show how the same spirit descended from father to son.

The Council of Paris, indeed, carries us in thought back a stage beyond the Council of Frankfort, and recalls us to a Council fifty years its senior—that of Rome, A.D. 775—where we saw both nomination to the popedom, and to all sees episcopal and archiepiscopal in his dominions, with subsequent investiture, conceded synodically to Charles the Great by the first Adrian, amid tacit understandings on both sides—on the part of the Pope, that possession of a certain amount of territory named by him was to be given and guaranteed for ever to his see; on the part of the monarch, that he was to remain autocrat throughout his dominions in both Church and State. No reference was made to the East in this covenant, and for a time the East interposed between it and its consummation. But events soon showed that it was merely the filling in of the outline which was delayed; and all through the middle ages the students of the great work of Gratian, after it had been approved as their text-book by Eugenius III., the friend of S. Bernard, must have believed that the actual relations of Church and State then dominating in Europe were but the natural products of what had been mapped out at Rome between Charles the Great and Adrian I., A.D. 775, in the first instance, renewed subsequently between his son and heir and Eugenius II., A.D. 825, and again assured to a new dynasty between Leo VIII. and the first Otho, A.D. 963.

Gallicanism, whatever it may have proved in modern times, was, in the hands of the founder of the Franko-German Empire and his son, unquestionably the parent of the Latin, the mediæval, and the modern Church of Europe to this day, by creating for it a temporal monarchy within itself and attaching to it all the splendour, with all the cares and all the entanglements, of an earthly crown, making it possible for its bishops and archbishops to become leaders of armed hosts, and its monks and abbots proprietors of vast domains, despiritualising as a body the entire hierarchy, narrowing the minds of all to the spots built upon or cultivated by themselves, and inspiring them with forgetfulness of the many races still outside the Christian pale and of the older Christian Churches with whom sacramental communion had long been in abeyance, and such occasional intercourse as was brought about by the course of events only served to widen the breach.

There was just one new feature developed in this system as time went on. The Popes, after a time, got the better of the purely temporal power, and then in right of their spiritual character claimed to be supreme: from which the final outcome was what might have been expected. They were not merely discrowned, but they were likewise stripped of their territorial possessions in due course by the representatives of the great founder of their temporal rule. The Reformation has often been taunted with having been indebted in every case to princes for its success, *nor can this be possibly denied as a fact*. But neither can it be denied as a fact that the papacy was indebted to crowned heads ages ago for all that crowned heads have taken from it in modern times.

On the other hand, the fact that it kept its vast endowments so long, without either swords or soldiers worth the name to defend them, affords unequivocal proof that Europe must have derived, for a considerable time, considerable benefits from the commanding influence thus accorded to it by common consent—benefits which it would be grossly dishonest in any member of the still glorious Universities of Oxford or Cambridge to pass over unacknowledged, or seek

RECONCILIATION ATTEMPTED BY GRATIAN.

to extenuate, in any review of the period of their respective foundations. God forbid also that anything should appear in these pages, having either for its object or for its effect to impeach the honesty, the learning, or the saintliness of individuals of any period whatsoever, who, born and bred in a system endeared to them by tender or pious associations from the cradle, loyally supported it through life, and resented with all their might all wanton and injurious criticisms of its foundations, and all flippant distrust of its constituted authorities. The system was in its origin and at its framing the work of a few, and it was no sooner firmly rooted in the soil than it claimed for itself prescriptive rights, and was accepted as a fact and carried out in detail by peace-loving men, ignorant and unsuspicious of the means which had been used in shaping it, and of the character of the foundations on which it ultimately reposed. Let us illustrate the situation by recalling it as it must have been presented to three friends and contemporaries—than whom the twelfth century produced none worthier, and whose good report has never yet been assoiled—S. Bernard, abbot of Clairvaux, Eugenius III., his devoted pupil both at Clairvaux and as Pope, and Gratian, the renowned monk of Bologna. In their day the interpolated Creed of Reccared and Charlemagne, received at last by the Popes, was the acknowledged Creed of the West. The pseudo-Decretals of the earliest Popes, with other pseudonyms of the same pretensions, passed everywhere for the highest exponents of Church law on every subject with which they dealt. Later enactments founded on them could not be questioned, while any that differed from them had to give way or be interpreted in their sense. Gratian, whose genius impelled him to the profession of canon law, noticing the conflict between this class of authorities and others which he felt equally bound to respect, endeavoured to strike the balance between them in his well-known work inaccurately called the 'Decretum,' but which he called, in the hope that it would be found to bear out its title, 'Concordantia Discordantium Canonum.' Now, to which class would his conscience naturally lead him to give the preference where they disagreed? Surely, to the very class which he believed to be most ancient: as regards their authorship perfectly genuine, and as regards their facts perfectly correct, but which we now know to have been put together on purpose to instil untrue notions respecting them on each point. His work consists of three parts, of which the first part occupies 300 pages, the second 820 pages, and the third 100 pages, in the edition of Boehmer, still its handiest edition.[1] The pseudo-Decretals of the earliest Popes are marked as much as 54 times in the first part, 279 times in the second, and 29 times in the third, making a grand total of 362 times in all, taken from the pseudo-Isidorian collection alone. But this was not the only source by any means from which his spurious quotations were drawn. In short, it was a complete network of forged documents which he sat down in perfect good faith, unconscious of the least flaw or fiction in their contents, and made the work of his life to reconcile with canons of Councils that were strictly genuine, and utterances of the Fathers that were truly primitive. Yet nobody can rise from a careful survey of his work and not feel convinced that it was compiled in all honesty; the life-long task of one who would have recoiled in horror at the bare thought of shielding imposture from exposure, to the full extent that it deserved. To nobody else but Satan could it be set down that a writer, *animated by the purest motives*, should have given not only currency, but authority, to so much falsehood without intending it. According to the learned annalist of the Cistercians, Angelo Maurique, whom Boehmer quotes,[2] it was S. Bernard who persuaded Gratian to undertake the task

---

[1] The edition of Richter, Leipsic, 1836, is founded on his, but the brand of spuriousness is transferred to the notes amidst other matter The edition of Friedberg is too overwhelming for practical purposes, and in spite of its pretensions to clear up everything, names Gratian only to say nothing further about him Leipsic, 1879.

[2] *Diss.* § x note, p

which it took him so many years of immense research to complete, and certainly the well-known treatise 'De Consideratione,' composed by S. Bernard for the edification of his old pupil Eugenius III. on becoming Pope, contains many passages demonstrating that S. Bernard was hard pressed himself to reconcile what he read in the genuine writings of the primitive Fathers, and the contemporary records of their times, with the *de facto* maxims and practices of his own day, without entering into vices and corruptions for which no plea could be made.

For instance, where pointing out how the extremities to which papal supremacy was now carried had absorbed all other lawful jurisdictions: 'I will not keep you in suspense any longer,' he says. 'I am speaking of the murmurs and complaints of the Churches. They cry loudly that they are being mutilated and dismembered. . . . Abbots are exempted from bishops, bishops from archbishops, archbishops from primates or patriarchs. Can this be good as regards appearance? It would be wonderful if it could be excused in practice. By doing so constantly, you may prove yourself possessed of a plenitude of power, but perhaps not of justice. You do so because you are able, but whether you ought is the question. . . . Can you possibly think it lawful for you to dismember the Church, confound order, disturb the boundaries which your fathers have set? If it be just for each to preserve his own rights, how can it accord with justice to take from a person what belongs to him? You err if you think that your apostolic power, because the highest, is the only power ordained by God. When the Apostle says, "Let every soul be subject to the higher powers," he says *not* to the higher power as one, but to the higher powers as many. . . .'[1]

Of appeals he says that the system as it existed had materially changed the apostolic character of the Popes themselves. Contrasting S. Peter with those who claimed

[1] III. 4.

to sit in his chair, he asks indignantly : 'Was it the case that there flocked to him from the whole world ambitious, covetous, simoniacal, sacrilegious, fornicators, incestuous, and other like monsters of men, in the hope that by his apostolical authority they might obtain or retain ecclesiastical honours?'[1] On another point of contrast he is equally stern :—

'This Peter it is who was never known to have gone into public adorned with silks or jewels covered with gold, riding upon a white horse, accompanied by soldiers, surrounded on all sides by garrulous servants. He believed that it was quite possible without these to fulfil the salutary precept, "If you love Me, feed My sheep." In these you have succeeded, not Peter, but Constantine!'[2] What would have been the feelings of the saint after this had he known that it was not even with Constantine, but with a counterfeit document, falsely bearing his name, that all this unedifying contrast began? He trusted, no doubt, that something might be done to stay the evils of the system over which he groaned by the publication of a work setting forth what the actual law of the Church was as a first step towards getting the penalties of that law enforced. And for the same reason he may well be supposed to have counselled its authorisation as a text-book for canon-law students on its completion by the Pope, to whom his own treatise was addressed.

There was another person also then at Rome who, we may be sure, would have seconded his views to the utmost— a native of Exeter—cardinal-presbyter, and chancellor of the Roman Church under previous Popes—to whom he addressed a characteristic letter, still extant, complimenting him on all the great things he had done for learning in other parts of the world, and begging that his old pupil might have the full benefit of his sage counsels.[3] This was the first English cardinal, Robert Pullen, who received his hat mainly for the regeneration which he had effected at

[1] Ib. 1 4   [2] Ib iv 3   [3] *Ep* 362, ed Migne.

Oxford in his younger days, causing both pupils and professors to abound there once more.[1] To his remarkable work we shall be brought back in due course. It is probable that he was alive when that of Gratian was completed, and, if so, then the licence given to it must have passed officially through his hands. Anyhow, the petition of Gratian in presenting his work to the Bolognese dignitaries on March 21, and begging them to get it licensed by the Pope so far that it might be publicly read and explained there, is registered in the official Calendar of Bologna for A.D. 1151, and the receipt of the apostolical letters of Eugenius III. in reply—'Per quas dabat suum *placet* super hoc'—is registered in the official Calendar of the same place for 1152.[2]

Here, too, we should do wrong to impeach the motives or the good faith of Eugenius in licensing the great work of Gratian for university lectures and students as a text-book at Bologna; for it had been compiled impartially with labour untold. It was conceived in a thoroughly comprehensive spirit. It appealed to no authorities but such as were then current, and believed to be trustworthy; while, so far as regards arrangement, it was vastly superior to any work of the kind as yet known.

Nobody wishing to found a school of canon law could have discovered anything in literature better adapted for giving impulse to its study then. Nor was this the only branch of learning that Eugenius has left proof of his wish to promote. His leisure hours were spent in getting approved works of the Greek Fathers translated into Latin.[3] Who can say, therefore, but that Gratian himself may have derived benefit from these very translations and reproduced them sometimes in his work? Nevertheless, it was a terribly calamitous day for Western Christendom when students who

[1] See the Proleg to his work in Migne, *Pat Lat* clxxxvi. 633-40, and Antony Wood, *Annals*, A D 1134, and Cave, *Hist Lit*. ii 222, both of whom Migne omits.
[2] Roehmer, *Diss* § 12, notes *f* and *g*
[3] *L'art de Vérif les Dates*, i 286

had devoured the work of Gratian became professors, and as professors lectured in what they had been so well schooled, and at length in many cases from professors became Popes; for then how could they help basing their Decretals on what they had taught or been taught in lectures on Gratian, and culling principles from documents coined by some miscreant of the ninth century, but circulated under high-sounding names?

The False Decretals are quoted by name—not often perhaps, yet often enough[1]—by the contributors to the collection of Gregory IX. to prove their continued study; and they are quoted still oftener in the earlier Decretals of Alexander III. and others, reprinted by C. Labbé, the lawyer, in 1608, with its preface to Gregory XIII. intact, where the 'two Isidores'—the saint and the forger—are singled out for special encomium as 'collectors of the letters of the Roman pontiffs and the decrees of all Councils.' This was barely twenty years before the Decretals of the forger received their *coup de main* from the French Blondel.

But it is not with canon law as a whole that we are concerned here, though it is with Gratian as a whole, and for this reason—namely, that his third part has for its special subject 'consecration,' which is our own likewise. Yet the method and the materials employed by him in discussing it have so much in common with the method and materials of his two former parts that we cannot study consecration in his work to advantage without frequently dipping into chapters on canon law for illustration. This observation will be fully substantiated further on.

There is another fact also connected with the work of Gratian and peculiar to it which should not be passed over. There was a movement in the fifteenth and following century for promoting its revival as a text-book, which, for various reasons, it was practically by then ceasing to be, yet nothing

---

[1] Friedberg's list is not quite complete, as it omits the *uniden-*fied quotations, Part II. Proleg. xii

could prove more clearly the estimation in which it was still held. After struggling with difficulties a whole century, this movement bore substantial fruit at last. A committee was formed, but unfortunately not till the Council of Trent was over, for bringing out a revised edition of the 'Decretum,' and this edition was at length given to the world, A.D. 1582, with a letter of Gregory prefixed to it ordering its publication, and saying of it, 'In quo magna ratio habita est operis ipsius dignitatis, et publicæ eorum præsertim qui in hoc studio versantur utilitatis.'

The list of names composing this committee given by Boehmer[1] may or may not be correct, but it is an imposing one, though it fails to include some that might have been added to it with advantage; and the work done by the 'Roman correctors,' as they are called, which takes the form of notes, is colossal enough, though it is not complete; for at that date the spuriousness of the False Decretals, though possibly suspected, had not been proved, and therefore the correction that was most desiderated in Gratian is still due from Rome. For the world this desideratum was supplied by the work of Berardus of Oneglia more than one hundred years ago.[2] Could the noble monk of Bologna have come back to life to peruse this work, he would have been the first to correct his own work by it for the benefit of all students of those high and holy subjects which he loved so well and laboured so devotedly to expound, with every regard to truth in his power, and in the way best calculated in his judgment to promote their edification.

[1] *Diss* § xvii note *c*.
[2] *Gratiani Canones Genuini ab Apocryphis discreti* (Venet. 1783, in 4 vols).

CHAPTER VIII.

GRATIAN, we have seen, quotes the False Decretals twenty-nine times at least in the third part of his work dealing specially with consecration and with the Eucharist, which comes first, and occupies about half of it under that head. Now, it is in treating of the Eucharist that his quotations from spurious works abound most. The False Decretals are quoted at least twenty times by name, though mostly for ritualistic observances. The most important of them has been anticipated—namely, that of Alexander I., who prescribes 'that the Lord's passion shall always be celebrated whenever the Lord's body and blood are consecrated.'[1] Another equally deserves particular notice—that of Telesphorus—which forbids any celebrations of the Eucharist on ordinary days before the third hour, *that* being the hour in which Jesus was nailed to the cross, and in which the Holy Spirit is said to have descended upon the Apostles.[2] These two contain the nearest approaches of any to the subject of Eucharistic consecration.

The subject of Eucharistic consecration is not formally discussed at all in the first distinction of the third part, nor in the second distinction till almost the middle. Then, two distinct—*discordant*, he would have called them, had he been asked, conformably with the title prefixed to his work—theories are propounded, which the student, if he can, must reconcile for himself, as the writer will not.

---

[1] *Dist* 11 c 1 'In sacramentorum oblationibus, quæ inter missarum solemnia Domino offeruntur, passio Domini miscenda est ut Ejus Cujus corpus et sanguis conficitur, passio celebretur' Where the last clause fixes the meaning of the first

[2] *Dist* 1 c 48

For the teaching of antiquity we shall find *but one* passage cited, and that one *from S. Augustine.* For the mediæval, a host of passages are given: (1) from alien or spurious pieces; (2) from very late but real authors, for whose names are substituted the names of S. Augustine or S. Gregory the Great. No passage from any genuine work of any known Father, Greek or Latin, is cited for what, on chronological grounds alone, must be called the mediæval teaching. The single passage quoted from S. Augustine for the teaching of the primitive Fathers is from his work on the Trinity, which, as it has been already given in full, need not be repeated. It maintains Eucharistic consecration to be due to the unseen action of the Holy Ghost on the elements invoked by prayer. Other passages in which the spiritual character of the sacrament is warmly maintained are given from him likewise, and presuppose this teaching; but it is asserted in no other passage quoted from him in so many words. Passages of an opposite character from Paschasius and Lanfranc are quoted *as from S. Augustine.* Colourless passages from S. Prosper, Gennadius, and Venerable Bede are quoted as from him too. Two passages from Lanfranc are given to S. Prosper, and one to S. Gregory the Great. Foremost of alien passages are two from Eusebius of Emesa, the semi-Arian, about whose writings so much has been already said. He was also called by some the '*Gallican,*' from the currency, no doubt, which his homilies obtained in France. For which reason, too, possibly, several of his homilies have been attributed to one French saint after another famed for his preaching—S. Cæsarius, or S. Eucherius, for instance— who may have borrowed from them or preached them entire, though the authority procured for them by being associated with such names plainly suggests another cause.

Foremost of spurious passages are those which come from works attributed falsely to S. Ambrose, or which have been interpolated in his genuine works.

Correct Gratian by removing these passages which are

spurious or alien, and by making Lanfranc alone speak for what Lanfranc wrote, and then, positively, the sole voucher for the specific teaching of the middle ages adduced by Gratian would be the predecessor of S. Anselm—his own senior, but contemporary. The Catechism of the Council of Trent, alas! appeals with most confidence to the passages most loudly calling for correction in Gratian, and passes over in unmerited silence the *only passage quoted by him from S. Augustine* giving expression to the teaching of the primitive Church in so many words. The effect of this is sad enough. For it rests the teaching which it upholds on the homilies of the semi-Arian Eusebius,[1] with the treatise 'De Sacramentis' of the pseudo-Ambrose, whom Gratian quotes at great length, and a third treatise, 'De Cœnâ Domini,' not known to Gratian, of the pseudo-Cyprian; its now acknowledged author being one with whom Gratian may have conversed himself. Surely such blots as these will not be permitted to remain uncancelled after the veil concealing them from view has been removed. Of the first, and what effects it must have wrought in the East had they not been almost entirely frustrated by the conservative spirit engrained there, which it could neither cajole nor subjugate, enough has been said in a foregoing chapter. Its companionship with the second in the West will be pointed out in dealing with the second.

About the last the only remark that need be added to the account which has been given of it in that same

[1] Part II c 4, § 3, as throwing light on the institution For the words, ib § 25

For a *consensus Patrum*, ib § 27 and 37, for the 'presence,' ib § 31; for the conversion of the elements, ib § 39 and 49; for effects, ib § 54 and 85, for frequent communions, ib § 63, for the name, ib § 4; for the elements, ib § 11, for the words, ib § 20 and 25 General references to Gratian include the first two

For the name 'supper,' ib § 5; for the words, ib § 25 Besides these, there are references to the False Decretals, to the Areopagite, to Isychius, to the doubtful sermon of S Chrysostom on Judas. All reference to the teaching of the Fathers on the action of the Holy Ghost is suppressed

[2] C. v. p. 166 *et seq.*

chapter, is that it shows to what extent ignorance or audacity could gain credit for its statements in mediæval times, for the glorious name of a venerated African bishop, saint, and martyr of the third century to be tacked to the tract of a Cistercian abbot of the twelfth century, dissociated in style from his well-known writings by phrases unknown in his day, and for the imposture to have escaped detection so long. If the pseudo-Cyprian stood his ground till the sixteenth century, the pseudo-Ambrose may, with more reason, be credited in some quarters still. For he comes to us in a dress which is specious enough. He poses as a Latin, not a Roman, discoursing on the liturgy then used in his Church, although failing to tell us where that Church was, and professing his utmost desire to follow the Roman Church in all that he could; only where custom is too strong for him will he permit any difference between it and him.[1] He calls his work, or it has been called for him, *De Sacramentis*, and we know, from unexceptionable testimony—that of S. Augustine—there was a work actually written by S. Ambrose bearing that name. Fortunately, S. Augustine makes copious extracts from this work in the second book of his own work against Julian, besides citing it there and elsewhere by name. Now, of the passages cited from it by him, not only can not one be found in the treatise which concerns us here, but all are foreign to its contents in every sense. Therefore, unless we can suppose S. Ambrose would have written two works essentially different, and called both by the same name, we must consider his own acknowledged work a decisive proof of the spuriousness of the other usurping his name, and regard that other an illustration of his own words directed against the '*tergiversating*' class from whom such words emanate. 'Solent,' he says, 'ut fallant, sub nomine clari alicujus viri epistolam fingere, ut auctoritas nominis possit commendari, quod per se ipsum recipi non possit.'[2]

---

[1] *De Sacram* in § 5.   [2] In 2 Thessal. ii. 1.

Cardinal Bona, whom nobody would accuse of wishing to undermine the credit of a liturgical authority, considered hitherto standard, and of no small importance so far as it goes, says of this treatise: 'Some years ago, fresh from the perusal of the works of S. Ambrose, which I had gone through in no perfunctory way, on arriving at this piece I seemed to myself to hear a man of another tongue, wholly different from that of S. Ambrose, speaking.' Other peculiarities are then pointed out by him, all pointing to the same conclusion. Notwithstanding, he will not depart from the received way of quoting it himself. Others possessed of knowledge superior to his own may decide whether he has misjudged its author.[1]

Certainly, till we can prove the attributing his six books to S. Ambrose to have been his own act, we must treat him as an unknown writer, in estimating whom we must be guided solely by what is found in his work.

His work, then, consists of six sermons on the model of the last five catechetical lectures of S. Cyril of Jerusalem, addressed to candidates for baptism, confirmation, and holy communion, and delivered by him when a presbyter, as we have seen. It is to be observed, however, that the last chapter of the fifth book once figured as a sermon by S. Augustine, and stands now eighty-fourth of the appendix to his sermons in the Benedictine edition, being an explanation of the Lord's Prayer. Whether the writer of these six sermons was a presbyter or bishop, and whether he preached as well as composed them, we cannot tell. The custom of washing the feet of the newly-baptised,[2] which, he says, was done by the 'summus sacerdos' in his Church—whom he avoids ever calling himself—though not practised at Rome, continued a custom in several Churches of the West for some time, so that it throws no definite light on the Church to which he belonged. But, in professing to recite the words

---

[1] *Rer Lit* 1 7, 4
[2] *Op S Amb.* ii 362, ed. Ben with the note

then used in consecrating the Eucharist by the celebrant at that Church, he testifies to the fact that, that either there were several versions of the Roman Canon at that time, or that his Church had not yet adopted the Roman Canon, word for word, as it exists now. For, according to him, the priest says, 'Fac nobis hanc oblationem adscriptam, rationabilem, acceptabilem; *quod figura est corporis et sanguinis Domini nostri Jesu Christi*'—a phrase copied from Tertullian.

This is a passage which neither Pamelius nor the Benedictine editors can face, as given in MSS. Pamelius omits 'ratam,' which the Benedictine editors put in; they put in the last sentence, which he changes. Pamelius is not consistent with himself in altering their text. The Benedictine editors take pretty much the same view of this work as Cardinal Bona. Pamelius, nothing doubting it all to have been written by the great Archbishop of Milan, transcribes the portion of the Canon which he finds in it for his edition of the Ambrosian liturgy, and heads the first three lines of it '*Invocatio sacerdotis*,' which he knew any Canon used by S. Ambrose must contain. Yet he changes the very phrase most characteristic of S. Ambrose which it exhibits—namely, 'quod figura est corporis et sanguinis Domini nostri Jesu Christi '—which Muratori was not slow to defend in another fragmentary version of the Ambrosian Canon which he prints. The words of this version speak of what was done by our Lord at the Last Supper—' dum panem et vinum in sacramentum sui corporis et sanguinis transformavit,' and Muratori quotes, in illustration of these words, two passages from *the indubitable works* of S. Ambrose, as he calls them, one of which may suffice now: 'Nos autem,' he says, in a treatise dedicated to the Emperor Gratian, ' quotiescunque sacramenta sumimus, quæ per sacræ orationis mysterium in carnem transfigurantur et sanguinem, mortem Domini annuntiamus.'[1] This passage was translated in a former chapter.[2] The other passage comes from

[1] *De Reb. Liturg. Diss.* c x pp 132-6   [2] Above, p 133.

the fourth chapter of his tract on the Incarnation. To transform or transfigure the bread into the sacrament under which Christ was received was precisely what the Holy Ghost was asked for in the primitive Church to do; whence that act of His was called 'conformatio sacramenti' by S. Isidore. But the writer of this treatise dispenses with His services altogether in the matter of consecration, and recites the 'Qui pridie,' &c. not, indeed, in all the fulness of the Roman Missal of our own times, but certainly with all the enthusiasm of a person exulting over a victory that had been lately won. 'How can bread become the body of Christ?' he asks. 'By consecration,' he replies. 'In what words and in whose words is consecration?' 'The words of the Lord Jesus . . . Therefore the *words of Christ consummate this sacrament* . . . Before consecration it is bread; the words of Christ have no sooner been pronounced than it is His body.'[1] The frequency and the fluency with which this is argued and reiterated is in marked contrast to the measured statement of Amalarius—' Hic credimus naturam simplicem panis et vini mixti verti in naturam rationabilem, scilicet corporis et sanguinis Christi.'[2] 'Not in all the Latin-speaking Churches,' says Cardinal Bona, with his eye fixed upon Milan, 'could the Popes get the Roman substituted for the provincial rite. In some places the struggle was vehement and sustained, and people fought for their national customs as for their hearths and homes, and as though salvation and the foundations of the faith were concerned in their maintenance.' Judged, therefore, from his work, the standpoint of this writer was clearly that of a partisan, who had been instrumental in getting the Roman rite substituted for the Ambrosian, and yet could no more help retaining a traditional phrase, stamped with the teaching of S. Ambrose, in the Canon, than the custom of washing the feet of the newly-baptised endeared to his Church. Oudin is, therefore, probably right in describing him as 'a

---

[1] *De Sacram* iv. 4, 5.   [2] *De Eccl. Off.* iii. 24.

Gallican,' not, indeed, of the eighth, but of the ninth century, nor a bishop either, but a monk.[1] There is another point on which Oudin has raised a learned discussion—namely, the relation of this treatise to the shorter but kindred one, 'De Mysteriis,' in which he finds evident tokens of the same pen. In many MSS., according to him, it is called the 'the first book of the sacraments,' or, at all events, considered with them as forming one work. He therefore would regard the shorter work as a sort of prefatory chapter to the longer one. But another explanation of their being so often found interwoven seems to be much nearer the truth —namely, that the author of the treatise 'De Sacramentis' interpolated the treatise 'De Mysteriis' in order that the spurious character of his own work might not be proclaimed by any divergence between them on the point for which the sponsorship of S. Ambrose was to be secured under the cloak of his name. The interpolation speaks for itself. It is introduced at the commencement of the ninth chapter, of which it occupies exactly five sections. Remove these, and the sixth section connects naturally with the last section of the preceding chapter, and proclaims its own homogeneousness with the whole. There is not a word in *this* treatise which is not in perfect harmony with all the acknowledged works of S. Ambrose, both in matter and style, when those five opening sections of the ninth chapter have been struck out.

S. Ambrose begins this treatise by referring to a well-known work of his connected with and containing references to several of his other works. The attention of the pseudo-Ambrose was therefore specially drawn to this work also,

---

[1] *De Script Eccl* 1 665 There was a Benedictine monk named Ambrose—though otherwise called Autpert—said to have been in great favour with Charlemagne, who died A D 778, leaving several tracts and sermons which are still extant; having been mixed up with the works of S Augustine and S Ambrose, but not at all in the style of the treatise 'De Sacramentis,' for which otherwise might have been found an author in him They may be read in Migne, *Patrol. Lat.* lxxxix. 1265 *et seq.*

with a view of accommodating it to his own. It is entitled 'De Benedictionibus Patriarcharum,' and the ninth chapter of this work, too, furnished him with his opportunity. These three lines—'Hunc panem dedit Apostolis, ut dividerent populo credentium; hodieque dat eum, quem ipse quotidie sacerdos consecrat suis verbis'—attest his hand; they are foreign to the manner of S. Ambrose. That they are not wanted there, that they interrupt the flow, is at once seen on their removal.

Both passages, it must be confessed, have been cleverly dovetailed into the text, and might have for ever escaped notice but for their more reckless counterpart in the six sermons.

Two more points remain to be noticed before quitting these sermons, which apparently never struck Oudin nor any subsequent critic of them, so far as my knowledge goes, and yet are facts: (1) their singular resemblance to the five lectures of S. Cyril of Jerusalem in point of form, and their flat contradiction to them on the special subject of Eucharistic consecration. In Cyril, consecration is attributed to the operation of the Holy Ghost, and the words of institution are not even named in connection with it. In the treatise 'De Sacramentis' all is attributed to the words of institution in the mouth of the celebrant, and all reference to the action of the Holy Ghost is left out.

(2) The absolute sameness of the teaching of these six sermons on that head with the two homilies of the Gallican or Emisene Eusebius, which clearly must have been the fountain-head from which their author drew. For, with the exception of S. Chrysostom, no other authority could have been quoted by him for his distinctive teaching at the time when it was first put forth; but he nowhere names nor seems to have had his eyes on S. Chrysostom. On the other hand, the following parallels tell their own tale:—

Hom. de Pascha, v.[1]

'Hic ergo Melchisedec, cujus genealogia vel origo notitiam illius temporis latuit, oblatione panis et vini hoc Christi sacrificium præsignavit. De quo propheta pronuntiat · "Tu es sacerdos secundum ordinem Melchisedec." Nam et beatus Moses de eo mysterio loquens vinum et sanguinem sub unâ appellatione significat in benedictione dominicam passionem multo ante demonstrante. . . .

'Quod si illius legis manna de quo legitur, " pluit illis manna ut ederent," hoc unicuique sapiebat, quod desideriis concupisset. . . . Qui tunc latuit præfiguratus in manna, sit tibi manifestatus in gratiâ Ipsum autem fuisse in mannæ illius specie præsignatum, etiam propheta evidenter testatur dicens " Panem cœli dedit iis panem angelorum manducavit homo," et quis panis angelorum est, nisi Christus qui eos cibo suæ charitatis et lumine suæ claritatis exsatiat? . . .

'Nam invisibilis sacerdos, visibiles creaturas in substantiâ corporis et sanguinis Sui verbi Sui secretâ potestate convertit ita dicens: " Accipite et edite hoc enim est Corpus Meum." Ergo sicut ad nutum præcipientis Domini repente ex nihilo substiterunt excelsa cœlorum, profunda fluctuum, vasta terrarum; pari potentiâ in spiritualibus sacramentis verbi præcipit virtus, et rei servit effectus . . . Quid autem mirum est, si quæ verbo creare potuit, verbo possit creata convertere? . . .'

[1] *Max. Bibl. Pat.* vi. 636-7

De Sacramentis.[2]

' Obtulit ergo Melchisedec panem et vinum. Quis est Melchisedec ? . . . sine patre, inquit, et sine matre est. Similis cui ? Filio Dei ' (§ 12).

'Quis habuit panem et vinum ? Abraham non habuit. Sed quis habuit ? Melchisedec. Ipse ergo auctor sacramentorum.' (§ 10).

'Forte aliquis dixerit: Judæis tantam gratiam præstitit. manna illis pluit de cœlo. Quid plus dedit fidelibus Suis ? Quid plus tribuit iis quibus plus promisit ? ' (§ 9).

'Magnum quidem et venerabile quod Judæis pluit de cœlo. Sed intellige. Quid est amplius, manna de cœlo, an corpus Christi ? Corpus utique Christi, qui auctor est cœli.' (§ 24).

' Sermo Christi hoc conficit sacramentum. Quis est sermo Christi ? Nempe is, quo facta sunt omnia Jussit Dominus, et factum est cœlum jussit Dominus, et facta est terra: jussit Dominus, et facta sunt maria. Vides ergo quàm operatorius est sermo Christi. Si ergo tanta vis est in sermone Domini Jesu, ut inciperent esse quæ non erant: quanto magis operatorius est, ut sint quæ erant, et in aliud convertantur.' (§ 15).

[2] S. Amb. *Op.* ii. 366 *et seq.*

The mediæval writers who flung themselves with enthusiasm into the teaching of these two sets of sermons on their first appearance were not slow to perceive their connection and to quote them consecutively, regarding them as both the clearest and earliest authorities for it to whom they could appeal. As such, Paschasius quotes them in his letter to Frudegard triumphantly by name.[1] But it was to the Emisene Eusebius in reality that the pseudo-Ambrose was due. His homilies had been unearthed in the search made for works of this description by order of Charlemagne, which had for its more formal result the '*Homilarius*' of Paul the Deacon,[2] but which also brought endless other pieces into notice, some with names attaching to them and some without, that had previously been hid, and hence began to be quoted in the ninth century for the first time, the more valued in proportion to their supposed antiquity, or else to their starting some new idea, congenial to the tastes of that age. The homilies of Isychius approved themselves on this account, though there was nobody to vouch for their author then any more than now. But for the Emisene Eusebius, as S. Jerome calls him, what more could be desired than the compliments paid him by the great Latin doctor, whose writings went hand in hand with his translation of the canonical Scriptures? It is true that in probably the least known of his works—his 'Chronicon'—the Emisene Eusebius curtly figures as 'the standard-bearer of the Arian party.'[3] But in the best known, his notices of illustrious men, he figures as one of the most elegant and best trained writers of his day; author of innumerable works that were popular and read with avidity; and, in addition, of short, but numerous, homilies on the Gospels.[4] In a letter to a celebrated Roman orator of his day, S. Jerome names the Emisene Eusebius actually next after S. Eustathius of Antioch, and

---

[1] Migne, *Pat Lat* cxx 1354
[2] Ib xcv 1159, with the circular of Charlemagne prefixed to it.
[3] A.D. 351
[4] C. 91.

S. Athanasius of Alexandria, as one of those learned men among the Greeks of whom people may doubt whether they are to be admired most for their secular erudition or for their knowledge of the Scriptures.[1] In another letter he tells S. Augustine that Eusebius of Emesa was one of those from whose commentaries on the Scriptures he may himself have borrowed,[2] and he repeats this in the preface to his own commentaries on Galatians, as though instances of what he stated would be found there. Might not any Latin, therefore, borrow to the same extent from his homilies that S. Jerome told the world without hesitation he had done from his commentaries? Their teaching on the institution of the Eucharist evidently commended itself at once to the judgment of the pseudo-Ambrose, and he had a special reason for wishing to be the means of propagating it far and wide, in his desire to both further and justify the adoption of the Roman Canon throughout the Frank Empire. The only thing wanting for that purpose was the shelter of a name that, being excepted against by none, would soon bespeak authority for it with all; and hence to justify the introduction of the Roman Canon at Milan, and at the same time to put an interpretation on it that would fix its meaning in future, he published his sermons under a title that would make them appear to have been preached by S. Ambrose, and then circulated copies of two genuine works of S. Ambrose, just enough interpolated to harmonise with these sermons, but yet too slightly to provoke suspicion. Partisans in all ages have considered artifices of this kind justifiable to make their opinions prevail, nor can it be denied that the pseudo-Ambrose managed most felicitously for the twofold end he had in view. But a miserable pitfall was thereby perpetuated for Western Christendom, by inundating it with conclusions on the highest subjects, drawn mainly from pseudonymous works, and ultimately from a semi-Arian source. One more question remains. When were these sermons made

[1] *Ep* lxx § 4, *ad Mayn*, ed Vallars [2] *Ep* cxii. § 4, ib

public? We seem furnished with a tolerable clue to their appearance by this twofold fact: (1) that Amalarius never appeals to them, though distinctly maintaining their teaching, and never failing to quote S. Ambrose wherever he can avail himself of his authority. (2) That Paschasius, having evidently drawn conclusions from them and from the homilies of the Emisene Eusebius in his well-known work, in answering objections made to that work by Frudegard quotes them both, and mentions the authors of both in the same breath by name.

Meanwhile, there would seem to be direct proof that the author of the Caroline Books was acquainted with the homilies of the Emisene Eusebius: for, though it is confined to a single phrase, writers of this period would be searched in vain for the same phrase, though it is appropriated also by Agobard in a slightly changed form.[1] Further, it is tolerably clear that the author of the Caroline Books had a well-known passage of the Areopagite in his mind at the same time, though his actual quotation from it amounts to no more than two words at most.[2] Towards the end of the homily for Easter, in a passage where the sacraments of baptism and the Lord's Supper are compared, the Eucharistic elements are said to be placed on the altar ' antequam invocatione summi Nominis consecrentur '—the action of the celebrant having been already dwelt on, which the author of the Caroline Books paraphrases thus: 'Cum scilicet corporis et sanguinis Dominici sacramentum . . . per *manum sacerdotis et invocationem Divini Nominis conficiatur*.'

We have thus a curious parallel to the False Decretals in the ups and downs of these homilies. Both were known to the advisers, and must have passed through the hands of Charlemagne, though the use to which they were turned in

---

[1] 'Ad invocationem summi Sacerdotis' A clear reason for this change has already been shown, above, pp 112 and 171-2

[2] *De Eccl Hierarch.* III § 12

Πρὸς αὐτὸν ἀναβοῶν, Σὺ εἶπας, &c, here rendered '*cum interno rugitu* memoriam faciat,' &c *Lib Carol* II 27.

his reign was far from conspicuous. For, though the introduction of the Roman rite throughout his empire was often talked about and in part commenced, and though promises of enlarged territory to the head of the Roman Church were freely made, still performance was delayed or toned down in each case by the pertinacity with which the Popes of his day resisted the introduction of the interpolated Creed. Both the Decretals and homilies, therefore, slept on the shelf for a time, till circumstances awakened attention to them anew and paved the way for their adoption. And then, just as the False Decretals became generally known through the Capitularies of Benedict the Levite, the homilies of the Emisene Eusebius became generally known through the sermons of the pseudo-Ambrose. Moreover, there was just one place likewise where the homilies of the Emisene Eusebius anticipated, in comparative privacy, the widespread influence, due to the pseudo-Ambrose, which they afterwards acquired, and that one place was Metz, in the quadrilateral. Here, too, the lines of the parallel force themselves upon us again. Mayence was the birthplace of the new canon law of the West; Metz was, earlier still, the birthplace of the new Canon of its Mass—as it was beginning to be called—or liturgy.

This, being a very recondite portion of history never before sifted, it cannot be too fully or too carefully worked out. Angilramn, the confidant of Charlemagne, for proof of whose secret dealings with Pope Adrian M. Wattenbach has already received our best acknowledgments, appears last on the list of bishops of Metz commemorated by Paul Wilfrid— or Warnefrid, whose Homiliarium was noticed a few pages back—his contemporary. He died A.D. 791. His see, for some reason which we can never hope to fathom, remained without a bishop for twenty-seven years, and when a bishop was appointed to it, A.D. 819, which was the fifth year of the Emperor Lewis and the year of his marriage with Judith, mother of Charles the Bald, it was one who left no memorial behind him but his name, Gundulph. On his death, A.D. 826, Drogo, brother of the Emperor, held the see for thirty-two years.

Metz was, it will be remembered, one of the schools of music where the Roman Chant was taught, and taught more efficiently than at Soissons. Members of the provincial choirs came from all parts of the empire to be trained there. Yet we shall soon find proof that it was much too near Aix to be Romanised—a contingency which, perhaps, its being left so long without a bishop was deemed the next best means of preventing.

Having brought general history down to this point, if we now go back and resume the question how Gallicanism was imported into the Roman Canon revised by S. Gregory from where we left it,[1] we shall find all the evidence we need of the process by which this change was carried out, concentrated in the writings and acts of two second-rate French ecclesiastics, Amalarius and Paschasius, who were contemporaries—concerned in what is called the Paschasian controversy—and a third, naturalised in France two centuries later, who became Archbishop of Canterbury, Lanfranc—concerned in what is called the Berengarian. Both controversies were waged with a want of honesty, with a contempt of Catholic belief and practices, with an amount of violence, conceit, and ignorance, most discreditable to the winning side, most disastrous to the entire Western Church. Of this trio we should naturally begin with Amalarius, as he comes first both in time and place.

A.D. 816, or three years before Metz was provided with a bishop again, there was a large gathering at Aix of bishops, abbots, and counts by order of the Emperor 'to sanction Capitularies for the good of the whole Church,' as it is expressed in the text of the Capitularies ;[2] or 'wisely and curiously to treat of many things for the emendation of holy Church,' as the preface to the Council has it ;[3] or 'although

---

[1] Above, p 256 *et seq*   [2] Baluze, 1 561   [3] Mansi, xiv 148

we have before now often ordained many things relating to the condition of the Churches and *their rites*, as much of this has since been hindered by the wiles of Satan, it is our duty to employ this time of peace for the common benefit of the Church of God, and of us all, so that what has been well begun by the blessing of God may obtain effect, and what has been imperfectly done may be corrected, and what has not been done, but is necessary, may be supplied,' as the Emperor says himself.[1] To get at the inner mind of all these converging declarations, we must go back to the no less important gathering at Aix in the reign of his father, A.D. 789, and construe them by the light shed upon them in the remarkable preface to that gathering of the great Charles and his Constitution of the preceding year—' De Emendatione Librorum et Officiorum ecclesiasticorum.' The son intended in this fresh gathering clearly to start in each case from the exact point where the purposes of his father, as then sketched by him, had hitherto been frustrated, suspended, or hindered in their full execution.[2] Accordingly, what is stated to have been the actual amount of work carried through by this Council in Mansi no doubt makes a great show, for it fills over 130 pages and forms two separate books, the first having for its subject the institution of canons regular, the second the institution of cloistered nuns. Still it is difficult to suppose that these two were the only subjects considered in an assembly convened professedly to do so much more. Nevertheless, taken as they stand, two things specially call for remark: (1) that there is no reference throughout to any power outside the empire, neither the see of Rome nor its head—if it had a head just then—being even named; (2) that the authorship of the two books promulgated by this Council has been attributed on no earlier authority than that of Ademar, the monk of Angoulême (who lived two centuries later, and therefore cannot be

[1] Baluze, i 562
[2] Ib. 203, with 209 *et seq.*

supposed to have been entirely well informed on matters of this sort), to 'Amalarius the deacon,' as he styles him.[1] We are told further by the same writer that 'a book on the Divine Offices and their variations, and on the order of the Psalms—*juxta clericorum antiquum usum*—was addressed by the said Amalarius to the same Emperor.' Thereupon Amalarius, of whom we know nothing previously, and who then was no more than a deacon, is presented to us as the inspiring mind of this large gathering. But, supposing him to have been this, we cannot avoid considering the two last works attributed to him due to this gathering also, though they may have taken him some time to mature, for both come strictly within the programme traced by the Emperor himself when he named ritual among the subjects that had occupied, and were still occupying, his thoughts. Anyhow, Amalarius tells the Emperor, in enumerating his reasons for dedicating his work on the 'ecclesiastical offices' of the Church of Metz to him, that the chiefest was, 'cum sciamus vos rectorem esse totius Christianæ religionis, quantum ad homines pertinet.' And, further, the whole character of his work shows how completely the writer was of this mind himself. This, we shall see presently, was the first edition of his work in one book—'De Ordine *nostræ* Missæ, quam consueto more celebramus'—and it may have been written A.D. 819, as Le Cointe shows, from the felicitations addressed to the new Empress at its close,[2] the only real clue to its date. Nor is anything said by him in any part of it incompatible with his being a deacon still, yet a deacon who was in high favour at Court. That he was attached to the Church of Metz is indisputable from this work alone: that he visited Rome to get particulars in its ritual explained to him *not before* but *after* having written this work, is his own explicit statement in the preface to the second edition of his work in the enlarged form it wears now; and that it is the earliest work of the kind in Latin extant, not anonymous, which

[1] *Hist* III 2, ap Migne, *Pat Lat.* cxli 29.   [2] A.D 827, n. 3

comments on what what is now called 'the Canon of the Mass' clause by clause, thereby putting us into possession of every word of it, from ' Quam oblationem Tu, Deus,' &c., with which he says expressly what he calls 'the immolation of Christ' commenced.[1] A further and most important fact is that all this part of the Canon, till we come to the ' Memento' for the dead, stands in the first edition of his work word for word as it stands in the Missals of the Church of Rome now. *In his work!* but who and of what Church was he? A deacon, not of the Church of Rome, but of Metz ; and, further, one who proclaims himself a sturdy Gallican all through, who speaks, even in his enlarged edition, of ' *our Sacramentary,*' not the Roman,[2] which he never once names ; and if he names a Roman ' Ordo,' it is one which omits all the earlier part of the Canon and only gives the first words of the prayers, from ' Nobis quoque peccatoribus,' just at the latest, though on points of ritual it is explicit and diffuse enough.[3] In Lib. III. c. 40 of his enlarged edition we meet with ' Auctor Missalis qui *vocatur* Gregorialis,' and in the thirtieth of the fourth book ' Missalis cujus auctorem credimus esse beatum papam Gregorium '; but in both cases the book, identical or not, is freely compared with his own, and where different he decides between them. What he has said of the Canon in his first edition is hardly varied in his second, except in this, that his comment on the words of institution pronounced by the celebrant follows, *not* exactly those words which are now held to effect consecration, but the parting command, ' in Mei memoriam facietis,' in his first edition ; whereas in the second it follows after an interval of seven lines of other matter, as if to indicate that the writer feared his comment might mislead persons in its previous place. My ideas of his first edition are taken from a rare MS. of the ninth century containing it, according to the description given of

---

[1] In the edition now used, iv. 24.
[2] Ib i 9
[3] Muratori, *Liturg Rom.* ii. 983-4.

it by himself[1] (which I have examined, but not yet had the means of collating), not from what Cochlæus first, and after him Nicolaus Aurificus, printed as such.

How long it was after the publication of his first edition that he went to Rome he omits to state; he omits even to state who was then Pope. He mentions no dealings with anybody but 'the ministers of the Church of S. Peter.' In the prologue to his next work, 'De Ordine Antiphonarii,' he tells us many more things relating to its composition than he had told us about his offices. He had been to Corbey in search of copies to compare with his own and had found four there. The Emperor Lewis thereupon sent him to Rome to make inquiries of Pope Gregory respecting these copies, and to ask for more copies to compare with them. *This visit to Rome, therefore, can be fixed with precision*; it took place A.D. 831,[2] soon after his visit to Corbey. Paschasius was discharging the duties of abbot there then, Abbot Wala being in exile for his complicity with the rebellion. Amalarius would seem to have remained on this occasion at Rome till he had finished his work, but he never mentions having seen the Pope but once, and his Gallican predilections are more strongly developed in this last work than in the first. 'In many things,' he says in his prologue, 'I have found *our* volumes arranged more rationally than the Roman. ... I was amazed to find such discrepancies between the mother and the daughter. ... I found our volumes considerably more ancient than the Roman with which I compared them. ... Where I thought the Roman preferable I wrote the letter *R* in the margin, where *our own* the letter *M* to stand for Metz.'

This, then, whatever explanations may be given of it, is an undeniable fact—that we must go for our earliest authentic introduction to the Canon of the Roman Missals of our own times, *not* to a Roman Pontifical or Sacramentary,

---

[1] Comp iv. 9, 'In libello de Officio Missæ,' where quotations from it occur.
[2] *De Ord Antiph.* c 58

nor to any comments upon either, whose dates can be fixed with any precision, dedicated to, or approved by the bishops of that Church, but to the work of a deacon of a Church of France, that had been twenty-seven years without a bishop when he compiled his book, and which he dedicated to the Emperor as 'ruler of the whole Christian world,' and that it was his Gallican pen which adventured this exposition—the earliest of its kind in any Church till then, being neither preceded nor even followed by any reference direct or implied to the action of the Holy Ghost—making consecration depend on the recital of those words by the celebrant, on which it has for so many centuries since been held by all Churches in communion with Rome to depend, as expounded by him.

'Here we believe the simple nature of the bread and of the mixed wine becomes by conversion a nature transcendental,[1] that of the body and blood of Christ.'

Amalarius quotes no Father or Doctor of the Church Latin or Greek for this unauthorised comment of his own on the recital of these words by the celebrant, nor could he have quoted any but S. Chrysostom, nor could S. Chrysostom, interpreted by himself, possibly be understood to exclude the concurrent action of the Holy Ghost. Again, till the ninth century, putting aside S. Chrysostom, all the Fathers and Doctors of the Church who have left anything extant on the subject declare the Real Presence to be the effect of the Holy Ghost on the Eucharistic oblation invoked by prayer. And to this teaching all the liturgies in existence that were used in other Churches when Amalarius wrote bore witness, as is proved from their remains, or from their then existing form—the Roman revised by S. Gregory, no less than the Mozarabic revised by his friend Leander, or the Constantinopolitan revised by S. Chrysostom. Accordingly, the Canon quoted so freely by Amalarius is proved, by the lack of any reference to this teaching, as great an exception to the

[1] 'In naturam rationabilem.'

liturgies of all other Churches then extant as his comments on it were to the teaching of all Christendom up to that time. Finally, what he states as its commencement, 'Quam oblationem Tu, Deus,' betrays his own hand in it, inasmuch as Paschasius, the monk of Corbey, is just as express in stating that the Canon in use *there*, when the first edition of his work was given to the world, commenced with the prayer 'Supplices Te rogamus,' then forming, and for two centuries longer at Rome, the Gregorian epiklesis, as will be shown further on. These two works, therefore—that of Amalarius and that of Paschasius—between them, by a special providence, furnish all the evidence that could be desired against their respective authors, and testify to the origin of the Canon of Amalarius, proving it essentially distinct from the true Gregorian, by what he had stripped of its meaning and transformed.

How his change became law must now be told; but first let me try to point out how it has come to pass that so many travellers in these parts, infinitely better equipped than myself, should have missed the road hitherto, and not scrutinised this Canon of Amalarius by the light of the candle which his acts supply. Gieseler, for instance, with his usual fulness, gives us a learned summary, backed by quotations of the controversy to which the work of Paschasius Radbertus gave rise;[1] but he has unconsciously misstated some things and omitted others, particularly these two points: (1) that the battlefield of the controversy was throughout confined to France; that even its effects never penetrated beyond North Italy; that Rome never stirred a finger in it at this time. (2) He never once refers to the teaching of the primitive Church on consecration; nor consequently notices the opposition to it of the new view derived from spurious or sectarian works on which Paschasius based his treatise. Gieseler has thus failed to see that, instead of a contest between the statements of Paschasius and S.

[1] Per III Div. I Part II c 3, § 14, with the notes

Augustine, it was a contest between the teaching of the entire primitive Church and the teaching of the Emisene Eusebius and the pseudo-Ambrose, countenanced in some sense latterly by S. Chrysostom, but inconsistent, even so, with his earlier and more standard works. It cannot be too often pointed out that *historically* the notion of a carnal Presence *dates* from the adoption of the teaching of the Emisene Eusebius and that of the pseudo-Ambrose on consecration by the Latin Church, and has never so much as obtained a footing in any part of the Church where the teaching of the primitive Church on consecration has been upheld.

Bearing all these facts in mind, it is possible that they may assist us in eliciting some conclusions from the Paschasian controversy respecting the liturgies of Metz, France, and Rome just at that time, which have not yet been drawn; commencing with Metz, and based on a review not merely of the works of Amalarius, but of his acts. The Gallican spirit breathing throughout his works has been already signalised. The minuteness with which each word of the Canon is set down and commented upon is another feature belonging to it, as though the writer was conscious that it differed *in some respects* from the Canon of other Churches at that time. From 'Quam oblationem' down to the recital of the words of institution, it is quoted entire, word for word as it stands now. His comment on the recital of the words of institution themselves has been already noticed. Then, what follows their recital is quoted entire from 'Unde memores' down to the end of the prayer 'Supplices Te rogamus' inclusive. After this, a few phrases and one short sentence form the sum of his quotations to the end of the post-communion prayers. Had it been his intention to impress upon his readers that the prayer 'Supplices Te rogamus' followed some way *after consecration* in his Canon, and that the action of the Holy Ghost was *nowhere invoked* in any part of it, he could not have explained his meaning more fully to them had he stated the fact. Even in describing how the oblation of the elements was made, the Holy Ghost is not so much as named by him. Between him and Paschasius there is a marked contrast in this respect, which we must never forget. The omission of all mention of the departed in his Canon is also to be noticed, and adds one more proof of what has already been stated as a fact,[1] that all the early copies of the Gelasian and Gregorian Sacramentaries that have yet been produced were written in France. A still further proof is, that he states the final benediction of the post-communion to be followed by the deacon saying, 'Ite, missa est,' a conclusion unknown to the Gelasian and Gregorian Sacramentaries, and to the first Ordo Romanus as well.

One more point to be noticed in the work now before us is its frequent quotations from the 'Gestis espiscopalibus,' or 'pontificalibus,' in other words, 'Lives of the Popes.'[2] It contains no quotations from their supposed Decretals. However, on ritual the statements of both are the same. The 'Eclogæ,' printed as a work of Amalarius, contain nothing connecting them with him; but many things, on the contrary, testifying to their later origin. The letters ascribed to him are purely conjectural.[3]

Passing from his books to his acts, he must be judged very differently from what he would have been had he left no record of himself besides his works. For by his acts he is proved to have been a fierce partisan, an itinerant intriguer, an unscrupulous proselytiser. Those who record them were certainly those who opposed them; but they were simply repelling his aggressions and defending their own. A huge mistake may be noticed here, which would seem to have been contrived by his friends in later times to add weight to his authority. Mansi scented it, but could not

---

[1] Daniel owns he could find no authority for its insertion, and his subterfuges would have been unnecessary, had he laid the fault of the omission on his French MSS.

Cod Liturg. i 38-9.
[2] Lib ii 16; iii. 5, 18, 21, 41–2; iv. 16 and 40.
[3] Migne reprints them without adding a word in their favour

say where the error lay.[1] How, he asks, could the same person be deacon of Metz and country-bishop of Lyons? Florus, deacon of the Church of Lyons, whose reputation for learning got him surnamed '*Magister*,' writes to tell the Council of Thionville that Amalarius came to Lyons professedly to examine their Office-books, but in reality to set everybody by the ears, to find fault with their ritual, to prove their Service-books replete with errors or defects, and to win all he could over to his heterodox opinions. All the presbyters, archdeacons, and country-bishops then present at Lyons joined in denouncing him; *one country-bishop of Lyons alone* was found willing to make copies of his books, and another, or the same dignitary, to defend and disseminate them.

In this letter there is no mention of Amalarius by name, but in a similar letter addressed to the Council of Quiersy he is both named and designated 'author of all the pestilent errors described in this letter,' but given no title whatever. In a third letter addressed to Drogo, bishop of Metz, and others, we have the following sentence: 'Præcessit enim in præfatâ nuper ecclesiâ' (Lyons) 'per prælatum ejus Amalarium error insanus et vanus,' &c. Here, by accident, or quite possibly by design, the genitive termination has been altered into the accusative. The true reading is, beyond any doubt, *Amalarii*. *His* error it was that was upheld by the 'prælatus ecclesiæ Lugdunensis' mentioned in the Thionville letter, placed here first simply from the light thrown by it on the other two.[2] The years in which these Councils were held cannot be fixed with any certainty, but they would all seem to have been held when Florus was left sole champion of a declining cause, for Agobard his bishop was in hiding, dispossessed of his see. Agobard himself had previously denounced the works of Amalarius in two separate treatises, the first on 'The Correction of the Antiphonary,' severely

[1] XIV 656-8
[2] Martene and Durand, *Vet. Script Collect.* ix 641-68.

APOCRYPHAL WRITINGS.

criticising his alterations, though without naming their author; the second professedly written against his four books on ecclesiastical offices, naming him again and again, but never once giving him any title.[1]

Florus calls that work 'a large codex, spun out into four volumes, composed and arranged by himself, which he placed in the hands of the Lyonnese to be *perused and transcribed*, asserting that he had been formally designated *the Official*, as having most wisely and elaborately commented on the sacred offices (of the Church). . . . Another work produced by him was an " Antiphonary," purporting to have been arranged and corrected by himself. . . . His latest production was a new volume which he had got ornately covered at Lyons, and wreathed with silk embroidery. This he called an " *Episode of his Works*," and this he meant to take with him to the palace, to present either to the emperor or to the president of the council. . . . His works could not fail to be known to all, as they had been carried about everywhere. . . . What he called his Episode was truly named, as it in fact recapitulated all the errors contained in them, and was, like the hump of a camel, their outcome.'[2]

The principal error charged on him by both may be called transubstantiation in embryo, because not yet formulated,[3] but with this we are not immediately concerned here. For what concerns us here most we should first note the strong and significant protest addressed to the bishops at Quiersy by Florus, 'against *apocryphal writings, circulated under the names of the Apostles*,' but *teeming with untruths*,

---

[1] 'Amalarii Abbatis' is merely the title given him in the heading of one MS., and therefore due to the scribe Migne, *Pat Lat* civ. 339 with note *b*

[2] *Ep* 1; Martene and Durand, ix 642

[3] 'Docet præceptor ipse Amalarius egregius, ita corpus Christi esse triforme et tripartitum, ut tria Christi corpora primum quod Ipse suscepit secundum in nobis, qui super terram ambulamus: tertium in illis, qui sepulti jacent Asserit in mysterio sacrificii hac de causa ties debere fieri partes unam calicis pro Christo, alteram in patena pro vivis, tertiam in altari pro mortuis '—Ib 643 It is difficult to suppose the work of Agobard against Amalarius has come down to us entire.

which ought, therefore, not only to be forbidden, but in every case seized and consigned to the flames, as being never free from poison, however pious in character they might seem to be.[1]

Fresh from the perusal of this strong and significant protest against 'apocryphal works circulated under the names of the Apostles,' let us turn, secondly, to the work ' De Expositione Missæ,' by Florus himself, which, for reasons overlooked, it would seem, by the learned authors of the ' Histoire Littéraire,' must be dated subsequently to this protest, and not before.[2] For it is, in effect, itself a protest all through against the very liturgical change most important to our inquiry—the removal of the prayer ' Supplices Te rogamus,' &c. from the position immediately preceding the words of institution assigned it by S. Gregory, to the position after consecration which it now holds—all reference to the action of the Holy Ghost being thereby cancelled. Amalarius had evidently got this change authorised by the Emperor Lewis at Metz without any difficulty some time before the reappointment of a bishop to that see, which took place A.D. 819, as we have seen. He came to Lyons many years after as a propagandist during the time when the Bishop of Lyons was away in disgrace, and, by the official authority which he then claimed to wield, got the same change carried out there too. Therefore, now the significant character of the protest against ' *apocryphal writings circulated under the names of the Apostles* ' comes out, as it furnishes us clearly with the grounds on which that change was made. For Amalarius had only to refer to the Clementine liturgy, which had reached the West by then, and he would see directly where the Roman Canon revised by S. Gregory departed from it, and where there was a grand opportunity for displaying his own superior learning in restoring the Clementine. ' Accipite et comedite, hoc est corpus meum,' of the Vulgate, from which S. Gregory never would have departed, would thus

---

[1] Martene and Durand, ix 664.   [2] Tom v 219

be changed by him into ' Accipite et manducate *ex eo* omnes,' though for some reason or other he shrinks from disclosing how those words stood in his revision. Similarly, the prayer ' Supplices Te rogamus,' transformed and made to precede those words by S. Gregory, should go back to the place designed for it by the pseudo-Clement in its original form, which it would suit equally well in the beautiful form since given to it, and which even an emperor might have refused permission to change, though he might applaud and appreciate the reason for restoring it to its old place. Amalarius would further see that no reference was made to the action of the Holy Ghost in the Clementine *before* the words of institution, and any reference to it after the recital of those words, fortified by the interpretation put upon them by the Emisene Eusebius, he might, in his rough and ready way of deciding such questions, deem quite superfluous. ' Quo ordine id perficiendum sit, *ex Domini institutione* addicitur,'[1] was a principle that would carry many with him still.

Florus, faithful to the traditions of his Church, while quite ready to profess the utmost reverence for those words, and even to admit that they had from the days of the Apostles formed part of the Canon, which it would not have been safe for him then to have denied, endeavours, nevertheless, to prove from passages of the Fathers and ancient liturgies which he quotes, that even in the excised form of the Canon forced upon Lyons, the Church must be understood to pray impliedly for the action of the Holy Ghost on the elements, as being essential to their consecration. His own words will be quoted further on, but they were soon forgotten. Of all the archdeacons and country-bishops who joined him in complaining of the acts of Amalarius, none dared contest them beside himself. Hilduin, abbot of S. Denys, gives us to understand what a terrible *razzia* there must have been of the old Officebooks in and about Paris, whenever the new use was intro-

[1] *Eccl Off* III 24

duced, though he forbears to say *when* that was, and it elicited no protest from him.

We have seen already that the Abbot of S. Denys, like the Abbot of Corbey, was exiled from his convent A.D. 830, for the same offence, viz. for siding against the Emperor Lewis with his rebellious sons. Wala passed six years in hiding. Hilduin, having been wanted to write the Life of the Areopagite giving name to his convent, was restored some years sooner, and we may be sure that, whatever changes the Imperial Official might order in his ritual would command his assent. But in the anarchy which then prevailed it would be impossible to fix any date for the tumultuous proceedings of Amalarius in the provinces with precision; all we can aver for certain is, that they commenced subsequently to his second researches at Rome, which resulted in his amended 'Antiphonary.' He must have left Rome with increased prestige, though it was only with the archdeacon that he had been closeted after his one reception by the Pope, for the Pope could not have possibly said him nay just then. But of his doings in the provinces all our information is comprised in this single, yet pregnant, assertion of Florus, that his doings at Lyons were just what they had been in all places previously visited by him; and where, indeed, had he not been? If any places had, then, been visited by him before Lyons, North Italy, with its capital Milan, must have been the first of these. Milan, with its time-honoured liturgy, must have engaged his special attention.

Milan, according to Landulph and others, had been rudely threatened with the loss of its heirloom soon after the conquest of Lombardy by Charlemagne; but, by dint of prayers and exertions in its behalf, this calamity was for a season averted.[1] Of what was now done, the treatise 'De Sacra-

[1] Ughelli says 'Ambrosianum siquidem Mediolanensis civitas atque diœcesis in hodiernum usque diem retinet' This however, as regards the Canon, is more than could be said with any truth.

mentis' is probably both the record and the first fruits. Some vestiges of the old Canon were condoned, but all reference to the part assigned in it to the Holy Ghost by the great archbishop, its reputed author himself, was expunged, and the interpretation to be put upon it in its new form henceforward by his successors was culled from the homilies of one whom he certainly would have repelled from communion. No such commentary, whoever composed it, could have been written till now.

From Lyons, Amalarius must sooner or later have turned northwards, and visited Paris and S. Denys, making it quite possible for Abbot Hilduin to report to the Emperor the survival of a few decayed copies of the old Office-books only since the introduction of what he calls the Roman, but in reality the Roman revised. Amalarius must have likewise visited Picardy, and with it Corbey once more, where Paschasius was still discharging the duties of abbot, as the Amalarian Canon had certainly been received there, where Paschasius published the second edition of his work dedicated to King Charles the Bald, as we shall see.

We must not underrate the influence then possessed by Amalarius, though Florus alone bears witness to it among contemporaries. Yet he must have organised a considerable following during his lifetime, for he inspired William of Malmesbury with all the warmth of a partisan so long after his death.

Let us now proceed to notice more particularly the points on which the contrast between Amalarius and his Gallican seniors or contemporaries is most sharply marked.

(1) Amalarius, as we have seen, rests his view of consecration on a single principle: 'We learn the order in which it is to be performed from the institution of the Lord,' and then asserts the change which takes place to be the immediate result of His words by the celebrant. (2) By dropping all reference to the action of the Holy Ghost at this time, he leaves us to infer that his own teaching had been in both

respects the teaching of the universal Church from the first.

On the second head, Agobard, bishop of Lyons, in a passage previously quoted, and written when he was in quiet possession of his see, and Amalarius was as yet unknown, distinctly testifies to the fact that the teaching of the whole Church in France, from the days of S. Irenæus downwards, had been different, and all earlier writers had testified to the same fact.

Engaged in controversy with Amalarius, prudence would seem to have dictated to him to reaffirm the principle laid down by him in strong terms, without, however, abandoning his own. His words are: ' So the Apostle received from the Lord, and delivered to the Church, that "our Lord Jesus Christ the same night in which He was betrayed, took bread. . . ." Whence the Church, from the tradition of the Apostles consecrating with these words the sacrament of the holy body and blood of the Lord, pointedly declares that the " Lord said to His Apostles, ' Take and eat of this all, for this is My body,' after the same manner also taking, after He had supped, this illustrious chalice." Let each faithful communicant mark what it is which He means by " *this* ": to wit, that the chalice consecrated by the celebrant is not another from that which the Lord gave to His Apostles. As therefore we think of the blood, we must also think of the body.'[1]

For his closing remark S. Agobard might have cited words to the same effect from S. Chrysostom; for his previous statement—' unde et ecclesia, ex traditione apostolorum his verbis consecrans,' &c.—he could have cited no patristic authority whatsoever, so far as my reading goes, nor is any such statement to be found in his other works.

Yet Florus, if he has not been interpolated, thought it advisable to use still greater explicitness on this head in expounding the Canon subsequently to the aggression of a secular official upon the Office-books of his Church on the

[1] *Cont. Amal.*

one hand and the statement of his bishop on the other. Accordingly, coming to the words 'Qui pridie' &c., we find him saying:—

'Therefore, that the universal Church may celebrate the perpetual memorial of its Lord and Redeemer, the Lord Himself delivered it to the Apostles and the Apostles generally to every Church in these words—in these words, without which no tongue, no country, no city, no part of the Catholic Church in fine, can consummate, that is consecrate, the sacrament of the body and blood of the Lord; the Lord Himself delivered it to the Apostles, and the Apostles generally to every Church, that the universal Church may celebrate the perpetual memorial of its Redeemer. It is thus, and will always be, consecrated by the power and words of Christ. His word it is which sanctifies the heavenly sacraments. He speaks in His priests daily. They act the part of ministers; He operates in majesty by Divine power.'[1]

But previously to this, and as if to compensate for the absence of any definite reference to the action of the Holy Ghost in the new form given to the liturgy that henceforth would have to be used in his Church by expounding such parts of it as he thought would bear that sense, conformably with the intention of the older, and to him much dearer, form—commenting on the words, 'uti accepta habeas et benedicas,' he says:—

'As though they should say suppliantly, we ask that Thou wouldest with Thy Spirit sanctify, and with Thy mouth bless, what is now offered unto Thee, that what is being done by our humble ministry may become effect by Thy power. . . .'

And, again, on 'Quam oblationem Tu, Deus' &c.

'Almighty God is invoked here that He would by the power of Him who descends so make the oblation placed on His sacred altars, and commended to Him by so many prayers, a regular and perfect Eucharist; that it may be

[1] Martene and Durand, *Vet Script.* ix 610–19, once for all

approved in all respects—in other words, numbered amongst those which have been accepted by Him; that it may also be valid—that is, firm and immovable for all time; that it may be likewise, by the power of the Spirit operating on it, both reasonable and in all these things specially grateful and well pleasing to God; that, though taken from the simple fruits of the ground, it may be made, by the ineffable power of the Divine benediction, the body and blood of the only-begotten Son of God. . . .'

And, immediately following his outburst on the words of institution, we read once more:

'He, whose offering that of Melchisedec prefigured, . . . He, by the power and benediction of the Paraclete Spirit, makes it His own body and blood. . . .'

Passing direct from these passages to the liturgical works ascribed to Alcuin or his disciples by his latest editor, we might almost date them from such comparison alone.

In the work 'De Divinis Officiis,' which he has placed last, *all* these passages are repeated nearly word for word, that on the words of institution having the extract here previously quoted from S. Agobard appended to it.[1]

In the work 'Confessio Fidei,' which he has placed first, we find them also repeated,[2] yet this is proved later by becoming distinctly controversial further on.

The second, or 'Disputatio puerorum,' proves itself earliest by making no reference to the words at all, and by being identic in teaching with the 'Liber Sacramentorum' of Alcuin; culled, as Frobenius shows ground for thinking,[3] from the Missal of his own monastery, and inspired throughout by the spirit of the following extract from the Mass of S. Augustine for Monday.[4]

'*Super oblata.*—We are mindful, Eternal God, Almighty Father, of the most glorious passion of Thy Son, of His

[1] C 40, ed Frob vol ii, but he never seems to have made this comparison.
[2] IV. 2–6
[3] *Monit Præv* p 2.
[4] Ib p 9

resurrection and ascension into heaven too. We therefore beseech Thy Majesty, O God, that our humble prayers may ascend to the throne of Thy clemency, and that the fulness of Thy Godhead may descend on this bread and on this cup. May the incomprehensible and invisible majesty of Thy Holy Spirit, O Lord, also descend on them as it descended on the offerings of our forefathers in olden times.'

Rabanus Maurus, who was a pupil of Alcuin in early life, and adhered loyally throughout life to his patristic teaching, has been anticipated in a former chapter. What part he took himself on the subject which concerns us most cannot be shown from any genuine work now extant of his; still William of Malmesbury, who thought the work of Amalarius on 'ecclesiastical offices' worth epitomising, and said of its author that 'another perchance might have described their varieties with more eloquence, but none with more knowledge,' must have thought ill of a work on the same subject by the Archbishop of Mayence, from which he quotes a few words, to have characterised his works in general as the productions of a mere plagiarist, who multiplied his quotations to prevent his readers from detecting his thefts. He therefore counsels his friend Robert to put aside Rabanus and attend to Amalarius, who has written on these matters *as a Catholic*. William himself is careful to point out in his epitome that Amalarius had made consecration of the elements consist in the recital of the words of institution by the celebrant.[1]

Haymo, bishop of Halberstadt, was another pupil of Alcuin, who, notwithstanding his see being German and at a considerable distance from Lyons, followed Agobard and Florus in denouncing the teaching of Amalarius, though without naming him, upon the same grounds as they, and clinging himself still more rigidly to the traditional teaching ignored by him; for on the effect ascribed by him to the

[1] Migne, *Pat Lat* clxxix 1771-4, and a MS. copy of his epitome in All Souls' College Library, n 28.

words of institution he is entirely silent, though everywhere maintaining the Real Presence.

Commenting on 1 Cor. x. 16, he says: 'The bread is first consecrated and blest by the celebrant and by the Holy Spirit, then broken, when, although it appears bread, it is in truth the body of Christ. All they who are partakers of that bread eat Christ's body.'

Again on c. xi. 24: 'As the flesh of Christ which He assumed in the womb of the Virgin is His true body that was slain for our salvation, so the bread which Christ delivered to His disciples and to all the elect, and which each celebrant daily consecrates in Church together with the power of the Godhead replenishing that true bread, is Christ's one body too.'[1]

The brief fragment 'De Corpore,' &c., printed as his, contains expressions never used by him in his other works; besides including a passage from the Emisene Eusebius whom he never elsewhere quotes. All the authority for ascribing it to him consists in its being appended to his sermons with 'Aimonis' written over it in a single MS.[2]

Walafrid Strabo was another pupil of Alcuin, afterwards monk of Fulda. He could have been no stranger to the controversy going on round him; but he is steadily reticent on all points connected with it. He says nowhere distinctly that the words of institution entered into the Canon, nor that it included a prayer for the descent of the Holy Ghost on the elements, nor in short to what agency the Real Presence, which he states as a fact, was due. The only passage forming any clue to his own opinions occurs in the sixteenth chapter of his work on 'Ecclesiastical matters,' where, speaking of the mysteries of the New Testament, he says that 'Christ at the Last Supper, previously to His betrayal, delivered the Sacraments of His body and blood to His disciples *in the substance of bread and wine*, and

[1] Migne, *Pat Lat.* xvii. 564 and 572.
[2] Migne, cxviii. 815, with the note.

enjoined their celebration in commemoration of His most holy passion.'

But when he comes to speak of the office for celebrating them, he says, that in Apostolic times, as far as he can discover, it consisted of prayers simply, with commemoration of the passion of the Lord.[1] Additions were made to it as time went on. On its general revision by S. Gregory the Great, and on the composition of the Canon in particular by him and others, some telling remarks of his and of Abbot Grimaldus have been already quoted, which should be recalled here,[2] particularly the later and incongruous insertions which he notices as then exhibited in the Gregorian Sacramentary; and the many Gallican Churches which he asserts still used their own prayers. But his own uncertainties and reserves in speaking of the formation of the Canon, whose very words he seems afraid to quote, and to the arrangement of whose prayers he shrinks from giving the least clue, can only be explained by the times in which he lived and the example set him by his own abbot, and afterwards archbishop, Rabanus Maurus, whose equanimity was as little disturbed by the turbulent innovations of the deacon of Metz as by the circulation of the False Decretals in and about Mayence within a few years of his own elevation to that see.

Before dealing with the well-known work of Paschasius, some few things must be said about himself and a work ascribed to him which is much less known. If the Life, now appended to his works, of Abbot Wala was really written by him, it must discredit him at once by containing much that is at variance with facts, besides representing himself in the character of an *intrigant*. On these grounds Le Cointe refuses to believe that the 'auctor vitæ seu concinnator fabularum,' as he calls him,[3] can have been the monk of Corbey, whose treatise 'De Corpore et Sanguine Domini' he

---

[1] C. 22, Migne, *Pat Lat* cxiv 943–51   [2] Above, p 243.
[3] A.D 826, n 3 and 830, n. 18 *et seq*

has taken such pains to describe.[1] Mabillon, however, whom Migne reproduces with approval, calls it an 'aureum opus,' apparently without having discovered these defects, so that his character has yet to be cleared. Another fact, unnoticed by Le Cointe, but noticed here some pages back, is, that while he places the first publication of the treatise 'De Corpore et Sanguine Domini' somewhere between A.D. 826-31, we learn from Amalarius himself that Corbey had been visited by him previously to his own second visit to Rome, A.D. 831. The dedication of this treatise on its first appearance calls for another remark, being addressed to an *incognito*.

That his second edition was brought out a considerable time—*dudum*—after the first, Paschasius himself tells us, and internal evidence confirms his statement. Parts of it read like interpolations and differ in principle so widely that it has actually been ascribed to Rabanus Maurus, his principal opponent.[2] But these discrepancies are cleared up much more naturally by his intimacy with Amalarius and by the new light let in upon him by the perusal of the homilies of the Emisene Eusebius and the 'De Sacramentis' of the pseudo-Ambrose during the interval between the first and second issues of his work, making the changes and additions afterwards introduced by him, on second thoughts, easily distinguishable from his original statements. His first edition was based on the true Gregorian Canon used in his monastery when he was monk; his second, on the Amalarian revision, introduced there when he became abbot. The dedication of his second edition is not altogether unlike that of the first, as it is addressed to an illustrious king, withholding his name. Some dedicatory verses, said to have been sent with his work, are more explicit, and in both he is explicit on one point—viz. in styling himself 'Abbot.' Both, therefore, must have been penned after A.D. 844, the

[1] A.D. 831, n. 40 *et seq*.   [2] Cave, *Hist. Lit.* ii. 32.

year of his election. Charles the Bald was just of age then, and his dominions practically comprised Western France down to the Pyrenees.

Coming to the contents of this treatise, then, it may be described as consisting of two distinct halves, with two or three stray sentences thrown into the first half here and there, for harmonising it with the second half. Chapter I. begins by declaring that 'Christ left nothing greater in mystery to His Church than the sacraments of baptism, and the Eucharist, and the Holy Scriptures; in all which the Holy Ghost, who is made surety to the whole Church, works inwardly the mysteries of our salvation to never-ending life.' In the next chapter, where the text is defective—probably from having been altered to suit the views of the second half—he speaks of sensible things being translated intelligibly by the power of God, divinely through the word of Christ, into His flesh and blood. In Chapter III. one explanation given by him of the word 'sacrament' is that 'the Holy Ghost, abiding in the body of Christ, imperceptibly works out all these mysteries of the sacraments under cover of what is visible for the salvation of the elect.' In Chapter IV. he says, 'Christ wished bread and wine in this mystery to be truly, by consecration of the Holy Ghost potentially created; and thus created, to be day by day offered mystically, for the life of the world; that, as His true flesh was created by the Spirit out of a virgin without human contact, so by the same Spirit the same body and blood of Christ might be mystically consecrated out of the substance of the bread and wine.'

These statements are reproduced almost word for word in the next ensuing chapters. The liturgical bearing of Chapter VIII. has been anticipated, but this is his statement in full:—

' *Never* is the flesh of Christ *rightly received, except from His own hand and the altar on high where Christ, the high priest of good things to come, assists for all.* Wherefore the celebrant, *on beginning to consecrate*,[1] says amongst other things, *Jube hæc perferri*, &c.'

The next section of the same chapter immediately following on this reads abrupt. It was interpolated clearly by himself in bringing out his second edition. Four chapters on he repeats his previous statement, to which we shall be recalled again, as having been quoted for another purpose. Chapter IX. § 2 repeats word for word a passage quoted already from Bede, testifying to the action of the Holy Ghost on the oblation, and from thence down to the end of the first section of Chapter XII. there is very little that we might not easily parallel in the writings of Venerable Bede or S. Gregory. Then we begin to encounter passages again which in another work we might consider interpolations; and from this point the attention of the reader is directed with marked emphasis to the 'words of institution,' as they are called, occurring in the Canon, which he begins quoting at the *exact same point* as Amalarius, to which coincidence we shall be brought back presently. The title prefixed to Chapter XV. is evidently borrowed from the interpolated sections of the work of S. Ambrose 'De Mysteriis,' and in Chapter XV. itself we have the fourth and fifth chapters of the fourth book of the 'De Sacramentis' of the pseudo-Ambrose paraphrased, but without ever naming that work. After this, we have the views of his second edition uninterruptedly to the end. On these views being challenged by Frudegard, a friendly critic, he defends them[2] by appealing openly to the Emisene Eusebius in opposition to what had been quoted against them from S. Augustine, but will not name the other work on which he relies further than this, that it is 'a book of S. Ambrose.' In his comments on S. Matt. xxvi. 26-30 there is a great change in his tone. It is no longer apologetic. In vindicating his speculations he hurls scorn

---

[1] '*Immolare* lit to strew the sacred cake, called *mola salsa*, upon the head of the victim.'—Schaller.
[2] *Ep ad. Frud.*

at every position of his evidently then numerous opponents at great length, but without quoting a single Father or Doctor of the Church in his defence. The appeal is to his own individual reason throughout.

We have thus got sufficient data for estimating the part played in this controversy by Paschasius, without touching on the question of his merits or demerits as a biographer. The audacity displayed by him in presuming to interpret S. Augustine by the writings of the semi-Arian Eusebius, his withholding the name of the work of S. Ambrose to which he had appealed, showing that he knew more than he liked his friend to know of its history, the defiant tone later assumed by him in exact parallel with the manner of acting attributed by Florus the Deacon to the Imperial Official. All these traits go far to confirm the inference which the latter part of his work would alone suggest, that he had introduced the Amalarian revision of the Canon at Corbey on becoming abbot, and considered himself thereby secure against any further interference from without, let his adversaries say what they pleased. But the testimony which he supplies himself against himself must be supplemented from his own cloister to be made complete.

Just about the time of the coming out of his second edition, we have several indications that Charles the Bald was occupying himself with liturgical questions when not engaged in war. Ratramn, another monk of Corbey, whose work has been already quoted in a former chapter, tells the king to whom he dedicates it—the king clearly to whom as ' King Charles' he had dedicated a previous work [1]—that it was written at his command, and on a thesis given by him too, from which we may infer that the work of Paschasius had already been perused by the king, and had led to his being asked his judgment on questions which that work had stirred. Ratramn, therefore, begins by telling the king how his conclusions would be gained. 'I will endeavour,' he

---

[1] *De Prædest.* Migne, *Pat. Lat.* cxxi. 13.

says, 'to answer the question put to me by your Majesty, not by dwelling on my own views, but by following in the track of the holy Fathers.' A short exposition of their teaching follows, which their *genuine* writings are subsequently quoted to bear out. Among them neither the Emisene Eusebius nor Isychius, whom Paschasius specially names, finds any place. In due course the works of S. Ambrose are reached,[1] and there the 'book' quoted, but not named, by his brother monk has a definite title given to it, 'The first Book of the Sacraments,' showing by his quotation from it, that in the MS. then used by him the short treatise now called 'De Mysteriis' was called and reckoned to be the first book of the treatise 'De Sacramentis.' And then all the quotations which he makes from it, even when drawn from one of its interpolated sections quoted by his brother monk, are rigidly confined to what might have been every word written by S. Ambrose, and easily paralleled from his genuine works. Similarly, when, further on, he quotes sentences from the actual fifth book of the treatise 'De Sacramentis,'[2] he studiously passes over, as though it contained none such, every passage where consecration is referred solely to the words of institution pronounced by the celebrant, and sums up the teaching of S. Ambrose in words already quoted in a former chapter, as being in full accordance with that of S. Jerome, S. Augustine, S. Fulgentius, and S. Isidore, who attribute consecration *uno ore* to the action of the Holy Ghost, without reference to any words but those of the prayer by which His descent was obtained.

How is this remarkable phenomenon to be explained? Paschasius and Ratramn, both members of Corbey, write, within a few years of each other, taking different sides on a controversy provoked by a work of the former. In this work the former had appealed to a treatise by S. Ambrose which he refrains from naming, or even quoting in its own words. Ratramn writing some years later, not merely names it, but

[1] C. 51   [2] C. 66.

actually quotes sentences from parts of it in which are found also statements favourable to his opponent, of which he takes no heed.

The case lies in a nutshell. Paschasius and Ratramn were both of them members of Corbey, but Paschasius was now abbot, while Ratramn was only monk, a single unit in a considerable body, from whom implicit obedience to their abbot was due, and penalties exacted in those days for disobedience, such as we cannot well now imagine compatible with religion. Let us give this circumstance full weight in estimating this work of the monk. As has been observed, he lays down carefully what the Fathers had taught, and then quotes a number of passages from their *genuine* works, naming each as he quotes it, and each a decisive testimony to their teaching. On coming to S. Ambrose he suddenly varies his method. He never quotes a single passage from his confessedly genuine works, but fixes on *two* given to him in a MS. of his own convent which he was then using, but described as *one*, which his abbot had forborne to name, but which he names in accordance with the title prefixed to it in this MS. 'De Sacramentis.' And from this he quotes in considerable detail, always explaining and arguing from each passage to show that the teaching of S. Ambrose was in full keeping with that of the Fathers, on whose general *consensus* he takes his stand, but passing over in the most marked manner every passage favourable to the novel views of his abbot, as much as to say, 'I know not how such passages as these got into this MS. of Ambrose which I am using, nor shall I inquire. All I know is that every genuine work of his would prove, were I to quote from it, that they can none of them have been penned by him. And though it might not be proper or expedient for me to contest all this with my abbot, posterity may well infer all this from my reticence.' Interpreted in this way, Ratramn will be seen by all to have administered a *coup de grâce* to the treatise 'De Sacramentis' as a whole, to the interpolations of what his MS. miscalls its first book, and to the malpractices of Amalarius and his own abbot, or some partisan in their confidence, from which they will not easily recover. More than this. From the marked emphasis with which Amalarius and Paschasius both quote the paragraph 'Quam oblationem Tu, Deus,' in the Canon, coupled with the piteous, because vain, attempt of Florus [1] to interpret it of the 'epiklesis,' of which Amalarius by his alteration had left no trace, we seem amply warranted in concluding that it was Amalarius who framed this paragraph, and inserted it and forced it upon other Churches, in transferring the beautiful prayer 'Supplices Te rogamus' to the place which it has held ever since.

We have thus unravelled the last thread of this Gallican tangle: with Amalarius and Paschasius between them, aided of course by others whose names were forgotten as soon as their work was done, the responsibility rests of the Roman Canon in its present unprimitive mould having been altered from the Gregorian by transposing the prayer on which consecration was made to depend by S. Gregory and his successors at Rome for a good deal longer than is commonly supposed, and by that alteration causing the Holy Ghost no longer to be invoked in the Roman liturgy, nor, in point of fact, for any purpose at all. Amalarius and Paschasius are the two names in the ninth century that must be made responsible for all this, for they not merely commenced the mischief, but took good care that it should survive them. At the same time we must not assume that either or both of them were Crypto-Macedonians or had any distinct conception of the unhappy results that would ensue from their act. Their act was probably dictated by conceit or ignorance, and, unless we disbelieve Florus, was based upon a mistaken estimate of the claims of the Clementine liturgy. The Macedonian framer of that liturgy, therefore, would have clapped his hands over their act, and not altogether regretted its

[1] Above, p. 388-9.

consequences. Again, what we must never think of condoning in them is their ruthless destruction of all the old Office-books and priceless copies of national liturgies that had been in use previously from time immemorial in every Christian and Western land, and their violent substitution for them of a liturgy recast by themselves, to reflect their novel and hybrid teaching; and, lastly, their unscrupulous ways of recommending it by interpolating the genuine works of the Fathers, and multiplying treatises in support of it under false names, to bespeak authority and antiquity for it, to neither of which it had the least claim.

Whether Amalarius asked for copies of the Roman Canon as well as of antiphons when last at Rome we are not told, nor whether any part of his mission, then or before, concerned the Canon. We shall see presently that the Roman Canon long survived his visits, first or last.

With Hincmar our survey of ecclesiastical France during this period may close, for it would not be complete without him. But he was greater as a canonist than a divine. Besides which, his see being of recent foundation compared with Lyons and Vienne, it had no traditions of such antiquity or so firmly rooted as theirs. Add to which that when he was elected to it, A.D. 845, it had been ten years without a bishop, having its affairs administered by two simple priests, over whom Amalarius may have ridden as roughshod as over Lyons in corresponding plight, and imposed his liturgical innovations there, for aught we know, in the absence of any stout-hearted deacon, Florus-like, to record his aggressions. Hincmar took evident pains to work in harmony with Charles the Bald on coming to his see. And of his predecessor Ebbo, we never seem able to get at the bottom of the misdemeanours for which he was eventually deprived. His greatest may have been that he withstood Amalarius and made no secret of his dissent from Paschasius.

Certainly we may infer that Hincmar knew more than he liked to notice publicly, from his never once quoting the

Canon nor giving his readers the least hint what the order of it was in his Church. As regards his own teaching he twice quotes Venerable Bede, word for word, on the action of the Holy Ghost on the oblation of bread and wine,[1] thereby testifying to the traditions in which he had himself been brought up. And in the second of these passages for the institution he quotes at great length the words of our Lord on different occasions, as we have them given by S. John, S. Paul, and S. Luke, but never in the form given to them in the Canon—his own comments on them being merely:—

'These things He said, and says and performs, Who spake, and they were made; He commanded, and they were created.'

Further on he adds:—

'The whole, therefore, which is enacted in this oblation of the body and blood of the Lord is a mystery; it is one thing which is seen and another which is comprehended. That which is seen has a corporal appearance, that which is comprehended a spiritual fruit.'

But in the very next chapter we have both views intermingled, the new and the old: passages from the genuine work against Faustus by S. Augustine and from the sermons of the pseudo-Ambrose thrown into close juxtaposition, but without naming either. It is not till we get to his twenty-fifth epistle that we find him quoting S. Ambrose thus: 'Ait enim in libro de sacramentis, sive mysteriis,' &c.[2]

But the chief interest attaching to him in this connection is that Sigebert tells us it was he who wrote back in reply to the Church of Ravenna 'sub personâ magni Caroli Imperatoris,'[3] thus vaguely designating Charles the Bald and alluding to a famous letter on which much has been built. There is also this further inaccuracy to be corrected—as we

---

[1] In *Fero Salom*, Migne, *Pat Lat* cxxv. 827, and *De Cav Vit* c 9, 1b 915, dedicated to Charles the Bald, when king
[2] *Ad Hild Ep Meld*, Migne, ib. cxxvi 165 and 7, where it is still called *liber*, though the quotation is from the second book of that work
[3] *De Script Eccl* c 99.

possess the letter of the clergy to him which elicited this reply, and they address him as king, not emperor [1]—which supplies the only clue to the date now remaining to us of this correspondence.

For beyond the stock passage quoted again and again from this letter of the king in our own days without further inquiry, not a word more seems forthcoming of the letter itself, and it is not certain either when it was last seen. Le Cointe omits to inform us how he came by the passage, which in modern times he was the first to quote; and as he died before he was half through the reign of Charles the Bald, we cannot tell whether he quoted it second-hand or not. To Professor Muhlbacher of Vienna my best thanks are due for favouring me with references to it at a much earlier date, by the Magdeburg Centuriators [2] and their presiding genius Flaccus Illyricus.[3] That he must have seen this letter entire cannot be doubted from his description of it; for he prints the letter of the clergy first, which is occupied entirely with questions about the monastic dress, begging to be left free to retain their own in some particulars, in others to conform to Rome. Charles, displeased with their freedom, he goes on to say, ' got a long reply written to them by his advisers, which, *owing to its excessive prolixity*, he must omit, though it contained some things good and noteworthy—for instance, *the seventh chapter*; . . .' where, say the Centuriators, ' the king testifies there was at that very time one way of celebrating Mass at Jerusalem, another at Milan, another in Spain at Toledo, besides indicating in express terms that, under his great-great-grandfather, Pepin, the Gallican Churches celebrated their divine services differently both from the Roman and the Milanese.' [4]

But this hardly tallies with the account given of it by Le Cointe, who professes to quote, not the substance, but

[1] *Max Bibl Pat* De la Bigne, xvi 765
[2] *Cent* ix c 4, § De Libris, c 6, § De Clave solvente, and § De Missa
[3] *Catal. Test Verit* lib ix p 23–6
[4] § De Missa

TWO VERSIONS OF THE STOCK PASSAGE. 403

the very words of the letter. This is his version of it, which all succeeding writers have followed:—

'Down to the times of our great-great-grandfather, Pepin, the Gallican Churches celebrated their divine services differently from both the Roman and the Milanese Church, as we have seen and heard from those who came to us from the neighbourhood of the Toletan Church and celebrated in our presence the sacred offices of that same Church.[1] There were likewise celebrated in our presence the sacred offices of the liturgies according to the Jerusalem order originating with S. James and according to the Constantinopolitan order originating with S. Basil, but our own opinion is that the Roman Church should be followed in the celebration of the liturgies.'

Who shall decide, till this letter can be found to speak for itself, which of these two versions of its seventh chapter is correct? Have the Centuriators unfairly suppressed any things in it that they should have supplied? Has Le Cointe supplied any things unwarrantably that he thought it should have contained? Or, again, did the context supply some things omitted by both that would have thrown light upon our present inquiry, and has this letter, therefore, been made away with by some later partisan historian of superior acuteness to both, who forecasted its being likely to prove some day mischievous for the unearthing of facts which he hoped devoutly might never be made public? Application to all the learned in Paris, Berlin, Vienna, and Ravenna, reported likely to be able to assist in discovering the whereabouts of this letter, has been made and courteously responded to, but hitherto this reference to the Centuriators has been its only fruit.

Accordingly, for the present, interpreting one version by

---

[1] 'Missarum,' both here and below, A D 601, n 18 It may fairly be doubted whether ' *Toletanæ ecclesiæ* ' is not a corrupt reading for 'Tolosanæ': *i e* Toulouse, captured by Charles, A D 844 (Le Cointe, ib n 53), when he published, before leaving, a Capitulary in nine chapters for its resettlement, ib. n 94 *et seq*

the other where they overlap, and recalling all that has been previously quoted and commented upon from Abbot Hilduin and from the Capitularies of Charlemagne for substituting the Roman Chant in his dominions for the Gallican, let us pay special attention to the events recorded of the years A.D. 844–5, and see whether they will not assist in fixing the date and interpreting the alleged contents of this letter. In A.D. 844 Paschasius is generally supposed to have brought out a second edition of his work on the Eucharist and dedicated it to Charles the Bald. Charles the Bald on receiving it commissioned Ratramn to draw up a work on the same subject, which he too dedicated to Charles the Bald. In A.D. 845 Hincmar, being elected archbishop of Rheims, is immediately found seconding the same king in getting extensive reforms carried out in every Church of his dominions,[1] and the province which then preoccupied Charles most was Aquitaine. There we find him legislating simultaneously for Churches in that province, as Toulouse, and even for Churches in Spain, as Gerona.[2] Gregory, the archbishop of Ravenna, who had taken part against the late Emperor, father of Charles, in the contest between him and the sons of his first wife, was still alive, but universally detested then by the Ravennatians, says Ughelli.[3] This would account for the letter of their clergy to Charles, and excellently fits in with his reply. For, if the treatises of Paschasius and Ratramn on the Eucharist then preoccupied him in his leisure hours, nothing could have been more natural for a ruler in his circumstances, or more congenial to the known tastes of Charles when not engaged in war, than to have invited the priests who came to him either from Toledo or Toulouse—whichever reading is preferred— to celebrate that sacrament in his presence according to the liturgy then used in their Church, and if any Greek priests chanced to be within call, to have invited them also to do

---

[1] Rohrbacher, *E H.* xii 69 *et seq* [2] Le Cointe, ib n 48–50
[3] *Ital Sac* ii. 346

the same by the liturgies of Jerusalem and Constantinople, that he might judge with his own eyes and ears of their respective merits. Again, in avowing his own preference for the Roman, he would naturally be supposed to mean the Roman as then used in France, or, if there were more recensions of it than one, then the recension which Amalarius, the 'Official' of the Emperor his father had installed at Metz and Lyons, and possibly Rheims too, seeing that Paschasius had elaborated a formal interpretation of it, which had caused a great stir, was everywhere being discussed, and in most places becoming more and more popular every day. Charles, after the manner of his father and of his grandfather, was never tired of professing how much he valued the consent of Rome to all his schemes for the public good in Church and State; but, like them, he took care to let the Pope feel how dangerous it might be for anybody to stand between him and his plans, when he had fully matured them, and was bent on giving effect to them in his own way. And the Popes, unless endowed with wills equally strong themselves, soon found it their best policy to keep on good terms at almost any price with the only power competent to lend them any real support in those troublous times.

Thus the attitude was threefold of parties in France during this controversy. There was the party led by Amalarius, that insisted on revising the Office-books in their own way, and on destroying all that had been in use previously, wherever they could lay hands on them. As these soon had Paschasius for their dogmatic exponent, and the strong arm of the Emperor Lewis and his son Charles for their support, their success was assured. Hence their language was as explicit as their views were decided. There was a second party that had several pupils of Alcuin belonging to it, represented by Rabanus Maurus and Walafrid Strabo, who clung to the teaching in which they had been brought up, but being men of peace, were too timid to defend it, and therefore were reserved or ambiguous. And there was a third party composed of devoted adherents to the teaching of the Fathers, who loudly protested against the changes that were being made, yet showed by their language that they were supporting a falling cause. Of these Agobard, Florus, and Ratramn are names that must always command respect.

The attitude of Rome during this controversy will now be shown to have been in remarkable contrast to that of France. There, neither questions of liturgy nor of dogma were stirred. No pen noticed, no tongue was heard on the disputes agitating France. Peace reigned in the cloister, everything went on as usual in church there. Moderns of course will declare this to have been due to the fact that at Rome there was nothing to change, that its teaching was then what it always had been, that its Canon had been correctly transcribed by Amalarius, and was then what it is now. Unfortunately for this explanation, it goes against recorded facts. The teaching of Rome was indeed then *what it had always been*, but this was *not* the teaching of Amalarius; it was the very teaching which Amalarius had first cast out of the Canon and then ignored, in explaining the Canon as altered by himself, a teaching which even Paschasius could not altogether ignore, because the Canon still used in his convent when he commenced writing, and was *identical with that of Rome*, maintained it. The calmness of Rome was due to the fact that she had not allowed Amalarius to tamper with her Canon, that it remained the *true* Gregorian, and that her teaching differed from it in no respect. Paul the Deacon, the collector of homilies for Charlemagne, and the biographer of S. Gregory the Great, knew nothing of the Amalarian Canon, but attributed to S. Gregory the very teaching which that Canon ignored. The story told by him of S. Gregory, quoted many pages back, testified faithfully to what the teaching of Rome, and consequently to what the Canon of Rome was, at the end of the eighth century. Pope Nicholas I.—*omni exceptione major*—heedless of all the controversy that was then raging on the subject in France, calmly testifies in the following words to what the teaching of Rome was in his day—the middle of the ninth century.

'The holy altar,' he tells the Emperor Michael, to whom he was then writing, ' on which we perform votive sacrifices to Almighty God, is a naturally common stone, differing in no wise from other tablets adorning our pavements and walls. But, God having co-operated at its consecration, on receiving the benediction it became the holy table that it is. Similarly the bread which is offered on it is common bread, but when it has been sacramentally consecrated, it becomes and is called in truth the body of Christ. So the wine before benediction is a small thing too, but *after sanctification of the Spirit*, it is made the blood of Christ.' [1]

Mansi gives up this passage, nor can we wonder at it, in despair. It is possible that the reading of it may be improved some day, but quite impossible that its meaning should be explained away. He is merely repeating S. Gregory, and repeats him because using *his* Canon, in *contradistinction* to what is used *now*.

When, and under whom, was the Canon of Amalarius and the teaching of Paschasius imported into Rome, and substituted in each case for the Gregorian ? *Not* earlier than two centuries later, when the same controversy burst forth again in France, and three French Popes in succession adjudicated upon it at Rome—Leo IX., Stephen IX., and Nicholas II. The first of these, Leo IX., was practically the first French Pope ; for Gerbert, or Silvester II., was too completly *sui generis* to be called anything but a citizen of the world, whereas Leo IX., who had formerly been bishop of Toul in France, filled Rome with his countrymen. Foremost of these was Humbert of Lorraine, whom he made cardinal in due course, and Frederick, brother of the Duke of Lorraine, whom he made chancellor. Humbert will always be remembered as head of the embassy that sped from Rome to Con-

[1] Mansi, xv. 166-7 ; *Ep.* ii. *ad Mich.*

stantinople, A.D. 1054, and which, after a series of intrigues and venal and violent transactions—venal in which Frederick, and violent in which Humbert, was most conspicuous—had the audacity, the Pope being dead who had sent them, to excommunicate the Greek patriarch Michael Cerularius, and actually deposit the document containing his excommunication on the high-altar of his church of S. Sophia, where it might be seen by all, before leaving for Italy.[1] Something was said of him and his works in a former chapter.[2]

Four years earlier it was that Berengarius (another Frenchman, of Touraine this time, not Lorraine) was condemned unheard in a Roman Council over which Leo presided, on the ground of a letter or letters addressed by him to Lanfranc, afterwards Archbishop of Canterbury. Lanfranc was a Lombard, not a Frenchman, but it was at Avranches in France that he won his spurs—Avranches, with its glorious outlook over the bay of the renowned Mount S. Michael, whose wondrous history commenced with the hermit who established himself on the neighbouring rock, hence called Robert of Tombelaine, and who was one of the many pupils that, with S. Anselm, flocked to that city to attend his lectures, and whose library still contains a fine MS. of the eleventh century, and in it a catalogue of the books at Bec when, to reward his services, he was made prior there.

A letter will be found in Mansi[3] purporting to be the one letter which Lanfranc received. It is but fair to say that Lanfranc uses the plural number 'letters.'[4] But then he adds that the correspondence, in whatever shape it reached Rome, was calculated to render him as much an object of suspicion as Berengarius, as it seemed to show that they were not on unfriendly terms, and this letter certainly contains nothing offensive. Be that as it may, Lanfranc was

[1] *Christendom's Divisions*, part ii c 1, supplies full details
[2] C v p 232 *et seq* It is also given in Gieseler, note 8 to Per. III.
Div II Part I c 3, § 29
[3] XIX 768.
[4] *De Corp. et Sang.* c 3.

present and allowed to clear himself, Berengarius was absent and was condemned. It was understood, says Lanfranc, from what was read out, that he approved of the work of John Scotus, and condemned that of Paschasius. More must have been read out by a good deal than is now found in this letter, to have caused the writer of it to be condemned unheard with anything like justice. Meanwhile, the treatise supposed in the eleventh century to have been written by John Scotus is now admitted generally to be the treatise by Ratramn[1] commented upon some pages back,[2] then held in abhorrence for its anti-Paschasian tone, but of which a very different estimate is given even in Migne now. And as for the work of Lanfranc, it must have been written at a comparatively late period of this dispute, for it recapitulates all the different professions exacted from Berengarius down to the last, at the sixth Roman Council under Gregory VII., A.D. 1079, which Lanfranc reports in full,[3] but on which he bestows no comment, still less informs us of anything else that passed at this Council. For Hildebrand, on becoming Pope, showed himself as good in heart a Roman as he was a Tuscan by birth, and abstained as far as he could from involving his compatriots in a controversy till then exclusively French. Moreover, a record of the proceedings of this Council, first published in the Royal Collection of Councils A.D. 1644, and afterwards in the continuation of Mansi, but evidently jotted down by one that was present, indicates in the clearest manner that Roman traditions were still cherished at Rome then, notwithstanding all the Gallicanism that had recently been forced on it, and was destined at last to take root there. For here we are told that all the members of this Council being assembled in the church of S. Saviour, a discussion took place respecting the body and blood of the Lord Jesus, when two views, and only two, were put forward: one, which was that of the majority, from which very few

[1] Gieseler, *E H*, Per III Div I Part II c 3, § 4, note 7.
[2] Above, p 396 *et seq.*   [3] Gieseler, ib

dissented at last, and with which all the authorities of the orthodox Fathers, Greek and Latin, were found in full accord, asserting that the bread and wine were through the words *of the sacred prayer*, and ministration of the celebrant, by *the action of the Holy Ghost*, converted into the body of the Lord that was born of a virgin and hung on a cross, and the blood which flowed from His side pierced with a spear, *substantively*; while the other, which was that of a few stricken with inveterate and immoderate blindness, endeavoured to prove that the substantive body, sitting on the right hand of the Father, was no more than a figure, deceiving themselves and others with sophistic pleas.[1]

Interpreting the first part of this report by the second, we shall find that the word *substantialiter* is to be construed with what follows, *not* with what precedes it, and that the Presence which follows on consecration, is that of a substantive *not* a figurative body, just what Irenæus and Tertullian had maintained against Marcion and his followers, 800 years before, without the least reference to the Paschasian view. Neither, in what is laid down on consecration, is there the least reference to what Paschasius taught. For it is here made dependent on the action of the Holy Ghost, obtained by the 'sacred prayer' for His descent, and the ministration of the celebrant in petitioning for it, and setting the elements apart for His action on them, all in exact conformity with what S. Gelasius, S. Gregory the Great, and Nicholas I. taught and practised in their day, and the whole Church long before.

More than this, there is at Avranches in MS. 84, folio 98, a discussion ascribed to S. Augustine, but which consists of dovetailed passages from the earlier half of the work of Paschasius,[2] and so put together as to form a running justification of the profession accepted from Berengarius at this Council, with which it ends. For here we find it

---

[1] *Ed Reg* xxvi 587-8; Mansi, xx 523, Migne, *Patrol Lat,* cxlviii 811.
[2] Cs 4 and 12

laid down that consecration is effected 'by the word of the Creator and the power of the Holy Ghost ; as, if it depended on the merit of the celebrant, it would not appertain to Christ. But now, as it is He who baptises, so it is He who, by His Holy Spirit, makes this His flesh, and transforms that into His blood. Whence the celebrant says : " Command these to be borne by the hand of Thy holy angel to Thy sacred altar on high in sight of Thy divine majesty." Why should he pray that they may be borne thither? In order that it should not be thought to be done by him, the celebrant.'

This, evidently the work of a contemporary, testifies to the place still filled at Rome by this prayer in the Canon when Gregory VII. was Pope.

No wonder Lanfranc said nothing of the proceedings of this Council on which the profession made subsequently by Berengarius, and the last ever exacted from him,[1] was founded. No wonder that it was afterwards said that the grand Pope who presided at this Council was condemned himself by the faction opposed to him at Mayence, '*quod antiquus discipulus Berengarii extiterit.*'[2] No wonder, finally, that the illustrious Mabillon, who must have read and pondered over the record of the proceedings of this Council, though he refrains from quoting it, should have been brought to the candid admission in the latest and most elaborate dissertation penned by him on this subject, that it was *not* the Real Presence, but only transubstantiation, that was denied by Berengarius.[3]

Yet France by that time was as completely with Lanfranc as Rome was of another mind. For, while this Roman Council of A.D. 1079 required no more from Berengarius than loyal adhesion to the teaching of the Catholic Church,

---

[1] 'Novissima quam habemus Berengari formula '—*Anom. Chifflet.* c 22, note 69

[2] *Ed Reg Concil* xxvi 590-1

[3] *Diss. de Bereng.* ap F A Zachar. *Thesaur. Theolog.* tom x part ii p 997 ' In omnibus scriptis suis totus est Berengarius, non ut realitatem impugnet, sed tantum conversionem substantiæ panis et vini in Christi corpus et sanguinem '

represented by the Latin and Greek Fathers practically to a man, a Synod of Orleans, A.D. 1017, condemned a number of poor simple Christians to be burnt alive for saying that the bread and wine placed on the altar by the hands of the priest, which was held to be made the Sacrament by the sanctification of the Holy Ghost, could not be 'converted into the body and blood of Christ,'[1] meaning, of course, could not be converted in the new sense put upon conversion by the Paschasian school—a sense quite foreign to the teaching of the early Church which Berengarius was required to profess at Rome, and also to what Ælfric was preaching about the same time to our Anglo-Saxon forefathers—'*not* bodily, but spiritually, made present '—in his own words.[2]

Two or three more facts relevant to the course that events took during the vicissitudes of this struggle in the West may be briefly noticed in concluding this chapter.

The first concerns several changes introduced into the ordination of presbyters in the Roman Pontifical, that may be said to supply proof of their own date. The earliest of these shall be reserved for the present, and inserted where we may trust it will tell most. The second is first supplied in a Vatican MS. of the eleventh or twelfth century, and may fairly be thought to have been placed there by one who mourned over, but could not prevent, the reception of the Amalarian Canon by Rome, and hoped, therefore, to compensate for it by anointing the hands of the presbyter to effect at every celebration of the Eucharist *without special prayer* on his part, what he had effected previously through special prayer at each celebration for the descent of the Holy Ghost. Immediately before delivery to him of the paten and chalice, the bishop anoints his hands solemnly with the oil used in anointing catechumens, saying over them:—

'Vouchsafe to consecrate and sanctify these hands by this unction and our benediction, O Lord, that whatever they

---

[1] Mabillon. *Analect* tom i 'De Conf Fid sub Alcuini nomine A D 1656 edita,' c 3, from Glaber Radulphus, whom he quotes, but evidently with pain.
[2] Above, p. 270.

have blest may be blest, and whatever they have consecrated may be consecrated and sanctified, in the name of our Lord Jesus Christ.'[1]

Professor Hoppe tried hard to get all the fruits of the Eucharistic epiklesis conveyed in a condensed form by this rite. Nor could we but wish well to his loyalty! Yet its contents go for nothing compared with its history; since, strange to say, it supplies one more proof—and a stiff proof into the bargain—of the amount of Gallicanism imported into the Roman ritual about that time. For this anointing of the hands of a presbyter at his ordination was a Gallican custom in the ninth century, whether owing its origin to the pseudo-Decretals or not. Theodulph, bishop of Orleans, speaks for the west of France;[2] Amalarius, in still plainer terms for the east,[3] A.D. 864. Rodolph, archbishop of Bourges, writes to Pope Nicolas I., asking whether only the hands of presbyters, or the hands of deacons too, should be anointed? Nicolas rejects the whole query with warmth. 'In this holy Roman Church, wherein we minister by the grace of God, *we do neither*. And, so far as our memory serves us, there is *no record of any such practice* by ministers of the New Testament.'[4] Not content with this, he refers his correspondent to the opening sentence of a letter of his predecessor, Innocent I., in answer to a suffragan of his own see.

'If priests of the Lord would only keep ecclesiastical institutions intact, which have been handed down to them from the blessed Apostles, there would be neither diversities nor varieties, either *in ordinations* or *consecrations.*'[5] Gratian could not have quoted this letter of Nicolas as

---

[1] Thus it stands in the *Pontif. Rom Clem VIII denuo Urbani VIII. auct recogn.* Ed Catalani (Paris Ed 1850) i 221, with the notes which however quite fail to answer Morinus on this point

[2] *Capit ab Presb Paroch Suæ* c 1 'Ut nec vestram consecrationem irritam faciatis, nec manus sacro unguine delibutas peccando polluatis'

[3] 'Qui uncti sunt, quorum repleta est consecratione manus,' &c *Eccl Off* ii 13

[4] Mansi, xv 390

[5] *Ep. ad Dec Ep Eugub*

having decided the point to which it refers,[1] had his successors departed from his ruling by then. Consequently, Muratori must have dated this part of his MS., if not the whole, two centuries earlier than it deserved.[2] One can only wish that a proposal had been made to Pope Nicolas to allow consecration of the Eucharist to be performed in his Church according to the Amalarian Canon, in preference to the Gregorian, and that his answer was still extant. For, though it is beyond even Popes to prevent the fabrication of counterfeit documents, or to defeat surreptitious and successful crusades against the genuine, there is just one thing that they always might do, and by doing earn the grateful acknowledgments of all good men; act in the spirit of their great predecessor Nicolas and condemn, and do their utmost to inhibit, the spread of every novel practice that has not unexceptionable grounds to recommend it; every departure from either primitive teaching or ritual against which no fault, defect, or exception of any kind has been made good; every document put forward as an authority, whose fictitious or false character has been established. Palimpsests are being continually discovered, which, having been stripped of their outer garment, prove the wilful effacement by partisan hands of some truthful but obnoxious tract; of some document exposing and inveighing against facts that had been studiously concealed; of some venerable, but violently displaced, liturgy; of some righteous burst of indignation against innovations, vices, or corruptions that had many powerful friends amongst contemporaries. Dr. Mone, whose learned dissertation on palimpsests is full of instruction, says, that in the Latin palimpsests of the fifth and sixth centuries alone, fragments of many sermons, liturgies, sacra-

---

[1] Dist xxiii c 12
[2] *Lit Rom* ii 406–14 It is the very last thing of all in this MS, and therefore may well have been added after it became fact The next MS which Muratori shrinks from dating specifically, contains it, with the rubric directing its use Ib p 429 None of the earlier rituals contain it Menard says nothing about the date of the MS. on which he comments containing this rite —*In Lib Sacram S Greg* notes 737 *et seq*

mentaries, and tracts upon the sacraments, have been brought to light, which can nowhere be found in a single whole copy now. In times of fierce controversy this 'massacre of the innocents' would be multipled tenfold. Thus the reason assigned by him in another place for the Gallican liturgies being so constantly written over is their having been everywhere displaced by the Roman. In conclusion he says, speaking generally, that it was not half so often lack of material or ignorance that gave rise to the palimpsest, as some special design on the part of its author to efface what he concealed by writing over.[1] Several fragments of the Gallican liturgy may be read in a work of the same author on the Latin and Greek liturgies, in the third of which the 'epiklesis' immediately follows what may or may not have been a recital of the institution; in another, the fifth, it is followed by a prayer evidently corresponding to the 'Supplices Te rogamus' of the Roman.[2] Anybody desirous of seeing for himself how things were done when controversy was at its highest may find some striking illustrations of erasure, *not* written over, at Avranches, in MS. 109—commented upon and extracted from by M. Ravaisson in his Report to the Minister of Public Instruction on the Libraries in the Departments of the West.[3] But the character of the erasures can only be studied on the spot. It is a fragment of some work on the Eucharist, possibly that of Rabanus Maurus, now lost. Unfortunately there is unexceptionable testimony to the fact that the *suppressio veri* prevailed in another form at Rome till quite modern times. For Renaudot, at the beginning of the last century, commenting on the editions of the Eastern liturgies published there previously to his own which he brought out at Paris, accuses the Roman editors of having wilfully misrepresented their MSS. in what they professed to have printed from them—in

[1] *De Lib Palimp* pp 21 and 37 Carlsruhe, 1855
[2] Pp 21 and 27, Frankfort-on-Main, 1850
[3] Paris, Joubert, 1841 Append p 374

short, he says there was not one liturgy that had been printed in exact conformity with the MS. of it; and he specifies two points in particular, where deviations from the original had been carried out in all the liturgies—viz. in the form given to the words of Christ and in the invocation of the Holy Ghost which they had in every single case—those cases excepted alone which had escaped their notice—changed from the Greek to the Roman form, or else accommodated to the Roman view. Where there was no difference between the rituals of the West and East, they had made no changes of any consequence.[1] It is sad, indeed, to think that works of *any kind* published at Christian Rome should exhibit such a departure from truthfulness—such marked tokens of an intention to deceive. But that ancient liturgies for commemorating the death of Christ, and communicating the benefits of that death to man, should have been brought out there with their most solemn portions so garbled, and in days so near our own, only shows with what tenacity the worst features of the Gallicanism of the ninth century maintained their hold on her system, and may go far to account for the catastrophe which may be said to have rained down brimstone and fire from heaven upon Western Christendom so soon afterwards. From that terrible catastrophe, which fell heaviest on France, and through no hands *more* heavily than his who supposed himself a second Charlemagne, 'omnipotent' to reconstruct the Court at Aix, there is no portion of Christendom that has not learnt some lesson, and this more particularly —to '*speak the truth,* every man to his neighbour.'[2] It has

---

[1] *Liturg Orient Collect* vol ii 'Diss de Syr Melch et Jacob Lit' § 10–14 (Paris, 1716). 'Omnes liturgias Romani editores duobus præsertim locis reformaverunt in forma verborum Christi Domini et in invocatione Spiritus Sancti. Illam quidem formam, quæ Græcis similis in plerisque est, *omnino sustulerunt* ut quæ in Latino canone est totidem verbis expressa substitueretur . Invocationem Spiritus sancti pariter immutaverunt, ita ut sententiam illius orationis, non ad efficiendam aut potius consummandam elementorum in corpus et sanguinem Christi transmutationem, sed ad fructum ex eorum digna susceptione percipiendum, retulerint . ' § 11

[2] Zech viii 16

cleared the air in many ways. Controversies are no longer carried on by Christians in the bloodthirsty, dishonest spirit that disgraced them formerly. Truthfulness is now admitted by all to be the condition on which the records of the past shall in future be studied ; and all who can correct errors of ignorance, or unravel errors of design, in whatever department of literature, sacred or secular, will henceforth be counted benefactors. Rome has already given proof that the lesson has not been lost on her. In a work recently printed at the Vatican, the spuriousness of the Sardican canons, by which her early Popes defended the right of appeal to their see, has been acknowledged at last with a frankness that is not at all likely to be lost on English hearts.

CHAPTER IX.

THE problem proposed has now been worked out sufficiently for all practical purposes, and the results, which are plain enough, may be summed up. They are plain because their standpoint throughout has been that they should be consistent with history. For the same reason there will be but one way of refuting them. Anybody dissatisfied with or doubting them will have to search history to disprove them. He will have to show either that the facts adduced are not facts, or that they have been incorrectly stated, or that other facts which should have qualified them have been suppressed or not given their due weight. Assuming that they *cannot* be disproved, however—although unquestionably we are brought face to face with much that is sad and humiliating in the extreme when we look back—we shall yet find more to take comfort and hope from in the sequel.

1. The facts, then, of a positive kind relating to the Eucharist that have been brought out in succession are the following :—

From Apostolic times to the first half of the ninth century—both, roughly computed, inclusive—consecration of the elements in celebrating the Eucharist was held to be the result of a prayer for the descent of the Holy Ghost to make them exactly what Christ had *called* them *after* consecrating them Himself. And we know for certain that His own words in *distributing them* to His Apostles were, with the mere change which their form required, invariably repeated by the celebrant in distributing them to each communicant, whose invariable reply was 'Amen' on receiving them. This, again, we have very good reason to think, was the *only* place where these words were reproduced in the primitive liturgies. Meanwhile the Holy Ghost had been invoked, not for a single, but for a twofold purpose. He was invoked first to effect what our Lord had effected by *blessing* and *giving thanks* over the elements in words that have *not* been recorded—by *eulogising* them, as S. Cyril has it; by *eucharistising* them, as S. Justin. There was no need for our Lord, even as man, to invoke the descent of the Holy Ghost on each occasion, either of instituting a sacrament or of performing a miracle. The Holy Ghost descended on Him at His baptism and never left Him from that time, but 'abode on Him,' as S. John tells us with marked emphasis.[1] It was 'in the power of the Spirit,' as S. Luke says,[2] that He commenced working in Galilee. The Church of the Fathers was very far from asserting that the Holy Ghost was with other men as with Him.[3] Hence there was an epiklesis, or special invocation of the Holy Ghost, always used by her ministers in both administering baptism and celebrating the Eucharist, and in each case the 'res sacramenti'—the gift conveyed in it—was ascribed to His action. The Holy Ghost was invoked, secondly, to make the soul of each communicant fit to receive with profit what was distributed after consecration. Not only consecration, but distribution of the sacrament was vested *uno ore* by the Fathers in the Third Person of the Trinity. For the Fathers gathered, and gathered rightly, from Scripture that all the benefits of the Incarnation procured for mankind by the Son were conveyed to the individual *ex officio* by the Holy Ghost. And they gathered further from Scripture, and gathered rightly, that He who prepared the body which the Son assumed at His Incarnation would effect the Incarnation of each individual Christian in succession, by

[1] I 32-33, twice repeated
[2] IV 14
[3] See particularly S Greg *Moral*

II c 56 'Dissimiliter ergo Spiritus in Illo manet, a Quo per naturam nunquam recedit.'

uniting his soul to the body prepared for Christ, which Christ offered for man and then bore with Him in triumph into heaven.

From their point of view, therefore, the Eucharist was a sacrament, just like baptism, consisting of two parts, as distinct from each other in kind as the two natures of Christ Himself, and neither, consequently, to be confused with, or absorbed in, the other: one material, outward, and earthly; the other spiritual, inward, and divine. The outward, contributed by the congregation, purveyed and set apart by the celebrant; the inward, due solely to the action of the Holy Ghost, obtained by prayer of the whole Church and addressed usually to the Father or to the Trinity, but now and then to the Son, as sender of Him jointly with the Father.

The outward remained to the last a figure, symbol, or sign of the inward—hence recognised as such in the liturgies. But, after consecration, as might with good reason have been expected, the inward was dwelt upon as though it existed alone, and the dominant idea that found expression in characterising it was its spirituality. For the 'Official' throughout was the Holy Spirit acting upon the life-giving body that He had prepared for Christ, preparing the souls of men for union with it, and accomplishing the union of each individual soul with it, whole and entire. Thus it was a process which carried its own explanation with it, though hid from view; for each individual who was the subject of it was reminded by it of the secret ties uniting his own body to his soul. Hence those rapturous, yet *not un*real, terms by which the Eucharistic oblation and the gift conveyed in it were designated by the Fathers, 'celestial mysteries, mystical, unbloody sacrifices, spiritual food or aliment, heavenly meat and drink.' Nothing carnal was ever associated with it either in their liturgies or in their minds. It is a fact that the word 'flesh' is never used in their liturgies except in a *bad* sense. Even in speaking of Christ, lest it might breed misconceptions, His *flesh* is *nowhere named.* He said Himself, 'Take'—*not* My flesh, but—' My body.' The material part of the sacrament entering in at the mouth, so passed into the bodily frame. The spiritual gift went direct to the soul, often called in Scripture the heart. '*Sursum corda*' was the key-note to all that followed.

Prayers for all estates of men in the Church militant, prayers for the departed, commemorations of saints and martyrs in the Church triumphant—of different length in different dioceses, but always ending with the Lord's Prayer —followed between consecration and distribution, and at last occupied so much time that their number had to be reduced and their contents abridged. S. Basil and S. Chrysostom, accordingly, we find credited with having been the first to take steps in this direction, and their example was followed in the West, though not by any means in their day.

But now, in connection with the change which concerns us here most, if anything has been brought out on distinct historical grounds in these researches, it is this weird-like coincidence: that all the liturgies of antiquity *now used* in the East as well as in the West—in the East through Constantinople, in the West through Rome—have been mainly borrowed, in respect of the form long since given to their most solemn part (consecration of the elements), from a Macedonian source—namely, from the liturgy that has come down to us in the eighth book of the Apostolical Constitutions, popularly called the Clementine. That whoever compiled it must have been a Macedonian has been shown in detail from its own contents, though it is in a service leading up to it, and affecting to emanate from S. Andrew, that the most decisive proof of this is found, where the First Person of the Trinity—the Father—is addressed as *God* of the Third, the Holy Ghost, which expression, as it was the Son, *not* the Holy Ghost, who 'took upon Him the form of a servant,' was rightly characterised *blasphemy* by Bishop

Montague, commenting on a kindred work.[1] Of Jesus the First Person of the Trinity was by S. Peter[2] and S. Paul[3] styled, with exquisite fineness and propriety, both ' God and Father '—being His Father as God, and His God as man—whereas of the Holy Ghost He could be styled *neither* God *nor* Father except by minds steeped in heterodoxy.

Read by the light of this phrase, the design of the liturgy which follows must have been to supplant, or at least discredit, the orthodox liturgies of older date, by professing to have been handed down to the Church through S. Clement of Rome from the Apostles in council assembled, and then making a recital of the acts and words of the Saviour in instituting the Eucharist on the night of His betrayal take precedence of the prayer invoking the descent of the Holy Ghost on the elements for their consecration, not hitherto found in that connection; the words of the Saviour having been used exclusively till then, as used by Himself, in distributing the consecrated elements to each intending communicant.

To the fact of their being absent in the older liturgies from the position assigned them in the Clementine, the concurrent testimonies of the two Cyrils—of Jerusalem and Alexandria—must be considered conclusive. A key to the sinister purpose contemplated in their new position—that of opposing the words of the Second Person of the Trinity to the action of the Third, and thereby producing the very consequences that have followed from it in the West—has come down to us in the homilies of Eusebius of Emesa, who showed such tact in opposing S. Athanasius, and was contemporary with, and shared the opinions of, the compiler of this liturgy, if not the actual compiler of it himself.

Proof has been given that this liturgy must have been known to S. Epiphanius, who commenced his great work

---

[1] Euseb Cæs *De Eccl. Theol.* iii. 6, note 65, ed Migne.
[2] 1 Pet. i. 3.   [3] Col i 3

against heresies A.D. 374; further proof has been given that it must have been known to S. Chrysostom while still at Antioch; and further proof, confirmed by internal evidence, that it was made by S. Basil and himself, believing it had been received from S. Clement, their model in revising the liturgy then used in their respective Churches in the heart of Asia Minor and at Constantinople. Naturally they both paid great deference to it in many ways on that account; and most in this—in the new form given there to the consecration of the elements, by reciting over them the acts and words of the Saviour at His last supper, *before* invoking the descent of the Holy Ghost on them for consecration. But, on the other hand, as if to compensate for this change, they both made their invocation not only much longer, but more distinct and emphatic, than it had been when it stood alone. To this intuitive foresight, more than anything else, the East owes its persistent adherence to the teachings of the older form.

The liturgy, thus revised by S. Chrysostom, became sooner or later that of Constantinople; and proof external and internal has been given, that both S. Gregory the Great, the founder of our Anglo-Saxon Church, and the future Metropolitan of Seville, Leander, used that of the supposed Clement, and that of the golden-mouthed prelate, whose prayer concludes our daily matins and evensong, at Constantinople, during their stay there together, in revising their own. But it has also been shown that they each took a higher line than either S. Basil or S. Chrysostom in the execution of their task. For they both decided on retaining the old prayer of their respective liturgies—then called in Spain 'the conformation of the sacrament:' by S. Gregory, 'the Catholic prayer'—for invoking the action of the Holy Ghost on the elements in its accustomed place; though both agreed to recast it each in the form he judged most suitable to his own Church, and then appended to it the recital of the acts and words of the Saviour, in pretty much the form—though not in the order—given to them in the Clementine.

Nothing could be more beautiful or more loyal than their decision in both respects: sad only to think how soon it was destined in each case to be consigned to oblivion; loyal, in upholding their own traditional prayer in its accustomed place; beautiful, even in their divergent address. Leander, addressing his prayer to the Son, by way of directing attention to the truth declared in the Gospel, and now set forth in the form of the Creed used in his own Church, that the Holy Ghost is sent by the Son as well as by the Father, to complete the purpose for which the Son died; and S. Gregory, supplicating the Father as he had hitherto done, but now, that the Holy Ghost might be commanded to raise the oblation of the Church on earth to the altar of the Son on high, that He might there, by His own act, effect the union of the faithful with His own body; and then, like Leander, reciting what was said and done by Him at His last supper on earth—in authorisation of the whole rite. God forbid that anything should here be said in disparagement of the recital of those acts and words in the liturgy; though they were first inserted in it with fell purpose by heretics, and a perverse turn given to their meaning by the position assigned them in a liturgy which is as false to their teaching as to the name which it bears. Place them once more where Leander and S. Gregory placed them with such exquisite discernment, and we may then say of their introduction into the liturgy, what S. Ambrose so finely said of the introduction into the Creed of the word Homoousios, after the objection taken to it by the Eusebians, 'that their heresy was decapitated with a sword which they had themselves unsheathed.'[1]

Up to this time there had been unity, continuous unity between the East and West; fidelity to the Creed that had been their joint work; loyalty to the ancient teaching and

[1] *De Fide ad Grat* iii. 15.

ritual that had come down to them both from Apostolic times. Whole nations were being converted by both. The churches everywhere, 'walking in the fear of the Lord, and in the comfort of the Holy Ghost,' were 'multiplied' as well as 'edified,' and edified as well as multiplied. It was the boast of S. Gregory that he reverenced the four first General Councils as the Gospels, and was not wanting in respect for the fifth also. His untiring devotion it was that gave the Anglo-Saxons their national Church. His large-hearted advice to its missionaries was that they should not hesitate to look round and see whether there was anything in ritual or discipline that they could borrow with advantage from other Churches. He told his critics boldly that his predecessors had borrowed from Constantinople, that he had, and would again, did it ever appear that he could do so with profit. As his friend Leander and he worshipped together in the great church of S. Sophia, which the Emperor Justinian had made the wonder of the world for size and magnificence, and assisted at, while there, celebrations of the Eucharist according to the liturgy revised by the far-famed preacher and theologian whose sermons had procured for him a surname that had become world-wide by common consent, they must have both felt assuredly that among all the inspiring things which they heard and saw, there were not a few worth taking back home with them to edify their respective flocks. Yet neither of them assuredly was pressed to adopt any part of the Constantinopolitan ritual, nor, when they returned home, did either of them seek to impose what they took from thence on any Churches besides their own. So matters went on for two centuries longer in the West without any further changes on this head, as was natural enough, for as Leander and S. Gregory both retained the invocatory prayer *in its accustomed place*, what they introduced subsequently with S. Basil and S. Chrysostom from the Clementine made no difference whatever in the teaching of their respective Churches; and so long as this was the case, there was no room for controversy, nor, in point of fact, is anything clearer from history than that of controversy there was *none*, respecting the Eucharist, in any part of the Church till the Gallicanism of the ninth century was developed in the West, giving rise to controversies that have not yet ceased.

2. Similarly, with regard to the Creed. To some, possibly, this close friendship between Leander and S. Gregory may seem hard to reconcile with the proceedings of the third Council of Toledo, A.D. 589, where the 'Filioque' was first inserted in the Creed, to which Leander subscribed, and also the apparent rejection of the fifth General Council by the Church of Spain at that time. But here S. Gregory cuts the knot for us himself, first, when he says that the *Latin words* 'mission' and 'procession' are convertible terms,[1] he as good as tells us that on going into this question with his friend, he found there was no difference between them in explaining it, and that under the circumstances he would do well not to press for explanations from the Church of Spain. Again, when he says that he 'venerates the fifth Council,' he gives us to understand that it had not as yet been received everywhere, and therefore was not as yet binding under anathema, though his own assent had been given to it. Nevertheless, he adds even of the fifth, that if any persons should attack its *de fide* pronouncements, he would anathematise them without scruple.[2] Finally, when he says that 'he received the first four Councils as the four Gospels,'[3] he proclaims his unqualified adhesion to all their *de fide* definitions, and to the Creed in which they were summed up, and that he would maintain them inviolate to the day of his death, as his consecration oath expressed it, '*usque ad unum apicem.*' The year in which S. Gregory became Pope

---

[1] 'Ejus missio ipsa processio est, quâ de Patre procedit et Filio — *In Evang* lib ii Hom xxvi § 2

[2] *Ep* lib iii x ad Savin 'Anathematizamus autem, siquis *ex definitione fidei*, quæ in eadem synodo prolata est, aliquid imminuere pra sumit, vel quasi corrigendo ejus sensum mutare sed sicut illic prolata est, per omnia custodimus'

[3] Ib

was A.D. 590, and as the letter containing these declarations was written in the third year of his pontificate, the proceedings of the third Council of Toledo could have been no secret to him when he penned them. This fact adds considerably to their force; nor could any proof be, therefore, stronger of his determination to uphold the Creed and dogmatic rulings of the first five General Councils intact under anathema, nor could their contents and bearings have been better known to anybody since than these to him. Just fifty years from the date assigned to his letter, Theodore, who was a Greek by birth, became Pope. The heresy which was then spreading elicited still stronger language from him. Addressing a synodical letter to the patriarch of Constantinople, named Paul, whose conduct he had grave cause to suspect, he breaks out into the following noble burst at its close:—

'Sufficient for us is the faith which the holy Apostles preached, which Councils confirmed, which the holy Fathers handed down, in which we were baptised and schooled ourselves, and which we teach, not allowing augmentation of any sort in the symbol of the faith, to which Councils have set their seal. Anathema to those who add aught to the sacred Creed or symbol; anathema to those who subtract aught from it, as it was defined at Nicæa, confirmed at Constantinople, and as at the first Council of Ephesus, and at Chalcedon, by the pious and orthodox Fathers who flourished then in the Catholic faith, it was established by favour of the Holy Ghost.'[1]

In addition to these weighty testimonies to its all-sufficiency for all practical purposes, after two centuries of experience, and to its unalterableness on principle, let us briefly recall the circumstances of its original promulgation and confirmation.

First of all it should be pointed out that, of all the articles in the Creed, this article relating to the Holy Ghost is just the one which received longest and most careful consideration

[1] Mansi, x, 705

before being ordered to form part of the Creed, the origin of it having been the 'tome' sent to the Church of Antioch by S. Athanasius, and the great synod under him, A.D. 362, at Alexandria, for restoring peace to the Church, in which the indivisibility of the Holy Ghost from the substance both of the Father and of the Son is distinctly set forth. This was followed ten years later by the 'tome' of the Westerns addressed by Pope Damasus to the Easterns, setting forth under anathema the same doctrine, and condemning all the various errors held by those who denied it. This again was read, approved, and acknowledged, by the Council of Antioch under S. Meletius, A.D. 380.[1] Hence, when ordered to form part of the Creed at Constantinople the year following, it had been previously discussed and agreed upon in synods at Alexandria, Rome, and Antioch.

No notice was taken of this at the Council of Ephesus, A.D. 431, under S. Cyril, for reasons which it is unnecessary to repeat here. But at the fourth General Council—that of Chalcedon, A.D. 451—the original Creed of Nicæa, and the enlarged form afterwards given to it at Constantinople, were both recited and ordered to be considered in future the one Creed of the Church, to the exclusion of any other for public use. The fifth, sixth, and seventh Councils each reaffirmed the same ordinance.

The extreme wisdom of this ordinance will appear by recalling the reasons on which it was evidently based. The first thought of the Fathers would naturally be to uphold the '*Monarchia*,' which all antiquity recognised in the Father, which Jesus Himself authorised in the clearest manner, by deferring in everything to His heavenly Father, and by giving us to understand that the difference between Himself and the Holy Ghost in relation to the Father consisted in this, that one was His only-begotten Son, the other the Spirit of Truth proceeding from Him. Jesus never speaks of Himself as *proceeding*, though He speaks of Himself as '*coming*

[1] Pagi ad Baron. A.D 369, n 7 *et seq*, endorsed by Mansi.

forth,' nor of the Holy Ghost as *begotten*, though He terms Him ' *another* Paraclete.'

Their next thought would be the diversities of expression current amongst themselves, neither easy to amalgamate, nor again to choose between, in speaking of the Holy Ghost; some speaking of Him as the Spirit of both, others that He proceeds from the Father and takes from the Son, others that He proceeds *principally* from the Father—in other words, from both, but not in the same sense. By restricting themselves to the *exact words of our Lord* in describing His procession, they would content all and offend none.

Then, those who met at Chalcedon would remember the sharp passage, not twenty years old, between Theodoret and S. Cyril on the subject of words used by the latter in the ninth anathema with which his celebrated letter to Nestorius closed. What was it that he meant in asserting, ' proprium esse Filii Spiritum '? For if by that phrase was meant that the Holy Ghost owed His existence through or to the Son, it was simple blasphemy, said Theodoret. S. Cyril declared in reply, that he meant no such thing; he admitted fully that the Holy Ghost proceeds from the Father, yet pleaded that He might be called the Spirit of the Father and the Son, as being consubstantial with both, and also sent by both.[1] Those who met at Chalcedon, therefore, must have felt sure they had S. Cyril with them in leaving that article just as the Constantinopolitan Fathers had published it.

Finally, the Constantinopolitan Fathers themselves had at least one reason that must have weighed extraordinarily with them, both in framing and in publishing that article when they did; and which it would be not only treason to truth, but injustice to them to suppress. Macedonius had been patriarch of the city where they met. His followers had been received into communion by Liberius, Bishop of Rome, A.D. 366, which was the last year of his life, without being required by him to renounce their heresy. S. Basil

[1] Mansi, v 122-26

may be said to have died of the troubles occasioned him by this act. The Macedonians unquestionably, who maintained that the Holy Ghost owed His existence to the Son, would have claimed a further victory for their founder in his own metropolis, had the Constantinopolitan Fathers included the procession of the Holy Ghost from the Son in their Creed.

Here we may stop in our review of the facts brought out in earlier chapters respecting the ritual and Creed of the primitive Church, supplemented, indeed, by some new facts bearing on the last, and all on the positive side. This similar remark, too, may be thrown in respecting the canons: namely, that the Western code, down to the days of S. Gregory, and for 150 years longer in round numbers, contained no canons but the Sardican that have not proved strictly genuine; and even against the Sardican that eminently truthful and accurate collector, Dionysius Exiguus, affixed this mark, that they were published in Latin, like the African, just as he had before said of the fifty with which he commenced 'qui *dicuntur* Apostolorum.' Those fifty certainly reflected all that we know from other sources to have been the discipline from Apostolic times observed in the Church; just as the Sardican, interpreted strictly by what took place, when S. Athanasius was in exile, with Julius, Bishop of Rome, for his unswerving mainstay, would be found in tolerable keeping with recorded facts, yet facts of a most exceptional kind.

What happened in the ninth century, and what have been its effects, must now be summed up—and summed up gently, to avoid wounding susceptibilities more than can be helped; yet summed up honestly, to avoid understating the truth. Borrowing a phrase, then, from days much nearer our own, we may say with truth that the whole Western Church was Gallicanised at that time; and with a Gallicanism that cleaves to much the larger half of it still; and such Gallicanism as adds one more knot to the tangle, by being the exact antithesis of the Gallicanism which for two centuries has been proscribed as such. For *that* Gallicanism was the righteous outburst of the most excellent of men, desirous of shaking off all the popular doctrines and practices in their system that were based on spurious documents, and of remodelling it by the genuine works of the Fathers, edited by them with such deep learning and reverence combined, a school that has in our own day produced a galaxy of distinguished men worthy—yes, well worthy—to be named in the same breath with the Benedictines of S. Maur for their high-souled writings and unsullied lives. Whereas the work of *this* Gallicanism was the wholesale destruction of a definite system of belief and discipline that had hitherto proved effectual for securing corporate union in the Church militant of every land, and the establishment of another, based on spurious documents of every kind, fabricated to secure prestige for it, wherever the new and the old clashed, and to forward the designs of a would-be master of the world.

Let full justice be done to all who can be shown to have been no parties to it. Let full justice be done to the Church of Rome for having been in each case *the last to succumb* to the tide. Let full justice be done to the memories of Popes Adrian I. and Leo III. for having struggled against it to the last. It took two full centuries to reconcile Rome to the interpolated Creed—a reconciliation which even Baronius in his day was not afraid to deplore. We learn from Hincmar, the great Archbishop of Rheims, that copies of the False Decretals of the early Popes were circulating in France long before he accepted them himself. It was not till after Hincmar had accepted them that credit was given to them at Rome by Pope Nicholas I. Finally, the Gregorian revision of the liturgy was not displaced at Rome by the Gallican version of it before the days of the French Pope, Leo IX., when Berengarius of Tours was condemned there by him for tenets as yet only considered heretical in France. Hence when Gregory VII., a Tuscan by birth, educated at Rome, became Pope, Berengarius signed a declaration which, being in accordance with Roman traditions, satisfied *him*, and was never again allowed to be molested for his opinions.

To dwell on each of these points with more fulness. It was *not heresy*, but empire, that Charlemagne proposed and was permitted to establish in the West, though he was not permitted to include the East in it, as he certainly proposed to do likewise. And, consciously or not, it is surprising in how many respects the means employed by him in furtherance of his designs would indicate that he mimicked the first king of Israel, Jeroboam. Religion he saw clearly was the only lever that he could employ with any success; and, till then, all the ordinances affecting the religion of Europe had issued from Constantinople. There the Creed of the Church had been discussed and put into final shape; there all the Councils as yet considered oecumenical had met; there all the canons binding the whole Church had been framed. All this must now be reversed or he could not succeed; and by his manner of reversing it he might, he hoped, add the East some day to his dominions. If authority could be found in existing documents for what he wanted done, well and good; if not, it must be supplied by his divines in the best way they could and at any cost. This is the real clue to the warmth with which he advocated the adoption of the interpolated Creed, which he found done to his hand in Spain, and to the general character of the False Decretals of the early Popes—fabricated nobody knows *exactly* when or by whom, but imported certainly by one in his confidence from the same quarter, and as certainly brought into play first at the scene preceding his own coronation as emperor, A.D. 800. His adoption of the interpolated Creed had its political side too. He wanted to add Spain to his dominions. As champion of its Creed, he had always a good excuse for intervening there. It was he who brought the errors of Felix, bishop of Urgel, and Elipandus, metropolitan of Toledo, to light and got them refuted. But simultaneously with their condemnation at the Council of Frankfort, A.D. 794, he discovered a far higher purpose to serve with his adopted Creed. It supplied him with a weapon of the first order against the decrees of the Seventh Council, though he must have known full well they had been confirmed seven years before by the Pope. But his policy required that the Pope should be detached at any cost from the East. Diplomacy, not theology, dictated the composition of the Caroline Books, and it is the defence of the adopted Creed of their inspirer that forms their centre-piece. But here we are reminded of the distinction once more between things ready to his hand and things of uncertain date. The authorship of his adopted Creed is well known, and of its first promulgation at the third Council of Toledo, A.D. 589, we have full details. Similarly the profession recited at full length in the opening chapter of the third Caroline Book in its defence can be dated to a year and has a well-known author. It is what is called the Creed of Pelagius, whose peculiar errors S. Augustine won so much fame by refuting that he has been called ever since 'Doctor of Grace.' Pelagius addressed this profession of his faith to the Roman bishop Innocent I., A.D. 417, in self-defence; and Cave says of it,[1] 'Pelagium de Trinitate *recte sensisse*, patet ex libello fidei ejus.' It is twice mentioned and quoted by S. Augustine. The Caroline divines, therefore, who knew his works so well, cannot with any reason be supposed ignorant of its authorship; hence the least that can be laid to their charge is that they connived at the fraud. For it is paraded in the Caroline Books as the '*Creed of S. Jerome*,' and, worse than this, it is itself interpolated, in its statement of the procession of the Holy Ghost, *with* the 'Filioque'—the word of four syllables sought to be justified in the Creed of Spain.

I know that there are some who contend that there was another Creed in existence which might have been used by Charlemagne, besides this profession of Pelagius, in support of his views—meaning of course the 'Quicunque vult'; or,

[1] *Hist Lit.* 1 383

as it has been for more than 1000 years called, the Athanasian Creed. When authentic proof, whose date cannot be challenged, has been produced of its pre-existence, *cadit quæstio*: but not before. Two centuries ago the False Decretals were credited with a similar pre-existence. But it is the *historical* relation of Charlemagne to both which should be pointed out first; for it is a clear historical fact that he employed both similarly. They were both published by him under false names. His publication of both, however, was not yet. They were meant to tell most against the Greeks; for both fairly represented the doctrine and discipline then received and enforced in *the West*. A few words may now be added on the pre-existence claimed for the 'Quicunque vult,' which was *brought out* by him first of the two. Persons have discovered a negative argument for its pre-existence from the lack in it of any reference to the errors of Elipandus and Felix; but he who decreed its publication as the Creed of Athanasius was too clever by half not to have perceived that any such reference would be fatal to the title that he designed for it, and therefore could not be permitted. On the other hand, it contains so much against their errors by anticipation, that, had it been a genuine work of the great bishop of Alexandria, the Council of Frankfort could not have passed it over in silence. But there is no reference to it whatever in the Caroline Books, nor in any other of the dogmatic utterances submitted to the Council of Frankfort, nor in any of the controversial treatises as yet published against Adoptionism. Had it been known to exist *before* A.D. 800, that heresy could not well have waited till *after* A.D. 800 to be confronted with it. Had it been found hid in a corner later, its discovery must have been hailed by numbers as a *eureka*. But history supplies no hint either of its pre-existence, nor of its subsequent coming to light. The positive facts on record point strongly to a later origin. Two years after the Council of Frankfort, as Pagi proves, Paulinus, bishop of Aquileia, convened a synod at Friuli, which he addressed at length in justification of the interpolated Creed, and then presented with a long exposition of 'the Catholic faith,' as he called it —not unlike the Athanasian Creed in some respects, but for which he certainly would have substituted the Athanasian Creed had he known of its existence then; and this he required all priests in his diocese to learn by heart.[1] It must have been soon found in practice much too long and involved for that purpose. Four years later—the year in which Charlemagne *was crowned Emperor*—Alcuin[2] writes in ecstasy to Paulinus, thanking him, in terms which I still consider decisive, for the ' symbolum Catholicæ fidei ' just received from him, and the very thing in his opinion for priests in every diocese to be required to learn by heart. And it so happens that there is in the Athanasian Creed just one word—' *suis* corporibus '—used in describing the resurrection of the body, which Rufinus[3] tells us was peculiar to the Church over which Paulinus presided: no small confirmation, therefore, that it was due to his pen. Then, two years later, among the things which all ecclesiastics are required to learn by heart in the Capitularies of A.D. 802, are: 'Fidem Sancti Athanasii, et cætera quæcunque de fide.' I have a letter by me from Pertz,[4] in reply to some criticisms that were forwarded to him, expressing his certainty that the date given by him to these Capitularies was correct. *Not* two years later—for Alcuin died A.D. 804—a tract now acknowledged to have been by him on the Procession,[5] written by command of, and dedicated to Charlemagne, twice quotes extracts at some length from what he calls an ' exposition of the Catholic faith, by the blessed Athanasius, bishop of Alexandria '; just as they are read now in what we call the Athanasian Creed. Finally, the monks of a

---

[1] Mansi, xiii 830–54
[2] *Ep* cxiii ed Migne.
[3] *In Symb Apost.*
[4] Pertz, *Mon. Germ. Legum*, i. 107.
[5] Migne, *Pat Lat.* ci. 63. It should be stated perhaps that the Paschasius quoted in c. 1 is Paschasius the Roman Deacon.

Latin convent on Mount Olives founded by Charlemagne, styled it by the name given to it in his Capitulary, when they appealed to it in justification of themselves for having given utterance to the interpolated Creed at Jerusalem, in the hearing of the Greeks, to their great annoyance, as they confessed in their letter to the Pope.[1]

All these converging facts would in ordinary cases be allowed by all to point one way; and of *authentic* evidence there has not been as yet a shred produced that suggests another. What weighs with most in withholding their assent from this is, that it implicates Paulinus and Alcuin in the publication of a work under a name which they both knew to be false. Yet they *cannot but* have known that the Creed of Pelagius was *not* that of S. Jerome. Suppose, then, that their lord and master insisted on making himself responsible for both names, and pointed out—what is perfectly true to this day—that there was nothing in either Creed to which S. Athanasius or S. Jerome could have taken exception, as being inconsistent with what each of them held and taught, is it likely that his divines would not have yielded the point? Let those who would dispute this, only peruse the savage letter addressed by the great autocrat to his devoted Alcuin, then within a year of his death, and to the monks of S. Martin, with his own piteous reply to it, and they will see what Charlemagne could be, when his ordinances, even when drawn from the False Decretals, were contravened, it mattered not by whom.[2]

As regards the authorship of those False Decretals, we know from history that Riculphus was both an antiquarian and diplomatist; but history suggests, further, that though

---

[1] It may be read in Neale, *Eastern Ch* Gen Introd ii 1155 *et seq*

[2] 'Sed et valde miramur, cur *vobis solis* visum sit nostræ sanctioni et decreto contraeundum cum liquido pateat et ex consuetudine veteri, et ex constitutione legum decreta rata esse debere, nec cuiquam permissum illorum edicta vel statuta contemnere' The enactment infringed is common to the pseudo-Decretals and the Capitularies of Angilramn (*Ep* clviii., ed Migne) The reply to it is misplaced, being given in advance, *Ep* cxlix

not possessed of sufficient ability to have composed them, he was quite competent, having procured and perused them, to have discerned and pointed out their use to his master. If the son of Pepin had any designs on the East, the *jure divino* claim set up in them for the bishop of old Rome—the acknowledged patriarch of the West, but now his subject—would make Constantinople beholden to him without fighting. There was no canon of Eastern Councils in existence that they would not over-ride. Sooner or later the affairs of the whole Christian East must be referred to him as their last appeal. It was needless to add how much his sway would be consolidated by them at home. Caution dictated that they should not be made generally known, till the Bishop of Rome was fairly detached from the East, otherwise the scheme for his ecclesiastical aggrandisement might produce results widely different from those which it was intended to secure.

Contrary to the general opinion formed of them hitherto, my facts, I venture to think, will be found to warrant the inference that, with whatever object the pseudo-Decretals were framed, temporal, *not* ecclesiastical, interests were what they were primarily designed to subserve, when they were first used, and canon-law, *not* of the West, but of the *East*, what they were meant to supplant. It has been assumed too hastily, that because the *Empire* came to be the smallest, and the *Papacy* the greatest gainer by these Decretals, that they were manufactured or first used by the Popes, or for their special benefit. 'One soweth, and another reapeth,' was a proverb when our Lord pointed out its application to His disciples.[1] It would not follow that in every case where the reaper had not been the sower the crop could not fail to be got in well, or the bread good.

That Riculphus, afterwards archbishop of Mayence, was employed on a mission in Spain by Charlemagne, and that it was he by whom the False Decretals were carried into

[1] S John iii 37.

France from Spain, are both of them historical facts. And there are some curious indications besides extant, but not noticed hitherto, that they were manufactured about that time to order. Their author tells us, in his preface, that to his collection of Councils he will subjoin the remaining decrees of the Roman prelates down to S. Gregory, by whom Hinschius takes it for granted, as all others had done before him, is meant the first Gregory. Ludicrous as it may appear, Charlemagne was imposed upon himself similarly. For he appeals in his Capitularies of A.D. 803 [1] to a letter ' of the blessed Pope Gregory '—by whom given him? by his friend Riculphus—on which he founds his decision. It proves to have been written, *not* by S. Gregory, but by Gregory II. And, further, this statement of the pseudo-Isidore turns out one of those passages which he has artfully travestied from the real Isidore, which will be seen below in parallel column with his.[2] The real Isidore speaks in general terms, without naming S. Gregory. Still, as matter of fact, he gives a few letters of S. Gregory, but a few only, bringing them just down to his own time. Why was the counterfeit Isidore so desirous of calling attention to them? Precisely because they related to the conversion of King Reccared, and the Council at which the Creed was interpolated. But did not his own collection stop there too? Certainly not, though Hinschius, because ' the deceiver ' had said it should end with S. Gregory, refuses insertion to anything further. But the editor of the False

[1] Baluz. *Capit. Reg Fr* 1 385.

[2] Isid. Hispal ap Migne, *Pat. Lat* lxxxiv 91.

' Subjicientes etiam decreta præsulum Romanorum, in quibus pro culmine sedis apostolicæ non impar conciliorum exstat auctoritas, quatenus ecclesiastici ordinis disciplina in unum a nobis coacta atque digesta et sancti præsulis paternis instituantur regulis, et obeientes ecclesiæ ministri vel populi pecialibus imbuantur exemplis....'

Isid Mercat. ap. Migne, cxxx 8.

' Subjicientes etiam reliqua decreta præsulum Romanorum, *usque ad sanctum Gregorium*, et quasdam epistolas ipsius, in quibus,' &c , just as on the other side , after which he interpolates more of his own He does stop with *a* Gregory, but it is not the first of that name.

Decretals in Migne was wiser in his generation. For he says, at the end of the Epistles of S. Gregory I., in a note, that he 'adds the decretals of Popes Gregory II., Vitalian, Martin, Gregory III., and Zachariah, because they are thus given in ancient MSS.' According to him, therefore, the False Decretals stop just at that very point where the Codex Carolinus begins, the first of that Codex being a letter of Gregory III., and the second a letter of Zachariah. It would, of course, never have done for the letters given in one collection to have been *identical* with those given in the other. Still the continuation of the series from one to the other cannot well have been the effect of chance. The natural inference plainly would be that the compiler in Spain and the compiler at Aix must have stood in some relation to each other for their lists to be continuous, and to dovetail so well. Anyhow, the compiler in Spain, by bringing his list down to Zachariah, proves himself to have been contemporary with him of Aix, so that Riculphus may well have conversed with the Spaniard, if Spaniard he was, and purchased his work from him too, when sent on a mission into Spain. It was by Popes Gregory II. and III. that the foundations of Gallican ascendency were laid in the person of Charles Martel, when his intervention in Italy was invoked by them; it was to Pope Zachariah principally that Pepin, the father of Charlemagne, owed his crown. The names of Martin and Vitalian would be put in deliberately, though they involved an anachronism, to prevent the simple from guessing why mention of the other three was superadded.

How the liturgy revised by S. Gregory came to be revised in France, and, after having been revised in France, became that of Rome, requires only to be succinctly stated, with a broad distinction observed between what is authentic and what is not, to command assent. Nobody needs to be told that numberless things would never have happened in Europe but for Charlemagne. What we want to know on this head is, how much was actually planned and executed during his reign, and what was filled in after his death. We have, then, authentic evidence that, following the steps of his father Pepin, he substituted the Roman for the Gallican Chant throughout his dominions, and that he contemplated a general correction of all the Office-books and Missals then used in France.[1] Not long after this, he applied for and received from Adrian I. a Gregorian Sacramentary,[2] for what purpose we are not told, but we find clear reference made to it in the Caroline Books.[3]

This is about the sum of what was done by him, or contemplated by him, in connection with Church services. He has been credited with more; he may have threatened more; he may have intended more, had his hands been free or had Rome proved more pliant. His son Lewis had barely mounted the throne when he summoned a great Council at Aix, A.D. 816, to carry through, as he says, what his father had purposed so many years before [4]—one of the things specially named by him being the correction or emendation of the Missals and Office-books. But so many things had to be taken in hand that the Council separated before this item was reached. Amalarius, we are told, put the different regulations made by the Council respecting the institution of canons and cloistered nuns into shape. He was then merely deacon of the Church of Metz, and Metz had been left without a bishop, which its proximity to Aix alone can explain, ever since the death of Angilramn, its last bishop under Charlemagne, A.D. 791. Soon after this Amalarius justified the confidence reposed in him by writing, first, a work on 'Ecclesiastical Offices' that went through two editions—a small and an enlarged one—and then a work on the book of Antiphons, or Antiphonary. Both works evidently were dictated by the programme traced by the

---

[1] *Constit de Emend. Lib*, with Capit. 78 and 70 (Aix), A D 789, ap. Baluz i 203 and 230.
[2] *Cod Carol Ep* xcix (the last), dated in Migne A D. 791.
[3] Lib ii 27
[4] *Prol Ludov Imp.* ap Baluz. i. 561-3 and Capit 28, ib. p. 569. Also Mansi, xiv 147-282.

Emperor at the late Council—traced, but not yet executed. In both he makes the Missal and Office-books of his own Church of Metz his standard. In his book—for it was published at first in one book—on 'Ecclesiastical Offices,' he gives the words of the earlier part of the Canon complete, and they will be found identical with the words of the Roman Canon as it exists now and has existed for more than 800 years. Hence the first observation which history forces on us respecting it will create surprise —namely, that it was, when published by him, the very first ever seen or used, including no prayer for, nor any mention of, the action of the Holy Ghost on the elements. A second observation— and this he takes special care to impress upon us—is that his Canon commenced with the paragraph, ' Quam oblationem Tu, Deus,' &c., which he quotes at length, and that it was immediately preceded by the three sentences due to S. Gregory. What, then, had he done with the Gregorian epiklesis, of which an account has already been given, showing that it had been recast from a prayer in the Clementine liturgy and made to stand where the old 'prayer' of the Roman invoking the descent of the Holy Ghost on the elements formerly stood ? Amalarius left the Gregorian epiklesis untouched, word for word with what it is now, but relegated it back to the place occupied by the prayer at the end of the Canon in the Clementine, from which it had been copied. By this step it was entirely robbed of its meaning and entirely dissociated from the purpose which it had been recast to serve.

Just after, or just before possibly, the completion of his second work Amalarius was appointed 'Imperial Official' for correcting the Office-books of the empire, and he forthwith acted on what he had written. The time chosen by him for entering on his visitorial progress should also be taken into account, for it was a time when everything was turned upside down in France. We read of bishops ejected summarily from their sees and abbots from their convents, of everybody living in bodily fear of his life, and nobody knowing what side to take. It was during the unnatural, but not unprovoked, rebellion of the sons of the Emperor by his first wife against their father. It is Florus, a well-known learned deacon of the Church of Lyons, who furnishes us with a painful illustration of these desolating years in what befel his own Church, the oldest in France, and then presided over by a truly primitive bishop, but who, for having incurred the wrath of the Emperor, was in hiding far away from his see. Florus, his deacon, had the sympathies of the whole diocese with him in denouncing the conduct of this overbearing official, whose doings and dealings with the ancient ritual of his Church he has described in such impassioned terms. Evidently the change that he sorrows over most in it is the excision of its epiklesis; for in his 'Exposition of the Mass,' which he wrote later, he vainly labours to discover this *implied* in a dozen places of the Amalarian Canon, by which from henceforth the Canon that had been handed down from S. Irenæus was to be supplanted; while to the bishops assembled at Quiersy, whither he forwarded a second philippic against Amalarius, he points out clearly what had led to this change by calling upon them to endorse what he quotes from S. Leo, directing that 'the circulation of *apocryphal writings passing under the names of the Apostles,* yet replete *with falsehoods,* should not only be forbidden, but they should be burnt or otherwise destroyed, as being never free from poison, in spite of the garb of piety which they may exhibit.'[1]

Here the Clementine liturgy, which from internal evidence alone could be shown to have dictated this change, is as clearly pointed at in connection with it. Florus tells us in conclusion that one province after another had been subjected to the same visitation as his own, and that in all alike the conduct of this Imperial Official had been identic.

[1] Martene and Durand, *Vet Script &c Collect* ix 664.

Hilduin, abbot of S. Denys, another exiled and but just restored contemporary, testifies to the wholesale destruction of the old Office-books in his part of the country—round Paris, that is. And that his onslaught was anything but confined to the north or south, the exceeding few and fragmentary survivals of them, exhumed two centuries ago, when convents were at their zenith of wealth and splendour in France, and the searchers for them in general among the most honoured of their own inmates, go far to substantiate.

Yet, by *a singular Providence*, just enough of them remains to show what their ancient ritual must have been, and to plead touchingly for its restoration. Also, by the flickering glimmer which they supply, we shall at last be able to *convict the reckless Official out of his own mouth and that of his friend.*

One witness may suffice for our purpose now, and, strange to say, it has come down to us intact. It is a short 'Exposition of the Roman Mass,' which, though written in France, Martene sees good cause to date prior to the introduction into France of the Roman liturgy. As it has been carefully described in a former chapter, all that need here be said of it is that it clearly recognises the prayer on which we are now engaged as an epiklesis, assigns it the place given to it by S. Gregory, and makes consecration depend on the action of the Holy Ghost on the elements for which it asks. Paschasius Radbertus, without knowing it, is in striking accord with this Expositor, and thereby, without intending it, exposes his friend. The Official and he became friends, when the Official visited Corbey, where Paschasius was at that time discharging the duties of its exiled abbot, to collate the different copies of the Antiphonary which it contained with his own of Metz. It was immediately after this that Paschasius brought out the first edition of his well-known work on the Eucharist; and in the earlier chapters of that work, which he must have forgotten to revise when he republished it in an enlarged form, he distinctly tells us that the prayer 'Supplices Te rogamus' occurred in the liturgy then used by him, 'where the celebrant began to consecrate'—'cum hæc *incipit immolare.*' Amalarius, in opposition to this, as distinctly tells us that the Canon *commenced* with the paragraph, 'Quam oblationem Tu, Deus,' which he recites entire to prevent any misapprehension. Let us only remove this paragraph, clearly due to him, and put in its place the prayer 'Supplices Te rogamus,' and we shall find the space filled to perfection, not a word too little nor a word too much, leaving everything that precedes and everything that follows unchanged. We bid adieu to the Imperial Official and return to the glorious unearthly conception of the saintly founder of our Anglo-Saxon Church. The Holy Ghost is honoured as the consecrator of the blessed Eucharist in the West again. In His hands the Real Presence presents no difficulty, but is in perfect accordance with Scripture and with nature too; for each of us carries about its explanation in his own personal experiences every day he lives. The stumbling-block occasioned by its perversion is taken out of our way.

And as it is Paschasius who thus, unawares, enables us to put our finger on this audacious patchwork of the Imperial Official in revising S. Gregory, so it is the Imperial Official himself who, no less unawares, enables us to date with precision the birth of the counterfeit work of most importance to Paschasius in upholding it on dogmatic grounds. For Amalarius never fails to quote S. Ambrose for his own conclusions, wherever he possibly can; yet he never once names or refers in any way to the treatise 'De Sacramentis,' which, of all works ever given to S. Ambrose, would have served his purpose best, had it been in existence, when his chapters on the Canon were penned; whereas Paschasius in the latter half of his work, which constituted its second edition, borrows largely from that treatise, though without naming it; and even in his reply to the friendly criticisms of his beloved Frudegard, he will refer to it no further than as a work of S. Ambrose, lest its authenticity should be challenged; though he quotes openly from the homilies of the Emisene Eusebius—the very source from which it was borrowed —in support of its views. But here Ratramn, one of his own monks, comes to our assistance, and explains all, in quoting this treatise deliberately by the title which it now bears, and testifying to its being included in the Corbey MS. he was then using, but utterly repudiating every word in it inconsistent with the teaching of S. Ambrose in his genuine works; even when citing extracts from the very chapters parading in other parts of them the un-Ambrosian views of his abbot.

Proof of all this having been already given, it need not be repeated. What became of Ratramn after this pitiless and scathing exposure of his superior is a question which we had perhaps best not raise. 'Nemo me impune lacessit' is certainly the tone which Paschasius assumes towards his opponents in his commentaries on S. Matthew. But at that time Paschasius had been driven out of Corbey himself, and some think his differences with Ratramn had contributed to his expulsion.[1] Anyhow, Ratramn outlived him; and must have commended himself to Pope Nicholas by writing against the Greeks at his request, A.D. 867. Of his sentiments on the Eucharist, too, Pope Nicholas could not have failed to approve, as he shared them himself. Yet on that subject his was a falling cause; and of his tract nothing more was heard, till it had been given to another author so long that it was universally believed two centuries later to have been by him—namely, by John Scotus—and was condemned as being his work. Nobody doubts now by whom it was written, and the fact authenticated in it which concerns us most is, that it was on the shelves at Corbey that a MS. including the treatise 'De Sacramentis' among the works of S. Ambrose was first discovered in the reign of Charles the Bald—never, till then, known to exist—and then it was dis-

[1] Mabillon, *Prol* c. iv.; ap. Migne, *Pat. Lat.* cxx. 12-16.

credited without loss of time by its discoverer, in a tract addressed to that king, on all the points for which it had already been and is still quoted.

Thus these two conspirators—for we could not in accordance with history designate them by a milder name—not animated, indeed, by heresy, but rather by mere conceit or party cabal, mutually convict each other; Paschasius, by testifying to the difference between his former Canon and the Amalarian, and Amalarius by testifying that when his own work on 'Ecclesiastical Offices' was written, the treatise 'De Sacramentis' quoted for the first time by Paschasius, and attributed by him to S. Ambrose, was not known to exist.

It was this poor and paltry piece, and its prototype the homilies of the Emisene Eusebius on which it was based, that between them guaranteed the reception of the Amalarian Canon, and of the teaching of Paschasius, its exponent, in process of time, by the whole West; though each literally was unknown to the Roman Church till events connected with the Berengarian controversy forced them both upon Rome, the truly Roman Hildebrand being apparently the *last to stand out*, for which he was forthwith traduced as a follower of Berengarius. Yet Berengarius himself, according to the mature judgment of Mabillon, cannot be charged with having denied the Real Presence. And the *Real Presence* it was that, down to the ninth century, was universally taught and upheld in every part of the Church, and the agent of it was as universally believed to be the Holy Ghost invoked by prayer—invoked, however, not only to consecrate the elements set apart solemnly for His action on them, but also to prepare the soul of each intending communicant for incorporation with the Divine body, prepared no less by the Holy Ghost, that was slain for man.

The fact that this catholic and divine teaching, yet so rational, natural, and easy to be explained by reference to the laws of our being in the highest degree, should have been as

SAD RESULTS OF THE NEW TEACHING. 447

completely torn in pieces, obliterated, and scattered to the winds as the venerable liturgies that were built on it, by two Gallican divines of such very moderate pretensions and standing in their own Church and outside their own Church all but unknown, with no sort of authority for their conclusions beyond two or three pseudonymous or heterodox pieces; the fact that these should have proved the means of ejecting the Holy Ghost from the sublime function assigned Him in all previous liturgies at each celebration of the most august of sacraments ordained by Christ, and of fixing on the very words of Christ Himself a meaning and a purpose different from His own in using them—different too from what had been given to them in the liturgies and in the teaching of every Christian Church till then; and, lastly, the fact that for refusing to attribute this wrong meaning and purpose to them, Christians should have been persecuted, tormented, and even burnt alive, within two centuries of its reception in the West—and how much longer, England and all European countries only know too well—these facts, though granting it was all blindly done by men who thought they were doing God service, rather than by men bent on ruining His Church, ought surely to fill us all, who are groaning under the disasters occasioned by it, with burning shame, and set us on active measures for the healing of those divisions which, planned and originated by the powers of evil, and worked out in ignorance by deluded men, would instantly disappear and be forgotten were the disused teaching and ritual of the Catholic Church that preceded them to be simply revived.

It is true that the *fons mali* was imported from the East in this case, but the East extracted its poison before receiving it, and it consequently produced there no noxious fruit. And even in the West it was received at first with like caution, till it was taken up and sown broadcast in France by reckless hands, and cultivated in such sort as to fall in and harmonise with other indigenous productions of the same kind. Anyhow, the mischief is not of our own making, nor of our immediate forefathers either, nor even of our remote forefathers, who took no part in its introduction. Nevertheless, our responsibility will be great if we let it remain; for the position occasioned by it constitutes a libel upon our orthodoxy, and the consequences still emanating from it are soul-destroying and Christianity-paralysing and compromising in the extreme. God forbid that we should be represented as winking at or encouraging heresy by merely succeeding to what has been handed down to us; but the position is too closely bordering on it to be tolerated any longer by those who love their religion. Macedonius, the cruel persecutor of all who opposed his errors in the Eastern capital, had he survived to the middle ages, would have clapped his hands over the blood that was shed by the Greeks and Latins in quarrelling over the interpolated Creed and the Procession of the Holy Ghost, and might have said with some truth that, if the consequences drawn by the Latins from His eternal Procession, as they held it, were correct, those who dogmatised with him could not be far wrong. For, of the practical consequences arising from it, one certainly was, that the Latins had excluded all reference to the action of the Holy Ghost on the oblation in their modern way of consecrating the Eucharist;[1] and of the speculative consequences arising from it, one certainly was that the Latins denied the right of the Holy Ghost to be called 'a principle' except in relation to the creation, which was precisely what his own followers taught.[2]

Eusebius of Emesa next, had he lived on till then, could not have failed to have dilated in his exuberant and

---

[1] When Amalarius revised the Canon, the 'Filioque' was accepted in all the West, except at Rome

[2] 'Spiritus Sanctus non ab æterno principium est, sed *esse cœpit* quia non dicitur principium nisi ad creaturas.'—Magist Sentent lib 1 dist. 29. S Augustine being quoted at starting, it might be thought he had authorised this inference But he goes no further than this, in the passage quoted from him: 'Pater est principium totius divinitatis vel si melius dicitur, Deitatis,' which is Catholic doctrine Further on S. John viii 25 is adduced, but mistranslated in a way which no schoolboy now would repeat.

attractive manner on the triumph achieved by his homilies to that extent in the West, so long after their delivery, that all the Latin doctors had to a man abandoned the ritual and the teaching of the whole Church during the first eight centuries of the Gospel for their teaching.

Finally, the Arians, had they lived on as a body till then, would have gloried over the fact that all the Œcumenical Councils said to have been inspired by the Holy Ghost that had condemned their teaching and legislated for the whole Church, had been abandoned, even in their dogmatic definitions, where claiming to be most perfect, by the Latins, in deference to the pronouncements of a few Court divines of their own—the very class held up to such withering scorn by the great Athanasius—and to a pseudonymous Creed produced by them bearing his name. Then, as for their legislation, that it had been entirely supplanted by a collection of decretals forged by the Latins themselves, but professing to have been issued by the earliest occupants of the Roman see.

These hypothetical reflections, which would have been perfectly natural in those mouths to whom they have been assigned, will bear drawing out still further in their application.

Of Court divines first: for Court divines are by no means an extinct class. Unquestionably Court divines would have constituted Arianism the religion of the whole Church in the fourth century, *had they not been withstood.* At one time Christendom was said to be fighting over an '*i*.' Yet till Liberius became Pope, neither by fraud nor by force could that *iota* be thrust upon those noble spirits, who were ready to lay down their lives sooner than betray the perfect Godhead of Him who had died for man. And Liberius was no sooner gone to his account than his successor, Pope Damasus, at once joined hands with the East in repudiating his act, by not only condemning all the errors of the Macedonians and Semi-Arians who had beguiled him in the most explicit terms, but by revising and enlarging the Creed to the exact form in which it is recited throughout the East still.

Why, then, were the Court divines of Charles the Great and his successors allowed to dictate the insertion of a whole word in the Creed of the Church, while the Court divines of Constantine the Great and his successors were not allowed to dictate the insertion of the single letter '*i*'? Let England and Rome ponder over this contrast, for it concerns them both. Again: why was that change permitted to be argued as though it had been a mere question between the Council of Frankfort and the second Nicene Council; or matter of contention and rivalry between the Greeks and Latins? Can this be denied to be the literal fact; that it was a crowned autocrat, first in Spain, and then in France, who claimed to set *the Son of God right*, in determining the relations of the Divine Persons in the Godhead to each other? Under the *flimsy veil of honouring Him*, they had the audacity to correct what He had revealed; and what, if He had not revealed it, human reason could never have guessed or discovered! Is not this, can it be denied to be, the naked truth, stripped of all its controversial integuments? Oh! the reverent wisdom of the Constantinopolitan Fathers and Pope Damasus, in restricting themselves to the exact words of the Second Person of the Trinity for defining the procession of the Third. Oh! the unerring foresight of the Chalcedonian Council, which defined, in commenting on their Creed, that its teaching on the subject of the Father, Son, and Holy Ghost was 'perfection'—in other words, could not be changed for the better by subtraction, addition, or alteration of any sort: a declaration enhanced by the fact that, on the subject of the Incarnation, no such pronouncement was made. Well might S. Gregory the Great say of the first four Councils after this that he reverenced them as the four Gospels; for if ever anything was ruled infallibly by the Church, it was this dogmatic definition of the Fourth Council which resumed them all. It is too late for a second

Damasus to be produced at Rome, to repudiate the act of Benedict VIII., who betrayed the last of them[1] no less unworthily than Liberius betrayed the first.

How piteous, too, by contrast, the bewilderments of a traditional maze that could lead a noble mind and devotional intellect so far astray as to let S. Thomas think of defending the indefensible, by putting into competition with the words of his Divine Master—can it be that he failed to realise their being His?—the metaphysics of Aristotle, and the 'ordo rerum,' as it appeared to himself; making it '*necessary*' between them, as he judged, that either the Son should proceed from the Holy Ghost, or the Holy Ghost from the Son.[2] And then, against all the rulings of Œcumenical Councils binding upon Christendom, claiming to settle the whole question by an appeal which the real Athanasius would have shrunk from entertaining, had it been made to him.

'Sed contra est, quod dicit Athanasius in symbolo suo: Spiritus Sanctus a Patre et Filio; non factus, nec creatus, nec genitus, sed procedens.'

The Reformation, it has been often said, was brought about by the joint action of Court divines and Crowned heads, and this, as a fact, admits of no dispute; but it is equally certain that the mediæval Church was the work of the Court divines of Charlemagne, and that Rome became the head of it by breaking with antiquity, and substituting for it those three changes in Creed, ritual, and Church government which, for the light which they receive from each other, have been, as it were, thrown into parallel columns here: first, as

---

[1] But for Berno, who seems to have been on the spot at the time, A D 1012, we should not have known that it was his act, or that he did it at the earnest request of his great benefactor, the Emperor Henry II, who was, as M Rohrbacher appositely reminds us, a lineal descendant of Charlemagne. —*E. H* xiii 331.

[2] What he says is '*In Scripturâ sacrâ* non exprimitur,' &c., though he refers to S John xv. *Sum Theol* Part I Quæst xxxvi art 2, with Quæst xxviii art. 4. I shall have to refer presently to his misstatements of history A good edition of the *Summa*, pointing out all these unintentional and unavoidable blots, would be invaluable

regards the authority which dictated them; secondly, the means by which they were brought about; and last, and not least, as being each of them what a Pneumatomachian, or fighter against the Holy Ghost, would consider so much gain to his cause.

It is on the first point connected with these changes that we are still engaged, and may conclude by saying that history, which photographs events as they occur, acquits Rome of having had any hand in *originating* these changes, but attributes them wholly to the founder of the Latin empire and his successors; and in regard of the second point, too, the means by which they were brought about—in other words, by false literature circulated to win acceptance for them —pronounces it to have been the work of their emissaries on the whole. Nevertheless, history testifies as clearly to their having been received one by one, without further inquiry, by Rome during the darkest period of her history, and then defended by her theologians as having been decreed in due form by her authority.[1]

Thus the position to which the Church of Rome was advanced in this way will, historically, compare with the position acquired by the Church of England since the Reformation. For they became both of them established Churches by the same process—one by means of Concordats with Crowned heads, the other by means of Statutes of the Realm: Rome, the established Church of Europe, and England, the established Church of Great Britain and Ireland, and of all countries under British rule. Charlemagne and his successors endowed the Church of Rome; Henry VIII. and his successors the Church of England. But in concessions to the sovereign, those made by Rome were far the most open to exception in principle and disastrous in their effects of the two; for in her case, schism with the East on fundamentals ensued; in that of England a breach, on secondary points only, with the Churches in com-

[1] See the first art already quoted from S. Thomas.

munion with Rome. Let both, accordingly, so far refrain in future from throwing stones at each other, and each only take thought how it may change for the better. England incurred a joint responsibility with Rome for the first schism, from which she has not yet cleared herself entirely, though in setting forth the Procession of the Holy Ghost from the Father and the Son in her fourth Article, the word 'eternal' has been omitted. A contrast is thus established between it and the generation of the Son described in her second Article, where the word 'eternal' is virtually supplied, and one stumbling-block of the first schism has been thereby removed.

As regards the second schism, it was Rome who put the weapon in her hands, which has been wielded by her with so much success.

Meanwhile Providence, that permitted both ruptures, has brought good out of both. The civilisation of the all-important continent of Europe was effected during the one, and constitutional freedom in Church and State for individuals, with a great religious revival for its undoubted product, has been effected in Great Britain during the other. Good men naturally would have desired that all these blessings had been secured in either case without a schism; but let good men everywhere now ask themselves this question honestly: Whose fault it will be *soon* if both schisms are not *soon* healed? For are there not indications in the course which events have taken, and are still taking in so many various ways, that the same Providence not merely suggests, but wills, nay, demands, their healing? One such conspicuous indication meets us in dealing with our next point—namely, the pseudonymous and spurious documents emanating in the ninth century from France, and on which all the Gallicanism of the ninth century was, and is still, based. How slowly, but surely, they have been one by one stripped of their sheep's-clothing and exposed! The stripping process commenced at the Reformation, but it was by no means confined to the Reformers. The good men of all schools worked at it, and are still working at it; yet who can say no more remains to be laid bare? For it takes some time, naturally, to complete the proofs of a forgery, and a still longer time for those proofs to be generally received, and longer still for the conclusions which have been built on it to be given up or swept away. Yet falsehood, even when its real character is unsuspected, works mischief in the mind, and its effects are doubly baneful where it is not abandoned after sufficient exposure. Insensibly they tell upon character, and indifference to truth on every subject soon becomes habitual by remissness on one. Again, stolen goods may be acquired honestly by persons ignorant of the means by which their vendors became possessed of them; but as soon as the theft has been legally proved, the purchaser cannot detain them, when the minister of justice or the director of conscience decides that restitution of them is to be made, though it may be that the rightful owner is also directed to return part of what the purchaser had acquired honestly with his own money, never dreaming that it had been stolen from another. Yet nobody can retain with a good conscience what he finds to have been unlawfully taken from another by fraud or force. It is not enough, therefore, that false pieces should be disowned; the mischief created by them must be, so far as can be, summarily stopped and prevented from ever again recurring. When the amended edition of Gratian was brought out, A.D. 1582, with the sanction of Pope Gregory XIII. prefixed to it, the spuriousness of the False Decretals had not been proved. Nobody doubts it now. Those False Decretals are cited in absolute ignorance of their fictitious character by Gratian as first-class authorities at least 54 times in his first part, 279 times in his second part, and 29 times in his third part—the part which concerns us most here—making a total of 362 times in all from the Pseudo-Isidorian collection alone. And there are numerous other references in his work to documents just as confessedly false.

Now, their continued presence must by its very juxtaposition discredit every genuine canon of the Church that is found in such company, cited either to explain or bear out their contents. The Roman communion could not fail to rise many degrees in public estimation if, by a formal act of its authorities, every false piece found in Gratian were relegated to an appendix specially prepared for such, as in the Benedictine editions of the Fathers.

But, as is well known to canon-law students, the third part of the 'Decretum' deals specially with 'Consecration.' Here correction is urgently needed in the interests of a much larger class than canon-law students; and here, too, notice should not fail to be taken of its omissions, which, though possibly just as unavoidable by its compiler as its commissions, have been ten times more disastrous in their effects. For of the forty-two Fathers and approved writers in every part of the Church down to the beginning of the ninth century, quoted at great length in my fourth chapter, attributing consecration of the Eucharistic oblation to the action of the Holy Ghost invoked by prayer, forty-one are passed over as though they had never lived or written, and but one passage to that effect, deprived of half its force by being incidental in form, is given from S. Augustine; while, for the view superseding it, Paschasius in the ninth century, with Lanfranc in the eleventh, are the only real vouchers, and even from them passages are quoted in support of *their view* now and then, not in their own names, but under that of S. Augustine. All the rest are spurious or alien pieces, from Eusebius of Emesa, the Semi-Arian, or from the pseudo-Ambrose. Supposing them all genuine, what would be their weight in comparison of that of the great phalanx of standard authorities passed over in silence? Practically, without intending it the least, Gratian may be said to have buried alive forty-one Fathers of the universal Church on this point.

Still, even so, the mischief would have been comparatively

trifling if it had stopped with him; but other illustrious writers, never having seen his errors corrected, have reproduced them unawares. They were passed on from Peter Lombard to the Schoolmen, and from the Schoolmen to the Council of Trent and its Catechism. The absence of any special prayer for the action of the Holy Ghost in the mediæval Canon of the Western liturgy no doubt caused the teaching of the Catholic Church on that point to be wholly forgotten. Peter Lombard quotes passages from S. Augustine containing it, without heeding their import. Neither in the decrees or canons of the Council of Trent, nor in its Catechism, is a single passage containing it quoted at all. In the second part of the Catechism which treats of the sacraments, we have, besides constant reference to the authorities quoted by Gratian, no less than forty-seven distinct appeals to spurious, pseudonymous, or even sectarian works: in particular, for the *institution of the Eucharist*, as was observed in a former chapter, we are referred to the homilies of Eusebius of Emesa, the Semi-Arian, by name![1]

Never was a *consensus Patrum* on any point more complete, never was it set aside more completely, nor in more complete ignorance. This is now the third point affecting the prerogatives of the Holy Ghost on which the Roman Church has, in deference to the fiat of two or three Gallican divines of the ninth century, broken, not only with the teaching of the universal Church of every preceding age, but with her own greatest Popes—S. Leo, S. Gelasius, and S. Gregory, to name no more—whose writings bespeak their unreserved agreement with the teaching of the Church of their day. Of all the breaches with antiquity, this was the most flagrant, and wears the worst appearance. For, as to the Creed, there were some Fathers who thought the eternal Procession of the Holy Ghost from the Son as well as from the Father deducible from Scripture; and as to the canons, we find many maxims scattered up and down the False Decretals

[1] Part II c. 4, § 3.

by no means at variance with canons which everybody respects. But on the Eucharist the teaching of the primitive Church was by those Gallican divines of the ninth century quite reversed. For they not only caused all reference to the action of the Holy Ghost to be expunged from all the liturgies allowed in the West, but the teaching of the Fathers on that point to be buried in oblivion, that it might not clash with their own. Further, they put a meaning upon certain words of our Lord, in which it is a simple fact that they were not used by Him, nor understood in any part of the Church at large before their time. Nevertheless, on both points the ritual and the teaching, which, aided by the civil power they imposed upon France, gradually, by means of the false documents circulated in its support, became the ritual and teaching of the whole West—everybody believing its credentials to be beyond suspicion. But the consequences of taking poison are the same whether taken in ignorance or with design, and we may well ask whether this abandonment of any reference to the action of the Holy Ghost in the liturgy may not have led to a corresponding lack in the Tridentine decrees and canons on Justification of any recognition of His special prerogatives as the 'Sanctifier.' For it was the teaching of the universal Church for at least eight centuries that the Holy Ghost came down from heaven to be the dispenser of all the benefits of the Incarnation to be had in the Church at large, and to apply them, through the sacraments, to each individual soul desiring them. S. Paul expounds this teaching at great length in his first Epistle to the Corinthians. How comes it, then, that in the tenth and eleventh chapters of the Council of Trent on Justification, treating of its increase, and of keeping the commandments, the Holy Ghost is not so much as named, nor in other chapters ever more than incidentally mentioned? Cardinal Newman, in his 'Lectures on Justification,' published as an Anglican, was evidently conscious of this deficiency, and therefore devotes three whole lectures to the indwelling of the

Holy Ghost in each of us and its effects.[1] Cardinal Manning might be thought from his book on the 'Temporal Mission of the Holy Ghost,' first published in 1865, to have advanced considerably further; but it is in reality confined to one branch of a subject greatly needing discussion as a whole. He has, however, given it a title.

No doubt the beautiful hymns 'Veni, Creator Spiritus' and 'Veni, Sancte Spiritus' were both composed by members of the Latin Church, and of these the first is sung at ordinations in the Roman and Anglican Churches alike, and in the Anglican at confirmations too. Still it is on the work of the Holy Ghost in the heart that both hymns enlarge so sweetly, neither touch on His work in the sacraments. Again, a beautiful litany will be found in Roman Catholic books of private devotion, addressed to the Holy Ghost, and appealing to Him as One ' by whom we are born again, who dwellest in us, who governest the whole Church.' Here there is a reference to the sacrament of baptism, but to that sacrament alone, where there were six more that might have been named. Adam of S. Victor, canon of Paris, sang of the Holy Ghost, unrebuked, in the twelfth century: 'Tu commutas elementa; Per Te suam sacramenta Habent efficaciam.'[2] But his was a 'Vox clamantis in deserto'—nobody responded to it; he had not, probably, the luck to be known to S. Anselm.

I have asked myself the question why Providence should have permitted the eyes of so many generations of good men in the West to be so ' holden ' as to have mistaken the teaching of those ninth-century divines in France for that of the Church of all previous ages and lands; Eusebius of Emesa for some Gallican saint, and the counterfeit Ambrose for the spiritual father of S. Augustine? Too quick by half to be my own the answer came: namely, that Providence—for reasons analogous to those which dictated a similar course to be pursued under the elder dispensation—*winked*, as S. Paul expresses it, 'at the times of this ignorance, but now com-

[1] Lect vi.–viii. [2] Daniel, ii. 73.

mandeth all men everywhere to repent'; in other words, to abandon all the errors from which 'the veil spread over all nations' has been removed. For its removal has been the act, not of man, but of Providence—an act which has preserved to us the declarations of so many venerable Fathers intact, and placed them as it were side by side with the venerable fragments of liturgies used in their day, testifying to the ritual on which their teaching was based, and then finally caused breath to enter into the 'dry bones' of a glorious race that one hundred years ago was believed extinct, but whose very language can never, till all the books of the New Testament written in it have been obliterated, cease to be studied, and whose living representatives, some rescued from bondage, others a perfectly new race, 'standing upon their feet, an exceeding great army,' protest in a voice that waxes louder and louder every day—and, as truth must always, will insist on being heard at last—that through all the vicissitudes of degradation, and oppression, and shame endured by their ancestors, they never have deviated one iota from the Creed, the Ritual, and the genuine Canons, believed, handed down, and held to be binding on the whole Church till a Latin empire was set up in France, which succeeded on false pretences in Gallicanising the whole West to this very day—claiming for their Church the right to apply to herself those magnificent words of their grandest orator and noblest patriot, $\Delta\iota\grave{\alpha}$ $\tau\alpha\hat{\upsilon}\tau'$ $\dot{\alpha}\xi\iota\hat{\omega}$ $\tau\iota\mu\hat{\alpha}\sigma\theta\alpha\iota$,[1] and moreover adding, that it is the voice of God.

Yes! it is not merely the Greek Church that demands reparation at our hands for the savage treatment it received from our Crusaders, denounced at the time by the reigning pontiff, Innocent III. himself,[2] and which eventually proved

---

[1] Demosth *De Coronâ*, circa fin

[2] 'You were forbidden,' he says, '*under pain of excommunication* to meddle with any territory belonging to Christians .. and you, apparently without having the smallest power or jurisdiction of any kind over the Greeks, have departed from the integrity of your vows, and waged war, not against Saracens, but against Christians; instead of recovering Jerusalem,

the means of handing over the fairest heirloom of the first Christian emperor—the capital called after him—to the Turk; but it is also God, in the person of the Holy Ghost, who demands the restitution of all the honour taken from Him surreptitiously more than 1,000 years ago, but which, being thus 'compassed about with so great a cloud of witnesses' to His prerogatives, we can no longer withhold from Him without sin.

Further, the same Providence that arranged for the preservation and accumulation of this unexpected array of witnesses to forgotten truth—demolishing error and falsehood in the same breath—has held them, nevertheless, in reserve till the moment most favourable to their production. The Oxford movement, as it was preceded by the Evangelical or Cambridge movement—which it might, perhaps, more fitly be called, from the widespread vitality conferred on it by the trustees of the late Rev. C. Simeon—so, when it collapsed, it was followed after a time by a double recoil: one generating a revival of the onslaught upon Christianity by the Deistical writers of the last century, but with keener weapons, and with enhanced bitterness, happily with no worse results as yet than that of confirming every reasonable man in his belief of the historic unassailableness of its credentials, and of the entire reasonableness of its supernatural claims; the other originating in the great, but prematurely cut short, work on the Eastern Church by the late Dr. Neale, than whom there never was a more learned or indefatigable, truthful, or conscientious Church historian, or *anybody* to whom Christendom, should it ever be reunited again, will owe more; for it was he who recalled attention at a very critical time from Rome to the condition of the Eastern Churches, and disclosed treasures in each that had

you have seized on Constantinople' Letter to the Marquis of Montferrat, on learning the news 'It never recovered the blow it received at the hands of the Latins,' says Mr. Hallam, *Middle Ages*, c vi. vol ii. 178–87; Mr. Finlay, *Byzant Emp.* ii 443, gives their atrocities in full detail.

never been brought into sunlight before. So far as controversy was concerned, indeed, the Rev. W. Palmer, Fellow of Magdalen College, Oxford, had in his masterly 'Dissertations on the Orthodox Communion' abundantly cleared the ground; but, till Dr. Neale brought out his book, English readers in general had no definite conception whatever of the area now in these days covered by that communion, its aggregate numbers, and their devotion to it; the existing dioceses of its still defined patriarchates; its modern ritual and various Office-books; the liturgy, that, like the Roman in the West, has supplanted all others—still, indeed, preserved as relics, but which are no longer used—its beautiful hymns, its canonical discipline, its history, with the literature that has grown up in it, since the schism. Dr. Neale was ably and dutifully seconded during his lifetime by Dr. Littledale, to whom, at his removal to a better world in 1866, he bequeathed the mantle that has since been worthily worn by him. Outside the limits of the Orthodox communion his labours have been likewise supplemented by Messrs. Badger, Denton, Malan, and quite recently by Mr. A. J. Butler, and others, to whom carefully-written accounts of the condition, past and present, of the Nestorian, Bulgarian, Coptic, Gregorian, Armenian, and Maronite communions are due, all serving to direct special attention to the East; so that, had not the Ritualistic school, which he was instrumental in forming at home, caused a diversion after his death by occupying themselves mainly with the ancient, though not strictly primitive, liturgies of this country, the appeal which it has fallen to my lot to make would have been doubtless anticipated, and in all probability by this time successful, as regards England; though, perhaps, in that case the Gallican origin of the liturgy now common to all Churches in communion with Rome might never have been brought to light, nor confronted with the general revision by S. Gregory the Great, which it has so long superseded. Further, it is just possible that both this fact and the appeal founded on it may now receive calmer and fuller consideration from those whom it concerns most than would have been accorded to it some years ago, from the marked interest and steadily-growing respect exhibited on the Continent for the work of Dr. Neale, to whom, more than anyone else, Dr Hoppe confessed his obligations in 1864 for his own special work on the ' Epiklesis'; but nine years earlier, Dr. Daniel, in bringing out the completion of his own learned work on liturgies generally—since then become standard with all—wrote thus of him, in quoting him at full length as a guide for all others in reference to the liturgies of the East:—

'At perspicuitate et evidentiâ ea liturgiarum dispositio, quam doctissimis operibus suasit nobis J. M. Neale: rerum sacrarum Orientalium hâc nostrâ ætate longe peritissimus: quem doctorem veneror et amicum.'[1] Such words are best appreciated untranslated.

Lastly, can any true lover of Christ hesitate or fail to perceive the course so plainly marked out by Providence for us to pursue, when that which is precisely the most palpable and least defensible change affecting the prerogatives of the Holy Ghost, inaugurated by fraud and coercion in the first instance, and then handed on in complete misapprehension from generation to generation in the Roman and Anglican communions alike, turns out to be the speediest and easiest healed in both—by each in its own way, yet by both in a way calculated not only to bring them together again in love, but to restore peace between them and the East and

---

[1] *Cod. Liturg* iv 35 In painful contrast to this the following, which is only too true, was penned on the day of his funeral, August 4, 1866 It appeared in the *John Bull* —

'So was buried John Mason Neale, one of the profoundest scholars amongst the English clergy He was not a D D of his own University of Cambridge, and, like John Keble, he was unrecognised by Church authorities and State officials He lived and died warden of a seventeenth-century almshouse, value 27l a year His name was known in Russia, in Greece, in Germany, in America, at Rome. Foreigners sought his correspondence, Orientals and Occidentals valued his profound learning. The Church of England has mightily benefited by his teaching, yet found no preferment for him But now he is in peace'

harmony with the saints in bliss? For on the part of the Church of Rome the restoration of a single prayer, word for word as it is printed now, to the place destined for it by S. Gregory when he recast it, is alone wanted to make the canon of her liturgy breathe the teaching of the whole Church in his day once more; while the Church of England, by simply going back to the first Prayer Book authorised in modern times for public use by the whole realm, would find herself using a Communion Office which the founder of the Anglo-Saxon Church, agreeably with his own instructions to her first Archbishop of Canterbury, could not have failed to approve. And then the Holy Ghost, invoked once more by both, as in the East by all, to bring Christ to us and us to Him, would soon open the hearts of all towards each other and inspire them with a burning desire for intercommunion with each other such as has never been felt hitherto since divisions commenced, and such as would speedily cause them to disperse like smoke. For divisions, *history tells us*, never became permanent in the Church of Christ till the high functions, attributed by the primitive Church to the Holy Ghost in consecrating and administering the sacraments ordained by Christ, as His Vicar under the Gospel, for communicating all the fruits of His Incarnation to each soul in every age redeemed by His death, had been transferred in the West to man. *Ego* 'baptizo te,' 'confirmo te,' 'absolvo te'[1]—such was the language from that time put into the mouth of man in the West till now—language which to this day has never been used by any but sectarians in the East.[2] Accordingly, from that time the word

---

[1] Martene, *De Ant Eccl Rit* lib 1 c. 1, art 14, and c 2, art 4; and c 6, art. 5 It is quite possible that the departure from the Greek 'cred*imus*' in the Creed to 'cred*o*' by the Latins in much earlier days may have suggested the *first person* in these cases also

[2] *Dict of Christian Biog* 1. 162, § 55 where the Copts, the Nestorians, and Æthiopians are credited with it, but even in their case we may safely assume that its adoption was the work of a Latiniser Mr. Butler, in his learned work on *Ancient Coptic Churches*, quotes a ritual of Severus, Patriarch of Alexandria, A D 646, showing that

'*spiritual*' wholly disappeared—except on a few special occasions, where relics of the old form are still preserved—from every part of the liturgy now binding on all Churches in communion with Rome. From that time the Real Presence too—which only the action of the Holy Ghost can explain in a way that every Christian can understand—has been denied by numbers in the West, proved a stumbling-block to more, and bred such degrading and interminable controversies as no pious Christian can contemplate without equal pain and shame. The Master of the Sentences himself meekly confessed in his day, on reaching the question 'De modis conversionis,' that he was all at sea, powerless to decide which way to turn.[1]

No such controversies ever stirred the primitive Church; no such controversies ever stirred the Greek Church; no such controversies, we may therefore reasonably conclude, would have stirred the Western Church had Eucharistic consecration, such as it was in primitive times, never been abandoned for the form now in use. Not a single Father can be quoted in support of the existing rituals either of England or Rome. S. Chrysostom, the only Father from any portion of whose genuine writings the least countenance for them can be produced, even he protests in a voice of thunder against vesting Eucharistic consecration in him who merely ministers at the altar. Our existing rituals put the Holy Ghost on one side. Now, had this been our own act, it would have been a direct affront done to Him on our part. But even *for unintentional affronts* men ask pardon of each other on earth: nor would it be considered good breeding in any made conscious of them to fail in this respect. Again, the Churches of England and Rome are both pledged in their formularies to be guided by a *consensus Patrum* in interpreting Holy Scripture wherever

the formula then in use was that of the Orthodox Church still (vol. ii 271), and adds in the next page that 'at the present day the ceremonies do not appreciably differ from those recorded by Severus.'

[1] *Sent.* iv. dist. 11, § 1

they can be proved unanimous.[1] What answer, therefore, will they make to the concurrent voices of all the Fathers and Divines—whose *ipsissima verba*, culled from their genuine writings, have been faithfully reproduced in these pages that they may be heard on this point—to S. Justin Martyr and S. Irenæus; to Tertullian and Origen; to S. Firmilian and S. Cyprian; to S. Cyril of Jerusalem and S. Ephrem; to the Greek Jerome and the Alexandrian Eusebius; to Peter, the successor of S. Athanasius, and S. Theophilus, the next but one bishop after him of the same see of Alexandria; to S. Isidore of Pelusium and S. Nilus, both pupils of S. Chrysostom, though subsequently resident in Egypt, showing that the teaching of both sees on this point was the same; to Didymus, appointed catechist of Alexandria by S. Athanasius; to S. Optatus, S. Augustine, and S. Fulgentius in North Africa; to S. Isidore and S. Ildefonse in Spain; to S. Agobard, Theodulph, and Alcuin in France; to Venerable Bede in this country; to S. Gregory the Great and his predecessors Vigilius, Agapetus, Gelasius, S. Leo, and Innocent I., bishops of Rome; to S. Ambrose, S. Gaudentius, and Maxentius in North Italy; to S. Jerome both at Bethlehem, Constantinople and Rome, and in Dal-

---

[1] Session IV of the Council of Trent: 'It decrees that no one shall in matters of faith and of morals pertaining to the edification of Christian doctrine presume to interpret Holy Scripture contrary to that which Holy Mother Church, whose it is to judge of the true sense and interpretation of the Holy Scriptures, hath held and doth hold, or even contrary to the *unanimous consent of the Fathers*, even though such interpretations were never intended to be at any time published.'

Bulla Pii IV super Formâ Juramenti Professionis Fidei 'Item sacram Scripturam juxta eum sensum quem tenuit et tenet sancta mater ecclesia, cujus est judicare de vero sensu et interpretatione sacrarum Scripturarum, admitto nec eam unquam, *nisi juxta unanimem consensum Patrum*, accipiam et interpretabor'

With us the golden rule of S. Vincentius of Lerins, which is, however, merely that of S Irenæus, Tertullian, and S Augustine, epitomised—'Quod semper, quod ubique, quod ab omnibus'—finds expression in some form or other, and cordial acceptance in all the works of our standard divines, forty-two of whom—just the number of Fathers quoted for 'primitive consecration' by me—may be read thereon in No 78 of *The Tracts of the Times*, emanating from Oxford in 1840. Comp Dr Pusey's Sermon on 'The Rule of Faith' (Oxford, 1878)

matia; to S. Basil, S. Gregory Nyssen, and Theodore in different parts of Asia Minor; to Theodoret in Syria; to Leontius of Byzantium and Anastasius of Mount Sinai; then, last, but not least, to S. Chrysostom and his amanuensis, S. Proclus, at Antioch and Constantinople—with whom we could not without gross injustice and hypocrisy refuse to admit the living witness of the fifty or sixty millions of orthodox Christians in the Russian and Eastern Churches to be still in entire, faithful, and loyal accord, their fundamental principle from the first and till now being what Hooker has long since translated for his English readers, though the tradition of its application to the incorporation of the souls of all faithful believers in Christ with the body that was offered on the cross for man, having been lost in his day, is nowhere noticed by him in connection with the dogma which he commends to our acceptance—namely, that 'Life and all other gifts and benefits, growing originally from the Father, come not to us but by the Son, nor by the Son to any of us in particular but through the Spirit'?[1]

They testified to its most august, most catholic, application when they taught that the descent of the Holy Ghost had from Apostolic times been invoked on the Eucharistic oblation by the Church to effect what Christ, in words that have not been recorded, effected by His acts of blessing and giving thanks over it at its institution. Hence some said with S. Justin that the oblation was eucharised by Him; others with S. Cyril of Alexandria that it was eulogised by Him; the majority that it was sanctified or consecrated by Him. All meant the same thing; all agreed that, after consecration by Him, what was distributed to all comers was precisely what Christ had distributed Himself to His Apostles—the Holy Ghost being also charged with its administration. Thus the doctrine that Christ was really given and received in the Eucharist was universal, and never doubted or disputed in any part of the Church as long as the descent of the blessed Paraclete was invoked in

[1] See above, p 5.

prayer, both to make Christ present in His sacrament to His faithful people, and to prepare their hearts for His reception. As long as the Holy Ghost was considered 'Official' of the union then effected between Him and them, it needed neither argument nor explanation, for it explained itself; being strictly paralleled by the union already subsisting between their own souls and their own bodies in each adult. For it was a process by which His sacred body was brought into communion, whole and entire, with each individual soul, conveying to it all the manifold benefits which that body, sacrificed on the cross, purchased for all mankind, and all those purifying and quickening influences, in addition, to be derived from contact with a body that had never known sin. Contact with their own mortal bodies was a savour of death unto death in each case; contact with His glorified body was a savour of life unto life unto all. From first to last the idea thus presented to the mind was spiritual, inspiring, and intelligible to the meanest understanding.

On what conceivable ground, then, I am entitled to ask in their name, could either England or Rome decline to quit a ritual and teaching introduced by a few Gallican divines in the darkest ages, for which not a single Father can be quoted, nor any writings earlier than their own, except such as avow themselves to have proceeded from a semi-Arian pen, or can be proved to have been circulated under false names, and to return to the undoubted ritual and teaching of the whole Church down to the ninth century, which the Roman Church herself for two centuries longer upheld? As she was clearly the last to abandon it, and abandoned it under pressure, in God's name let her be the first to set the example of going back to it: seeing especially that everything will remain in her Missal as before, save only that a beautiful prayer will be restored to its proper place, and be given the true meaning which it was intended to bear when it was inserted there. Surely Rome will not be deterred from adopting a course so simple lest it should be interpreted as a concession made to the Church of Constantinople. For was not this very charge brought against S. Gregory? 'Talk of his keeping the Church of Constantinople within bounds, *when he makes her customs his model in all things.*'[1] His noble reply to it would be found just as convincing as it was then. But, further, let me submit respectfully that again traces of an over-ruling Providence manifest themselves too visibly to be denied, when attention has been once drawn thereto. The Roman Church, in spite of all that has happened to her during the Middle Ages, has retained *just enough* of the old Catholic form to prevent her being unreservedly committed to the new. Let me point out—not as a controversialist, but—solemnly, for grave consideration by her authorities, the marked difference which exists between the words of the first and third chapters of the Council of Trent on the Eucharist and the Catechism professing to be their exponent. They will be best shown in parallel columns:—

Chapter I. says:—	The Catechism says curtly:—
'All our forefathers, as many as were in the true Church of Christ who have treated of this most Holy Sacrament, have most openly professed that our Redeemer instituted this so admirable a Sacrament at the last supper, when, *after the blessing of the bread and wine*, He testified in express and clear words that He gave them His own very Body and His own Blood—words which recorded by the Holy Evangelists, and afterwards repeated by S. Paul, whereas they carry with them that proper and most manifest meaning in which they were understood by the Fathers, it is indeed a crime the most unworthy that they should be wrested by certain con-	'A sanctis Evangelistis Matthæo et Luca, itemque ab Apostolo docemur, *illam esse formam*: "Hoc est Corpus Meum." Scriptum est enim: "Cœnantibus illis, accepit Jesus panem, et benedixit, et fregit, deditque discipulis suis: et dixit: Accipite et manducate: Hoc es corpus Meum." Quæ quidem consecrationis forma, cum a Christo Domino servata est, ea perpetuo Catholica Ecclesia usa est.' It adds that passages from the Fathers supporting this view could not be numbered, and refers to chap. i. of the Council of Trent, given on the other side. Consecration of the wine follows, § 21, where the words of our Lord relating to it are given. In neither

[1] *Ep.* lib ix 12.

tentious and wicked men to fictitious and imaginary tropes, whereby the verity of the flesh and blood of Christ is denied, contrary to the universal sense of the Church.'

Chapter III. adds:—

'This faith has ever been in the Church of God, that *immediately after consecration*, the veritable body of our Lord and His veritable blood, together with His soul and Divinity, are under the species of bread and wine: the body under the species of bread, and the blood under the species of wine, *by force of the words*. . . .'[1] viz. the words spoken by our Lord in distributing each kind, in the manner just described.

case are the citations of His words by the Catechism identic with those cited by the Council.[2]

The statement of the Catechism could hardly be more pronounced than it is.

'We are taught,' it says, ' by the Evangelists S. Matthew and S. Luke, and also by the Apostle S. Paul, that the form is as follows: " This is My body "'; that is to say, consecration of the contents of the paten takes place when those words have been pronounced over them by the celebrant. Such has unquestionably been long since the received teaching of the Church of Rome. But this is as unquestionably *not* the teaching of the first chapter of the Council of Trent, to which the Catechism refers us; for there consecration is supposed *to have been effected* by the previous act of our Lord in ' blessing the bread and wine.' *After* having done this, He 'testified' that what He distributed was 'really' what He called it in each case. This is primitive doctrine ; this interprets those words subsequently spoken by our Lord in strict accordance with the primitive Church by making them a formula for distribution, *not* consecration. This is

---

[1] Sess. XIII. Waterworth's Tr.   [2] Part II. c. 4, § 20–21.

the doctrine which is still affirmed in the Roman Church every time presbyters are ordained. Their ordination service closes in the Gelasian Sacramentary with this benediction: [1] —

'Do Thou, Lord, upon these Thy servants, whom we dedicate to the honour of the presbytership, bestow the hand of Thy benediction severally, that they may preserve the gift of Thy ministry pure and undefiled, and through the suffrages of Thy people may, by the immaculate benediction of Thy Son, transform His body and blood '—in the sacrament, that is.

The Latin text has been already given of this striking passage and its relevancy commented upon in part.[2] Some further details may be filled in here. Though we possess no copies of the Gelasian and Gregorian Sacramentaries as yet older than the ninth century, we find some things in both that proclaim their own date. Gelasius became Pope A.D. 492. His predecessor Celestine, to whose zealous cooperation with S. Cyril of Alexandria the third General Council held at Ephesus was due, died A.D. 432. But the crowning letter of S. Cyril which settled everything there was, twenty years later, incorporated together with the no less famous letter of S. Leo, bishop of Rome, to Flavian into the definition of the Council of Chalcedon, thereby conferring upon it œcumenical celebrity. As such it was translated in the old Latin version of canons, revised by Dionysius Exiguus, just about the time when Gelasius became Pope; and the translation in both versions of this letter which concerns us here will be found identic—viz. *ad mysticas benedictiones*—being the phrase by which S. Cyril designated the prayer invoking the descent of the Holy Ghost used in his Church, and then held to supply what was effected by our Lord Himself in blessing the bread and wine.

There can be little doubt, therefore, that it was from

[1] Muratori, *Lit. Rom.* i. 514.   [2] Above, p 87-9.

this phrase of his that the formula first found in the Gelasian Sacramentary was copied, though S. Leo might just as well be credited with having appended it to the Ordinal as S. Gelasius. This venerable relic, therefore, still binds the Church of Rome to the old ritual, and, further, by making 'the suffrages of the people' form part of it, she not merely perpetuates the Alexandrian type, but that of Jerusalem in addition; for it is S. Cyril of Jerusalem who tells us that the people joined in the invocatory prayer by their 'Amens.'

But, again, the Council of Trent in its third chapter calls the Eucharist 'the spiritual food of souls,' which is another point in favour of my contention. Lest, however, the construction which I have put upon these chapters, and the contrast pointed out between them and the Catechism professing to be their exponent on this, as on other subjects, should be disputed, I have reserved a decisive testimony to bear me out, and it is that of an old Oxford man, or rather of Oxford's second founder—Robert Pullen, first English cardinal of the Roman Church and its chancellor under three successive Popes—whose common sense revolted at using the recorded words of our Lord in a sense and for a purpose different from what had been intended by Him, though all traces of the primitive ritual had disappeared when he wrote for the edification of S. Bernard, Gratian, and Eugenius, his juniors in the twelfth century, all of whom came to him for instruction. 'The Lord, by the *power of His benediction*, both by Himself and by His servants, converts bread into His body and wine into His blood . . . and as, prior to His benediction, it was bread, so, *subsequently to His benediction*, He pronounced it His body.'[1] Thus these three chapters of the Council of Trent alone prove to demonstration that on the subject of consecration the Roman Church has not yet irremediably broken with the primitive Church. When the breach can be repaired at so little cost, will she hesitate to mend it? There is a

[1] *Sent* viii. 5; ap. Migne, *Pat. Lat.* clxxxvi. 965-6.

homely proverb of this country which says '*One stitch* in time saves nine'; and it is but *one* stitch that is wanting in this case.

The Church of England would have fewer difficulties probably to face than the Roman in making that change which would render to the Holy Ghost His due; for her first Book of Common Prayer contains a Communion Office ready to hand which is in full accord with antiquity both on that subject and on all others. Of none of the ancient liturgies, with their numberless *accretions*, could the same be said; of all existing liturgies, as its own loyal children in Episcopal Scotland and the United States would be the first to admit, it is *facile princeps* without addition or subtraction; and of living men who could draw up another less open to question? For, though hoary with age, no changes, except possibly that of spelling, would be required in it previously to the re-adoption of that entire book for public use. The consent of the whole realm having been given to it in due form at its first publication, it would scarcely need to be taken through all these formalities a second time. Legal sanction for its use, subject to the control of the bishop in churches petitioning for it, so that it might in no case be forced on unwilling or numerously dissenting congregations, might be had by the mere insertion of a permissive clause to that effect in the Act of 35 & 36 Vict. c. 35 for shortened services—under which head its own morning and evening services might claim to be included—in its favour.

Further than this, I would not for many reasons be understood to press for the present. Things that have long been disused must first have their prescriptive title made good, and not be precipitately or peremptorily brought back, or they will be thought innovations, and treated as such. Again, our present communion office is so thoroughly Scriptural, that none who profess themselves satisfied with it, and unable to go beyond the limits so carefully traced in its ritual, should be disturbed in its use.

Nevertheless, in commending and respecting their stedfastness, it may be permitted to me to submit in turn for their favourable consideration, on behalf of a change demanded imperatively from us all on higher grounds than that of mere ritual, and certain to be welcomed by numbers amongst us on every ground, two remarkable testimonies to its intrinsic merits, of which they could scarce fail to approve, delivered in times, too, more keenly critical and revolutionary than our own. First, Bishop Taylor—Jeremy Taylor is the name by which he is best known—not the least learned, but the most deservedly popular of our standard divines, compiled, during the Commonwealth, when the public use of the English Book of Common Prayer was interdicted, what he called 'an Office for the Administration of the Holy Sacrament of the Lord's Supper, according to the way of Apostolical Churches, and the doctrine of the Church of England,' and published for use in private houses. In this, his prayer of consecration runs as follows:—

'Have mercy upon us, O heavenly Father, according to Thy glorious mercies and promises, send Thy Holy Ghost upon our hearts, and let Him also descend upon these gifts: that by His good, holy, and precious presence, He may sanctify and enlighten our hearts, and may bless and sanctify these gifts, that this bread may become the holy body of Christ. Amen.

'And that this chalice may become the life-giving blood of Christ. Amen. That it may become unto us all that partake of it this day a blessed instrument of union with Christ, of pardon and peace, of health and blessing, of holiness and life eternal, through Jesus Christ our Lord.'[1]

This is a paraphrase from the Greek liturgies—not, however, as we have them now, but as they stood in the days of the two Cyrils of Jerusalem and Alexandria, before the words of institution had come to form part of them, and

[1] *Works*, xv. 300-1, ed. Heber.

when by the word '*make*' was meant *not change* the outer, but, under cover of it, supply the inner part of the sacrament —as is shown to demonstration by what was inserted long afterwards in a subsequent clause.[1]

Jeremy Taylor says of this office, that it is 'according to the way of the Apostolical Churches, and the doctrine of the Church of England,' in recommending it for use, when Holy Communion according to our present Office might not be had; and such is its consecration-prayer, one which he must therefore be understood to have placed at least on a par with our own. That of the first Prayer Book of Edward VI., though identic in principle, is not half so full.

What Jeremy Taylor is to most members of the Church of England, Calvin is to most professing Christians outside the Church of England amongst our countrymen. Calvin composed no such office for his followers. He simply went as far from the Roman Mass of his day as he could. But in his teaching on this subject, which was unreservedly that of the Fathers and of the primitive Church, he has bequeathed us the strongest testimony that we could desire to the 'apostolical' character of the consecration-prayer approved by the learned Bishop of Down and Connor. 'Our *souls*,' said Calvin, 'are fed by the flesh and blood of Christ just as our bodily life is maintained in health and vigour by bread and wine. For our souls must find their aliment in Christ, or the analogy of the sign will not hold: nor can this be, except Christ *really becomes one with us*, and refreshes us with His flesh as meat, and His blood as drink. And, although it may seem incredible that the flesh of Christ locally so far off can penetrate to us to be our food, let us remember how vastly the hidden power of the Holy Spirit transcends our senses: and how foolish it would be to subject His immensity to our rule. Let faith accordingly grasp what our mind cannot comprehend, that a *real union* between things locally parted is effected by the Spirit. And

---

[1] Μεταβαλὼν τῷ Πνεύματί Σου τῷ Ἁγίῳ See above, p 193

so, that sacred communication of His own flesh and blood by which He transmits His life to us, as though intused into our very bones and marrow, Christ both testifies and guarantees to us in His supper, and that not by a vain object or empty sign, but by evoking the action of His Spirit there, to make good His promise.'[1]

Calvin was oppressed by the act of carnal manducation, and had not realised the analogy between the union of the soul with Christ through union with His body, and the union of the soul with its own body. When he calls Christ 'the *spiritual* aliment of *souls*' in the Eucharist, he is at one literally with the Tridentine Fathers in their second chapter already quoted. Further, had he *but* seen the beautiful prayer 'Supplices Te rogamus,' placed where S. Gregory placed it in the Roman Mass, and given the interpretation which he designed for it in recasting and placing it there, that Mass would never have been the stumbling-block to him that it was. For, in point of fact, it was *the absence* of any such teaching in it that drove him from it. It was that same absence of any such teaching on their part that he denounced with equal vigour in the Lutherans.

'They put about falsely,' says he, 'that what we teach on spiritual manducation is opposed to what they are pleased to call the real and the true. Since what we say refers solely to the mode, which with them is carnal, as they include Christ in the bread, with us it is spiritual, as it is the hidden action of the Spirit which is our bond of union with Christ. . . . Indeed, it were no small injury to the Holy Spirit were we not to believe that it is by His incomprehensible power that we are made partakers of the flesh and blood of Christ in communicating. . . .'[2]

To Calvin, therefore, belongs the credit of having been the first Western in modern times to revive the teaching of the primitive Church, ascribing Eucharistic consecration to

[1] *Inst* iv c 17, § 10 [2] Ib. § 31–33.

the action of the Holy Ghost on the elements, with the Real Presence for its effect. Virtually this teaching is also that of the first and third chapters of the Council of Trent, and formally that of the second. On the other hand, the only modern ritual framed in accordance with this teaching was the *Edwardine*. Almost all the Reformed Confessions—the Helvetic, the Gallican, the Scottish, the Declaration of Thorn, the Catechisms of Heidelberg and Geneva, with the short English Catechism of 1553,[1] give their unqualified adhesion to this teaching, yet, strange to say, admit no prayer based upon it into their rituals. It is perfectly true that *no such prayer* was enjoined by our Lord, but where do we find *any prayer enjoined* by Him, either for the indwelling of the Spirit in our hearts, or for any of the manifold gifts and graces which S. Paul bids us consider *His* 'work'? Which of the Gospels, for instance, records our Lord commending to His disciples for constant use a prayer similar to the collect for Whitsunday? Yet what Christian of any denomination is not in the habit of using a prayer asking for similar guidance at times? How, then, can any Christian who believes it is the Holy Ghost who brings Christ to us and us to Him in the Eucharist object to pray in Church for His coming to do both?

'He shall glorify Me,' said our Lord, 'for He shall take of Mine, and shall show it unto you.'[2]

And again: 'He shall teach you all things and bring all

---

[1] Its date deserves special notice, being one year after the Prayer Book of 1549 had been superseded by that of 1552, yet this Catechism upholds the teaching of the first book ' *Q* How came these things to pass? *A* These things came to pass in a certain hidden way, and by the lively working of the Spirit *Q* You seem to wish to say that faith is the mouth of the soul, whereby we receive this heavenly meat, well-nigh full of salvation and immortality, and communicated to us by the Act of the Spirit . ' Its author was, according to Heylyn, Poynet, bishop of Winchester *The Two Liturgies, &c.* edited for the Parker Society by Rev Joseph Ketley, Cambridge, 1844; for the English copy, p. 517; for the Latin, p 564–5

[2] See the meaning of this verse drawn out in c. 11 p 15–7, and illustrated from S Chrysostom.

things to your remembrance whatsoever I have said unto you.'

Such benefits having been confided to Him to distribute, can we suppose that it is *not* expected that we should apply for them at all, or for both classes in the same breath, but only for one?

Unquestionably the recognition of a great principle like this, after it has been buried in oblivion for so many centuries, is a step in the right direction—and a forward step too—still prayer based on it must shortly follow, or it will be speedily forgotten again. And never, after having been made clear to our apprehensions, can it really be forgotten again without sin. For our present attitude, were we responsible for it, could not be described otherwise than as a flagrant offence committed against the Godhead, *in the person of the Holy Ghost*. It is divested of this character *solely* by being unintentional on our part. Otherwise to confound the Persons in the Godhead is not more wrong than to confuse their offices, or merge their prerogatives. This is, at present, what has been done systematically by the Churches of England and Rome for ages in celebrating the Eucharist. Yet hitherto we are without blame in the matter. It is not our fault. It is the result of a deep-seated and long-standing delusion. Even our remote forefathers were bound hand and foot by it as well as ourselves. It occasioned numberless things to be done that never ought to have been done, and cannot now be contemplated without shame, though the doers of them, who acted under a complete misapprehension, and in perfect good faith, not only committed no crime, but were constantly God-serving men, and God constantly permitted good to flow from their acts.

We must strike the balance very carefully between reprobating and condoning and visiting with unqualified praise, before we can estimate things as we ought in these days. We must not shrink from reprobating the thinly-veiled hypocrisy manifested in the conduct of those who could, under pretence of doing honour to our Lord, assume to themselves the function of setting Him right in what He had propounded to His own disciples on the Procession, and with which one General Council after another had shrunk from meddling; of those who rudely seized and made words used by Him in distributing what He had previously consecrated their own unauthorised formula for consecration; of those, finally, who took upon themselves to exclude the Holy Ghost from the part attributed to Him by the primitive Church in that rite, notwithstanding that our Lord had specially revealed Him to His disciples, as the Paraclete who would be sent from heaven to act for Him when He had gone thither.

We may not charge Gratian with hypocrisy, for his eyes were blinded by the spurious authorities passing for standard in his day. Again, we must not shrink from entering a stern protest against the delusions of an age that inveigled so spiritual a saint as S. Bernard of Clairvaux into preaching a crusade, while condoning his act. Again, when we call to mind and exult over the undoubted fact that the all-important continent of Europe, standing between the old world and the new, was consolidated, in its Christianity, and sown all over with the seeds of a civilisation whose development has placed the rest of the world at its feet, by the mediæval Church, whose head was the Pope, and the regulars of whose spiritual army were quartered in monasteries that once crowned every hill or securely nestled in every vale—whose loss good men therefore deeply deplore—let us not, however, forget that there is another side to the picture. First of all, let us consider that, had S. Paul and his companions anticipated the mediæval Church by restricting their missionary labours to Asia Minor, and passed their lives in studding it over with gorgeous cathedrals and convents—instead of crossing over into Macedonia—Europe might have continued to be, from then till now, pretty much what it was when Julius Cæsar invaded Great Britain. Next, let us not shut our eyes to another fact in the annals of Christian Europe, not less patent or noteworthy than the former one—viz. that missions to the heathen wholly ceased in Europe *just when* monasteries were most numerous, fullest of monks, and richest, and cathedrals most ornate. No session was devoted to the unconverted nations of the world at the Council of Trent. It was only during the first quarter of the seventeenth century that the Propaganda with its seminary for missionaries was founded at Rome; to be followed at no great interval in this by the Society for the Promotion of the Gospel in Foreign Parts. What, then, was the appalling discovery which this resumption of missionary work in both Churches very soon brought to light? It was that three-fourths of the world were still heathen! But this was no discovery to Him who died for man; and Who, when His parting precept had been put on one side by those who should have remembered it most, permitted the destruction and disbanding of all those monasteries and convents on which the wealth of nations had been expended, that the souls of nations might be cared for again.

But this, again, is by no means all. After more than two centuries of renewed work and enlarged experience, aided by all the various facilities which commerce and science have joined hands in placing at their disposal, what is the crucial fact to which the missionaries of every Christian Church and land must perforce bear testimony but this: that in no case can a whole nation be named that has been won to the Gospel? Roman Catholic missionaries are just as powerless as Anglicans, Greeks, Russians, and Americans to effect the conquest of a whole nation to the faith of Christ. Conversion by driblets is the only result as yet attained in any quarter of the globe; and even these require to be superintended by clergy from the West to be kept in life. Proselytisms of baptised Christians from one community to another have, from the final separation of the East and West down to our own times, evoked far more zeal, been prosecuted with far more cost of time, money, and labour, and probably far exceeded the aggregate number of all the conversions, during the same period, from heathenism. Such a phenomenon as that of the Anglo-Saxon Church in the days of Bede—that is to say, within about two generations of its foundation; and in days when all travelling was on foot—is unknown in all the missionary reports of the seventeenth, eighteenth, and nineteenth centuries. But in the days of Bede *national* conversions were *not* the exception, but the *rule*.

The truth is, it is permitted to *no portion* of the Church, however considerable, to effect, in the present disunited condition of the Church, what was effected habitually by any portion of the Church, when all Churches being in full communion with each other acted together as one man. This is the last and most urgent of all the lessons sought to be impressed upon us all alike by Divine Providence for the last three centuries. Without intercommunion with each other, *we might just as well hope to convert whole nations as hope to fly*. All the zeal so praiseworthily brought to bear upon missionary work abroad and at home would find it quite worth its while to attempt nothing further in that direction till it had succeeded in getting the great question of intercommunion actively taken up by all it could influence. Divine Providence as good as tells us we can do nothing without union, worth the name. The longer we neglect it, the greater responsibility we shall all incur; the more difficulties we shall have to face; the fewer blessings will attend our labours. God calls us to union by making the conversion of nations impossible to rival Churches. How *are* we to settle our differences? By *beginning* at the right end! By making peace with God first, and then peace with man will ensue without a word. Providentially—*most* providentially —for the Roman and Anglican Churches, a door has been discovered ajar in their respective liturgies for making peace with God. The Holy Ghost restored in their respective liturgies and in their general teaching to the high functions assigned Him in the Primitive Church, based on the words of the Saviour Himself, interpreted by S. Paul, witnessed to by all the Fathers, would cause scales to fall from their eyes, and old sores to be healed in their hearts. Eucharistic controversy would be no longer possible between them. All stumbling-blocks connected with it would be removed from all outside their pale. Intercommunion with each other, and with all other Churches, could not but follow soon, on the basis of the old landmarks of the Church accepted by all, and of liberty for all to regulate their own concerns within those limits.

The temporal mission of the Holy Ghost, rightly set forth and cordially received, will answer every question relating to grace conveyed through the sacraments; to grace conveyed through His indwelling in each regenerate soul; to grace conveyed without the sacraments, where the Gospel has never been preached, or where for other causes the sacraments cannot be had, the *baptismus Flaminis*, as it has been called.[1] Once let all Churches work together again in love— love such as the Holy Ghost alone can inspire—for the conversion of the heathen, and the inherent power of Christianity to triumph over every barrier but that of the stubborn heart will burst forth like lightning from between the clouds in resistless force; the effete nation of China will be vanquished after infinitely less fighting, and in infinitely less time than old Rome; the forbidding continent of Africa than the mighty but undisciplined hordes that had to be Christianised and civilised when old Rome fell. A solemn act of reparation to the Holy Ghost for the disrespect unwittingly shown Him for so many centuries in the West could hardly fail to stir up Christian Europe to a fuller sense of her duties to mankind both as an evangeliser and a civiliser than has yet been brought home to her.

[1] S Thom. *Sum Theol.* III. quæst 66, art 11

For Europe was clearly Christianised and civilised herself during the Middle Ages that she might afterwards impart her own enlightenment, her superior faith and culture, to the nations lying in darkness, wheresoever discovered by her children.

I have thus been allowed to discover my way through a puzzle which it has taken me many years to unravel—namely, the causes of the rise and fall of the mediæval Church; for it had no sooner attained its zenith and dazzled all by its splendour than decay set it, and in collapsed. It was *not* founded upon a rock, but upon sand—upon sand collected and cemented in 'miry clay' during the ninth century. Conclusive proof has been given that its foundations were not the work of Rome, but of France, and that it was not till its origin had been forgotten and its worst features disguised beyond detection that Gallicanism was first accepted and then defended by Rome. England, it should be added, had been taken in by it at least two centuries before Rome succumbed; but it was Rome, not England, that committed Europe to its maintenance. Gallicanism I have called it for want of a better name, and under Gallicanism the feudal system and all other kindred measures tending to secularise the Church would properly come, were this the place for discussing them; but it is only with its insidious aggressions upon spiritual things that we are now concerned, from which neither the unreformed Church of Rome nor yet the reformed Church of England have shaken themselves free. Judged by the standard of the primitive Church, both would be found equally needing reform. As to their respective merits, I say without hesitation that I much prefer the English Church to the Roman, *supposing them to remain separate.* Nevertheless, in the interests of all Christians in general and for the general conversion of those who are not yet Christians, I should at all times be willing to work cordially for the reunion of the Roman and the English Church on terms honourable to both and in accordance with sober truth. Failing that, a *modus vivendi* might possibly be arranged between them on friendly terms sufficient to enable them to work heartily side by side for the propagation of the Gospel abroad and the suppression of wickedness and crime at home.[1]

As to the Church of Rome being *the only Church* on earth, when the Church of Rome can point out *the nations* converted by her since communion was broken off between her and the East the statement may be worth considering seriously, but not till then. Meanwhile there are many sterling qualities in those who have been born and bred in the Church of England that are wanting or rarely found in Roman Catholics, and there are some good qualities likewise common amongst Roman Catholics that Anglicans might copy with advantage. I respect and sincerely love the good men of both communions, and, so far as my experience goes, they might, left to themselves, amalgamate, and would agree very well together. But there is one thing on whose interests I set a far higher value than on the interests of either communion, and that one thing is Christianity. To its interests all rival communions are bound to give way. There is no religion to compare with it on earth of any that I have known or whose books I have ever read. It was meant to be and it is admirably fitted to be, it deserves to be and it ought therefore to be, the religion of all mankind. When people point triumphantly to the many truths contained in other Creeds, which they therefore contend are worthy to be placed in the scales with it, I have one answer for all—' It is always the worst lie that contains most truth.' A really good Christian is the best specimen of a man in

---

[1] In the words of the late Bishop Dupanloup · 'What would not be our power for preaching the Gospel to those who know it not, if we were at one amongst ourselves! The majority of mankind remain buried in darkness because we bring them a Gospel divided, disputed, cut up into fragments If England, France, and Russia were agreed in the truth, and therefore in the charity and zeal of the Apostolate, the face of the East, of the whole world would be changed' Quoted by Oxenham: *Short Studies*, &c , p 424 (Chapman & Hall, 1885).

whatever part of the earth he may be found and to whatever Church he may belong. I will add, a good Jew is the next best. Accordingly, my last words in this, my probably last book on the subject, shall be what stood in the title-page to my first—

'CHRISTIANUS SUM : CHRISTIANI NIHIL A ME ALIENUM PUTO.'

Feast of the Purification, 1885.

www.ingramcontent.com/pod-product-compliance
Lightning Source LLC
Chambersburg PA
CBHW071221290426
44108CB00013B/1245